Genealogical Resources of the
Civil War Era

Genealogical Resources of the
Civil War Era

Online and Published Military or Civilian Name Lists, 1861-1869, & Post-War Veteran Lists

by

William Dollarhide

Family Roots Publishing Company
Bountiful, Utah

Published by Family Roots Publishing Co.
PO Box 830
Bountiful, UT 84011
www.familyrootspublishing.com/

Library of Congress Control Number: 2008926801
ISBN: 978-1-933194-45-5
ISBN: 1-933194-45-6

Printed in the United States of America

Books by William Dollarhide

Published by Genealogical Publishing Co., Inc., Baltimore, MD:
- *Map Guide to the U.S. Federal Censuses, 1790-1920*
  (with William Thorndale) (1987)
- *Managing a Genealogical Project* (1988)
- *Genealogy Starter Kit* (1993);
  also published with the title, *Getting Started in Genealogy* (2001)
- *Getting Started in Genealogy ONLINE* (2006)
- *New York State Censuses & Substitutes* (2006)

Published by Heritage Quest, North Salt Lake, UT:
- *Seven Steps to a Family Tree* (1995)
- *Map Guide to American Migration Routes, 1735-1815* (1997)
- *British Origins of American Colonists, 1629-1775* (1997)
- *America's Best Genealogy Resource Centers*
  (with Ronald A. Bremer) (1998)
- *The Census Book: A Genealogist's Guide to Federal Census Facts, Schedules, and Indexes* (1999)
- *Grow a Family Tree!* (2001)

Published by Family Roots Publishing Co., Bountiful, UT:
- *Census Substitutes & State Census Records*, Vol. 1 - Eastern States (2008)
- *Census Substitutes & State Census Records*, Vol. 2 - Western States (2008)
- *Genealogical Resources of The Civil War Era* (2009)

Contents

Foreword

by Leland K. Meitzler

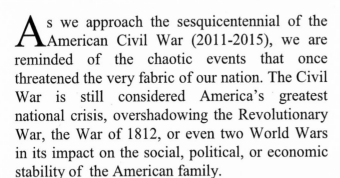

As we approach the sesquicentennial of the American Civil War (2011-2015), we are reminded of the chaotic events that once threatened the very fabric of our nation. The Civil War is still considered America's greatest national crisis, overshadowing the Revolutionary War, the War of 1812, or even two World Wars in its impact on the social, political, or economic stability of the American family.

The South's peculiar institution of slavery, the Northern states' overwhelming opposition to it, Abraham Lincoln's election, and the eventual secession of the eleven states forming the Confederacy, all had a dramatic effect on all Americans. For most of us, our ancestors were not just the participants of the war as soldiers and sailors, but also included civilian families of men, women, and children. Whether military or civilian, many of our ancestors suffered terribly. And, although a century-and-a-half has gone by, it seems it has not been all that long ago that our ancestors fought, bled, and died.

I remember clearly the centennial celebrations of 1961 through 1965. At the time, I wondered what part my great-grandparents and great uncles may have played. I wondered about what life was like for my great-grandmother, Abigail, who was left a widow as a young woman. I wondered what it was like for my grandmother, and her brother, both born during the war, and neither having any memories of their father. There were a few family stories, but no written records in our family's possession.

It was another decade before I began my search for my Civil War roots. The search was not easy. The books that were written on the subject aided my search at the time. Now, several decades later, acclaimed genealogical author, William Dollarhide, has written another book – one that could not have been written in 1975. This book is written for the Twenty-first Century family historian interested in locating information on their Civil War ancestors.

A staple of American genealogical research has long been the search for one's Civil War ancestors. Most American Civil War genealogy books were written in the pre-Internet era, and therefore lack reference to online tools that genealogists have come to expect. These volumes are still valuable, and should still be referenced by genealogists. However, Dollarhide recommends that the modern family historian should start their Civil War search on the Internet – in fact, the Civil War Soldiers and Sailors online database is the first Resource Group found in this volume.

This book was not written as a guide to Civil War narratives as such, but a guide to the various records in which one will find the lists of names of both soldiers and civilians. Those lists include records created during the War, records produced immediately after the War, Veteran Censuses, State Censuses taken (1885-1945) with Civil War Veterans listed, and numerous Internet resources.

Keep in mind that the War directly touched not only the men who fought, but their wives, parents, children, and often, their extended families. Civil War genealogy research, therefore, is the study of families of the era, and Dollarhide has written this book specifically to help in that research.

The book is divided into four parts. Part One is the Introduction, with commentary on Free vs. Slave States, jurisdictions, U.S. expansion, the Confederacy, and Civil War era families. Part Two is unique, in that Bill Dollarhide has identified twenty sets of records called "Resource Groups." Ten of these Resource Groups are nationwide in scope, while the other ten are statewide in nature. Detailed descriptions as well as facsimile examples are given for each Resource Group. Most of the statewide Resource Group descriptions include specific references (including page numbers) to resources found in Part Three.

Part Three is made up of a bibliography of published statewide name lists, 1861-1869, as well as post-war veteran lists. It's laid out by state, Alabama through Wyoming Territory. For each state/territory, the entries are for online resources, followed by published resources. Much of Part 3 was originally printed in serialized form in issues of *Everton's Genealogical Helper*, 2006 through 2008, though updates and revisions have since been made.

Since the book is made up of national and statewide records sources, Part Four details the best places to search for county and local resources. The top resource centers are identified, including three large genealogical libraries, two specialized military facilities, and dozens of Civil War Parks and Historic Sites.

If you haven't started the search for your Civil War ancestor, this book is a great place to begin. If you're a seasoned researcher, the volume may inform you of additional resources and places to look. And, hundreds of web addresses are used in the book, enabling a researcher to quickly locate the latest resources currently available on the Internet.

May your search be profitable and lead to a greater understanding of your Civil War era families.

Leland K. Meitzler
Publisher

Part 1

Introduction to the Civil War Era

Most genealogical resources of the Civil War era are related to the soldiers and regiments of the Union and Confederate military jurisdictions. But there are many records relating to the entire populations of the states as well. This review identifies places to look for people during the decade, 1861-1869, and post-war veterans; first for the national name lists, and then a state-by-state listing.

Before reviewing the many resources available, it may be useful to look at the jurisdictions (keepers of records) of the Civil War era, and some history of how these jurisdictions evolved.

Free vs. Slave States: A Line Divides the Nation

A joint survey of the colonial boundary line between the proprietary lands held by William Penn and Charles Calvert was completed by surveyors Charles Mason and Jeremiah Dixon in 1767. The line remains the current east-west Pennsylvania-Maryland border, and the part of the Maryland-Delaware border that runs approximately north-south. The Mason-Dixon Line became the division between the northern free states and southern slave states.

The division line was extended in 1787 to the length of the Ohio River upon the creation of the Northwest Territory. The **Northwest Ordinance** (formally, *An Ordinance for the Government of the Territory of the United States, North-West of the River Ohio),* was the most important legislative act to come out of the Continental Congress prior to the Constitution of the United States of 1789. The Northwest Ordinance dictated that the first territory would be a "free" territory, that is, forbidding slavery.

The Northwest Ordinance also set up the methods by which new states could be admitted into the Union States. First, Congress would have to pass an enabling act which called for a local convention to be convened, a state constitution prepared, and a local vote of approval. This method was used for the admission of the state of Ohio in 1803, taken from the area of the old Northwest Territory and followed for all subsequent territories that became states.

But the Northwest Ordinance did not apply to the original thirteen states, and any new state taken from their original bounds had to have custom enabling acts by Congress, as well as the parent state. For example, the 14th state of Vermont was admitted (as a free state) to the Union in 1791, taken from land claimed and relinquished by both New York and New Hampshire.

The slavery issue had been a major dividing force in colonial America and for the first seven decades of the United States. Specific religious and ethnic groups in the original thirteen colonies tended to migrate to newly opened lands according to their beliefs relating to the slavery issue. For example, in the early 1800s, Virginia and North Carolina Quakers left for the free states of Ohio and Indiana; while the Scots-Irish from those same areas headed south to found the slave states of Alabama and Mississippi. New lands opened in the slave states of Kentucky and Tennessee were occupied by both slave and anti-slave proponents, and these "crossroad" states remained intermixed until the time of the Civil War.

From the very beginnings of the United States, the issue of slavery created an intense competition between congressional represent-atives over the admission of new states. New states were often admitted in twos, one free of slavery, the other permitting slavery. The evolution of slave versus free states at the time of each census year, 1790-1860 shows this balancing act:

1790. The population figures from the 1790 census revealed that 94 percent of the 698,000 U.S. slaves lived below the Mason-Dixon Line. But de facto slavery still existed in a few of the northern states. Of the fourteen states in early 1791, six were slave states, that is, slavery was officially recognized as legal.

1800. With the addition of the slave states of Kentucky in 1792 and Tennessee in 1796, the U.S. now had eight states south of the Mason-Dixon Line and eight states north of the line.

1810. By the time of the 1810 census, the states north of the Mason-Dixon Line had all abolished slavery. The admission of the free state of Ohio in 1803 brought the numbers to nine free and eight slave states.

1820. The admission of the free states of Indiana (1816), Illinois (1818), and Maine (1820), brought the free total to twelve; the new slave states of Louisiana (1812), Mississippi (1817), and Alabama (1818), to eleven slave states.

The **Missouri Compromise of 1820** allowed Missouri to become a slave state while adding Maine as a free state, and set the limits for further expansion in the West. The northern boundary of Missouri lay almost exactly on the latitude of the Mason-Dixon Line of Pennsylvania-Maryland, and the division line from Kentucky at the Mississippi River now moved north up the river to the present Missouri-Iowa line, and then west. By the terms of the Missouri Compromise of 1820, the northern Missouri line was supposed to be the new division between any future slave and free states, continuing that line of latitude as far as the western boundary of the United States (the Continental Divide).

1830. With Missouri's admission as a slave state in 1821, the total went to a balance again with twelve free and twelve slave states.

1840. The admission of the free state of Michigan in 1836, and the slave state of Arkansas in 1837 continued the balance to thirteen slave states and thirteen free states.

1850. In March 1845, Florida was admitted as a slave state. The Republic of Texas, 1836-1845 had permitted slavery, and when Texas was annexed to the U.S. in July 1845, it entered the Union as a slave state. The admission of the free states of Iowa (1846), Wisconsin (1848), and California (1850), brought the totals to sixteen free states and fifteen slave states.

Texas was the last slave state to enter the Union. The fragile agreements between the two factions in Congress fell apart completely when the **1854 Kansas-Nebraska Act** was passed, allowing these two new territories to choose whether they would be slave or free states. This Act had the effect of revoking the Missouri Compromise of 1820.

Clearly, the balance of free vs. slave issues in Congress was worsening for the South. After the

1854 Kansas-Nebraska Act, Southerners began meeting and discussing the possibility of leaving the Union. The term *Southern Confederacy* began to appear in print about this time.

1860. With the addition of the free states of Minnesota (1858) and Oregon (1859), the imbalance increased to eighteen free states and fifteen slave states. In addition, the U.S. included five territories destined to become free states: Kansas, Nebraska, New Mexico, Utah, and Washington. With an even more imbalance of power in Congress and no hope of seeing any more slave states added to the Union States, the break-up of the Union was a goal of Southerners.

One other jurisdiction was that of the five civilized tribes of what was unofficially called *Indian Territory*. Although not a state or a territory, and with no representation in Congress, the Cherokee, Choctaw, Chickasaw, Creek, and Seminole Nations all permitted slavery. During the Civil War, the Nations held sympathies for the South.

Southern historians are known for their claim that the Civil War was not fought over the issue of slavery – it was fought over the issue of "States' Rights." But northern historians come back with, "Yes, it was fought over the states' rights to keep slaves." But, since the precise division line between slave states and free states was not maintained during the Civil War, both northern and southern historians are only partially correct.

Jurisdictions of the Confederate States of America

The departure of southern states from the Union began in December 1860, with South Carolina's secession; fulfilling their promise to secede if Abraham Lincoln were elected as President. Over the next two months, South Carolina was followed by Mississippi, Florida, Alabama, Georgia, Louisiana, and Texas. Delegates of these seven states met in Montgomery, Alabama to form the provisional government of the Confederate States of America in February 1861, naming Jefferson Davis as the provisional President and Alexander Stephens as Vice-President.

"DAVIS AND STEVENS, PRESIDENT AND VICE-PRESIDENT OF THE SOUTHERN CONFEDERACY. [PHOTOGRAPHED BY BRADY]" (*Harper's Weekly,* Feb. 3, 1861)

In April 1861, Virginia joined the Confederacy, followed by Arkansas, Tennessee, and North Carolina in May 1861, for a total of eleven states. The capital of the Confederacy was designated as Richmond, Virginia in May 1861, and the first general election took place on November 6, 1861, in which Jefferson Davis of Mississippi was elected President, and Alexander Hamilton Stephens of Georgia as Vice-President.

The Confederate States accounted for only eleven of the fifteen slave states as part of the United States before the Civil War. The slave states of Kentucky and Missouri were both officially recognized by the United States of America, and the Confederate States of America, but neither of these border states formally seceded from the Union, and both had rival Union and Confederate state governments during the war years. The other two slave states were Maryland and Delaware, and both remained with the Union, although the U.S. federal government felt it necessary to impose martial law upon Maryland's state government to prevent their secession.

An early map produced showing the area of the northern and southern states, was first printed in *Harper's Weekly,* Feb. 23, 1861. Note that the slave states of Maryland, Delaware, Kentucky, Missouri, and Indian Territory were all expected to become part of the Confederacy. Of the fifteen slave states in the U.S., eleven states seceded to form the Confederate States of America by May 1861.

The only territory officially added to the Confederate States of America was the Territory of Arizona, an area encompassing the southern half of pre-Civil War New Mexico Territory from Texas to California. In March 1861, the territory was self-proclaimed at a local convention and asserted its desire to join the Confederacy. The Confederate Congress recognized the Territory of Arizona in February 1862. But it lasted only until July 1862, when it was occupied by Union forces, and the area returned to the jurisdiction of the U.S. New Mexico Territory.

The five civilized tribes of the Indian Territory were officially recognized as "Indian Protectorates" by the Confederacy, but the existing treaties the tribes had with the U.S. remained in effect during the Civil War. The tribes, however, supplied troops only to the Confederate side, rather than supporting the Union cause. After the Civil War, the United States revoked their treaties, created new ones, reduced their lands substantially, and began a program to integrate individual Indians into U.S. society as "farmers."

Union States and Expansion, 1861-1864

After the secession of the eleven southern states in early 1861, the Union was composed of the New England states of Connecticut, Maine, Massachusetts, New Hampshire, Rhode Island, and Vermont; the Mid-Atlantic states of New

York, New Jersey, Pennsylvania, Delaware, Maryland, and the District of Columbia; the Old Northwest states of Ohio, Indiana, Illinois, Michigan, Wisconsin, and Minnesota; the state of Kansas, admitted in January 1861; and the far west states of California and Oregon, for a total of twenty states. Of that group, only Maryland supplied soldiers to the Confederate cause, the others were represented by Union troops only.

Kentucky and Missouri were claimed by both the Union and the Confederacy, and both states had competing state governments for the duration of the Civil War period. About 67% of the troops formed in Kentucky were Union, and 33% Confederate; while the Missouri representation was about 75% Union and 25% Confederate.

Two states were admitted to the Union during the Civil War. First, the anti-slavery counties of Virginia split off as West Virginia in June 1863, joining the Union as its twenty-first free state. Then came Nevada, which had been designated a U.S. territory in March 1861, mainly as a means of securing Nevada's rich gold and silver deposits for the Union. President Lincoln saw statehood for Nevada as a means of obtaining the necessary votes for his upcoming election for a second term. In less than a month, a rush constitution was prepared, voted on, telegraphed to Washington, and ratified in October 1864. Nevada increased the total of Union states to twenty-two. Earlier in 1864, Lincoln had pushed through Congress enabling acts for statehood for both Colorado and Nebraska Territories, but these two territories voted against statehood.

During the course of the Civil War, the Union also included the four pre-Civil War territories of Nebraska, New Mexico, Utah, and Washington, all of which supplied only Union troops to the war. New territories established by the Union during the Civil War were Colorado Territory, Feb 1861; Dakota Territory, March 1861; Arizona Territory (US), February 1863; Idaho Territory, March 1863; and Montana Territory, May 1864. Dakota and Colorado territories supplied Union troops. In the case of the U.S. Arizona Territory and its predecessor, the Confederate Territory of Arizona, both supplied troops to the war. And, some early Union soldiers from the areas of Idaho and Montana were drawn from their parent territories of Washington and Dakota.

The War Years:
April 1861 to May 1865

During the formation period, Dec 1860 – April 1861, southern state forces seized eleven federal forts and arsenals ranging from South Carolina to Texas, all without resistance from Union forces. The first shots of the Civil War were fired at Union-occupied Fort Sumter, South Carolina on April 12, 1861, marking the onset of a conflict that continued until the surrender of the forces by Confederate General Robert E. Lee to Union General Ulysses S. Grant at Appomattox, Virginia on April 9, 1865. The last Confederate forces surrendered and Jefferson Davis was captured a month later, essentially ending the Civil War and the Confederate States of America.

The Thirteenth Amendment to the United States Constitution, ratified December 6, 1865, abolished slavery throughout the United States. Ratification of the 13th Amendment was a condition of the return of local rule to those states that had seceded.

Civil War Era Families in the
Federal Censuses

Family historians looking for evidence of their ancestors at the beginning of the Civil War decade have at their disposal the names of the inhabitants of the United States from the 1860 Federal Census. This census was taken for every household in America, with a census day of June 1, 1860. As a result, it may be possible to identify every future Union or Confederate soldier and their families about ten months before the Civil War began.

However, a family historian jumping to the 1870 Federal Census to identify the same soldiers or families ten years later faces a difficult task. The reason for this difficulty can be attributed to at least three factors:

First, the 1870 Federal Census is considered the worst national census ever taken in terms of completeness and accuracy. It is estimated that 5 to 10 percent of the population of the Union states was missed, and 15 to 20% of the former Confederate states was missed. The official population figures of the U.S. increased from about 31.4 million in 1860 to 38.6 million in 1870, thus an additional 7.2 million names were not part of the 1860 census figures. It is estimated that most of the increase was due to post-war immigration, 1865-1869, rather than a burgeoning birth rate after the Civil War.

Second, from 1861-1865, the Civil War was responsible for at least 620,000 deaths on both sides, a major disruption in the population, and a large statistical bubble over and above the normal mortality attrition rates from the previous decade. In the Confederate states, the number of Civil War deaths were as high as 10% of their total population; and added to the people not counted, as much as 30% of the total people of 1860 who could have been named in the 1870 census, had there been no Civil War.

And third, the devastation and disruption of people and their homes, whether soldiers or civilians, had a major impact on the population and where they lived after the war. Unfortunately, the 1870 Federal Census identifies a population with little continuity to compare with 1860 names and places.

Follow the Rules

A rule in genealogy is to treat the brothers and sisters of your ancestors as equals. That means that we should spend an equal amount of time and effort finding a brother's genealogical events, i.e., births, residences, marriages, deaths, etc., as we do for the direct ancestor. By working on close family members, our goal is to find the details about the same set of parents.

This rule is even more important when you learn there was a brother of an ancestor who was a soldier in the Civil War. Your own ancestor may have been too young, or too old, or perhaps wealthy enough to buy himself a substitute to serve in his place. But if a brother were a soldier in the Civil War, there are records available that will aid in identifying an entire family, their places of residence, their migrations, and more. So, even if your direct ancestor did not serve in the Civil War, a close family member may have served, and collecting the wealth of information about that soldier may provide the answers you need.

Start with the Place

All genealogical research requires three things about a genealogical event for every person: 1) The **name** of the person, 2) an approximate **date** of the event, and 3) the **place** where the event occurred. In most genealogical research tasks, the **place** of the event needs to be known before you will ever find any records – the place of the event is where a written record was created.

Locating the home of a Civil War soldier is important. The first genealogical event, therefore, may be the day the soldier joined the Army. To be thorough, we need to know his name, date of enlistment, and the place where he enlisted. Since nearly all military regiments were locally raised, finding the regiment a soldier joined ties that person to a local town, county, or region of a state. This was true for both the Union and Confederate states. Both forces included a Regular Army, and the Union side had separate troops from Colored Troops, Veteran Reserve Corps, and specialist Volunteers; but a large majority of all Civil War records listing the names of participants are related to the local regiment in which a soldier served. For example, on the Confederate side, 96 percent of the soldiers were drawn from state regiments; and on the Union side, about 87 percent of the soldiers were from state regiments.

Knowing the place of enlistment also means that the neighbors of your ancestor can be followed to assist in finding records for both, and used as clues in locating the right person after the war. So, immediately after you have a name of a soldier, the date of his enlistment, the place where he enlisted, and the name of the regiment he joined, go back to the 1860 census to find that person in a family. In some cases, a 13- 14-year-old boy may be shown in the 1860 census who later participated in the Civil War. Thus, the 1860 census may be an aid to understanding the local participants, the place where the regiment was first organized, when they joined, and where they may have landed after the war.

Fortunately, there are now resources available that give the name of a soldier and the regiment to which he was attached. And, there are many nationwide and statewide name lists available to help identify people and family groups during and after the Civil War.

Identifying the Resources Available

For this review, genealogical resources of the Civil War era are identified and described in twenty (20) different categories. Half of these categories, or **Resource Groups,** are related to nationwide records, i.e., those resources that cover multiple states and were generally originated and maintained by the national government. The second half of the Resource Groups are related to statewide records, maintained either by the National Archives or a particular state facility.

Refer to **Table 1 – Summary of Resource Groups Available for Each State** (pp. 52-53). All twenty Resource Groups are listed; with an indication of any originals, microfilm, or online databases available for each state/territory.

A more detailed description of each resource follows, with facsimile examples of the twenty Resource Groups of the Civil War era.

Part 2

Descriptions and Examples of Resource Groups Available

NATIONWIDE SOURCES:

RG 1 – **Civil War Soldiers & Sailors System** (online database). Combined Union and Confederate soldier lists; plus Regimental Histories & Unit Rosters.

RG 2 – **American Civil War Research Database** (online database). Soldier lists from Adjutant General Reports; Regimental Histories & Unit Rosters.

RG 3 – **Official Records of the War of the Rebellion**. 70 printed volumes, full text online, completely indexed.

RG 4 – **General and Organizational Indexes to U.S. Pension Files, 1861-1934**.

RG 5 – **1883 List of U.S. Pensioners on the Roll**. 5 vols. of reprints plus CD-ROM.

RG 6 – **1890 Federal Census (Special Schedules) of Union Veterans**. Microfilm, CD-ROM.

RG 7 – **Roll of Honor & Veteran Burials for all States**. CD-ROMs, online databases & VA's Nationwide Gravesite Locator.

RG 8 – **1865-1867 Confederate Amnesty Papers**. Includes Applications for Presidential Pardons, Loyalty Oaths, and more.

RG 9 – **Consolidated Lists and Records of Confederate Soldiers & United Confederate Veterans Association**.

RG 10 – **Index to Compiled Service Records** (all states). Union Regulars, Veteran Reserves & U.S. Colored Troops.

STATEWIDE SOURCES:

RG 11 – **Compiled Service Records** (by state). Microfilm of the contents of the original packets for each soldier in 24 states.

RG 12 – **Index to Compiled Service Records** (by state). Microfilm of the General Index Cards for each soldier in 44 states.

RG 13 – **1861-1869 State Censuses**, entire state populations (20 states); and any **1885-1945 State Censuses** with Civil War veterans noted (8 states).

RG 14 – **1861-1869 Statewide Name Lists**. Voter registrations, tax lists, etc., and **1890-1910 Territory Lists** (Alaska & Hawaii).

RG 15 – **1862-1869 Internal Revenue Assessment Lists**. Name lists from all states & territories during the Civil War era.

RG 16 – **Statewide Militia Lists**. Alternative lists of soldiers of the Civil War for 35 states.

RG 17 – **Confederate Pension Applications, Name Lists, and Censuses of Confederate Veterans**. 14 states.

RG 18 – **Indexes to Statewide Records** (Census Substitutes). Vital records, probates, or other statewide name lists in 36 states.

RG 19 – **Statewide Lists of Veteran Burials**. Listings available for 29 states.

RG 20 – **State Adjutant General Reports**. Rosters of soldiers, regiments for 29 States/Territories.

Refer to **Table 1 – Summary of Resource Groups Available for Each State** (pp. 52-53). All twenty Resource Groups are listed; with an indication of any originals, microfilm, or online databases available for each state/territory. A more detailed description of each Resource Group follows, with facsimile examples of the genealogical resources of the Civil War era.

NATIONWIDE SOURCES
RG 1

Civil War Soldiers & Sailors System – National Park Service

Home page:
  www.civilwar.nps.gov/cwss
Soldier search:
  www.civilwar.nps.gov/cwss/soldiers.cfm
Sailor search: (pending)

The Civil War Soldiers & Sailors System (CWSS) is an online index to the names from all military troops found in the microfilm series, ***Index to Compiled Service Records***, a group of indexes that came from the General Index Cards created in the early 1900s by the Pension Bureau. The microfilmed indexes are described in RG10 (all states) and RG12 (non-state records).

This free online searchable index combines all names into one database, and has become the first place to look for a Civil War soldier. At this writing, the CWSS site has a combined list of all Union and Confederate soldiers, with the list of sailors still in development. The soldiers search screen is shown on the next page.

Historians have determined that about 3.5 million Union and Confederate soldiers actually participated in the Civil War. A soldier serving in more than one regiment, serving under two names, or spelling variations resulted in the fact that there are 6.3 million General Index Cards for 3.5 million soldiers. Indexed are a total of 6,270,639 names of participants, (4,206,779 Union and 2,063,860 Confederate).

A breakdown of the numbers of named soldiers from each participating state/territory is shown, taken from the CWSS state lists. Forty-four of the modern fifty states are represented. The six states not listed had no Civil War soldiers, or were formed after the war: Alaska, Hawaii, Idaho, Montana, Oklahoma, and Wyoming.

Confederate State or Territory / U. S. State or Territory	Union Troops	Confederate Troops	Total Troops
Alabama	2,842	197,427	200,269
Arizona Territory (USA)	655	—	655
Arizona Territory (CSA)	—	271	271
Arkansas	12,946	108,020	120,966
California	21,405	—	21,405
Colorado Territory	8,461	—	8,461
Connecticut	65,220	—	65,220
Dakota Territory	269	—	269
Delaware	16,223	—	16,223
District of Columbia	10,607		10,607
Florida	2,199	35,245	37,444
Georgia	195	244,812	245,067
Illinois	370,624	—	370,624
Indiana	277,220	—	277,220
Iowa	97,165	—	97,165
Kansas	40,281	—	40,281
Kentucky (USA)	108,074	—	108,074
Kentucky (CSA)	—	51,605	51,605
Louisiana	14,686	128, 256	142,942
Maine	83,289	—	83,289
Maryland	53,557	6,089	59,646
Massachusetts	164,434	—	164,434
Michigan	142,969	—	142,969
Minnesota	30,972	—	30,972
Mississippi	903	173,935	174,838
Missouri (USA)	195,303	—	195,303
Missouri (CSA)	—	70,691	70,691
Nebraska Territory	5,275	—	5,275
Nevada	1,684	—	1,684
New Hampshire	45,616	—	45,616
New Jersey	96,901	—	96,901
New Mexico Territory	12,970	—	12,970
New York	512,150	—	512,150
North Carolina	5,217	197,314	202,531
Ohio	464,270	—	464,270
Oregon	2,754	—	2,754
Pennsylvania	508,215	—	508,215
Rhode Island	26,497	—	26,497
South Carolina	93*	133,602	133,695
Tennessee	54,086	195,805	249,891
Texas	4,370	159,031	163,401
Utah Territory	96	—	96
Vermont	43,663	—	43,663
Virginia	2,598	281,205	283,803
Washington Territory	1,524	—	1,524
West Virginia (1863)	47,334	—	47,334
Wisconsin	127,559	—	127,559
NON-STATE RECORDS			
Confederate Regulars	—	80,552	80,552
Union Regulars	139,441	—	139,441
Union Vet. Reserves	107,563	—	107,563
Union Colored Troops	228,096	—	228,096
Union Non-state Vols.	48,401	—	48,401
Total Soldier Records	**4,206,779**	**2,063,860**	**6,270,639**

* SC drawn company of Colored Troops

A "Print Screen" image of the CWSS solider search box is shown above. To reach this screen, go to the CWSS Home Page at **www.civilwar.nps.gov/cwss/** and select "Soldiers." Or, you can go directly to this webpage at: **www.civilwar.nps.gov/cwss/soldiers.cfm**. You can search for just a surname, or add a first name, whether Union or Confederate, the state of origin (of a regiment, etc.), unit (regiment, company, etc.), or function (infantry, cavalry, etc.). A search in this database for the surname Dollarhide and no other information presents a results list of 26 names in the format shown below:

No.	Soldier Name	Side	Function	Regiment Name
1	Dollarhide, A.	Confederate	Infantry	45th Regiment, Virginia Infantry
2	Dollarhide, A. C.	Confederate	Cavalry	25th Regiment, Texas Cavalry (3rd Texas Lancers)
3	Dollarhide, Charles	Union	Infantry	130th Regiment, Indiana Infantry
4	Dollarhide, Cornelius	Confederate	Cavalry	25th Regiment, Texas Cavalry (3rd Texas Lancers)
5	Dollarhide, Eyre	Confederate	Infantry	2nd Battalion, North Carolina Infantry
6	Dollarhide, H.	Confederate	Artillery	Jeffress' Company, Virginia Light Artillery
7	Dollarhide, Harrison	Confederate	Infantry	51st Regiment, Virginia Infantry
8	Dollarhide, Henderson	Confederate	Infantry	48th Regiment, Virginia Infantry
9	Dollarhide, Ira F.	Union	Infantry	116th Regiment, Indiana Infantry (6 months, 1863-4)

NATIONWIDE SOURCES
RG 1 – continued

Regimental Histories and Unit Rosters
of Union & Confederate Soldiers at the CWSS Website

The first place to find a Civil War soldier is in the combined Union & Confederate soldier lists indexed at the Civil War Soldiers & Sailors (CWSS) online database. After finding a Union or Confederate soldier in the CWSS database, you will learn the soldier's name, state of origin, arm of service, and any regiment(s) in which he served.

The CWSS website has included all Union regimental histories from Frederick Dyer's *A Compendium of the War of the Rebellion*. In addition, many Confederate regimental histories are included, from several published sources.

Dyer's *Compendium*, the leading historical reference to the Union military units of the Civil War, includes a brief history of each unit, marching orders, battles engaged in, mustering in dates and places, and mustering out dates and places. The Confederate regimental histories follow about the same format.

Since the CWSS site has the names of all soldiers linked to a regiment, a special search can list the names in a separate webpage devoted to a single regiment. These regimental name lists then act as Unit Rosters, but are actually a compilation of names from the main database. There may be other publications that give the official unit rosters of soldiers in a particular regiment, and any comparisons between the official rosters and the CWSS rosters may not always agree.

A Regiment Search allows a researcher to find out more about the regiment in which a soldier may have served, plus an understanding of other soldiers serving in the same regiment.

Since most state regiments, Union or Confederate, were formed from a local area, the soldiers in a particular regiment were usually all from the same town, county, or region of a state.

Search for a regiment. Start at the Home Page of the CWSS site: **www.civilwar.nps.gov/cwss**. Click on "Regiments" to go to the Search Regiments screen. Select Union or Confederate, and the State (of origin). With just this information, a search will present a list of all regiments for one state. To go to a specific Unit, type the Unit Number or Ordinal as just a numeral, i.e., "25" rather than "25th", and a Function (i.e., Cavalry, Infantry, etc.).

As an example, a search in the CWSS soldier list for soldiers from Texas revealed an A.C. Dollarhide and a Cornelius Dollarhide, both soldiers in the **25th Regiment, Texas Cavalry (3rd Texas Lancers) (Gillespie's).** Going to each soldier's individual record indicated that A.C. Dollarhide was also known as Cornelius, so there were two entries for the same man. Going to the Regiments page, a search for the 25th Regiment, Texas Cavalry, brought up a regimental history, and a link to the list of all soldiers, adding a third entry for Cornelius with a variable spelling of Dollyhide. Examples of the results from that search are shown on the opposite page. The top box is an example of the regimental histories available for Union and Confederate regiments. The lower box shows an example of a name list for one regiment.

FEATURED EXHIBIT

FLAGS

Symbols in Battle
★ CIVIL WAR FLAGS IN ★
☆ NPS COLLECTIONS ☆

CONFEDERATE TEXAS TROOPS

25th Regiment, Texas Cavalry (3rd Texas Lancers) (Gillespie's)

25th Cavalry Regiment [also called 3rd Texas Lancers] was organized by C.C. Gillespie early in 1862. The unit was soon dismounted and ordered to Arkansas. Here it was captured in January, 1863, at Arkansas Post. After the exchange the regiment was consolidated with the 17th, 18th, and 24th Texas Cavalry Regiments (dismounted) and was placed in Deshler's, J.A. Smith's, and Granbury's Brigade, Army of Tennessee. This command fought with the army from Chickamauga to Atlanta, moved with Hood to Tennessee, and saw action in North Carolina. The 25th was organized with about 900 men and had 552 in action at Arkansas Post. At Chickamauga the 17th/18th/24th/25th suffered 200 casualties and in December, 1863, totalled 690 men and 520 arms. Only a remnant surrendered on April 26, 1865. The field officers were Colonel Clayton C. Gillespie, Lieutenant Colonel William M. Neyland, and Majors Joseph N. Dark and Edward B. Pickett.

Click here to search for soldiers in this unit.

Click here for a listing of all soldiers in this unit.

25TH REGIMENT, TEXAS CAVALRY (3RD TEXAS LANCERS) (GILLESPIE'S)

Displaying records 481 to 500 of 2361

No.	Last, First	Company	Rank_In	Rank_Out
481	Doiris, J.		Private	Private
482	Dolgado, Sevara	D	Private	Private
483	Dollard, J. J.	B	Private	Private
484	Dollarhide, A. C.	A	Private	Private
485	Dollarhide, Cornelius	A	Private	Private
486	Dollyhide, A. C.	A	Private	Private
487	Donahoe, C. C.	G	Private	Private

NATIONWIDE SOURCES
RG 2

The American Civil War Research Database (ACWRD)

Home page:
  www.civilwardata.com/
Soldier Search:
  Subscription required. One week pass: $10.00;
  Annual membership:$25.00.

The ACWRD is a private website operated by Historical Data Systems, Inc. of Duxbury, MA. The main database, a work in progress online for the last ten years, contains a list of Union and Confederate soldiers found under the category of "Personnel Directory." The number of soldiers are identified here in a single searchable database, currently with over 4.2 million officers and enlisted men of the Civil War. The main source for the names comes from rosters found in the various statewide Adjutant General reports, and for several state lists, from the *Index to Compiled Service Records* (same lists found in RG1). Users of the database are encouraged to add information about a particular soldier, and updates to the database takes place on a semi-monthly basis. As a result, the information about one soldier in the ACWRD system (RG2) is usually much greater than the CWSS System (RG1).

In addition to information on individual soldiers, the ACWRD also has extensive data about the various regiments of the Civil War, both Union forces and Confederate forces. The complete list of categories of special lists at this site includes the following:

● **Analytical Report List** – A list of Analysis Reports as well as a list of every available report and screen in the system.

● **Regiment Lookup** – Regiments listed by state, providing access to individual regiment information such as casualty analyses, experience charts, rosters, and histories.

● **Regimental Dynamics** – Regimental statistics for comparative purposes searchable by state, regiment type, and enlistment time.

● **Battle Directory** – Obtain battle statistics from the databases and battle synopses.

● **Battle Order Directory** – Battle Order and Reports for both Union and Confederate forces. Currently covers Shiloh, Antietam, and Gettysburg.

● **Personnel Directory** – Access to over 4.2 million officers and enlisted men of the Civil War, their war histories, battles, personnel histories, and information (when possible) about the town they came from and the units they fought in. In some cases indexes to pension records are available.

● **Photo Directory** – Access to the soldiers for whom a photograph is available.

● **Generals Directory** – Access to the General officer database. Contains personnel who attained a rank of Brigadier General or higher. Profiles and pictures for many are available. All other officers are in the Personnel Directory.

● **Medal of Honor Soldiers** – Access to the soldiers in the Database that were awarded the Medal of Honor. Stories about some of these soldiers are also available. (Source: *Deeds of Valor*)

● **Roll of Honor Soldiers** – Access to the Union soldiers in the Database that appear in the U.S. Quartermaster's Department *Roll of Honor* and can be identified as such. (See RG7).

An example of the search screen to locate one soldier is shown on the opposite page. Each soldier may lead you to biographical information from several sources.

Results from the search for Union soldiers with the surname Dollarhide, where seven names are listed. Another search was necessary for Confederate soldiers.

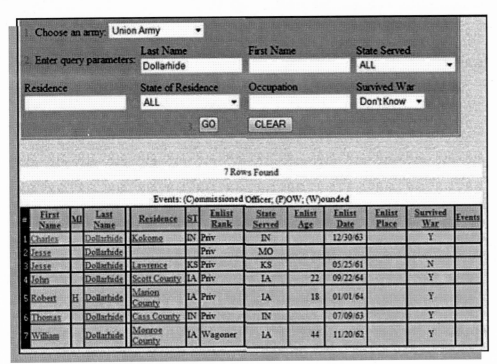

1. Choose an army: Union Army

2. Enter query parameters:

Last Name	First Name	State Served
Dollarhide		ALL

Residence	State of Residence	Occupation	Survived War
	ALL		Don't Know

GO   CLEAR

7 Rows Found

Events: (C)ommissioned Officer; (P)OW; (W)ounded

#	First Name	MI	Last Name	Residence	ST	Enlist Rank	State Served	Enlist Age	Enlist Date	Enlist Place	Survived War	Events
1	Charles		Dollarhide	Kokomo	IN	Priv	IN		12/30/63		Y	
2	Jesse		Dollarhide			Priv	MO					
3	Jesse		Dollarhide	Lawrence	KS	Priv	KS		05/25/61		N	
4	John		Dollarhide	Scott County	IA	Priv	IA	22	09/22/64		Y	
5	Robert	H	Dollarhide	Marion County	IA	Priv	IA	18	01/01/64		Y	
6	Thomas		Dollarhide	Cass County	IN	Priv	IN		07/09/63		Y	
7	William		Dollarhide	Monroe County	IA	Wagoner	IA	44	11/20/62		Y	

Click on any name to see a biography of that person, if available, as shown below:

Example of a biography of one soldier. The main source for the military information came from the Iowa Adjutant General's reports, with added personal information from other sources, including user-submitted data from private researchers.

Other information about the soldier is added, but the amount of information will vary from one soldier to the next.

William Dollarhide

Residence Monroe County IA; 44 years old.

Enlisted on 11/20/1862 as a Wagoner.

On 4/28/1863 he mustered into "D" Co. IA 7th Cavalry
He was Mustered Out on 12/23/1865 at Omaha, NE

Promotions:
* Private 6/28/1864 (Reduced to ranks)

Other Information:
born in Indiana
died in Douglas County, OR
Buried: Roseburg National Cemetery, Roseburg, OR

After the War he lived in Douglas County, OR

Sources used by Historical Data Systems, Inc.:

 - Roster & Record of Iowa Soldiers in the War of Rebellion
 - Research by Harold Slavik
(c) Historical Data Systems, Inc. @ www.civilwardata.com

NATIONWIDE SOURCES
RG 3

The War of the Rebellion: Official Records of the Union and Confederate Armies and Navies

■ *The War of the Rebellion: A Compilation of the Official Records of the Union and Confederate Armies,* originally published under the direction of the Secretary of War, printed by the Government Printing Office, Washington, D.C., 1880-1901, The original volumes were organized into four series with a total of 70 volumes. FHL has entire series, FHL book 973 M29u Series.1- 4. The volumes were microfilmed by the National Archives, series M262, and also filmed by the Genealogical Society of Utah, 1971, 120 rolls, beginning with FHL film #845206. The *War of the Rebellion* brings together extracts of the official written documents relating to the activities of the U.S. Army and the Confederate Army, including a myriad of correspondence, field orders, reports of battles, prisoners, reports and returns, and all operations in the field. The extracts are not generally related to the common soldier, but to the communication between officers of the Armies, at all levels of the command structures. The records are massive, cumbersome, and not well indexed.

■ ONLINE TEXT: *The War of the Rebellion (Armies).* Researchers now have access to a complete electronic version of the *War of the Rebellion* series, and with the wonder of Optical Character Recognition (OCR), every word in the 70-volume series is indexed. **The Making of America** service sponsored by Cornell University is a gathering of historical documents on the Internet. The Browse Page for the *War of the Rebellion* is at: **http://cdl.library.cornell.edu/ moa/browse.monographs/waro.html**. At the Browse page, a Table of Contents highlights the volumes, dates, chapters, etc., to navigate directly

to the text. The Cornell University database is available with free access. See also *The War of the Rebellion* (not all volumes) at the Ancestry.com subscription site.

■ *The Civil War CD-ROM: The War of the Rebellion, a Compilation of the Official Records of the Union and Confederate Armies,* designed by Philip Oliver, published by Guild Press, Carmel, IN, 1996, 2006, FHL CD-ROM No. 51. The CD-ROM also includes the complete text of Dyer's *Compendium of the War of the Rebellion; Regimental Losses in the American Civil War,* by William F. Fox; and *Military Operations of the Civil War,* by Dallas Irvine. Every word in the text in all books is OCR searchable.

■ *Official Records of the Union and Confederate Navies in the War of the Rebellion,* published by the Department of the Navy, printed by the Government Printing Office, 1894-1922, 30 vols. Index at the back of each volume. Content is similar to the Army series. FHL book 973 M2unr v.1-30. Also on microfilm, beginning with FHL film #1490058.

■ *General Index to Official Records of the Union and Confederate Navies in the War of the Rebellion,* reprint of original volume published by Government Printing office, 1927, 457 pages. Reprint by Antiquarian Press, New York, 1961, FHL book 973 M2unr index, and FHL film #924604.

The example on the opposite page is from *The War of Rebellion (Armies),* Series 1, Chapter 53, page 301.

CARROLLTON, *October 28, 1864.*

Brigadier-General CRAIG:

I am still without information of any rebel forces in this county. I will march southwest for about two hours, when, if I hear of no force farther west, I will change my direction to the east, with the view, first, of sweeping out any small force that may be lurking in the Sugar-tree bottom, and, second, of passing over to the eastern part of the county to Grand River, to release some loyal men said to be still hid in the brush in that neighborhood.

J. H. SHANKLIN,
Colonel, Commanding.

HDQRS. SIXTY-SEVENTH REGT. ENROLLED MISSOURI MIL.,
Wellsville, October 28, 1864.

Adjt. Gen. JOHN B. GRAY:

GENERAL: Some two weeks ago information was brought to me from Callaway County, which I have often found reliable, that this place was doomed, but that the attack would not be made for several days for the reason that I had strengthened my post by erecting a good stockade around the block-house, and they to be sure must have artillery, and that they had six pieces on Blackfoot, in Boone County. One week later 100 camped on Hickory Creek, six miles from here, who told Charles Clarke that they were on their way to re-enforce Dorsey, and that this place is doomed, and that they had sent for artillery this morning. Word was here that Bill Anderson was moving from Boone into Callaway, and that bodies of men, probably recruits, were going up the Missouri (bank) from Warren to concentrate near here. This p. m. I got word again that they had cannon, and were to meet Dorsey and his force here. I am advised of the move against Dorsey, and that may delay the threatened attack; but I will say that I am ordered to watch the movements of Dorsey's force, which I am on the lookout for night and day by trusty men. If I learn his coming in time and he takes the creeks up, he will be bushwhacked. I have been thus full in my statement to you, general, that the authorities may be better able to decide upon my call for artillery. The last messenger advised me to take and hold some persons prisoners, as then they will not attack me for fear I will shoot those in confinement. I trust, general, you will excuse me for being so lengthy, as I felt it my duty to impart all the information I possessed to those who know more than I do, and consequently better able to judge; but let them come as they may, they can get a fight.

I am, with respect, your obedient servant,

C. H. CANFIELD,
Colonel Sixty-seventh Regiment Enrolled Missouri Militia.

NATIONWIDE SOURCES
RG 4

Indexes to Pension Files – U.S. Veterans/Widows

In the early 1900s two major card indexes were compiled by the Pension Bureau, one set arranged by the veteran's name; the other arranged by the unit/organization in which a pensioner served during active service. These original card indexes were microfilmed, complete sets available, along with recent online indexes/images as indicated below:

■ *General Index to Pension files, 1861-1934,* microfilm of original records of the Veterans Administration, Washington, D.C., now at the National Archives. Includes index cards for all states, but a reference to pension records for Civil War veterans is limited to Union soldiers, or Union Colored Troops. Each card gives the soldier's name, rank, unit, and terms of service; names of relationships of any dependents; the application number; the certificate number; and the state from which the claim was filed. The index cards refer to pension applications of veterans who served in the U.S. Army between 1861 and 1917. The majority of the records pertain to Civil War veterans/widows, but they also include veterans of the Spanish-American War, the Philippine Insurrection, Indian wars, and World War I. Filmed by the National Archives in 1953 as Series T288, 544 rolls of 16mm film, beginning with FHL film #540757 (Abbott, Clifford - Ackerman, Garrett).

■ **ONLINE INDEX** (Ancestry.com): National Archives and Records Administration. *Civil War Pension Index: General Index to Pension Files, 1861-1934* [database on-line]. Provo, UT, USA: The Generations Network, Inc., 2000. Original data: *General Index to Pension Files, 1861-1934.* Washington, D.C.: National Archives and Records Administration. T288, 544 rolls.

■ *Organizational Index to Pension Files of Veterans Who Served Between 1861 and 1917,* microfilm of original manuscripts for all states at the National Archives, Washington, D.C. Filmed by the National Archives, series T289, 1949, 765 rolls (16mm). The information provided here is virtually the same as that in the *General Index to Pension Files, 1861-1934,* T0288. Unlike the alphabetical General Index, however, this index groups the applicants according to the units in which they served. The cards are arranged alphabetically by state, thereunder by arm of service (infantry, cavalry, artillery), thereunder numerically by regiment, and thereunder alphabetically by veteran's surname. Use the online index (RG1) to Civil War soldiers to locate a Union soldier, which will give the exact unit in which the person served. If the person applied for a pension, this series of records will give additional information about the person. Each card gives the soldier's name, rank, unit, and terms of service; names of relationships of any dependents; the application number; the certificate number; and the state from which the claim was filed.. The majority of the records pertain to Civil War veterans/widows, but they also include veterans of the Spanish-American War, the Philippine Insurrection, Indian wars, and World War I. The series begins with FHL film #1725491 (ALABAMA: Unassigned; 1st Alabama Colored Infantry; and Company C, 29th Alabama Infantry).

■ **ONLINE IMAGES:** *Organizational Index to Pension Files of Veterans Who Served Between 1861 and 1917,* digitized images from all 765 rolls of microfilm. Digitized for the National Archives by Footnote.com. Visit their site at **www.footnote.com** for details.

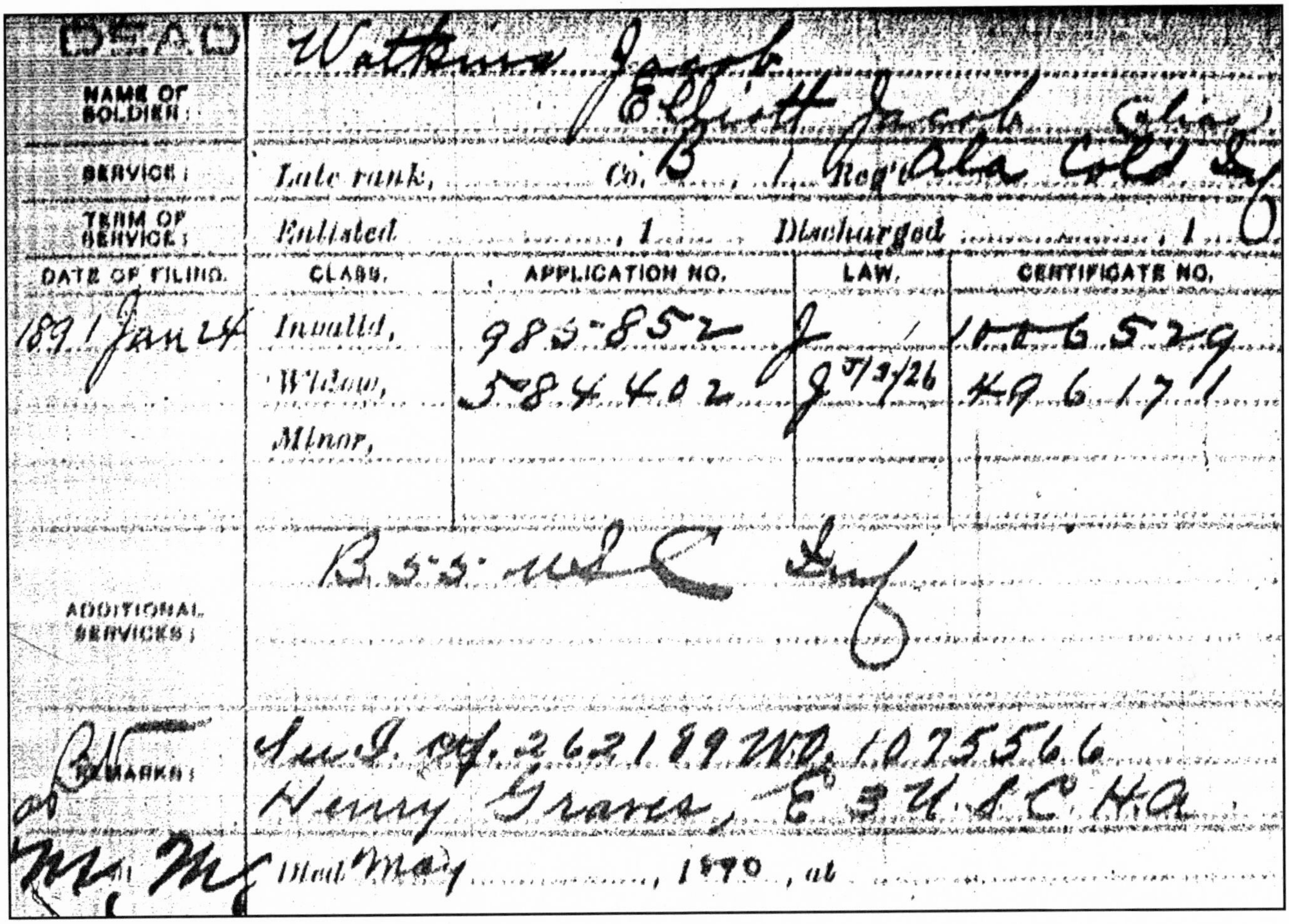

DEAD

NAME OF SOLDIER: Watkins Jacob / Elliott Jacob alias

SERVICE: Late rank, Co. B, 1 Reg't Ala Col'd Inf

TERM OF SERVICE: Enlisted , 1 Discharged , 1

DATE OF FILING	CLASS	APPLICATION NO.	LAW	CERTIFICATE NO.
1891 Jan 24	Invalid,	985852		1006529
	Widow,	584402	7/3/26	496171
	Minor,			

ADDITIONAL SERVICES: B 55 U.S.C. Inf

REMARKS: See I. Ctf. 262189 WO. 1075566 Henry Graves, E 3 U.S.C.H.A.

Died May , 1890, at

Example of an index card from ***Organizational Index to Pension Files of Veterans Who Served Between 1861-1917***. The cards are available on microfilm, but all 765 rolls of microfilm were recently digitized and made available online at **www.footnote.com**.

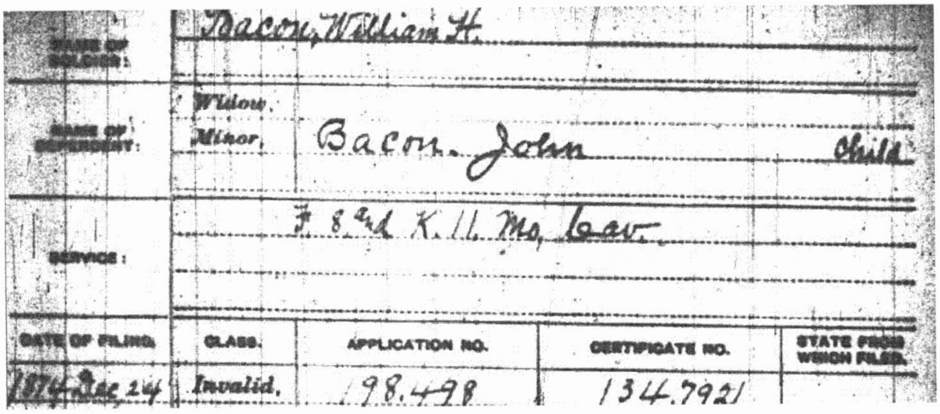

NAME OF SOLDIER: Bacon, William H.

NAME OF DEPENDENT: Widow, Minor, Bacon John Child

SERVICE: F 8 K 11 Mo Cav.

DATE OF FILING	CLASS	APPLICATION NO.	CERTIFICATE NO.	STATE FROM WHICH FILED.
1874 Dec 24	Invalid,	98498	134792	

Note that there are index cards for the soldier, any widow who applied for a pension, and any minor children eligible for a pension. The example shown here is for a child, John Bacon, eligible for a pension based on the service of William H. Bacon, the soldier. The word "child" on the line for John Bacon confirms that he was a son of the soldier.

NATIONWIDE SOURCES
RG 5

1883 List of Pensioners on the Roll

The 1883 *List of Pensioners on the Roll* was published by the U.S. Pension Bureau in five volumes. Although the volumes have been reprinted, both in book form and CD-ROM, the publication has never been microfilmed, except for the portion of volume 4 containing pensioners residing in Minnesota. (See FHL fiche #6334560).

■ *List of Pensioners on the Roll January 1, 1883: Giving the Name of Each Pensioner, the Cause for Which Pensioned, the Post-Office Address, and the Date of Original Allowance,* 5 vols., 3,952 pages, originally prepared by the United States Pension Bureau, published in 1883 as Senate Executive Document 84, Parts 1-5, reprint by Genealogical Publishing Co., Inc., Baltimore, 1970. FHL book 973 M2Lp v. 1-5.

This is the official Pension Roll of 1883, the major genealogical source for Civil War and War of 1812 pensioners. Arranged by state or territory, and thereunder by county, it contains the full names of approximately 300,000 persons who were on the Pension Rolls as of 1883, with such information as set forth in the subtitle above. Pensioners residing in the New England states, New Jersey, and the District of Columbia listed in the first volume; those residing in New York and Pennsylvania in the second; those residing in Iowa, Ohio, and Illinois in the third; and those resident elsewhere (including foreign countries) in the fourth and fifth.

■ See also *Federal Pensioners' Roll of 1883,* prepared by James N. Jackson, a CD-ROM publication by Heritage Quest, North Salt Lake, UT, 1998, which includes a searchable name index and the full textual content of all five volumes. The list contains the names of all people receiving federal pensions for military service. In 1883 most of the pensioners were Civil War veterans, but this list includes pensions for service in the Mexican War, the Cherokee Removal of 1836, the War of 1812 and even a few from the Revolutionary War. FHL CD-ROM No. 135.

■ **ONLINE INDEXES:** *List of Pensioners on the Roll,* **Statewide Indexes.** There are a few statewide lists from the Pensioners on the Roll listings posted at various websites. A review of those linked at **www.censusfinder.com** (and other portals) shows statewide name lists for Arizona Territory, California, Colorado, Indiana, Kansas, Michigan, South Dakota, and Wyoming.

LIST
OF
PENSIONERS ON THE ROLLS JANUARY 1, 1883.

NEW YORK.
ALBANY COUNTY.

No. of certificate.	Name of pensioner.	Post-office address.	Cause for which pensioned.	Monthly rate.	Date of original allowance.
125, 272	Keenan, Thomas	Albany	g. a. w. l. hand, &c	$2 00	Oct., 1873
147, 915	Wall, Benj	do	g. a. w. l. thi	4 00	Aug., 1877
177, 428	Bates, Otis	do	injury to abdomen	8 00	Oct., 1880
161, 071	Mortimer, Richard	do	g. a. w. l. breast	4 00	June, 1879
112, 094	Low, Edw	do	chr. rheum	8 00	July, 1871
121, 770	Smith, Wm. H	do	wd. lft. hand, &c	8 00	Nov., 1873
133, 221	Ball, Jno. J	do	cut l. ft. with an axe	5 00	Apr., 1875
156, 213	Burr, Samuel G	do	chr. diarr	2 00	Oct., 1878
21, 448	Dodge, Charles B	do	loss r. arm	24 00	
161, 033	Hill, Loren C	do	g. a. w. l. arm	2 00	June, 1879
130, 557	Brown, Milton	do	epilepsy	8 00	Jan., 1878
2, 360	Reed, Joseph P	do	wd. rt. side	8 00	
181, 929	Scace, Jno. B	do	g. a. w. l. thi	4 00	Feb., 1881
25, 899	Steeve, Marquis E	do	wd. rt. lung	8 00	
125, 905	Tyler, Elnathan B	do	wd. rt. hip	2 00	
23, 446	Bassett, Geo. S	do	loss forefin. l. h.	2 00	
45, 679	Leahy, Thomas M	do	wd. rt. leg	2 00	
188, 665	Miller, Charles W	do	g. a. wd. r. leg. & shell wd. r. side.	18 00	May, 1881
37, 962	Hillsgrove, Albert H	do	g. a. w. face, loss l. eye	12 00	
	Wheelock, Cyrus	do	wd. r. wrist	5 00	
	Jacobs, Maurice H	do	g. a. w. r. breast & r. arm	8 00	Jan., 1881
	Greene, Franklin L	do	partial deafness both ears & inj. of spine.	6 00	July, 1881
114, 958	Barber, Robt. P	do	wd. of rt. hip & head	8 00	
64, 610	Lake, Jno. W	do	g. a. w. rt. arm	8 00	
32, 553	Brusseau, Sirrell	do	wd. l. forearm	8 00	
142, 701	Sheehan, Jno	do	gen'l debility	8 00	Oct., 1876
173, 018	Morris, Watkins J	do	g. a. w. l. knee	4 00	Apr., 1865
213, 432	Curtis, Geo. B	do	dis. of spine	12 00	Aug., 1863
185, 949	Deller, Wm	do	g. a. w. l. arm	4 00	July, 1865
125, 562	Becker, James H	do	g. a. w. thi. and r. leg	2 00	Apr., 1873
160, 884	Gallagher, Jane	do	g. a. w. l. forearm	4 00	Oct., 1864
60, 140	Springer, Edw	do	wd. lft. leg	2 66⅔	Aug., 1865
191, 424	Neideck, Albert	do	dis. of eyes	4 00	June, 1864
124, 588	Mattison, Luca V. S	do	sunstroke	4 00	May, 1873
140, 004	McMillan, Alex	do	dis. of lungs res. inter. fever.	4 00	July, 1865
142, 199	Parmelee, Dennis A	do	rheum	12 00	Aug., 1876
59, 339	Clifford, Jno. M	do	g. a. w. of face	4 00	June, 1865

Sample page from *List of Pensioners on the Roll*, Vol. 2.

NATIONWIDE SOURCES
RG 6

1890 Federal Census (Special Schedules) of Union Veterans

An Act of March 1, 1889, provided that the Superintendent of the Census in taking the Eleventh Census should "cause to be taken on a special schedule of inquiry, according to such form as he may prescribe, the names, organizations, and length of service of those who had served in the Army, Navy, or Marine Corps of the United States in the war of the rebellion, and who are survivors at the time of said inquiry, and the widows of soldiers, sailors, or marines."

Most of the 1890 population schedules were destroyed as a result of a 1921 fire in the Commerce Building in Washington, D.C. Surviving the fire were about half of the Special Schedules for veterans, which were organized in bound volumes and stored in alphabetical order by state. The Special Schedules for the states of Alabama through Kansas and approximately half of those for Kentucky were lost.

■ *Special Schedules Enumerating Union Veterans and Widows of Union Veterans of the Civil War,* microfilm of original records at the National Archives, Washington, D.C. Each schedule calls for the following information: name of the veteran (or if he did not survive, the names of both the widow and her deceased husband); the veteran's rank, company, regiment or vessel, date of enlistment, date of discharge, and length of service in years, months, and days; post office and address of each person listed; disability incurred by the veteran; and remarks necessary to a complete statement of his term of service. Surviving schedules beginning with Kentucky through Wyoming were filmed by the National Archives, 1948, as series M123, on 118 rolls. The FHL has the entire set, beginning with

FHL film #338160 (**Kentucky:** Boone, Bourbon, Bracken, Campbell, Clark, Fayette, Franklin, Gallatin, Grant, Harrison, Jessamine, Kenton, Owen, Pendleton, Scott, and Woodford Counties).

■ See also *1890 Veterans' Schedules, Selected States,* a CD-ROM publication by Genealogy.com, CD131, 1998. This CD contains an index of approximately 385,000 war veterans and veterans' widows who were enumerated on the special veterans' schedule of the 1890 United States census. Although the 1890 veterans' schedule was meant only to record information about Union soldiers and their widows, it also lists information about some Confederate soldiers, as well as soldiers who served in other wars, such as the War of 1812 and the Mexican-American War. States represented include AL, DC, IL, KY, LA, MD, ME, MI, MS, MT, NC, ND, NE, NH, NJ, NM, NV, OK, OR, RI, SC, SD, TN, TX, UT, VA, VT, WA, WI, WV, and WY. In addition, there are a few records from the states of CA, CT, DE, FL, GA, ID, IN, KS, MA, NY, OH, and PA. Each indexed entry includes the individual's first and last name, age, sex, microfilm page number, state, county, and locality of residence at the time of the enumeration.

■ **ONLINE INDEX** (Ancestry.com): The contents of the CD-ROM above is also an online database at Ancestry.com.

■ **Statewide Indexes, 1890 Veterans Census.** Most of the state name lists have been indexed in separate volumes. Refer to **Part 3 – Statewide Name Lists** for a state of interest.

Special Schedule.—Surviving Soldiers, Sailors, and Marines, and Widows, etc. PAGE

S. D.: 4 ; E. D.: 14 ; Minor Civil Division: *Millersburg Precinct 3*

House No.	Family No.	Names of Surviving Soldiers, Sailors, and Marines, and Widows.	Rank.	Company.	Name of Regiment or Vessel.	Date of Enlistment.	Date of Discharge.	Length of Service.			
1	2	3	4	5	6	7	8	Yrs.	Mos.	Days	
197	223	*George Mack alias* *George Mack Fawn*	—	—	—	—	186—	186—	—	—	—	27
224	254	*Peter O'Connell* ✓	Priv	C	21 Ky Reg Col 4	186— Jan—	186—	4	—	—	28
241	271	*John Donaldson* ✓	Priv	—	—	—	186—	186—	—	—	—	29
358	388		Priv	E					3			30
289	325	*Ama Martin*	Priv	E	16 Ky Inf Co 1	186— July 1	186—	3	6	0	31
314	349	*Julius H. Calamese* ✓	Corpl	E	114 Ky Inf Reg 80	1864 Apr 2	1867	2	11	29	32
328	363	*Thomas Grant* ✓	Priv	—	—	—	186—	186—	—	—	—	33
329	365	*Asa St Louis* ✓	Priv	I	28 Ky Reg	—	1861 Sept—	1865	4	2	0	34
363	400	*James Honahu* ✓	—	—	—	—	186—	186—	—	—	—	35
404	443	*John M. Jameson* ✓	Captain	D	21 Ky Reg Div 2	1862 Jan 6	1866	4	1	4	36
25	29	*Alford Allen alias* *Alford Williams*	Priv	B	107 Ky Reg Inf 30	1864	—	186—	—	—	—	37
38							186—	186—				38
39							186—	186—				39
40							186—	186—				40

	Post-Office Address.	Disability Incurred.	Remarks.
	10	11	12
27	*Millersburg Ky*	—	X
28	*Millersburg Ky*	*Gun Shot*	X
29	*Millersburg Ky*	x	X
30	*Millersburg Ky*	*Gun Shot*	X
31	*Millersburg Ky*	*Pick a dorn through hand*	X
32	*Paris Ky*	*Sentry and fever*	X
33	*Paris Ky*	x	X
34	*Millersburg Ky*	x	X
35	*Millersburg Ky*	x	X
36	*Millersburg Ky*	*None*	X
37	*Millersburg Ky*	*Rheumatism*	X
38			
39			
40			

Sample page from the 1890 Special Schedules, showing Union Veterans and Widows
living in the precinct of Millersburg, Bourbon County, Kentucky.

NATIONWIDE SOURCES
RG 7

Roll of Honor & Veteran Burials for All States

■ *Roll of Honor: Names of Soldiers Who Died in Defense of the American Union,* originally published by the Government Printing Office, 1865-1871, Washington, D.C., 27 volumes. Recently reprinted by Genealogical Publishing Co., these books reference the names of over 200,000 Union soldiers who were buried in national cemeteries, soldiers' lots, and garrison cemeteries. The *Roll of Honor* is the only official memorial to the Union dead ever published, and in spite of some omissions and discrepancies, it remains the most comprehensive source of information on Civil War fatalities. Originally compiled by the U.S. Quartermaster's Department, it was published volume by volume as battlefield sites were surveyed, graves exhumed, and bodies identified and reburied. Information given for each cemetery includes the soldier's name, rank, regiment, company, date of death, and original place of interment. Filmed by the Genealogical Society of Utah, 1981, 3 rolls, FHL film #1445832, 1311589, and 1311590. The first roll contains an alphabetical index to places of interment of deceased Union soldiers, by state.

■ *The Unpublished Roll of Honor,* compiled by Mark Hughes, published by Genealogical Publishing Co., Baltimore, MD, 1996, 326 pages. This book continues the listing of burials of soldiers in post cemeteries and burials of civilians in national and post cemeteries that was begun by the Quartermaster's Department in the *Roll of Honor,* giving the researcher access to previously unpublished records of both soldiers and early settlers on the frontier. FHL book 973 M2oha.

■ *Roll of Honor: Civil War Soldiers,* a CD-ROM publication by Genealogical Publishing Co., Inc., Baltimore; and Family Tree Maker Family Archives, Broderbund, 1998. This CD contains images of the pages of all 27 volumes of

the *Roll of Honor* as well as *The Unpublished Roll of Honor.* A name index to all 27 volumes and *The Unpublished Roll* is also included on the CD. See FHL CD-ROM No. 9 part 351.

■ See also, *Index to the Roll of Honor,* compiled by Martha & William Reamy; with foreword and an index to burial sites by Mark Hughes, published by Genealogical Publishing Co., Inc., Baltimore, 1995, 1,164 pages. FHL book 973 M2roh.

■ **Online Index to Veteran Burials,** Veterans Administration. The *Nationwide Gravesite Locator* is a free website to locate any U.S. veteran, including many Civil War era veterans. Burial locations of veterans and their family members include those in VA National Cemeteries, state veterans cemeteries, Department of Interior cemeteries, and for many veterans buried in private cemeteries when the grave is marked with a government grave marker. Visit the search form at: **http://gravelocator.cem.va.gov/j2ee/servlet/NGL_v1.**

MISSOURI.

No.	Name.	Rank.	Co.	Regiment.	Date of death.	Section.	No. of grave.	No. of disinterment.	Original Place of Interment.
1	A——, D. C.					47	15	953	St. Louis, Mo.
2	A—ger, Wm.	Private	E	47th Indiana inf.	July 10, 1864	8	130		Jefferson Barracks, Mo.
3	Aaron, N.		A	3d Kentucky inf.	May 18, 1862	12	73	2,731	St. Louis, Mo.
4	Abbott, C.			33d Illinois inf.		35	1	187	Butler County, Mo.
5	Abbott, Henry		I	35th Illinois	Jan. 3, 1862	27	185	3,026	St. Louis, Mo.
6	Abbott, James M.		F	4th Missouri guards	June 25, 1862				
7	Abbott, James M.	Corporal	K	136th Illinois inf.	Oct. 23, 1864	34	230		Jefferson Barracks, Mo.
8	Abbott, John		F	13th Illinois	Feb. 1, 1863	35	20	219	St. Louis, Mo.
9	Abbott, Richard		F	31st Iowa	Feb. 1, 1863	51	18	155	Do.
10	Abbott, Samuel W.	Private	F	130th Illinois inf.	Nov. 1, 1863	5	162		Jefferson Barracks, Mo.
11	Abbott, Tho. J.		I	18th Indiana	Jan. 8, 1862	59	51	3,038	St. Louis, Mo.
12	Abbott, W.		I	1st Nebraska	May 2, 1862	36	29	1,054	Do.
13	Able, Datus E.		D	31st Iowa inf.	Mar. 2, 1862	38	257	3,342	Do.
14	Able, John B.	Private	L	9th Iowa cav.	Aug. 15, 1864	34	155		Jefferson Barracks, Mo.
15	Ables, Theodore		K	15th Iowa	Jan. 2, 1862	51	33	1,060	St. Louis, Mo.
16	Abner, Jesse	Private	I	30th Illinois inf.	Oct. 11, 1863	33	62		Jefferson Barracks, Mo.
17	Abraham, Ezekiel	do	E	83d Indiana	June 22, 1863	2	169		Do.
18	Abrams, Elijah		A	38th Illinois	June 28, 1862	35	107	2,314	St. Louis, Mo.
19	Ackerman, Jacob		A	13th Missouri inf.	Dec. 22, 1862	26	133	2,963	Do.
20	Acres, A.		D	29th Missouri inf.		24	293	1,112	Cape Girardeau, Mo.
21	Adair, Benj.	Private	H	35th Missouri inf.	April 17, 1863	2	49		Jefferson Barracks, Mo.
22	Adams, David		B	8th Indiana inf.	Oct. 29, 1862	58	140	2,865	St. Louis, Mo.
23	Adams, George R.	Sergeant	D	6th Minnesota inf.	Oct. 11, 1864	32	157		Jefferson Barracks, Mo.
24	Adams, James	Private	L	6th Missouri cav.	Dec. 4, 1864	8	208		Do.
25	Adams, James A.	do	F	47th Iowa inf.	Sept. 18, 1864	33	146		Do.
26	Adams, Jesse		D	30th Indiana	April 21, 1862	58	86	1,220	St. Louis, Mo.
27	Adams, Jos.		E	46th Indiana	April 27, 1862	53	91	1,372	Do.
28	Adams, Porter		E	13th Illinois	Feb. 17, 1863	35	135	3,919	Do.
29	Adams, Samuel		K	21st Missouri	July 1, 1862	39	124	1,140	Do.
30	Addison, Israel T.	Private	B	81st Illinois, (pris.)	Nov. 3, 1863		89		Jefferson Barracks, Mo.
31	Aeson, A. J.		F	56th Illinois	Sept. 4, 1862	27	123	2,426	St. Louis, Mo.
32	Agee, Chas. H. B.	Private	A	1st Indiana cav.	Nov. 3, 1864	31	179		Jefferson Barracks, Mo.
33	Ager, G.		H	15th Wisconsin	Aug. 28, 1862	37	65	1,154	St. Louis, Mo.
34	Aggee, W.		G	32d Missouri	Nov. 21, 1862	39	61	279	Do.
35	Aglor, Peter		G	29th Iowa	Feb. 3, 1863	37½	5	4,025	Do.
36	Agner, Wm. J.		D	2d Missouri cav.	Mar. 31, 1862	26	159	3,405	Do.
37	Ahas, Charles	Private	K	11th Missouri cav.		26	305	775	Rolla, Mo.
38	Aichel, Philip		K	7th Illinois cav.	June 3, 1862	27	48	1,477	St. Louis, Mo.
39	Aiken, John		K	32d Illinois	June 22, 1862	35	112	2,310	Do.
40	Aikin, John	Private	C	37th Iowa	May 25, 1865	2	120		Jefferson Barracks, Mo.
41	Ainsworth, M.		I	48th Indiana	Nov. 20, 1862	58	36	429	St. Louis, Mo.
42	Akers, Harvey	Private	K	12th M. S. M. cav.		39	14	230	Jackson, Mo.
43	Akers, John	do	A	10th Indiana cav.	July 13, 1862	45	351		Jefferson Barracks, Mo.
44	Akers, R.		A	1st Missouri art.	Nov. 11, 1862	25	22	323	St. Louis, Mo.
45	Albee, Albert C.	Sergeant	D	9th Minnesota inf.	Nov. 13, 1864	32	188		Jefferson Barracks, Mo.
46	Albers, Albert	Private	A	119th Illinois inf.	Aug. 17, 1863	31	60		Do.
47	Alberson, Solomon	do	K	12th Missouri cav.	April 11, 1863	8	29		Do.
48	Albert, Dennis	do	G	2d Missouri art.	April 7, 1863	1	22		Do.
49	Albertson, Alfred	do	G	12th Illinois cav.	Mar. 3, 1864	7	233		Do.
50	Albertson, Wm.	do	H	34th Indiana inf.	July 22, 1863	31	9		Do.
51	Albright, Ferdinand	do	E	21st Iowa inf.	Aug. 30, 1863	5	124		Do.
52	Albro, Jno.		H	24th Missouri inf.	Nov. 3, 1862	26	123	2,864	St. Louis, Mo.
53	Aldridge, Jas. J.		G	14th Iowa	Dec. 29, 1861	51	135	3,064	Do.
54	Aldridge, W. J.	Private	B	49th Illinois	Aug. 15, 1864	34	160		Jefferson Barracks, Mo.
55	Alexander, Chas. C.		H	29th Illinois	May 4, 1862	29	60	2,559	St. Louis, Mo.
56	Alexander, Christ.		F	28th Illinois	Dec. 1, 1862	35	44	621	Do.
57	Alexander, J. M.		F	77th Pennsylvania	May 9, 1862	48	19	1,201	Do.
58	Alexander, John	Private	D	29th Iowa	April 28, 1863	1	46		Jefferson Barracks, Mo.
59	Alexander, John	do	B	26th Indiana inf.	Aug. 11, 1863	7	86		Do.
60	Alexander, N.		H	46th Ohio inf.	April 17, 1862	65	39	1,261	St. Louis, Mo.
61	Alexander, Samuel M.	Private	K	9th Iowa inf.	Jan. 11, 1864	6	191		Jefferson Barracks, Mo.
62	Alexander, W. C.		A	1st Arkansas	Oct. 11, 1862	49	43	718	St. Louis, Mo.
63	Alford, Isaac L.		E	18th Indiana	Nov. 3, 1862	58	190	3,668	Do.
64	Alger, Abner	Private	A	8th Iowa	July 12, 1862	6	48		Jefferson Barracks, Mo.
65	Alger, Abraham	do	I	17th Michigan inf.	Mar. 4, 1864	7	230		Do.
66	Allan, T. C.		A	32d Missouri	Nov. 27, 1862	25	30		St. Louis, Mo.
67	Allen, Albert		C	42d Indiana	Dec. 8, 1861	58	300	373	Tipton, Mo.
68	Allen, August G.	Private	A	39th Missouri inf.	Feb. 23, 1865	45	26		Jefferson Barracks, Mo.
69	Allen, Daniel W.		E	12th Michigan		53	13	1,438	St. Louis, Mo.
70	Allen, F. A.		B	Curtis Horse	Jan. 18, 1862	48	42	2,113	Do.
71	Allen, Geo.		A	1st M. S. M.	Jan. 5, 1862	26	49	1,065	Do.
72	Allen, George	Corporal	A	178th New York inf.	Aug. 24, 1864	8	140		Jefferson Barracks, Mo.

Sample pages from the *Roll of Honor: Names of Soldiers Who Died in Defense of the American Union*, Vol. XX, pages 196-197, showing "Missouri: Union Soldiers Interred in the National Cemetery, Jefferson Barracks, Missouri."

NATIONWIDE SOURCES
RG 8

1865-1867 Confederate Amnesty Papers

■ **1865-1867 Confederate Amnesty Papers. See** *Case Files of Applications From Former Confederates for Presidential Pardons,* microfilm of original records of the U.S. Adjutant General's Office, now at the National Archives, Washington, DC. Includes alphabetical name index to the pardon application files (on roll 1). A Presidential pardon would restore a citizen to his former civil rights and would also provide immunity from prosecution for treason and from confiscation of property. The records consist of approximately 14,000 files containing pardon applications and related papers submitted to President Johnson, 1865-1867, by persons excepted from his amnesty proclamation of May 29, 1865, together with a few applications submitted to President Lincoln by persons excepted under his earlier proclamations. Included with each application is an oath of allegiance signed by the petitioner and, in many cases, recommendations from prominent citizens for clemency or letters from relatives or friends containing pleas for compassion. In some instances, there are notations by the President or his assistants indicating action on a particular case. The individual files often contain considerable information on a pardon applicant's background, his activities during the war years, and his attitude in defeat. Filed at the end of the alphabetically arranged records under each state, are various types of special files. For most states there are applications bearing the names of two or more individuals (Two-or-more name files) and/or documents relating to the business of pardoning (Miscellaneous files). Under South Carolina there is also a separate alphabetically arranged group of amnesty oaths (Special file) for persons whose applications are not included in the alphabetical name file. In group 2 under

the District of Columbia, there is a separate alphabetically arranged set of application files from persons excluded by the 10th exception (passing into the Confederacy from U.S. territory to aid in rebellion) but recommended for pardon by Mayor Richard Wallach. The pardon application files are divided into three groups: (1) applications submitted by persons from the South (Alabama, Arkansas, Florida, Georgia, Kentucky, Louisiana, Maryland, Mississippi, Missouri, North Carolina, South Carolina, Tennessee, Texas, Virginia, and West Virginia); (2) pardon applications submitted by persons from the North and West (California, Delaware, District of Columbia, Illinois, Indiana, Iowa, Kansas, Massachusetts, Michigan, Nebraska, New Jersey, New Mexico Territory, New York, Ohio, Pennsylvania, and Rhode Island); and (3) applications submitted by persons who designated no state or territory. Group 1, by far the most voluminous, is filmed on rolls 1-72; groups 2 and 3 are filmed on roll 73. Each of the first two groups is arranged alphabetically by state, territory, or district and thereunder alphabetically by surname of petitioner; the third group is arranged alphabetically by surname of petitioner. Beginning in 1867 Loyalty Oaths, or pardon applications, were taken by former Confederates, and provide the name of person, county of residence, number of months of residence in the state, the exact birth date, generally the county and state of birth, and naturalization date and place. Filmed by the National Archives, series M1003, 73 rolls. FHL has entire series, beginning with FHL film #1578739 (Name index to Pardon Application files. Group 1: Pardon applications submitted by persons from the South, Alabama Ab – Bo).

Examples of certain Confederate Amnesty Papers: An "Application for executive clemency and pardon," submitted by John Matlock of Camden, Arkansas, dated October 28, 1865.

As part of application process, John Matlock was also required to swear allegiance to the United States. Generally, it was property owners who applied for presidential pardons, because the pardon would restore civil rights to former Confederates citizens.

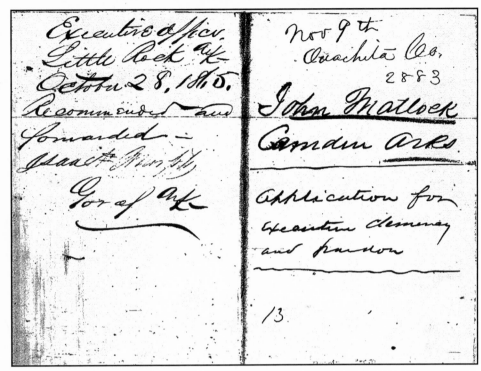

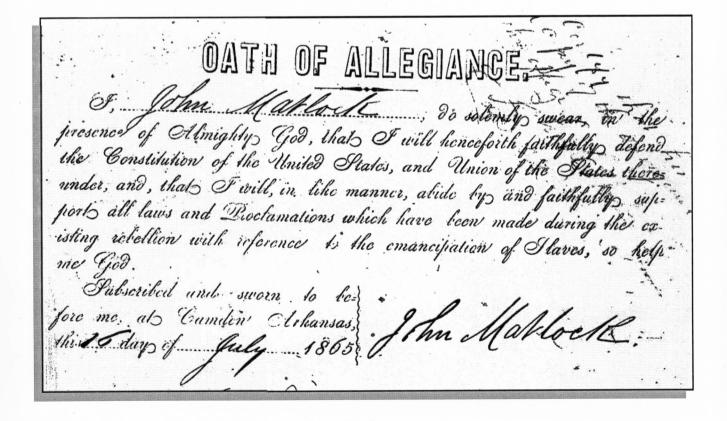

NATIONWIDE SOURCES
RG 9

Consolidated Lists and Records of Confederate Soldiers & United Confederate Veterans Association

■ *Consolidated Index to Compiled Service Records of Confederate Soldiers,* microfilm of original records at the National Archives, Washington, D.C. A typical General Index Card gives the name of the soldier, his rank, battalion, regiment, company, or other organization to which he belonged. In the early 1900s, indexing projects by the Bureau of Pensions combined the Confederate and Union Service Records. For each state, an index was prepared, using the General Index Cards for both Union and Confederate soldiers. Another set of General Index Cards was created for the Confederate soldiers from all states, which is the source of this *Consolidated Index.* Filmed by the National Archives, series M253, 536 rolls. FHL has entire set, beginning with FHL film #821594 (A-Adaholts).

■ *Compiled Service Records of Confederate Soldiers Who Served in Organizations Raised Directly by the Confederate Government (1861-1865),* microfilm of original records at the National Archives, Washington, D.C. Contains records of Confederate soldiers who served in military organizations formed by the Confederate Government and therefore not identified with any one state. Includes units of the Confederate Regular Army, several units raised among residents of Indian Territory, and one for foreigners recruited among Union prisoners of war. Filmed by the National Archives, series M258, 123 rolls. FHL has entire series, beginning with FHL film #880207 (First Confederate Cavalry, A-C).

■ *Compiled Service Records of Confederate General and Staff Officers and Enlisted Men,* microfilm of original records at the National Archives, Washington, D.C. Contains the compiled service records of Confederate officers and enlisted men who did not belong to any particular regiment, separate company or special corps. This class of military personnel included general officers, staff officers and enlisted men of the staff departments; and various appointees with a special status such as aides-de-camp, military judges, chaplains, agents, and drillmasters. Filmed by the National Archives, series M331, 275 rolls. FHL has entire series, beginning with FHL film #881105 (A-Adams).

■ *1895-1899 Membership Rosters, United Confederate Veterans,* microfilm of original records housed at the Jackson Barracks Military Library/Museum, New Orleans, LA. The records are organized by the state of residence of the veteran. Filmed by the Genealogical Society of Utah, 1990, 2 rolls, FHL film #1710607 (Rosters 1895-1899 Alabama – Mississippi) and FHL film #1710608 (Rosters 1895-1899, Missouri – West Virginia, miscellaneous).

Note: An early official in charge of memberships for the United Confederate Veterans Association, was also the Adjutant General of the state of Louisiana. A collection of the original applications for UCV membership from Confederate veterans nationwide were maintained at the Louisiana Adjutant General's office. The original applications for membership contain genealogical information about a Confederate veteran that may not be known from any other source. The applications have never been microfilmed, but the *1895-1899 Membership Rosters* from all states would indicate if an application document exists. A request for a copy could then be made to the Jackson Barracks Military Library, Building 53, Jackson Barracks, New Orleans, LA 70146.

The example to the right is for a document found in the **Compiled Service Records** series, in this case an expense voucher for the travels of a Confederate captain, with several hotel stops paid out-of-pocket. The document was issued by the Confederate States of America.

The sample page to the left is from the *1895-1899 Membership Rosters, United Confederate Veterans*.

NATIONWIDE SOURCES
RG 10

Index to Compiled Service Records,
Union Regulars, Veteran Reserve Corps & U.S. Colored Troops

On the chart showing the number of soldiers for each state in the CWSS database (RG1, page 10), the non-state units are indicated as Union Regulars, Veteran Reserves, Colored Troops, and non-state Volunteers. Together these non-state units represent about 13 percent of the total of Union soldiers who served in the Civil War. The names are included in the CWSS website index, and the microfilmed images of the original General Index Cards are found in three separate publications, as shown below:

■ *Index to Compiled Service Records of Volunteer Union soldiers Who Served in Organizations Not Raised by States or Territories,* microfilm of original records at the National Archives, Washington, D.C. The compiled service records to which these indexes apply consist of a jacket-envelope for each soldier, labeled with his name and containing the cards and original records, if any, pertaining to him. A typical General Index Card gives the name of the soldier, his rank, battalion, regiment, company, or other organization to which he belonged. This series of microfilm includes 14 alphabetical card name indexes to the compiled service records of volunteer soldiers who served in Union organizations not raised by states or territories, excepting the Veterans Reserve Corps and the U.S. Colored Troops. These 14 organizations were: 1) U.S. Sharp Shooters; 2) Signal Corps; 3) U.S. Volunteers; 4) Pioneer Brigade (Army of the Cumberland); 5) U.S. Veteran volunteers, engineers; 6) U.S. Veteran volunteers, infantry; 7) Confederate prisoners of War who enlisted in the U.S. Army; 8) brigade bands; 9) Indian home guards; 10) Mississippi Marine Brigade/Marine regiment; 11) U.S. volunteers; 12) enlisted men transferred to the Mississippi Flotilla, February 21, 22, and 23,

1862; 13) Departmental Corps (Department of the Monongahela); and 14) Varner's Battalion of infantry and Captain Turners Company. Filmed by the National Archives, series M1290, 37 rolls. FHL has complete series, beginning with FHL film #1604884 (U.S. Sharpshooters, A – K).

■ *Index to Compiled Service Records of Volunteer Union Soldiers Who Served in the Veteran Reserve Corps,* microfilm of original records at the National Archives, Washington, D.C. The Veteran Reserve Corps was composed of deserving officers and enlisted men who were unfit for active field service because of wounds or disease contracted in the line of duty, but who were still capable of performing garrison duty. The Corps also included officers and enlisted men borne on the Army rolls who were absent from duty and in hospitals, in convalescent camps, or otherwise under the control of medical officers, but who were capable of serving as cooks, nurses, clerks, or orderlies at hospitals and as guards for hospitals or other public buildings. When the Corps was first authorized in April 1863, it was known as the Invalid Corps. Its name was changed to the Veteran Reserve Corps in March 1864. Filmed by the National Archives, series M636, 26 rolls. FHL has entire series, beginning with FHL film #120358 (A – Ba).

■ *Index to Compiled Service Records of Volunteer Union Soldiers Who Served with United States Colored Troops,* microfilm of original records at the National Archives, Washington, D.C. Does not include Union soldiers serving with state units or in the regular army. Filmed by the National Archives, series M589, 1964, 98 rolls. FHL has complete series, beginning with FHL film #1266617 (A – Alk).

J. | **3 Cav.** | **Md.**

M. W. Sayers

Bugler 1 Regt. S.C. Cav

Confederate.

Appears on a

Roll of Prisoners of War

at Fort Delaware, Del., turned over by Brig. Gen. A. Schoepf, U. S. Vols., to Lieut. Col. C. C. Tevis, 4th Del. Infantry, and commanding 3d Maryland Cavalry, September 5, 1863.

Roll dated ____Not dated____

_____, 186 .

Where captured _Centerville, Tenn_

When captured _____June 27_, 1863.

Where born ____Ireland____

Remarks: ____Conscript____

Letter filed under 838 S. (O. C. G. P.), 1863, shows that the men whose names are borne on this roll were transferred to the 3d Maryland Cavalry by order of Secretary of War.

Number of roll:

248; sheet ____3____   C. J. Harris

(689b)   Copyist.

J. | **U.S.V.**

A. J. M. Sandy

Prt. ..., Co. J. , 22 Reg' Tenn. Inf.

(Confederate.)

Appears on a roll of

Prisoners of War

enlisted at Camp Chase, Ohio, in the U. S. Army, April 22, 1865.

Roll dated ____Not dated____, 186 .

Where captured _Pulaski, Tenn._

When captured _____Feb'y 16____, 1865.

Remarks: _Enlisted in U. S. A. April 22, 1865._

Book mark : _____

_____   S. A. Boyd

(567)   Copyist.

Examples of the microfilmed Index Cards from the series, *Index to Compiled Service Records of Volunteer Union Soldiers Who Served in Organizations Not Raised by States or Territories*. Both cards identify former Confederate soldiers who joined the Union Army after spending time in a prison camp.

STATEWIDE SOURCES
RG 11

Compiled Service Records,
Union & Confederate Soldiers from State Units

Two months after the capture of the Confederate capital in Richmond, Virginia, virtually all Confederate War Department records were transported to Washington, D.C. The U.S. War Department carefully preserved their own records pertaining to individual Union soldiers, as well as the acquired Confederate records – they were essential in confirming a record of service for any applicant for veteran benefits or pensions after the war.

The *Compiled Service Records* group for the period 1861-1865, came about because of this need, and the records were used heavily by the U.S. Pension Bureau well into the 1930s. Compiled into packets for each soldier, the files included any war documents that mentioned a soldier by name, i.e., enlistments, rosters, hospital visits, prisoner records, promotions, orders, desertions, discharge orders, and more. The papers were folded and inserted into a jacket-envelope (or packet). On the outside of the packet was written the name of the solder/sailor, date of service, and state and unit of service. By the 1880s, the Pension Bureau had 6.3 million packets in their files. Obviously, with a total of 3.5 million soldiers, many of the soldiers had more than one packet, due to variable spellings of a name, aliases, or service in more than one regiment.

The *Compiled Service Records* packets were organized in groups, by Confederate Army Records, Confederate Navy Records, Union Army Records, and Union Navy Records. Within each of these groups were divisions for the states of service, then the military units under each state. As a result, the *Compiled Service Records* for both Union & Confederate soldiers are basically all organized by state. Exceptions are those pertaining to special groups of Union soldiers (see RG10), and special groups of Confederate soldiers (see RG8).

To assist in locating a packet for one soldier, in 1903 the Pension Bureau began a program to index them. Over the next twenty years, the card indexes that were created became known as the General Index Cards, later divided into state groups as *Index to Compiled Service Records*.

Combining the General Index Cards from the RG12 group, plus RG10 and RG8, is where the total of 6.3 million packets comes from. The microfilmed General Index Cards from these three groups were used as the source for the online index at the CWSS site (RG1).

This Resource Group 11 is for the original packets of papers for each soldier. As statewide resources, any *Compiled Service Records* (the jacket and contents) that have been microfilmed are identified in **Part 3 – Statewide Name Lists**, under the applicable state heading. Table 1 (pp. 52-53) shows that 44 states have a microfilmed *Index to Compiled Service Records* publication, while only 24 states have the *Compiled Service Records* on microfilm.

It should be noted that the ***Index*** *to Compiled Service Records* series is not organized the same as the *Compiled Service Records* themselves. There are several national indexes, identified in RG8 and RG10. Meanwhile, the statewide indexes related to this Resource Group 11 are titled within one of these two groups in RG12:

- ***Index*** *to Compiled Service Records of Volunteer Union Solders Who Served in Organizations from* (name of state or territory).
- ***Index*** *to Compiled Service Records of Confederate Soldiers Who Served in Organization from* (name of state or territory).

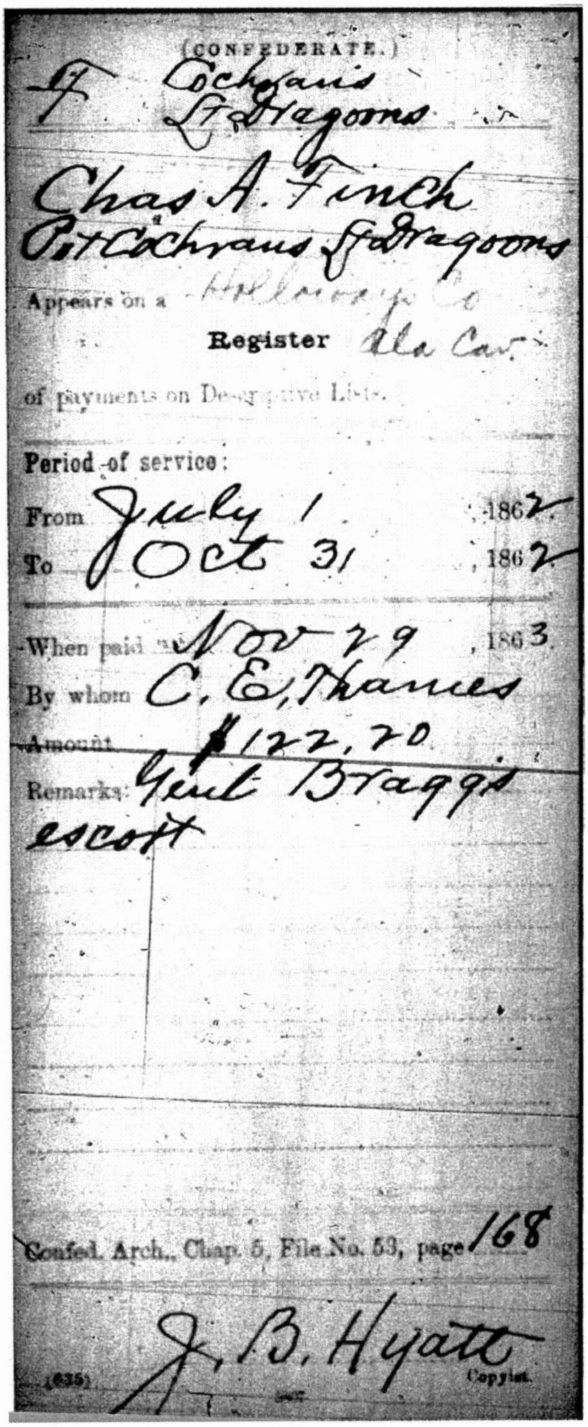

(CONFEDERATE.)

Cochrane's
Lt Dragoons

Chas A. Finch
Prt Cochrans Lt Dragoons

Appears on a

Register Ala Cav.

of payments on Descriptive Lists.

Period of service:

From July 1 , 1862

To Oct 31 , 1862

When paid Nov 29 , 1863

By whom C. E. Thames

Amount $122.70

Remarks: Genl Bragg's escort

Confed. Arch., Chap. 5, File No. 53, page 168

J. B. Hyatt
Copyist

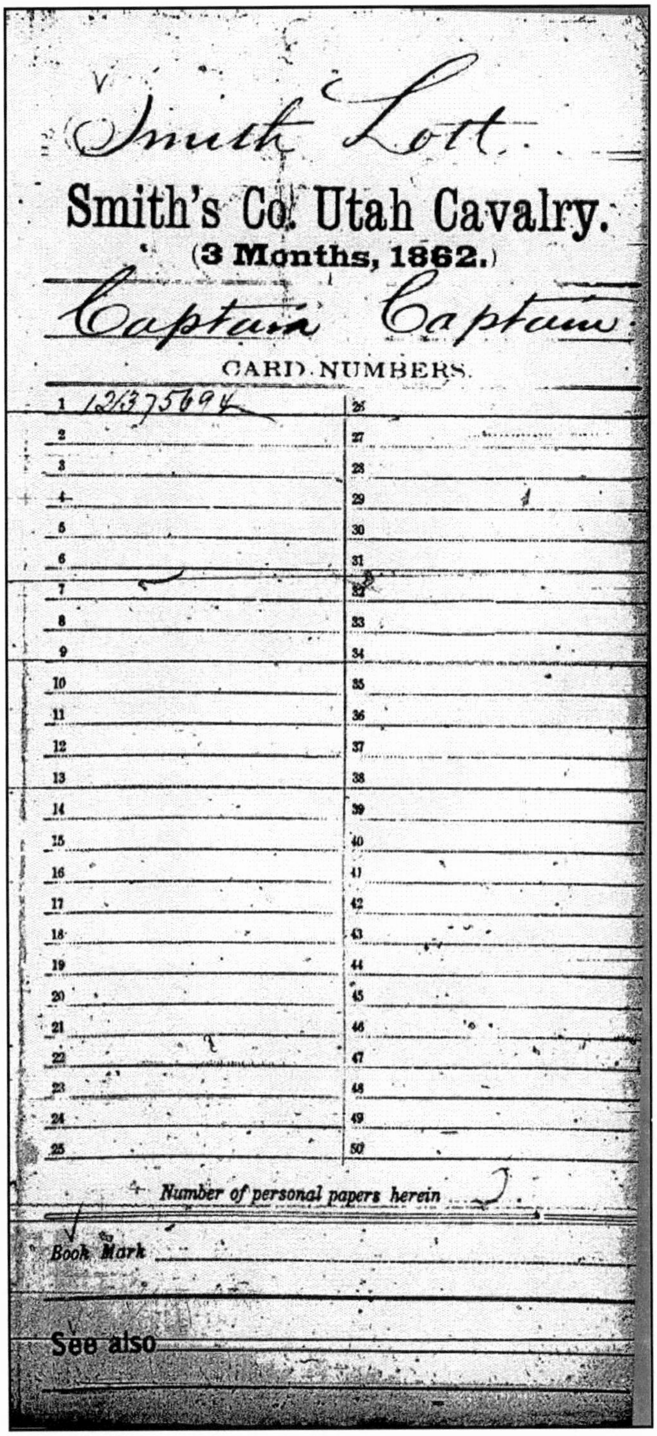

Smith Lott

Smith's Co. Utah Cavalry.

(3 Months, 1862.)

Captain   Captain

CARD NUMBERS.

1	1237 56 94	26	
2		27	
3		28	
4		29	
5		30	
6		31	
7		32	
8		33	
9		34	
10		35	
11		36	
12		37	
13		38	
14		39	
15		40	
16		41	
17		42	
18		43	
19		44	
20		45	
21		46	
22		47	
23		48	
24		49	
25		50	

Number of personal papers herein

Book Mark

See also

Examples of documents from the microfilmed *compiled Service Records* packets, one for a Confederate soldier, part of Cochrane's Dragoons, the escort group for General Bragg. Another document is for Captain Lott Smith, a card that indexes the numbered papers in his packet. (For a bit of history about Capt. Lot Smith, see Utah Territory, page 156.)

STATEWIDE SOURCES
RG 12

Index to Compiled Service Records,
Union & Confederate Soldiers from State Units

Most of the General Index Cards compiled by the Pension Bureau in the early 1900s were grouped by state. After they were transferred to the National Archives, the state groups were microfilmed as part of the series, *Index to Compiled Service Records*. There is at least one microfilm publication for 44 of the modern 50 states plus one for the District of Columbia. As a group, this state series has about 87% of the Union soldier records; and about 96% of the Confederate soldier records indexed at the Civil War Soldiers & Sailors System (CWSS) website (see RG1). For several of the states, there is one title for *Volunteer Union Soldiers*, and another for *Confederate Soldiers*. A breakdown of the numbers of Union and Confederate soldiers from each participating state/territory is shown on a chart with the CWSS system description (see page 10). The six states not listed had no Civil War soldiers, or were formed after the war: Alaska, Hawaii, Idaho, Montana, Oklahoma, and Wyoming. As part of **Part 3 – Statewide Name Lists**, an annotated citation to each title can be viewed with more details about each. The *Index to Compiled Service Records* for the states/territories listed below can be reviewed at the page indicated:

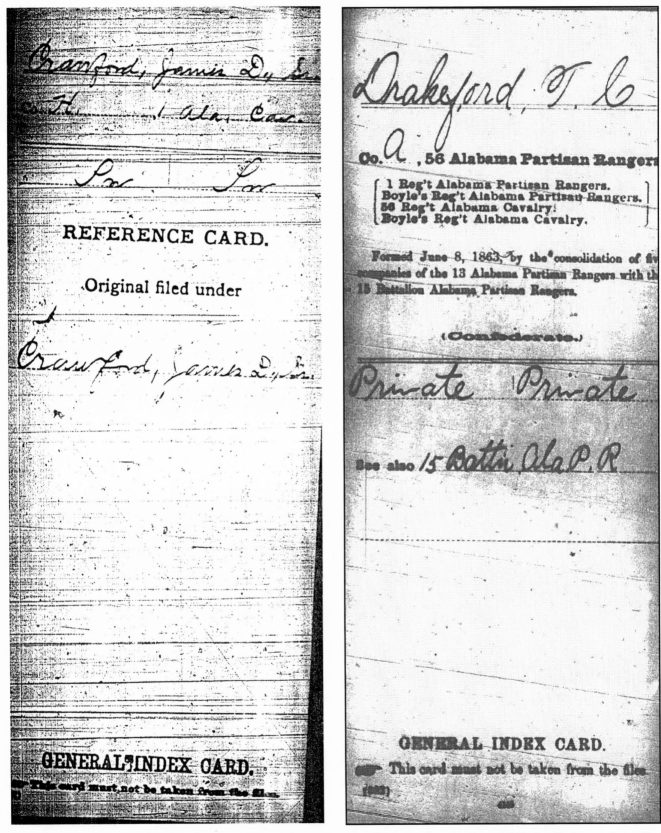

Examples of General Index Cards microfilmed for 44 states. These cards were located in the *Index to Compiled Service Records for Confederate Soldiers Who Served in Organizations From Alabama.*

STATEWIDE SOURCES
RG 13

1861-1869 State Censuses, and 1885-1945 State Censuses with Civil War Veterans Noted

Between the 1860 and 1870 federal censuses, there were state censuses conducted by both Union and Confederate states that may help identify people, family groupings, and places of residence. As part of **Part 3 – Statewide Name Lists**, an annotated citation to each title can be viewed with more details about each. The state censuses taken during the period 1861-1869 are useful for locating the names of residents, family members, and may even include the name of a soldier away from home. The later state censuses, 1885-1945, are valuable for locating a Civil War veteran after the war – these are state censuses that have an indication of a person's war service. (The first post-Civil War federal census that did this was the 1890 Veterans Schedules, shown in RG5). The full citation to each surviving state census for the states/territories listed below can be reviewed at the page indicated:

1861-1869 State Censuses:

1885-1945 State Censuses (with Civil War veterans noted):

---

* Not all counties, but good name lists for a sizeable portion of the state.

Upper Example: 1925 Iowa State Census, with veterans of the Civil War noted.

Lower Example: Military pages, 1865 New York State Census.

STATEWIDE SOURCES
RG 14

1861-1869 Statewide Name Lists & 1890-1910 Territory Lists

Statewide Name Lists include tax lists, voter registrations, city directories, or other name lists covering a large portion of one state. These name lists could be considered "census substitutes," because they list the names of residents for a specific area, along with some personal information. As part of **Part 3 – Statewide Name Lists**, an annotated citation to each title can be viewed with more details about each, and for all states. The name lists compiled during the period 1861-1869 are useful for locating the names of residents, usually head of households. Although Hawaii and Alaska were not part of the U.S. during the Civil War era, their later name lists may include Civil War veterans. The surviving statewide name lists for the 34 states/territories listed below can be reviewed in more detail at the page indicated:

A List of Persons and Property Assessed for Taxation

OWNERS OF LANDS TAXED.	Persons liable to pay a Poll	¼, ½, or part of ½ Section	¼ or ½ Section	No. of Section	No. of Township	No. of Range	No. of Acres	No. of Hundredths	Total value of land and improvements	Years Taxable	No. of town or city lots	Value of town or city lots and improvements	No. of shares of stock under the 30 value of etc.	Value of shares, stock	No. of slaves, etc.	Value of slaves
									$			$		$		$
Smith Abraham L	1															
Smith Albert	1	NW NE	10	12	32	40			120							
Smith Feh.	1											1	400			
Smith William	1											½	130			
Smith J. F.	1															
Smith Elvis	1	NW NW	9	9	31	40										
		SW NW	17	8	31	40		240								
Smith William	1															
Smith John P	1															
Smith B. H.	1	½ NE	34	7	31	80		240								
Smith G. B	1	NE NE	6	9	30	40		200								
Smith L. B	1															
Smith Philip	1										2,150					
Smith L. F.	1															
Smith J. E.	1															
Stokes J. B.	1															
Stokes H. S.	1															
Stokes W L	1															
Sharp Andrew R.	1	NW NE	16	12	31	40										
		SW NE	16	12	31	40		240								
Sharp James L	1															
Shankin James	1	N½ NW	26	12	33	80										
		NW	27	12	33	17	24	500								
Shannon Mc Elizabeth		NE	28	12	32	135	90									
		SW SW	17	10	32	80										
		SE	18	11	32	20		1300			7	1000				
Shannon W. H.	1															
Shannon Rufus	1															
Shannon William G.		N½ NW	18	10	31	80										
		SW NW SW	18	10	31	11										
		S½ SE	16	9	31	80										
		SE NW	16	9	31	40										
		SE NE	13	10	32	40		1000			1	600	1	150		
Smith Solomon Jr	1															
Snider James & Solomon Admrs of William Snider decd		NW	5	11	32	122		700								
Snider James E	1															

From *Arkansas Tax Records, 1821-1884,* microfilmed name lists that look much like a census, showing the names of property owners for a county area or city, town or precinct, etc. The document title at the top of this example page reads: "List of Persons and Property Assessed for Craighead County."

STATEWIDE SOURCES
RG 15

1862-1869 Internal Revenue Assessment Lists

In 1795, Congress levied a direct tax on American citizens to help pay off the debts left over from the Revolutionary War. Sixty-seven years later, Abraham Lincoln used that earlier "war tax" as justification for Congress to do it again, this time to help pay for the expenses of the Civil War. Beginning in 1862, the U.S. federal government levied a direct tax on manufactured products at the level of production and distribution, for any product with a value greater than $600. In addition, individuals were taxed, based on their annual income and the value of their personal property. For individuals, male or female, a person had to have an annual income over $600 to be subject to the tax. The value of an individual's personal property subject to the tax also had to exceed $600. After the first annual assessment of the direct tax in 1863, the United States government had collected about $20 million dollars.

To collect the tax, a large bureaucracy had to be created, with federal districts established in all states, based on the population of an area. Detailed tax lists were created. Assistant assessors prepared the lists in alphabetical order on large sheets. Alphabetical lists were prepared showing the names of persons, partnerships, firms, associations, or corporations; with several columns of information, including a full name, post office address, value of property, and amount of taxes levied.

For a genealogist, the Internal Revenue Assessment Lists provide about the same information as a head of households census. But the names listed will not include the poor farmer or low-paid worker – these lists of names are for people of property. As a federal agency, Internal Revenue records of historic value ended up at the National Archives. The National Archives undertook the project to microfilm the Internal Revenue Assessment Lists, organized by state. The microfilmed name lists exist for 39 states and the District of Columbia. The eleven modern states not included in the microfilming: Alaska, Arizona, Dakota Territory (SD & ND), Hawaii, Massachusetts, Nebraska, Ohio, Oklahoma, Wisconsin, and Wyoming. The records from the states that were filmed have been posted at **Ancestry.com** as U.S. I.R.S. Tax Assessments. The state lists that were included in the microfilming are all described in more detail in **Part 3 – Statewide Name Lists**, at the page indicated below:

1. Federal & state copies exist.

2. State's copy, filmed by the National Archives.

3. State's copy, filmed for the FHL, of Salt Lake City.

Example of the format used for the **Internal Revenue Assessment Lists**. Organized by district, the names of persons and businesses are listed within the districts in alphabetical order.

STATEWIDE SOURCES
RG 16

Statewide Militia Lists

The first source for locating information about a particular soldier who served during the Civil War is the *Index to Compiled Service Records,* with a combined index online at the CWSS website (RG1*).* A second major tool is a report of the State Adjutant General for the various states, listing rosters of all regiments formed in a particular state. Adjutant General reports from most states were combined into one database online at the American Civil War Research Database (RG2).

A third choice for locating a soldier are the state-generated rosters and military records related to a state's militia. The state militia records are unique, not copies of the *Index to Compiled Service Records*, or the *State Adjutant General Reports*. Published state militia lists are available from 35 states. The state lists that have been published are all described in more detail in **Part 3 – Statewide Name Lists**, at the page indicated below:

States with Published Militia Lists:

RECORD OF SOLDIERS AND OFFICERS

NAMES. (Give Middle Name in full.) RESIDENCE, TIME AND PLACE OF BIRTH.	PRESENT RANK. REGT. Battery	E.—WHEN ENLISTED. M.—WHEN MUSTERED. AND RANK.	Enlisted for Re-Muster Y—Years	PLACE OF ENLISTMENT.	W—Wndd O—Colored	Bounty Paid by Town	Bounty Paid by State Authorized to Organize
Name: Albert A. Von Putthammer Residence: Albany N.Y. Time and Place of Birth: 1816 19 Prussia	Capt 11th N.Y. Light Artillery	E. Oct 26th 1861 Jan 6th 1862 Captain	3 years	Albany N.y	W	none	none
Name: John E. Burton Residence: Albany N.Y. Time and Place of Birth: 1840 18	Capt 11th Indft Light Artillery	E. Oct 26th 1861 M Jan 6th Oct 22 1862 1st Sergeant	3 years	Albany N.y	W	none	none
Name: George Wm Davey Residence: Albany N.Y. Time and Place of Birth: Oct 26th 1837 Poughkeepsie N.y	Captain 11th Indft Light Artillery	Reenlisted Jan 23d 1864 E. Oct 23d 1861 M Dec 3 1861 Private	3 years 3 years	Albany N.y	W	none	none
Name: Robert A. Wormington Residence: Ashtabula Ohio Time and Place of Birth: 18 1819	1st Lieut 11th Indft Light Artillery	E. Sept 18th 1861 M Oct 26 " 1st Lieut	3 years	Ashtabula Ohio	W	none	none
Name: James Rodgers Residence: Albany N.Y. Time and Place of Birth: 18 1834	1st Lieut 11th Indft Light Artillery	E. Oct 26th 1861 M Dec 9th 1861 1st Lieut	3 years	Albany N.Y	W	none	none
Name: James T. Wyatt Residence: Greenbush N.y Time and Place of Birth: 1834 18 Newfoundland	1st Lieut 11th Indft Light Artillery	E. Oct 21 1861 M Dec 3 1861 2d M: Sergt	3 years	Albany N.Y	W	none	none
Name: James A. Manning Residence: Ashtabula Ohio Time and Place of Birth: 1836 18 Ireland	1st Lieut 11th Indft Light Artillery	E. Sept 18th 1861 M Oct 26 " Sergeant	3 years	Ashtabula Ohio	W	none	
Name: Gabriel Nathaniel P. Gale Residence: Albany N.Y. Time and Place of Birth: 1830 8	1st Lieut 11th Indft Light Artillery	E. Nov 18 1861 M " 12 "	3 years	Albany N.Y	W	none	
Name: Galen A. Knapp Residence: Ashtabula Ohio Time and Place of Birth: 18 1824	2nd Lieut 11th Indft Light Artillery	E. Sept 18th 1861 M Oct 5 " 2nd Lieut	3 years	Ashtabula Ohio	W	none	none
Name: Wadmore Redhead Residence: Ashtabula Ohio Time and Place of Birth: 1836 England	2d Lieut 11th Indft Light Artillery	E. Sept 18th 1861 M Oct 21st " Sergeant	3 yrs	Ashtabula Ohio	W	none	none

Examples from the *1865-1867 New York Town Clerks Registers*, with detailed information about each soldier. These militia lists were compiled by the town clerk in every town of the 62 New York counties. The original books are now preserved at the New York State Archives.

STATEWIDE SOURCES
RG 17

Confederate Pension Applications, Name Lists, and Censuses of Confederate Veterans

The first pensions granted to veterans of the Civil War were for Union soldiers only. In 1883, the first listing of nearly 300,000 Union veterans was published by the Pension Bureau, with the title, *Pensioners on the Roll* (see RG3). The U.S. Government had specifically excluded Confederate veterans, leaving the responsibility for Confederate pensions to the states. Between the 1880s and early 1900s, all of the eleven (11) former CSA states had passed acts to grant pensions to Confederate veterans of the Civil War. In addition, the Civil War border states of Kentucky, Missouri, and Oklahoma provided pensions for Confederate veterans. The lists of Confederate veterans are primary genealogical sources, usually giving vital statistics about the veteran, his wife and children, and details about any surviving widow.

Lists of Pensioners recorded by the fourteen (14) states that granted pensions to Confederate soldiers are listed below. The state, years, and titles of the published veteran lists are shown below with an indication of the page number where the full citation is found:

State	Year(s)	Title of Confederate Veterans List	Page of full citation
Alabama	1880-1930s	Confederate Pension Applications	56
Alabama	1907	Census of Confederate Soldiers	58
Arkansas	1891-1936	Confederate Veterans & Widows Pension Applications	61
Arkansas	1893-1939	Ex-Confederate Pension Records	61
Arkansas	1901-1929	Confederate Pension Records	61
Arkansas	1911	Census of Confederate Veterans	61
Florida	1885-1955	Pension Claims, Confederate Veterans and Their Widows	72
Georgia	1879-1891	Confederate Pension Rolls	75
Kentucky	1912-	Civil War Pension Applications	90
Louisiana	1911	Enumeration of Ex-Confederate Soldiers and Widows	93
Louisiana	1898-1929	Records of Pensioners of the State of Louisiana	93
Louisiana	1898-1944	Applications for Pensions	93
Louisiana	1912-1936	Louisiana Confederate Veterans Pensions	93
Louisiana	1924-1933	Civil War Pensions in Louisiana: Veterans and Widows	94
Mississippi	early 1900s	Confederate Soldiers & Sailors, Widows Pension Applications	107
Missouri	early 1900s	Confederate Pension Applications and Soldiers' Home Admissions	110
No. Carolina	1885-1953	Applications for Confederate Soldier's and Widow's Pensions	130
Oklahoma	1915-1919	Confederate Pension Applications for Soldiers and Sailors	135
So. Carolina	1888-1906	Civil War Pension Applications	148
So. Carolina	1901	South Carolina's Confederate Pensioners in 1901	148
So. Carolina	1921	South Carolina State Pension List of Confederate Veterans for 1921	148
Tennessee	1891-1965	Confederate Pension Applications: Soldiers and Widows	152
Texas	1861-1865	Texas Confederate Index: Confederate Soldiers of the State of Texas	154
Texas	1870-1930	Confederate Pensions (Texas): Applications Approved and Rejected	156
Texas	1895-1899	Texas Rosters, United Confederate Veterans	156
Virginia	1888-	Confederate Pension Rolls, Veterans and Widows (online database)	160
Virginia	1888-	Confederate Pension Rolls, Veteran and Widows (online index)	160
Virginia	1888-1934	Confederate Pension Applications	163
Virginia	1917-1926	Commonwealth of Virginia Civil War Pensioners	164

WIDOW'S CLAIM FOR PENSION.

STATE OF NORTH CAROLINA,

County of _Durham_

On this _30th_ day of _June_, A. D. 1885, personally appeared before me, _W. J. Christian_, C. S. C., in and for the State and County aforesaid, _Elizabeth Addison_, age _43_ years, and a resident at _Durham_ post-office in said County and State, and who being duly sworn, makes the following declaration in order to obtain the pension under the provisions of an act entitled "An Act for the relief of certain soldiers in the late war between the States," ratified March 11th, 1885, that she is the widow of the late _John H. Addison_ who enlisted in Co. _"I"_, _47_ Reg. N. C. State Troops, on or about the _1st_ day of _March_, 186 _2_, to serve in the armies of the late Confederate States, and that while in performance of duty in said Company and Regiment, in the State of _Virginia_, on or about the _28th_ day of _August_, 186 _2_, he received a wound or wounds, which terminated his life. _Died at Petersburg Hospital in Virginia, Disease Brain Fever_

She further states that she holds no office in the United States, State or County, from which she is receiving the sum of three hundred dollars in fees or as a salary, that she is not worth in her own right or the right of her late husband, property at its assessed value for taxation to the amount of five hundred dollars ($500), and that she has never remarried.

Sworn and subscribed to before me, this _30th_ day of _June_, 1885.

W. J. Christian
Signature of C. S. C.

Elizabeth her X Addison mark
Signature of Claimant

Also, personally appeared before me, _W. H. Morris_, who resides at _Durham_ post-office, in said County and State, a person whom I know to be respectable and entitled to credit, and being by me duly sworn, says that he is acquainted with _Elizabeth Addison_, the widow of the late _John H. Addison_ of Company _"I"_, _47_ Regiment, North Carolina State Troops, and that he believes her to be the identical person she represents herself to be, and that the facts set forth in her affidavit are correct to the best of his knowledge and belief, and that he has no interest direct or indirect in this claim.

Sworn and subscribed to before me, this _30th_ day of _June_, 1885.

W. J. Christian
Signature of C. S. C.

W. H. Morris
Signature of Witness.

STATE OF NORTH CAROLINA,

Durham County.

To the Auditor of the State of North Carolina:

We certify that we have carefully examined the application of _Elizabeth Addison_ the widow of the late _John H. Addison_ who enlisted in Company _I_, _47_ Regiment, North Carolina State Troops, for a pension under the provisions of an act entitled "An Act for the relief of certain soldiers in the late war between the States," ratified the 11th day of March, A. D. 1885, and the proofs filed in support thereof; that we are satisfied that the said _Elizabeth Addison_ is the widow of the late _John H. Addison_ who enlisted in Company _I_, _47_ Reg. N. C. State Troops, on or about the _1_ day of

Example of a widow's application for a pension. From *North Carolina, 1885-1953, Applications for Confederate Soldier's and Widow's Pensions.*

STATEWIDE SOURCES
RG 18

Indexes to Statewide Records

Shown below is a selected list of indexes to statewide records for 37 states. The list includes indexes such as biography indexes, vital records indexes, military databases, etc. Visit each state in **Part 3 – Statewide Name Lists** for the complete list for each state.

State/Territory	Year(s)	Title of Statewide Record	Page of full citation
Alaska Territory	1900-1912	Alaska Gold Rush CD: Census and Directory Index	58
Arizona	1860s	Arizona Biographical Index	58
California	1860s	Index to Great Registers of Voters	62
California	1849-1900	Index of Burials	62
Colorado Terrritory	1860s	Colorado Historical Records Database (online)	63
Connecticut	1641-1948	General Index to Probate Records	65
Connecticut	1860s	Index to the Hale Collection (Connecticut Vital Records)	65
Dakota Territory	1860s	South Dakota Naturalization Records Index	66
Dakota Territory	1860s	North Dakota Biographical Index	66
Delaware	1795-1932	Naturalization Records	70
Florida	1826-1865	Territorial and State Election Records	72
Georgia	1854-1877	Tax Digest and Compilation	76
Illinois	1860s	Online searchable databases: Civil War Veterans, Muster Rolls. Navy	77
Indiana	1860s	Online searchable databases: Biography, Cemeteries, Newspapers	79
Kansas	1860s	Kansas Biographical Index	87
Kentucky	1860s	Kentucky Index of Biographical Sketches in Histories	90
Maryland	1860s	Archives of Maryland (online)	95
Massachusetts	1841-1910	Index to Vital Records (online)	98
Michigan	1860s	Military Databases (online)	100
Michigan	1860s	Michigan Surname Index, Library of Michigan	102
Missouri	1860s	Military Databases (online)	108
Montana	1860s	First Families of Montana and Early Settlers	111
Nebraska	1860s	Nebraska History Index Search (online)	112
Nevada	1860s	NV State Library/Archives: Newspapers, Naturalizations (online)	114
New Hampshire	1860s	NH State Archives: military databases (online)	116
New Hampshire	1640-1900	New Hampshire Vital Records Indexes	118
New Jersey	1848-1900	Records of Births, Marriages, and Deaths of New Jersey	120
New Mexico	1844-1933	Parish Registers, Diocese of Santa Fe	123
New York	1634-	New York State Biographical, Genealogical, and Portrait Index	126
North Carolina	pre-1914	Cemetery Inscription Card Index	131
Oregon	1860s	Oregon Historical Records Index	136
Oregon	1860s	Oregon Pioneers Card Index, Multnomah Co Library	138
Oregon	1842-1902	Oregon Statewide Delayed Filings of Births	139
Pennsylvania	1860s	Civil War Databases at State Archives (online)	140
Rhode Island	1900-1950s	Rhode Island Vital Records: Birth Certificates, Birth Index, Deaths	145
South Carolina	1860s	State Archives Military Database (online)	146
South Carolina	1695-1925	Combined Alphabetical Index	147
Tennessee	1908-1925	Vital Records Indexes (online)	149
Texas	1836-1935	Index to Republic of Texas Claims (online)	153
Vermont	early to 1870	General Index to Vital Records of Vermont	159
Virginia	1853-1950	Vital Records Indexes	164
Washington	1853-	Washington Digital Archives Master Index (online)	165
Wisconsin	1830s-1990s	Wisconsin Genealogy Index (online)	170
Wyoming	1860s-1970	The Historical Encyclopedia of Wyoming	174

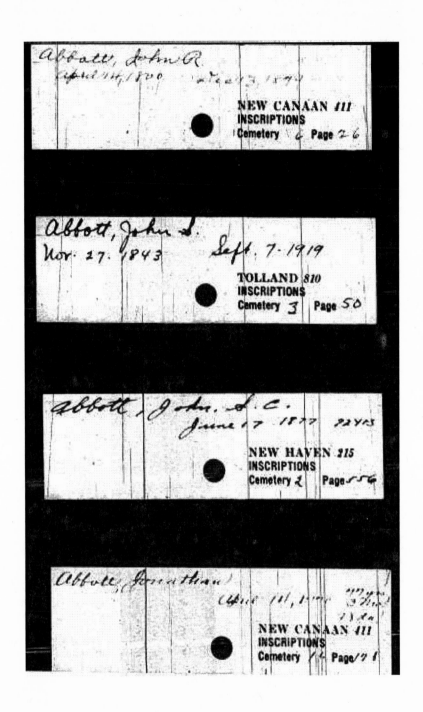

Taken from the microfilm, these are Index Cards to the **Hale Collection** (Connecticut Vital Records), originals located at the Connecticut State Library in Hartford, Connecticut.

STATEWIDE SOURCES
RG 19

Statewide Lists of Veteran Burials

Shown below is a selected lists of veteran burials in 30 states. The list includes indexes such as cemetery indexes, obituary indexes, GAR death rolls, etc. Go to **Part 3 – Statewide Name Lists** for the details for each title.

State/Territory	Year(s)	Title of Statewide List	Page of full citation
California	1849-1900	Mortuary Records for Northern California	62
Colorado Territory	1860s	Civil War Veterans from CA, NV, OR, WA; buried in Colorado	63
Connecticut	1860s	Vital Records Index (in the Hale Collection)	65
Delaware	1854-1864	Deaths from the Delaware Gazette	70
Florida	1860s-1940s	Register of Deceased Veterans	73
Indiana	1860s	Confederate POW burials	80
Indiana	1882-1948	Indiana Civil War Veterans: Transcription of the Death Rolls (GAR)	83
Indiana	1816-1928	Civil War Veteran Obituaries	83
Iowa	1883-1948	Iowa Civil War Veterans: Transcription of the Death Rolls (GAR)	85
Kansas	1883-1948	Kansas Civil War Veterans: Transcription of the Death Rolls (GAR)	88
Kentucky	1860s	Kentucky Cemetery Records Database (KHS, online)	89
Maine	1860s-1930	Cemetery Index of Veterans	95
Michigan	1860s-1900s	Sons of Union Veterans of the Civil War graves database (online)	100
Michigan	1860s-1900s	Michigan Wartime Deaths (online)	101
Michigan	1861-1930	Civil War Graves Registration Index Cards	103
Minnesota	1857-1975	Veteran Graves Registration Index (online)	104
Mississippi	1860s-	Confederate Dead and Other Confederate Records	107
Mississippi	1860s-	Mississippi Confederate Grave Registrations	108
Missouri	1860s-	Missouri Veterans Buried in Other States (online)	108
Missouri	1860s-	Veterans Buried in Missouri (online)	108
Missouri	1860s-	Confederate Roll of Honor, Missouri	109
Missouri	1882-1940	Index to Death Rolls, GAR, Missouri Division	110
Nebraska	1883-1948	Nebraska Civil War Veterans: Transcription of the Death Rolls (GAR)	113
Nevada	1860s-	Nevada Cemetery Transcriptions (statewide)	114
New Hampshire	1860s-	Civil War Cemetery Records	116
New Hampshire	1861-1865	Honor Roll of New Hampshire Union Soldiers, with burial locations	117
New Jersey	1860s	Card Index to Civil War Soldiers' Graves (NJ Hist. Society)	120
North Carolina	pre-1914	Cemetery Inscription Card Index (statewide WPA project)	131
North Carolina	1860s-	Confederate Gravestone Records	131
Ohio	1860s-	Grave Registrations of Soldiers Buried in Ohio	133
Ohio	1860s-	List of Ohioans killed during Civil War, buried Andersonville, GA et al	133
Oklahoma	1860s-	Civil War Union Soldiers Buried in Oklahoma	135
Oklahoma	1860s-	Veteran Burials in the State of Oklahoma	135
Pennsylvania	1860s-	Pennsylvania Civil War Veteran Burials	142
Rhode Island	1860s-	Honor Roll of Rhode Island Soldiers Who Died During Civil War	144
South Carolina	1860s-	Broken Fortunes: SC Soldiers Who Died (Civil War)	148
South Carolina	1860s-	Cemetery Records of Confederate Soldiers Buried in South Carolina	149
Tennessee	1860s-	Tennessee's Confederate Dead	151
Texas	1860s-	Civil War Burial Sites in Texas	155
Utah Territory	1860s-	Civil War Veteran Burials from AZ, NE, NV, NM, OR, UT, & WA	157
Virginia	1860s-	Virginia Military Dead Database (online)	160
Virginia	1860s	Men in Gray Interments	163
Washington Terr.	1860s-	Burial List of the Members of the 1st WA Terr. Infantry	166

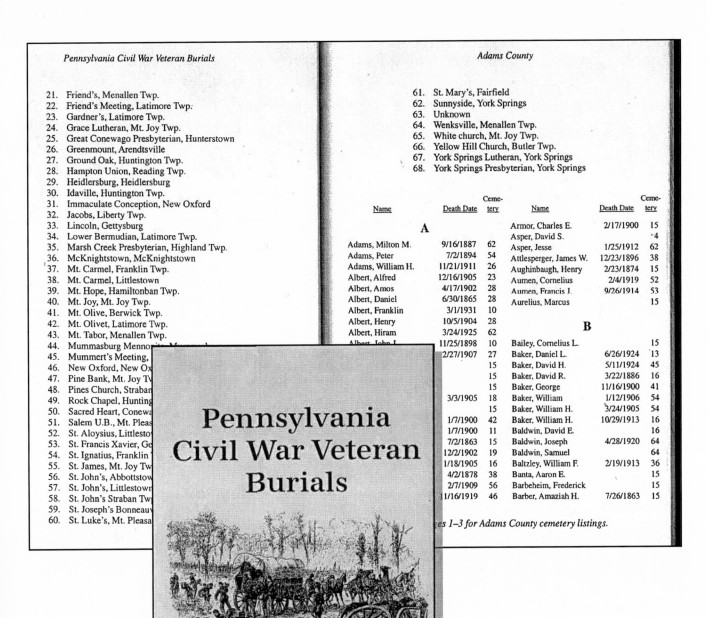

Pennsylvania Civil War Veteran Burials

21. Friend's, Menallen Twp.
22. Friend's Meeting, Latimore Twp.
23. Gardner's, Latimore Twp.
24. Grace Lutheran, Mt. Joy Twp.
25. Great Conewago Presbyterian, Hunterstown
26. Greenmount, Arendtsville
27. Ground Oak, Huntington Twp.
28. Hampton Union, Reading Twp.
29. Heidlersburg, Heidlersburg
30. Idaville, Huntington Twp.
31. Immaculate Conception, New Oxford
32. Jacobs, Liberty Twp.
33. Lincoln, Gettysburg
34. Lower Bermudian, Latimore Twp.
35. Marsh Creek Presbyterian, Highland Twp.
36. McKnightstown, McKnightstown
37. Mt. Carmel, Franklin Twp.
38. Mt. Carmel, Littlestown
39. Mt. Hope, Hamiltonban Twp.
40. Mt. Joy, Mt. Joy Twp.
41. Mt. Olive, Berwick Twp.
42. Mt. Olivet, Latimore Twp.
43. Mt. Tabor, Menallen Twp.
44. Mummasburg Menno...
45. Mummert's Meeting,
46. New Oxford, New Ox
47. Pine Bank, Mt. Joy Tw
48. Pines Church, Straban
49. Rock Chapel, Hunting
50. Sacred Heart, Conewa
51. Salem U.B., Mt. Pleas
52. St. Aloysius, Littlesto
53. St. Francis Xavier, Ge
54. St. Ignatius, Franklin
55. St. James, Mt. Joy Tw
56. St. John's, Abbottstow
57. St. John's, Littlestown
58. St. John's Straban Tw
59. St. Joseph's Bonneau
60. St. Luke's, Mt. Pleasa

Adams County

61. St. Mary's, Fairfield
62. Sunnyside, York Springs
63. Unknown
64. Wenksville, Menallen Twp.
65. White church, Mt. Joy Twp.
66. Yellow Hill Church, Butler Twp.
67. York Springs Lutheran, York Springs
68. York Springs Presbyterian, York Springs

Name	Death Date	Cemetery	Name	Death Date	Cemetery
A			Armor, Charles E.	2/17/1900	15
			Asper, David S.		4
Adams, Milton M.	9/16/1887	62	Asper, Jesse	1/25/1912	62
Adams, Peter	7/2/1894	54	Attlesperger, James W.	12/23/1896	38
Adams, William H.	11/21/1911	26	Aughinbaugh, Henry	2/23/1874	15
Albert, Alfred	12/16/1905	23	Aumen, Cornelius	2/4/1919	52
Albert, Amos	4/17/1902	28	Aumen, Francis J.	9/26/1914	53
Albert, Daniel	6/30/1865	28	Aurelius, Marcus		15
Albert, Franklin	3/1/1931	10			
Albert, Henry	10/5/1904	28	**B**		
Albert, Hiram	3/24/1925	62			
Albert, John J.	11/25/1898	10	Bailey, Cornelius L.		15
	2/27/1907	27	Baker, Daniel L.	6/26/1924	13
		15	Baker, David H.	5/11/1924	45
		15	Baker, David R.	3/22/1886	16
		15	Baker, George	11/16/1900	41
	3/3/1905	18	Baker, William	1/12/1906	54
		15	Baker, William H.	3/24/1905	54
	1/7/1900	42	Baker, William H.	10/29/1913	16
	1/7/1900	11	Baldwin, David E.		16
	7/2/1863	15	Baldwin, Joseph	4/28/1920	64
	12/2/1902	19	Baldwin, Samuel		64
	1/18/1905	16	Baltzley, William F.	2/19/1913	36
	4/2/1878	38	Banta, Aaron E.		15
	2/7/1909	56	Barbeheim, Frederick		15
	11/16/1919	46	Barber, Amaziah H.	7/26/1863	15

...ges 1–3 for Adams County cemetery listings.

Pennsylvania Civil War Veteran Burials

Adams County
Perry County

Book cover and pages from *Pennsylvania Civil War Veteran Burials*,
Adams County, PA, a series planned for all of Pennsylvania's counties.

STATEWIDE SOURCES
RG 20

State Adjutant General Reports

The selected list below shows several states for which Adjutant General reports are available. Go to **Part 3 – Statewide Name Lists** at the page indicated below for more details about each title.

State/Territory	Year(s)	Title of State Publication	Page of full citation
Arkansas	1866	Report of the Adjutant General for the Period of the Late Rebellion	60
California	1861-1867	Records of California Men in the War of the Rebellion	62
Colorado Territory	1861-1865	Official Army Register of the Volunteer Forces (Colorado)	63
Connecticut	1889	Record of Service of Connecticut Men in the Army and Navy	64
Illinois	1900-1902	Report of the Adjutant General of the State of Illinois	78
Indiana	1867-1869	Report of the Adjutant General of the State of Indiana	80
Iowa	1908-1911	Roster and Record of Iowa Soldiers in the War of the Rebellion	84
Kansas	1896	Report of the Adjutant General of the State of Kansas, 1861-1865	87
Kentucky	1915	Report of the Adjutant General of the State of Kentucky, Confederate	89
Kentucky	1866	Report of the Adjutant General of the State of Kentucky, Union	89
Maine	1862-1867	1861-1866 Annual Reports of the Adjutant General, State of Maine	95
Maryland	1898-1899	History and Roster of Maryland Volunteers, War of 1861-1865	96
Massachusetts	1861-1937	Massachusetts Soldiers, Sailors and Marines in the Civil War	98
Michigan	1882	Michigan in the War	102
Michigan	1915	Record of Service of Michigan Volunteers in the Civil War, 1861-1865	102
Michigan	1872?	Michigan Volunteers Descriptive Rolls, 1861-1866	103
Minnesota	1866	Minnesota Adjutant General's Report	105
Nebraska	1891	Roster of Soldiers, Sailors and Marines...War of the Rebellion	113
New Hampshire	1895	Revised Register of the Soldiers and Sailors of New Hampshire	117
New Jersey	1876	Record of Officers and Men of New Jersey in the Civil War	119
New Mexico	1867	Official Army Register of the Volunteer Forces (New Mexico)	123
New York	1896-1906	Reports of the Adjutant General, 1895-1906	125
New York	1912	New York in the War of the Rebellion, 1861-1865	125
Ohio	1895?	Official Roster of the Soldiers of the State of Ohio	133
Pennsylvania	1869-1871	History of Pennsylvania Volunteers, 1861-5	141
Rhode Island	1866	Official Register of Rhode Island Soldiers	144
South Carolina	1913-1930	South Carolina Troops in Confederate Service	148
Tennessee	1966?	Report of the Adjutant General of the State of Tennessee	151
Vermont	1892	Revised Roster of Vermont Volunteers	159
Washington Terr.	1867	Official Army Register of the Volunteer Force (Washington Territory)	166
West Virginia	1898	Report of the Adjutant General of West Virginia, 1897-1898	169
Wisconsin	1914	Wisconsin Volunteers, War of the Rebellion, 1861-1865	171

COMPANY B—Continued.

NAME.	Rank.	Place of Enrollment.	Date of Enlistment.	Date of Muster.	Remarks.
Juan Francis Guirado	1st Lieut.	San Francisco	Aug. 16, 1861	Sept. 11, 1861	Mustered out at Fort Union, N. M., Sept. 30, 1864, expiration of term of service.
Ephraim C. Baldwin	1st Lieut.	Santa Fe, N. M.		Aug. 29, 1864	Mustered out at Santa Fe, Dec. 31, 1866, per Dept. of California, S. O. No. 258.
Chauncey R. Wellman	2d Lieut.	San Francisco	Aug. 16, 1861	Sept. 2, 1861	Promoted to Capt. of Co. E, same Regt., Aug. 15, 1862.
Elisha E. Latimer	2d Lieut.	Fort West, N. M.	Jan. 26, 1863	Feb. 9, 1863	Promoted from 1st Sergt.; mustered out at Fort Union, N. M., Sept. 30, 1864, expiration of term of service.
Charles J. Croft	2d Lieut.		Aug. 14, 1865		Never mustered as an officer; mustered out as Hospital Steward, March 27, 1866.
Elisha E. Latimer	Sergeant	San Francisco	Aug. 26, 1861	Sept. 2, 1861	Promoted 2d Lieut. Feb. 9, 1863, with rank from April 1, 1862.
Henry H. Roberts	Sergeant	San Francisco	Aug. 26, 1861	Sept. 2, 1861	Discharged Feb. 20, 1863, for disability.
John S. Ashmead	Sergeant	San Francisco	Aug. 26, 1861	Sept. 2, 1861	Reduced to the ranks Mar. 17, 1862; mustered out at Fort Union, N. M., Sept. 30, 1864, ex. term of service.
Nathan Zorkowsky	Sergeant	San Francisco	Sept. 5, 1861	Sept. 9, 1861	Discharged at Fort Union, N. M., Feb. 11, 1864, by reënlistment; mustered out at San Francisco, Dec. 31, 1866, per S. O. No. 258, Dept. of Cal., of Dec. 29, 1866.
John E. Calhoun	Sergeant	San Francisco	Sept. 5, 1861	Sept. 9, 1861	Discharged at Fort Union, N. M., Nov. 30, 1863, by reënlistment as a Vet. Vol.; mustered out at Ft. Sumner, N. M., Aug. 17, 1866, by order of Dept. Com.
Aaron V. Peck	Sergeant	Las Cruces, N. M.	Sept. 13, 1864	Sept. 24, 1864	Vet. Vol.; for former service see Co. A, same Regt.; promoted Sergt. May 11, 1866; mustered out at San Francisco, Dec. 31, 1866, per S. O. No. 258, Dept. of Cal., of Dec. 29, 1866.
Charles Christopher	Sergeant	Santa Fe, N. M.	Oct. 5, 1863	Oct. 5, 1863	Reënlisted as a Vet. Vol. from Co. E, same Regt.; mustered out at Fort Sumner, N. M., Aug. 24, 1866, services no longer required.
David P. Andrews	Sergeant	Rio Miembres	Jan. 1, 1864	Jan. 28, 1864	Reënlisted as a Vet. Vol. from Co. E, same Regt.; mustered out at San Francisco, Dec. 31, 1866, per S. O. No. 258, Dept. of Cal., of Dec. 29, 1866.
George M. Carpenter	Sergeant	Rio Miembres	Jan. 1, 1864	Jan. 28, 1864	Reënlisted as a Vet. Vol. from Co. E, same Regt.; discharged at Santa Fe, June 25, 1866, for disability.
James W. Green	Sergeant	San Elizario, Tex.	Jan. 12, 1864	Jan. 12, 1864	Reënlisted as a Vet. Vol. from Co. A, same Regt.; mustered out at Fort Sumner, N. M., Aug. 17, 1866, by direction of Dept. Commander.
Sydney M. Webb	Sergeant				Drop'd by excess of organization; turned over to Co. C.
James Botsford	Sergeant				Drop'd by excess of organization; turned over to Co. C.
Thomas T. Bartlett	Sergeant	Santa Fe, N. M.	Nov. 15, 1863	Nov. 15, 1863	Promoted 2d Lt., 1st Cav., N. M. Vols., July 3, 1865.

RECORD OF CALIFORNIA TROOPS.

98

Philip W. Sampson	Sergeant	San Francisco	Aug. 29, 1861	Sept. 5, 1861	Discharged at Fort Union, N. M., Dec. 1, 1863, by reënlistment as a Vet. Vol.; appointed Corp. Oct. 1, 1863; promoted Sergt. July 28, 1865; discharged December 10, 1865, per S. O. No. 101, War Dept.
James Longhead	Sergeant	San Francisco	Sept. 5, 1861	Sept. 9, 1861	Promoted Sergt. Sept. 1, 1862, and 1st Sergt. Feb. 9, 1863; mustered out at Fort Union, N. M., Sept. 30, 1864, expiration of term of service.
Charles Mason	Sergeant	San Francisco	Aug. 26, 1861	Sept. 2, 1861	Appointed Corp. Aug. 26, 1861; promoted Sergt. March 17, 1862; mustered out at Fort Union, N. M., Sept. 30, 1864, expiration of term of service.
Henry W. Easton	Sergeant	Santa Fe, N. M.	Oct. 5, 1863	Oct. 5, 1863	Reënlisted as Vet. Vol. from Co. D; promoted Sergt. from Corp. July 28, 1865; mustered out at Fort Union, N. M., Sept. 10, 1866, with company.
John McDonald	Sergeant	Santa Fe, N. M.	Dec. 12, 1863	Dec. 12, 1863	Reënlisted as Vet. Vol. from Co. E, same regiment; promoted Sergt. from Corp. Aug. 17, 1866; mustered out at San Francisco, Dec. 12, 1866, per S. O. No. 258, Dept. of Cal., of 1866.
Thomas Scott	Sergeant	San Francisco	Aug. 26, 1861	Sept. 2, 1861	Appointed Corp. Feb. 1, 1863; promoted Sergt. Jan. 1, 1864; mustered out at Fort Union, N. M., Sept. 30, 1864, expiration of term of service.
William F. Taylor	Sergeant	Santa Fe, N. M.	Nov. 30, 1863	Nov. 30, 1863	Reënlisted as a Veteran Volunteer from 5th U. S. Inf.; promoted Sergt. from Corp. Aug. 17, 1866; mustered out at Fort Union, N. M., Sept. 10, 1866, with Co.
Andrew J. Hayes	Sergeant	Franklin, Texas	Feb. 10, 1864	Feb. 11, 1864	Vet. Vol.; for former service see Co. E, same regiment; disch'd at Fort Union, N. M., Sept. 10, 1866, with Co.
Victor Dontremont	Sergeant	San Francisco	Sept. 2, 1861	Sept. 5, 1861	Appointed Corp. Aug. 26, 1861; promoted Sergt. July 1, 1863; died at Fort Stanton, N. M., Aug. 28, 1863, from saber wounds.
Orrin W. Simms	Corporal	Santa Fe, N. M.	Dec. 12, 1863	Dec. 12, 1863	Reënlisted as a Vet. Vol. from Co. D, same Regt.; discharged at Fort Leavenworth, Kan., Dec. 6, 1865, while on detached service.
William Warneck	Corporal	San Francisco	Sept. 5, 1861	Sept. 9, 1861	Discharged at Fort Union, N. M., Dec. 9, 1863, by reënlistment as a Vet. Vol.; mustered out at Fort Sumner, N. M., Aug. 24, 1866, by order of Dept. Com.
Charles Brakebill	Corporal	Santa Fe, N. M.	Oct. 5, 1863	Oct. 5, 1863	Reënlisted as a Vet. Vol. from Co. D, same Regt.; mustered out at Santa Fe, N. M., Aug. 8, 1866, by order of Dept. Commander.
Henry Feldwick	Corporal	San Francisco	Sept. 5, 1861	Sept. 9, 1861	Discharged at Fort Union, N. M., Nov. 30, 1863, by reënlistment as a Vet. Vol.; appointed Corp. July 28, 1865; mustered out at Fort Union, N. M., Sept. 10, 1866, with company.
John Cleveland	Corporal	Santa Fe, N. M.	Oct. 24, 1864	Oct. 25, 1864	Reënlisted as Vet. Vol. from Co. D; appointed Corp. July 28, 1866; mustered out at Fort Union, N. M., Sept. 10, 1866, with company.

FIRST REGIMENT OF CAVALRY.

99

This is a reproduction of a two-page spread (table) showing officers and enlisted men of Company B, First California Cavalry Regiment, from *Records of California Men in the War of the Rebellion*, compiled by Brig. Gen. Richard H. Orton, California Adjutant General's Office, 1890 edition. Typical of most of the Adjutant General reports, this is a roster of soldiers within various units from California. This, and several other state reports are the source of the soldier name lists online at the American Civil War Research Database (RG2). The "Remarks" column in all of the Adjutant General reports usually have more personal details about a soldier than the *Index to Compiled Service Records*.

TABLE 1

Summary of Resource Groups Available for each State

ALABAMA to MINNESOTA

RESOURCE GROUPS

- ♦ Originals & Microfilm Available
- □ Originals Only Available
- ■ Online Database Available

Section	RG No.	TITLE	Alabama	Alaska Territory	Arizona Territory	Arkansas	California	Colorado Territory	Connecticut	Dakota Terr./ND/SD	Delaware	District of Columbia	Florida	Georgia	Hawaii Territory	Idaho Territory	Illinois	Indiana	Iowa	Kansas	Kentucky	Louisiana	Maine	Maryland	Massachusetts	Michigan	Minnesota
NATIONWIDE SOURCES	1	Civil War Soldiers & Sailors System (Online Database)	■		■	■	■	■	■	■	■	■	■	■			■	■	■	■	■	■	■	■	■	■	■
	2	American Civil War Research Database (Online Database)	■		■	■	■	■	■	■	■	■	■	■			■	■	■	■	■	■	■	■	■	■	■
	3	War of the Rebellion, Official Records	■		■	■	■	■	■	■	■	■	■	■		■	■	■	■	■	■	■	■	■	■	■	■
	4	Indexes to Pension Files, 1861-1934	■		■	■	■	■	■	■	■	■	■	■			■	■	■	■	■	■	■	■	■	■	■
	5	1883 List of Pensioners on the Roll	□		■	□	■	□	□	□	□	□	□	□		□	■	■	□	■	□	□	□	□	□	■	■
	6	1890 Federal Census, Special Schedules, Union Veterans																			■	■	■	■	■	■	■
	7	Roll of Honor Burials (books) & VA Grave Locator (all online)	■	■	□ ■	□ ■	□ ■	□ ■	□ ■	□ ■	■	□ ■	□ ■	□ ■		□ ■	□ ■	□ ■	□ ■	□ ■	□ ■	□ ■	□ ■	□ ■	□ ■	□ ■	□ ■
	8	1865-1867 Confederate Amnesty Papers	♦			♦	♦				♦	♦	♦	♦			♦	♦	♦	♦	♦	♦		♦	♦	♦	
	9	Consolidated Lists of Confederate Soldiers & Vets	♦		♦	♦							♦	♦							♦	♦		♦			
	10	Index to Compiled Service Records, Union Regulars, et al					♦	♦	♦	♦	♦	♦					♦	♦	♦	♦			♦			♦	♦
STATEWIDE SOURCES	11	Compiled Service Records (by State)	♦		♦	♦		□	□	□	♦	♦	□	♦			□	□	□	□	♦	♦	□	♦	□	□	□
	12	Index to Compiled Service Records (by State)	♦		♦	♦	♦	♦	♦	♦	♦	♦	♦	♦			♦	♦	♦	♦	♦	♦	♦	♦	♦	♦	♦
	13	1861-1869 State Censuses	♦		■	♦	♦						♦	♦					■						♦	♦	■
	13	1885-1945 State Censuses								♦									■	■						♦	■
	14	1861-1869 Statewide Name Lists & 1890-1910 Territory Lists	♦	♦			♦	♦			♦	♦	♦	♦	♦		♦	♦	♦	♦	♦	♦	♦	♦	♦	♦	♦
	15	1862-1869 Internal Revenue Assessment Lists	■		■		■	■	■		■	■	■	■		■	■	■	■	■	■	■	■	■		■	■
	16	Statewide Militia Lists	♦				♦	♦	♦	♦			♦	♦		■	♦	♦	♦	♦	♦			♦	♦	♦	
	17	Confederate Pension Applications, Censuses	♦			♦							♦	♦							♦	♦					
	18	Indexes to Statewide Records		♦	♦		♦	■	♦	♦	♦		♦	♦			■	■			♦	♦			♦	■	■
	19	Statewide Lists of Veteran Burials					♦	♦	♦				♦				♦	♦	♦		■			♦		■	♦
	20	State Adjutant General Reports				♦	♦	♦	♦								♦	♦	♦	♦			♦	♦	♦	♦	♦

From *Genealogical Resources of the Civil War Era*, by William Dollarhide, published by Family Roots Publishing Co., Bountiful, UT.

TABLE 1 – Continued

Summary of Resource Groups Available for each State

MISSISSIPPI to WYOMING

RESOURCE GROUPS

- ♦ Originals & Microfilm Available
- □ Originals Only Available
- ■ Online Database Available

	RG No.	TITLE	Mississippi	Missouri	Montana Territory	Nebraska	Nevada	New Hampshire	New Jersey	New Mexico Territory	New York	North Carolina	Ohio	Oklahoma & Ind. Terr.	Oregon	Pennsylvania	Rhode Island	South Carolina	Tennessee	Texas	Utah Territory	Vermont	Virginia	Washington Territory	West Virginia	Wisconsin	Wyoming Territory
NATIONWIDE SOURCES	1	Civil War Soldiers & Sailors System (Online CWSS)	■	■		■	■	■	■	■	■	■	■	■	■	■	■	■	■	■	■	■	■	■	■	■	
	2	American Civil War Research Database (Online Database)	■	■		■	■	■	■	■	■	■	■	■	■	■	■	■	■	■	■	■	■	■	■	■	
	3	War of the Rebellion, Official Records	■	■	■	■	■	■	■	■	■	■	■	■	■	■	■	■	■	■	■	■	■	■	■	■	■
	4	Indexes to Pension Files, 1861-1934	■	■	■	■	■	■	■	■	■	■	■	■	■	■	■	■	■	■	■	■	■	■	■	■	■
	5	1883 List of Pensioners on the Roll	□	□	□	□	□	□	□	□	□	□	□	□		□	□	□	□	□	□	□	□	□	□	□	■
	6	1890 Federal Census, Special Schedules, Union Veterans	■	■	■	■	■	■	■	■	■	■	■	■	■	■	■	■	■	■	■	■	■	■	■	■	■
	7	Roll of Honor Burials (books) & VA Grave Locator (online)	□ ■	□ ■	□ ■	■	□ ■	□ ■	□ ■	□ ■	□ ■	□ ■	□ ■	□ ■	□ ■	□ ■	□ ■	□ ■	□ ■	□ ■	□ ■	□ ■	□ ■	□ ■	□ ■	□ ■	■
	8	1865-1867 Confederate Amnesty Papers	♦	♦		♦			♦	♦	♦	♦	♦	♦		♦	♦	♦	♦	♦		♦			♦		
	9	Consolidated Lists of Confederate Soldiers & Vets	♦	♦							♦						♦	♦	♦			♦					
	10	Index to Compiled Service Records, Union Regulars, et al		♦		♦	♦	♦	♦	♦	♦			♦		♦	♦	♦				♦		♦	♦	♦	
STATEWIDE SOURCES	11	Compiled Service Records (by State)	♦	♦		♦	♦	□	□	♦	□	♦	□	♦		♦	□	□	♦	♦	♦	♦	□	♦	□	♦	□
	12	Index to Compiled Service Records (by State)	♦	♦		♦	♦	♦	♦	♦	♦	♦	♦	♦	♦	♦	♦	♦	♦	♦	♦	♦	♦	♦	♦	♦	
	13	1861-1869 State Censuses	■	♦		♦	■		♦		♦				■		♦									♦	♦
		1885-1945 State Censuses															♦									♦	
	14	1861-1869 Statewide Name Lists & 1890-1910 Territory Lists			♦	♦	♦	♦	♦		♦				♦	♦	♦	♦	♦	♦		♦		♦			♦
	15	1862-1869 Internal Revenue Assessment Lists	■	■	■		■	■	■	■	■	■			■	■	■	■	■	■	■	■	■		■	■	
	16	Statewide Militia Lists	♦	♦		♦		♦	♦		♦	♦	♦		♦	■	♦	♦	♦	♦		♦	■	♦	■	■	
	17	Confederate Pension Applications, Censuses	♦	♦							♦			♦			♦	♦	♦				■				
	18	Indexes to Statewide Records		■	♦	■	■	■	♦	♦	♦	♦			♦	■	♦	■	■	■		♦	♦	■		♦	♦
	19	Statewide Lists of Veteran Burials	♦	■		♦	♦	♦	♦		♦	♦	♦		♦	♦	♦	♦	♦	♦	♦		■		♦		
	20	State Adjutant General Reports				♦		♦	♦	♦	♦		♦			♦	♦	♦				♦			♦	♦	♦

From *Genealogical Resources of the Civil War Era*, by William Dollarhide, published by Family Roots Publishing Co., Bountiful, UT.

Part 3

Statewide Name Lists, 1861-1869 & Post-War Veteran Lists

Most genealogical resources available for the Civil War era are those related to the military units, with many name lists of soldiers from rosters, state militia lists, or the service records of individual soldiers. But, between the 1860 and 1870 Federal Censuses, there were also state censuses, statewide tax lists, voter registrations, and other statewide name lists produced that include names from the civilian population as well as the military.

The name lists found at the state level are the main sources for finding a reference to an ancestor during the Civil War era. Therefore, a review of the online or published name lists for all states begins below. Identified are the following resources for each state:

Online Resources:
- The State Archives and/or the State Library website; and any Civil War related databases available online at that website.
- Any Civil War website for a state.
- Any 1861-1869 online name list or Post-War veteran list for a state.

Published Resources:
- Any published Compiled Service Records, Militia Lists, Pension Records, or Veteran Records specific to the state.
- Any statewide name lists 1861-1869, including State Censuses, Tax Lists, or Voter Registrations.
- Any published guides relating to the Civil War for a state with resource lists.

ALABAMA

Online Alabama Resources

State Archives. Alabama Department of Archives and History (ADAH), Montgomery, AL. ADAH website: **www.archives.state.al.us/index.html**.

■ **Online Databases at the ADAH Website:**
- Alabama Civil War Service Cards File. (surnames A-L only).
- Brief Historical Sketches of Military Organizations Raised in Alabama During the Civil War.

■ **Alabama Civil War Roots.** Go to: **www.rootsweb.com/~alcwroot/**. Description at the Home Page: "Designed to provide you with the information – tools to do your own in-depth research, concerning the Civil War service of your Alabama ancestors, both Union and Confederate."

Published Alabama Resources

■ *Compiled Service Records of Confederate Soldiers Who Served in Organizations from the State of Alabama*, microfilm of the original records at the National Archives, Washington, D.C. Filmed by the Archives, 1961-1962, microcopy series 311, 508 rolls, beginning with FHL film #880330 (1st Cavalry, A – G, 1861-1865). The names from this series are included in the CWSS system.

■ *Index to Compiled Service Records of Confederate Soldiers Who Served in Organizations from the State of Alabama,* microfilm of original records at the National Archives, Washington, D.C. Filmed by the National Archives, series M253, 49 rolls, beginning with FHL film #821949 (A – All). The Alabama entries are incorporated into the national index at the National Park Service website at: **www.itd.nps.gov/cwss/**.

■ *Compiled Service Records of Volunteer Union Soldiers Who Served in Organizations from the State of Alabama,* microfilm of the original records at the National Archives, Washington, D.C. Filmed by the Archives, 1958, series M276, 10 rolls, beginning with FHL film #880848 (Index, A – Z) and FHL film #1276611 (1st Cavalry, A – Br). The names from this series were indexed at the NPS website at: **www.itd.nps.gov/cwss/**.

■ *Index to Compiled Service Records of Volunteer Union Soldiers Who Served in Organizations from the State of Alabama,* microfilm of original records at the National Archives, Washington, D.C. Filmed by the National Archives, series M263, 1 roll, FHL film #880848. Alabama entries are incorporated into the national index at the National Park Service website at: **www.itd.nps.gov/cwss/**.

■ *Confederate Service Records (for out-of-state soldiers who served in Alabama units),* microfilm of original records compiled by the ADAH, filmed by the Genealogical Society of Utah, 1987, 1 roll, FHL film #1411532. The out-of-state soldiers are listed within 17 state groups, each in alphabetical order. Name lists were compiled for soldiers organized on the roll as follows: Item 1: Arkansas; Item 2: Florida; Item 3: Georgia; Item 4: Illinois; Item 5: Indiana; Item 6: Kentucky; Item 7: Louisiana; Item 8: Maryland; Item 9: Michigan; Item 10: Mississippi; Item 11: Missouri; Item 12: North Carolina; Item 13: Ohio; Item 14: South Carolina; Item 15: Tennessee; Item 16: Texas; and Item 17: Virginia.

■ *Alabama State Militia, 1820-1865,* microfilm of originals at the ADAH, Montgomery, AL. Alphabetical card file of those serving in the state militia. Information was compiled by the ADAH from various sources. Filmed by the Genealogical Society of Utah, 1986, 11 rolls, beginning with FHL film#1462797 (State militia, A-Boardman, Volney).

■ *1865-1867 Amnesty Papers: Name Index to Pardon Application Files. Group 1, Pardon applications submitted by persons from Alabama.* FHL has entire series, described for all states in RG8 (page 24). Applications from Alabama residents organized on the microfilm as follows:
- Ab – Bo, FHL film #1578739.
- Br – Col, FHL film #1578740
- Coo – Fa, FHL film #1578741.
- Fe – Gw, FHL film #1578742.
- Ha – Ho, FHL film #1578743.
- Hu – La, FHL film #1578744.
- Le – Ma, FHL film #1578745.
- Me – Pe, FHL film #1578746.
- Ph – Ry, FHL film #1578747.
- Sa – Sw, FHL film #1578748.
- Ta – Wal, FHL film #1578749.
- Wan – Yo, Two-or-More Name File, Miscellaneous File, FHL film #1578750.

■ *Confederate Pension Applications, ca. 1880-1930's,* microfilm of records of the Alabama Pension Commission, now located at the ADAH. Through the years the Alabama General Assembly passed various types of legislation approving pensions to Confederate veterans and their widows. Most of these applications were made ca. 1880's-1930's, though a few were made or reviewed as late as the 1940's-1960's. Pensions were paid to surviving widows up into the 1970's in some cases. The Pension Applications were organized in alphabetical order by the surname of the applicant. Filmed by the Genealogical Society of Utah, 1987, 276 rolls, beginning with FHL film #1502476 (A – Adams, F. L.).

■ *Applications for Relief by Maimed Confederate Soldiers,* microfilm of originals at the ADAH, Montgomery, AL. Applications are arranged alphabetically by county, then alphabetically by surname. The Alabama General Assembly approved acts in 1867, 1881, and 1885 providing Confederate veterans artificial limbs or compensation for loss of limbs and other disabling wounds. This series, from the State Auditors Office, consists of applications by responding vets to said relief acts. Filmed by the Genealogical Society of Utah, 1990, 2 rolls, FHL film #1653552 (Autauga – Talladega counties); and FHL film #1653553 (Tallapoosa – Winston counties).

■ *Confederate Soldiers [Pensioners] in Alabama, 1907, 1921, & 1927,* microfilm of originals at the ADAH, Montgomery, AL. Resident veterans of the Confederate army in Alabama were eligible for a state pension under certain conditions Upon approval of the pension applications, the state auditor prepared an alphabetical record by county of all pensioners. Each probate judge received a copy of his county's pension record.

The **1907 Series** includes the pensioner's full name, present address, birthdate and place, rank and date of entry into military service, name and letter of company and regiment, and date and place of discharge or separation. Re-enlistment information is also given, if any.

The **1921 Series** is a questionnaire returned by Confederate pensioners concerning military and personal histories. Personal information reported on includes pensioner's name, place and date of birth, length of Alabama residency, wife's age and place of birth, marriage date and place, lists of living children, place of residency, and occupation. The 1921 Series is arranged numerically and alphabetically by military unit, thereunder alphabetically by pensioner's name. Military units are filed in the following sequence: infantry, cavalry, navy, coast guard, marines, artillery, out-of-state commands. Researchers can determine a pensioner's military unit by referring to the *Confederate Pension Applications,* which are arranged alphabetically by pensioner's name.

The **1927 Series** was created when the state legislature, in considering changing pensioner classifications, needed to establish the birthdate and marriage date of each Confederate widow pensioner. The survey was conducted by the probate judge of each county. The record provides the veteran's name, the widow's name, her age and birthdate and the marriage date. The record is arranged alphabetically by county, thereunder alphabetically by the name of the widow. Filmed by the Genealogical Society of Utah, 1988, 10 rolls, beginning with FHL film #1533727 (Autauga County, 1907).

■ *Internal Revenue Assessment Lists of Alabama, 1865-1866,* microfilm of originals at the National Archives in Washington, D.C. From intro: "On the 6 rolls of this microfilm publication are reproduced bound volumes of tax assessment lists for the three collection districts established for the state of Alabama by Executive order dated May 16, 1865. The lists were created in the offices of assessors and assistant assessors of Internal Revenue during the period 1865-66." Names arranged alphabetically within division and then within months. District 1: Baldwin, Barbour, Butler, Choctaw, Clarke, Coffee, Conecuh, Covington, Dale, Henry, Marengo, Mobile, Monroe, Pike, Washington, and Wilcox counties. District 2: Autauga, Bibb, Chambers, Coosa, Dallas, Greene, Lowndes, Macon, Montgomery, Perry, Pickens, Randolph, Russell, Shelby, Sumter, Talladega, Tallapoosa, and Tuscaloosa. District 3: Blount, Calhoun, Cherokee, DeKalb, Fayette, Franklin, Jackson, Jefferson, Lauderdale, Lawrence, Limestone, Madison, Marion, Marshall, Morgan, St. Clair, Walker, and Winston counties. Filmed by the Archives, 1987, series M754, 6 rolls. FHL has complete set, beginning with FHL film #1578453 (District 1, divisions 1-21, annual, monthly, and special lists, Jan – Jul 1866).

■ *1866 Alabama State Census,* microfilm of originals at the ADAH, Montgomery, AL. Includes name of head of household for African-Americans and whites; with the number of females and males in age categories. There were four schedules: 1) listed whether a soldier was killed or injured during the Civil War. 2) listed Colored population. 3) listed white population, and 4) a recapitulation of numbers. Not every county took all four schedules, and there is no published statewide index. Filmed by the Genealogical Society of Utah, 1988, 8 rolls, beginning with FHL film #1533830 (Autauga County).

■ *1866 Voter Registration Lists.* Available on microfilm at ADAH, only. This series was created in accordance with an act passed by Congress on March 2, 1867, "to provide for a more efficient government of the rebel States," and particularly to extend suffrage to the millions of freedmen across the South. All adult black and white males who had sworn an oath of loyalty to the United States were eligible to register to vote. Included is the person's name, race, length of residence in the state, county and precinct, the book and page where his oath is recorded, naturalization information, and reasons for rejecting some registrants. Arranged alphabetically by county, then chronologically by date of registration

■ *1907 Alabama Census of Confederate Soldiers,* transcript compiled from ADAH microfilm, published by Gregath, Cullman, AL, 1982, 5 vols. Contents: Vol. 1: Autauga thru Clay counties; Vol. 2: Cleburn thru Greene counties; Vol. 3: Hale thru Monroe counties; Vol. 4: Marshall thru Randolph counties; Vol. 5: Russell thru Winston counties. FHL book 976.1 X22c. Also on microfilm, 5 rolls, beginning with FHL film #1421815. Indexed in *Master Index to 1907 Census of Alabama Confederate Soldiers,* Indexed and compiled from Alabama State Archives microfilm, published by Gregath, Cullman, AL, 2000, 100 pages. FHL book 976.1 X22c.

ALASKA TERRITORY

Purchased from Russia in 1867; District of Alaska, 1867-1912; Territory of Alaska, 1912-1959; State of Alaska, 1959. Although not part of the United States during the Civil War, there were Civil War veterans who migrated to Alaska after the war. The best overall finding aid to early Alaska people is the following:

■ *Alaska Gold Rush, Extracted from the Original U.S. Federal Census Schedules: Alaska 1900 Census Index; Alaska 1910 Census Index; Alaska People Index; Alaska Polk Directories Index,* a CD-ROM publication by Heritage Quest, North Salt Lake, 2001. Contains 105,574 entries in the database. Alaska-Yukon Polk directories, 1902-1912. Also includes: History and timeline of the gold rush era, with population growth tables – articles from Heritage Quest Magazine: *Genealogy Project in Alaska* / by David A. Hales; *The Klondike Gold Rush - Finding Grandpa in the Crowd* / by Wenonah Finch Sharpe; *National Archives-Alaska Region* / by Patricia Brown Darling; *National Archives-Alaska Region* / by Donna Potter Phillips – Additional resources.

ARIZONA TERRITORY

The only territory officially added to the Confederate States of America was the Territory of Arizona, an area encompassing the southern half of pre-Civil War New Mexico Territory from Texas to California. In March 1861, the territory was self-proclaimed at a local convention and asserted its desire to join the Confederacy. The Confederate Congress recognized the Territory of Arizona in February 1862. But it lasted only until July 1862, when it was occupied by Union forces, and the area returned to the jurisdiction of the U.S. New Mexico Territory. The U.S. Territory of Arizona was created by Congress in February 1863 with bounds about the same as the present state of Arizona, a state since 1912.

Online Arizona Resources

Arizona State Library, Archives and Public Records in Phoenix, AZ, has two divisions with major genealogy collections:

■ **The Law and Research Library Division.** This is the AZ State Library, with many published materials relating to Arizona history. Website: **www.lib.az.us/is/genealogy/index.cfm**.

● **Arizona Biographical Index,** available online at the AZ State Library site. Includes Arizona people from the Civil War era. To access the webpage for the index, go to: **www.lib.az.us/Bio/index.cfm**.

■ **The History and Archives Division.** This is the AZ State Archives, with many collections of original manuscripts relating to Arizona history. Website: **www.lib.az.us/archives/**.

■ **1883 Pensioners List (Arizona Territory),** an online database extracted from *List of Pensioners on the Roll January 1, 1883 – Giving the Name of Each Pensioner, the Cause for Which Pensioned, the Post-Office Address, and the Date of Original Allowance,* United States Pension Bureau,. Go to: **www.jengod.com/genealogy/**.

■ **Arizona Civil War Website.** This is a private website that includes web pages for Brief History, Websites, Books, Manuscripts, Benjamin Sacks Collection, and Map of the Confederacy. Go to: **http://jeff.scott.tripod.com/civil.html**.

Published Arizona Resources

■ *Compiled Service Records of Confederate Soldiers Who Served in Organizations from the Territory of Arizona,* microfilm of originals at the National Archives, Washington, D.C. Filmed by the Archives, 1961, series M0318, 1 roll, FHL film #536241 (AZ Confederate Volunteers, A – Z).

■ *Index to Compiled Service Records of Confederate Soldiers Who Served in Organizations from the Territory of Arizona.* Filmed by the National Archives, series M375, 1 roll, FHL film #821837. The Arizona entries are incorporated into the national index at the National Park Service website at: **www.itd.nps.gov/cwss/**.

■ *Compiled Service Records of Volunteer Union Soldiers Who Served in Organizations from the Territory of New Mexico,* microfilm of original records at the National Archives, Washington, D.C. Includes U.S. Arizona Territory regiments. Filmed by the National Archives, series M427, 46 rolls, see FHL film, beginning with film #821883 (Index, E – L), and FHL film #471538 (1st Cavalry, A – Aq).

■ *Index to Compiled Service Records of Volunteer Union Soldiers Who Served in Organizations from the Territory of Arizona, 1861-1865,* microfilm of original records at the National Archives, Washington, D.C. Filmed by the National Archives, series M532, 1 roll, FHL film #881608. The Arizona entries are incorporated into the national index at the National Park Service website at: **www.itd.nps.gov/cwss/**.

■ *A Brief History of the Independent Arizona Territory Confederate States Battalions in Arizona Territory, 1861-1862,* compiled by Sherman Lee Pompey, published by Pacific Specialties, Kingsburg, CA, 1971, 7 pages. FHL book 979.1 A1 No. 3. Also on microfilm, FHL film #874332.

■ *1864 Territorial Census of Arizona,* microfilm of original records at the Arizona Department of Libraries, Archives & Public Records in Phoenix, Arizona. This census was provided for in the federal organic act establishing Arizona Territory, one of only three such censuses ever conducted by the federal government between decennial census years. The results of the enumeration were used in forming judicial districts and for the election of members to the territorial legislature and other offices. The census schedule questions include a person's name, age, sex, marital status, where born, how long a local resident, citizenship status, occupation, residence of all married individuals, and value of personal and real estates. Filmed by the Arizona Department of Libraries, Archives & Public Records, 1997. FHL has 1 roll, FHL film #2114989. See also *The 1864 Census of the Territory of Arizona,* extracted by the Historical Records Survey, division of Women's and Professional Projects, Works Progress Administration, 1938, 210 pages, FHL book 979.1 X2p 1864. Also on microfilm, filmed by the Genealogical Society of Utah, 1973, 1 roll, FHL film #897437.

■ *1866 Arizona Territorial Census,* microfilm of original records at the Arizona Department of Libraries, Archives and Public Records, Phoenix, Arizona. This was the only census authorized by the territorial legislature. (The 1864 territorial census was a federal enumeration). Includes schedules for all five counties in place in 1866: Mohave, Pah-Ute, Pima, Yavapai and Yuma counties. Filmed with *An Index to the 1866 Census of Arizona Territory,* by Jim Schreier. Filmed by the Genealogical Society of Utah, 1976, 1 roll, FHL film #928107. See also *Arizona 1866 Territorial* [Index], edited by Ronald Vern Jackson, et al., published by Accelerated Indexing Systems, North Salt Lake, 1982, 64 pages, FHL book 979.1 X2j 1866.

■ *Arizona 1867 Census Index,* by Ronald Vern Jackson, et al., published by Accelerated Indexing Systems, Salt Lake City, UT, 1983, 54 pages. This was taken from what appears to be a census of Pima County (Tucson) only. FHL book 979.1 X2j 1866.

■ *Arizona 1869 Territorial Census Index,* by Ronald Vern Jackson, et al., published by Accelerated Indexing Systems, Salt Lake City, UT, 1983, 100 pages. No territorial census was taken in Arizona in 1869. This appears to be a county census taken in Yavapai County only. FHL book 979.1 X22a.

ARKANSAS

Online Arkansas Resources

State Archives. Arkansas History Commission (AHC), Little Rock, AR AHC website: **www.state.ar.us/ahc/index.htm**.

■ **Online Civil War Databases at the AHC Website:**
  • Index to Arkansas Confederate Home Records
  • Request Form for Photocopies of Arkansas Confederate Pensions

Published Arkansas Resources

■ *Internal Revenue Assessment Lists for Arkansas, 1865-1866; 1867-1874,* original records filmed by the National Archives, series M755 (1865-66); and series T1208 (1867-74). No film at FHL.

■ *Compiled Service Records of Confederate Soldiers Who Served in Organizations from the State of Arkansas,* microfilm of original records at the National Archives, Washington, D.C. Filmed by the Archives, 1960, series M317, 256 rolls, beginning with FHL film #821811 (Index A, 1861-1865), and FHL film #880849 (1st [Crawford's] Cavalry, A – C, 1861-1865).

■ *Index to Compiled Service Records of Confederate Soldiers Who Served in Organizations from the State of Arkansas,* microfilm of original records at the National Archives, Washington, D.C. Filmed by the National Archives, series M376, 26 rolls. FHL has entire set, beginning with FHL film #821811 (A). The Arkansas entries are incorporated into the national

index at the National Park Service website at: **www.itd.nps.gov/cwss/**.

■ *Compiled Service Records of Volunteer Union Soldiers Who Served in Organizations from the State of Arkansas,* microfilm of original records at the National Archives, Washington, D.C. Filmed by the Archives, 1962, series M399, 60 rolls, beginning with FHL film #881488 (Index, A-F); and FHL film #1380847 (1st Battalion, Infantry A-K). The Arkansas entries are incorporated into the national index at the National Park Service website at: **www.itd.nps.gov/cwss/**.

■ *Index to Compiled Service Records of Volunteer Union Soldiers Who Served in Organizations from the State of Arkansas,* microfilm of original records at the National Archives, Washington, D.C. Filmed by the National Archives, series M383, 4 rolls. FHL has entire set, beginning with FHL film #881488 (A-F). The Arkansas entries are incorporated into the national index at the National Park Service website at: **www.itd.nps.gov/cwss/**.

■ *Report of the Adjutant General of Arkansas, For the Period of the Late Rebellion, and to November 1, 1866,* microfiche of original published by the Government Printing Office, Washington, D.C., 1867, 278 pages. Includes rosters of soldiers who were mustered into service for each of the Arkansas regiments. Filmed by University Publications of America, Bethesda, MD, 1990, on 3 microfiche, FHL fiche #6082312.

■ *Confederate Service Records* (for Arkansas soldiers who served in Alabama units), microfilm of original records compiled by the ADAH, filmed by the Genealogical Society of Utah, 1987, 1 roll, FHL film #1411532 (Item 1, Arkansas soldiers).

■ *1865-1867 Amnesty Papers: Name Index to Pardon Application Files. Group 1, Pardon Applications Submitted by Persons from Arkansas.* FHL has entire series, described for all states in RG8 (page 24). Applications from Arkansas residents organized on the microfilm as follows:
  • Arkansas, Ad – Lu, FHL film #1578751.
  • Mc-Yo Two-or-More Name File, Miscellaneous File, FHL film #1578752.

■ *Index to Arkansas Confederate Pension Applications,* compiled by Desmond Walls Allen, published by Arkansas Research, Conway, AR, 1991, 322 pages. FHL book 976.M22adl. Also on microfilm, FHL film #16979621.

■ *Inmates in the Arkansas Confederate Home, ca. 1890-1963,* microfilm of original records at the Arkansas History Commission, Little Rock, AR. Filmed by the Commission, ca 1975, 17 rolls. FHL has complete set, beginning with FHL film #2310463 (Inmates in the Arkansas Confederate Home, ca. 1890-1963; Index: Abel, William Randolph Sr. – Blaylock, Susan E. (ends with the folder only for Francis A. Bledsoe).

■ *Arkansas Confederate Veterans and Widows Pension Applications, 1891-1936,* compiled by Frances T. Ingmire, published by F. T. Ingmire, St. Louis, MO, 1985, 442 pages. Arranged in alphabetical order by surname of veteran. FHL book 976.7 M28f.

■ *Ex-Confederate Pension Records, 1893-1939,* microfilm of original records at the Arkansas History Commission, Little Rock, AR. Includes a digest of the statutes of Arkansas embracing all laws of a general nature in force at the course of the regular session of the General Assembly of 1937, vol. 2; Chapter 129. Filmed by the Genealogical Society of Utah, 2000, 11 rolls, beginning with FHL film #2209370 (Minutes of the State Board of Pensions, containing a list of pension claims allowed: Feb. 3, 1893-Aug. 9, 1939 [in volume with records of the State Insurance Bureau: 1873-74]; 1891-1896 Registers of warrants for pension issued; 1891-1896 Pension listings, Arkansas – Cleveland).

■ *Arkansas Confederate Pension Records, ca. 1901-1929,* microfilm of original records at the Arkansas History Commission, Little Rock, AR. These files were kept by the State Auditor of Arkansas. Files are in alphabetical order, for the most part, within each roll of film. The films are generally in alphabetical order from roll to roll except the J's and K's where order is disrupted. Filmed by the Arkansas History Commission, 121 rolls. FHL has complete set, beginning with FHL film #1722443 (Aaron – Adams, John J.).

■ *Arkansas Tax Records, 1821-1884,* microfilm of original records at the Arkansas History Commission, Little Rock, AR. Filmed by the Genealogical Society of Utah, 1994, 2002, 72 rolls, beginning with FHL film #1954757 (List of available county tax records Arkansas County – Yell County), and FHL film #1955034 (List of available county records (revised) Arkansas County – Yell County).

■ For the only county with extant records from the 1865 state census, see *Washington County, Arkansas Sheriff's Census for 1865,* compiled by Nancy Maxwell, published by Heritage Books, Bowie, MD, 1993, 74 pages. Includes surname index. FHL book 976.714 X2m.

■ *Arkansas 1911 Census of Confederate Veterans,* transcribed and edited by Bobbie J. McLane and Capitola Glazner, published 1977-1981, extracted from the original records at the Arkansas Historical Commission prior to microfilming. Gives quite extensive information on veterans and their families. 3 vols. Contents: vol. 1: A-D; vol. 2: E-Mc; vol. 3: M-Z. FHL book 976.7 X2m v.1-3. Also on 3 microfiche, FHL fiche #6019335. Indexed in *An Index to the Three Volumes, Arkansas 1911 Census of Confederate Veterans,* by Bobbie Jones McLane, published by Arkansas Ancestors, Hot Springs, AR, 1988, 245 pages. FHL book 976.7 X2m.

CALIFORNIA

Online California Resources

State Library. California State Library, Sacramento. Go to the "California History Section" webpage at: **www.library.ca.gov/calhist/**.

State Archives. California Archives & Museum, Sacramento. Website: **www.ss.ca.gov/archives/archives_e.htm**.

■ **California Civil War Website.** A private website with general information about California's role in the Civil War. Go to: **www.militarymuseum.org/HistoryCW.html**.

■ **1883 California Pensioners List.** Names from Colusa, Kern, Lake, Lassen, Los Angeles, Marin, and Monterey counties are online at: **www.arealdomain.com/california1883.html**.

Published California Resources

■ **1860s Great Registers of Voters.** All California counties in place during the Civil War decade have voter registration lists on microform. Go to the Family History Library's website at: **www.familysearch.org**. From the main page, access "Family History Library," then "Family History Library Catalog." Use the place search, and type "California" to get a list of topics available for that state. Click on "View Related Places" to get a list of California counties. Click on a county to see a list of topics, including "Voting Registers."

■ *Records of California Men in the War of the Rebellion, 1861 to 1867,* compiled by Brig.-Gen. Richard H. Orton, California. Adjutant General's Office, 1890 edition published by the State Office, Sacramento. Reprint by Gale Research, Detroit, MI, 1979, 887 pages, FHL book 979.4 M2a. Also on microfiche, 17 fiche, FHL fiche #6118432. Indexed in *A Personal Name Index to Orton's "Records of California Men in the War of the Rebellion, 1861 to 1867,"* compiled by J. Carlyle Parker, published by Gale Research, Detroit, MI, 1978, 153 pages. FHL book 979.4 M2a.

■ *Index to Compiled Service Records of Volunteer Union Soldiers Who Served in Organizations from the State of California,* microfilm of original records at the National Archives, Washington, D.C. Filmed by the Archives, 1964, series M533, 7 rolls. FHL has series, beginning with FHL film #881609 (Index, A – Cl, 1861-1865). The California entries are incorporated into the national index at the National Park Service website at: **www.itd.nps.gov/cwss/**.

■ *California State Militia Index to Muster Rolls, 1851-1866,* compiled by Root Cellar, Citrus Heights, CA, 1999, 4 vols. Contents: vol. 1: Abachuco to Earl. J.; vol. 2: Earl, J. to Laux, C.; vol. 3: Laux, C. to Scott, W.; vol. 4: Scott, W. to Zwieback. FHL book 979.4 M2cs v. 1-4. Also on microfiche, index to muster rolls, 21 fiche; unit summary, 1851-1866, 2 fiche.

■ *The Civil War Veterans of San Diego, CA: Including Citations to Genealogical Research Sources in San Diego, California,* by Barbara Palmer, published by the author, San Diego, CA, 1999, 382 pages. Contains alphabetical listings of veterans, compiled from cemetery inscriptions and other public and vital records, giving name of veteran, rank, units served in, names of spouse or parents, if available, etc. FHL book 979.498/S1 M2p. Also on microfilm, FHL film #1425462.

■ *1862-1866 Internal Revenue Assessment Lists for California,* microfilm of original records located in the National Archives, Washington, D.C. Lists are arranged alphabetically by surname of those being assessed for each period. Filmed by the National Archives, 1988. FHL has 33 rolls, beginning with FHL film #1534664 (Annual lists, 1863).

■ *1865-1867 Amnesty Papers: Name Index to Pardon Application Files. Group 2, Pardon applications submitted by persons from California.* Refer to the National Confederate Lists for a detailed description of the records. FHL has entire series, described for all states in RG8 (page 24), applications from California residents on FHL film #1578811.

■ *Index to Naturalizations in the U.S. District Court for the Northern District of California, ca. 1860-1989,* microfilm of records located at the National Archives, Pacific Sierra Region, San Bruno, California. Index cards give name, residence address, age, date of order of admission, date certificate issued, petition number, signature of citizen, alien registration number and citizenship certificate number. Filmed by the Genealogical Society of Utah, 1992-1993, 165 rolls, beginning with FHL film #1852274 (A – Acio, Nunila 1860-1989).

■ **Index of Burials, 1849-1900.** See *Mortuary Records 1849-1900 (Northern California),* microfilm of card file located at the Special Collections section, California State Library, Sacramento, CA. Contains a card file arranged in alphabetical order by surname of burials in the northern California area ca. 1849-1900. Includes name of deceased, age and date of birth, date and cause of death, name of attending physician (if known), and place of burial: along with a listing of the various sources for burial information. The title "Mortuary records" was supplied by the Special Collections Section of the California State Library, Sacramento. The file actually indexes burial records from a variety of sources in the library's collection. Filmed by the Genealogical Society of Utah, 1991, 13 rolls, beginning with FHL film #1683914 (A – Battly).

■ *Index to the California Information File, 1846-1986,* microfiche of index cards at the California State Library, Sacrament. Contains an index to the California Information File which contains 717,000 cards bearing about 1.4 million citations to information in California periodicals, newspapers, manuscript collections, selected books, vertical file collections, county histories, government documents, theses, biographical encyclopedias, biographical files, etc. *A User's Guide to the California Information File,* is available under FHL call no. 979.4 A1 No. 127. Card file filmed by Commercial Microfilm Service, Bellevue, WA, 1986, 550 microfiche, beginning with FHL fiche #6333977 (A. – Adams, Charles). To locate film numbers for all 550 fiche, use the **www.familysearch.org** site. Go to Library / FHL Catalog / Film/Fiche Search – "6333977" (first film number in the series).

COLORADO TERRITORY

Online Colorado Resources

State Archives. Colorado State Archives, Denver, CO. Go to: **www.colorado.gov/dpa/doit/archives/**.

■ Search the **Colorado Historical Records Database** by Name, County, Time Span or Record Type. Go to: **www.colorado.gov/dpa/doit/archives/**.

■ **Colorado Civil War Website.** Go to: **www.earthstation9.com/index.html?colorad2.htm**.

■ **Online 1883 Colorado Pensioners List.** Go to: **www.arealdomain.com/colorado1883.html**.

Published Colorado Resources

■ **Colorado Civil War Soldiers.** See *Official Army Register of the Volunteer Forces of the United States Army for the Years 1861, '62, '63, '64, '65,* microfiche of original published: [Colorado], Washington, D.C.: U.S. Government Printing Office, 1867. 7 p., Contains Part VIII (Colorado) only. Published Bethesda, MD: University Publications of America, 1993, 1 microfiche, FHL #6118445.

■ *Civil War Veteran Burials from California, Nevada, Oregon and Washington Regiments: Buried in Colorado,* by Sherman Lee Pompey, published by Historical and Genealogical Publishing Co., Independence, CA, 1995, 4 pages. FHL book 978.8 A1 No. 106. Also on microfilm, FHL film #2055284.

■ *Colorado Territory Civil War Volunteer Records: A Comprehensive Index to the Twelve Volumes of Military Clothing Books Found in the Colorado State Archives Containing the Historical Background of the Volunteers of Colorado Territory During the Civil War Period, 1861-1865,* records extracted by Columbine Genealogical and Historical Society, published by the society, Littleton, CO, 19094, 454 pages. FHL book 978.8 M22c.

■ *Civil War Index Cards, 1861-1865,* microfilm of original records at the Colorado State Archives in Denver, CO. Each card gives a soldier's name, rank, age, organization, when and where enrolled, by whom enrolled, when and where mustered, by whom mustered, book and page numbers, and other information. Filmed by the Genealogical Society of Utah, 1992, 4 rolls, as follows:
- Civil War index cards: A – Franklin, Ashley M., FHL film #1862946.
- Civil War index cards: Franklin, Ashley M. – McFadden, Owen, FHL film #1862947.
- Civil War index cards: McFadden, Owen – Shock, Adam L., FHL film #1862948.
- Civil War index cards: Shock, Adam L. – Z, FHL film #1862949.

■ *Index to Compiled Service Records of Volunteer Union Soldiers Who Served in Organizations from the Territory of Colorado,* microfilm of original records at the National Archives,

Washington, D.C., filmed by the National Archives, Series M0534, 1964, 3 rolls, as follows:
- Index, A – Hap, 1861-1865, NARA M534 roll 1, FHL film #821998.
- Index, Har – O, 1861-1865, M534 roll 2, FHL film #821999.
- Index, P – Z, 1861-1865, M534 roll 3, FHL film #822000.

The Colorado entries are incorporated into the national index at the National Park Service website at: **www.itd.nps.gov/cwss/**.

■ *1862-1866 Internal Revenue Lists for the Territory of Colorado,* microfilm of originals at the National Archives, Washington, D.C. Filmed by the National Archives, 1968, Series M0757, 3 rolls, as follows:
- Revenue name lists, divisions 1-14, Annual, monthly, special 1862-1863 (NARA M757 roll 1), FHL film #1578500.
- Revenue name lists, divisions 1-14, Annual, monthly, special 1864 (NARA M757 roll 2), FHL film #1578501.
- Revenue name lists, divisions 1-14, Annual, monthly, special 1865-1866 (NARA M757, roll 3), FHL film #1578502.

■ *1865-1867 Taxpayers, Clear Creek County, Colorado Territory,* name list published in *Foothills Inquirer,* Vol. 16, No. 1 (Spring 1996) through Vol. 16, No. 3 (Fall 1996), a publication of the Foothills Genealogical Society of Colorado, Lakewood, CO.

■ *1866 Heads of Families, Jefferson County, Colorado Territory,* name list published in *Foothills Inquirer,* Vol. 17, No. 3 (Fall 1997) and Vol. 18, No. 4 (Winter 1998), a publication of the Foothills Genealogical Society of Colorado, Lakewood, CO.

CONNECTICUT

Online Connecticut Resources

State Archives. Connecticut State Archives/ Connecticut State Library, Hartford, CT. Website (Home): **www.cslib.org/archives/**.

■ **Online Civil War Databases at the State Archives Website:**
- Noble Pension Database. Go to: **www.cslib.org/noble.asp**.

- Fitch's Home for Soldiers and Orphans (1863-1940). Go to: **www.cslib.org/fitch.asp**.

■ **Connecticut Military Department.** Website: **www.ct.gov/mil/cwp/view.asp?a=1351&q=270354**.

Published Connecticut Resources

■ *The Military and Civil History of Connecticut During the War of 1861-1865: Comprising a Detailed Account of the Various Regiments and Batteries, Through March, Encampment, Bivouac and Battle: Also Instances of Distinguished Personal Gallantry, and Biographical Sketches of Many Heroic Soldiers: Together with a Record of the Patriotic Action of Citizens at Home, and of the Liberal Support Furnished by the State in its Executive and Legislative Departments,* by W.A. Croffut and John M. Morris, published by Ledyard Bill, New York, 1868, 891 pages. Includes index. FHL book 974.6 M25c. Also on microfilm, FHL film #1698072.

■ *Catalogue of Connecticut Volunteer Organizations (Infantry, Cavalry and Artillery) in the Service of the United States, 1861-1865: With Additional Enlistments, Casualties, &c., &c., And Brief Summaries Showing the Operations and Service of the Several Regiments and Batteries,* prepared from records in the Adjutant General's Office, published by Brown & Gross, Hartford, CT, 1869, 936 pages. FHL book 974.6 M25cc. Also on microfilm, FHL film #1033670.

■ *Record of Returns from Towns and Payments to Soldiers and Families During the Civil War, Vol. 1-2, 1861-1866,* microfilm of original records at the Connecticut State Archives, Hartford, CT. Includes index arranged alphabetically by name of town. Contains name of each soldier, name of wife, names and ages of children, regiment and company, rank, date of muster, term of enlistment, changes in service, and payments made. Filmed by the Genealogical Society of Utah, 1988, 1 roll, FHL film #1533593.

■ *Record of Service of Connecticut Men in the Army and Navy of the United States During the War of the Rebellion,* photocopy of original compiled by authority of the General Assembly under the direction of the Adjutant-General, published by Lockwood & Brainard, 1889, 1,071 pages. Includes index. FHL book 974.6 M2c. Also on microfilm, FHL film #982124.

■ *Connecticut Men in War of Rebellion, Corrected, Amended or Additional Records,* typescript (photocopy), 41 pages. Includes "Connecticut men in the Spanish War, Philippine Insurrection and China Relief Expedition, April 1898 to July 1904; corrected, amended or additional records" pp. 37-41. FHL book 974.6 M2c supp. Also on microfilm, FHL film #982124.

■ *Index to Compiled Service Records of Volunteer Union Soldiers Who Served in Organizations from the State of Connecticut,* microfilm of original records at the National Archives, Washington, D.C. Filmed by the Archives, series M535, 1964, 17 rolls, beginning with FHL film #821909 (Index, A – Bem). The Connecticut entries are incorporated into the national index at the National Park Service website. Go to: **www.itd.nps.gov/cwss/**.

■ **Vital Records Index,** see the Charles R. Hale Collection at the Connecticut State Library. microfilmed as the *Hale Collection,* includes many records from the Civil War era, including vital records (newspaper notices and cemetery inscriptions) with surname index to cemetery inscriptions referring to places and newspapers; index to death notices from newspapers (not included above); index, marriages by newspapers; general index to marriage notices arranged alphabetically; cemeteries by localities; newspapers. Filmed by the Genealogical Society of Utah, 1949-1950, 360 rolls, beginning with FHL film #3076 (Surname Index, Death and Inscriptions Aa – Alb).

■ *General Index to Probate Records: All Districts in Connecticut, 1641-1948,* microfilm of originals at the Connecticut State Library, Hartford, CT. Alphabetically arranged. Filmed by the Genealogical Society of Utah, 1957-1958, 67 rolls, beginning with FHL film #166000 (Aal, Abraham – Amidon, Raymond Holt).

■ *1862-1866 Internal Revenue Assessment Lists for Connecticut,* microfilm of original records at the National Archives, Washington, D.C. District 1

contains Hartford and Tolland counties; district 2, Middlesex and New Haven counties; district 3, New London and Windham counties; and district 4, Fairfield and Litchfield counties. Filmed by the Archives, 1968, series M758, 23 rolls. FHL has entire series, beginning with FHL film #1534625 (District 1, Annual lists 1862-1864).

DAKOTA TERRITORY, NORTH DAKOTA & SOUTH DAKOTA

Dakota Territory, created in 1861, formed the First Battalion of Dakota Cavalry for the Union Army, in 1862 and 1863. North Dakota and South Dakota both became states in 1889, dividing the original Dakota Territory in half. Surviving Civil War records relate to the war years when it was part of Dakota Territory, as well as subsequent records relating to veterans living in the states of North Dakota and South Dakota.

Online Resources

■ **State Historical Society of North Dakota – Archives Genealogy Page. http://history.nd.gov/ archives/genealogy.html.**
Genealogy Resources are described at this webpage, none of which are available as digital databases. But, the SHSND is one of the few state archives in the country that will actually conduct research for you. This is the webpage to get the information necessary to access many of their archival collections. Most collections of interest to genealogists are accessible at the Orin G. Libby Memorial Reading Room of the North Dakota Heritage Center in Bismarck. For those unable to visit this library in person, the reference staff will attempt to answer specific requests by mail. From Home Page: "Due to the small number of staff and the large number of requests, search time cannot exceed twenty minutes per letter. Therefore, please do not include more than three requests per letter and provide us with as much information as possible, including names, precise locations and dates. No general or surname searches will be attempted. A list of genealogical researchers can be

provided if desired." Sources available for research include:

- **Public Death Index** (at ND Dept. of Health website).
- **Census Schedules.** Research request forms available.
- **Pioneer Biographies/ Historical Data Project (WPA) Biography files.**
- **North Dakota Biographical Index.**
- **Oral History Project Collection.**
- **Naturalization Records.**
- **Land Office Tract Books.** Not indexed. Township/Range description of property must be provided. No Homestead records (but this site provides a link to the Billings, MT Bureau of Land Management website.
- **Newspapers.** Marriage and birth announcements, obituaries or other items from the newspapers can be searched only if the month, day, year and location of the event can be provided. Most newspapers are on microfilm and can be borrowed on Interlibrary loan.

■ **South Dakota State Archives – "For Genealogists" Page.** www.sdhistory.org/arc/archives.htm. As part of the website for the South Dakota State Historical Society in Pierre, SD, the State Archives webpage is the starting point for genealogists. Click on "For Genealogists" for a review of the online databases available:

- **Naturalization Records Index** – Search through First Papers & Second Papers to find individuals.
- **Newspaper Database** – Search the index to find which South Dakota newspapers are microfilmed and available for searches or interlibrary loan.
- **Newspaper Vital Records Index** – Search for newspaper articles. Main topics include birth, marriage, and death, along with various other categories.
- **Guide to American Indian Research in South Dakota** – This guide is intended to describe both the archival holdings of the South Dakota State Archives, and other information sources regarding the Lakota, Nakota, and Dakota.
- **Genealogy Resources – Archival Collections:** Naturalization Records, Federal Census, Veterans Census, State Census, BIA Indian Census, WPA Graves Registration, County Records, Women's History.
- **Genealogy Resources – Library Collection:** Newspapers, Centennial Atlases, City directories, Yearbooks, County Histories, Family Histories, Microfilm, Links.
- **Genealogy Resources - Services/Information:** Surname Reference File, Research Request Forms, Facilities, and Assistance.

■ *Civil War Veterans in South Dakota Counties in 1885,* a recent webpage at the State Historical Society site. Plans include the listing of 5,875 Union soldiers living in 45 South Dakota counties as of 1885. **www.sdhistory.org/arc/civilwar/1885.htm.**

■ **Dakota Territory in the Civil War.** **www.rootsweb.ancestry.com/~cwahgp/states/ dakindex.htm.** Dakota Territory's role in the Civil War. Includes mailing lists for the discussion and sharing of information regarding the Civil War.

■ **American Civil War – North Dakota.** **www.archaeolink.com/north_dakota_in_the_ civil_war.htm.** Includes the following links:

■ **Civil War Rosters – Dakota Territory.** This is a link to a directory of Civil War Rosters/Muster Rolls available on the Internet: Go to **www.geocities. com/Area51/Lair/3680/cw/cw-k.html**.

■ **North Dakota American Civil War – Map of Battles.** You will find click-to-read histories, locations of battles, and more. Go to: **http://americancivilwar.com/statepic/nd.html**.

■ **Online Index – 1885 Dakota Territory Census (North Dakota Counties).** This is a searchable index sponsored by the Institute for Regional Studies, North Dakota State University, Fargo, ND. Schedules have survived for fifty of the fifty-six counties which existed in the northern half of Dakota Territory. All fifty counties are now indexed and contained in this database. The missing county schedules include Boreham, DeSmet, Flannery, Hettinger, Sheridan, and Stevens. Go to the following website: **http://library.ndsu.edu/ archives/databases**.

■ **Civil War Rosters – Dakota Territory Links.** **www.geocities.com/Area51/Lair/3680/cw/cw- dk.html.** This private website has a directory of Civil War Rosters/Muster Rolls that have been found on the Internet. Links include South Dakota, North Dakota, Nebraska, Iowa, and other areas with a Dakota Territory connection.

■ **1883 Pensioners on the Roll (South Dakota counties).** Go to: **http://files.usgwarchives.org/sd/military/1883ndx.txt.**

Published Resources

■ **"1861 Dakota Inhabitants, A-D,"** in *WyMonDak Messenger*, a periodical of the Tri-State Genealogical Society, Belle Fourche, SD, (Summer 1989); **"1861 Dakota Inhabitants, D-M,"** (Fall 1989), **"1861 Dakota Inhabitants, M-Z,"** (Winter 1990).

■ *Dakota Territorial Census of 1885: From the Original Records on File at Bismarck, N.D.,* from "Collections of the State Historical Society of North Dakota," Vol. 4 (1913). Information includes name, sex, age, relationship to head of family, occupation, birthplace, father's birthplace, mother's birthplace. Census returns for the counties of Allred, Bowman, Buford, Dunn, McIntosh, McKenzie, Mercer, Mountraille, Oliver, Renville, Stanton, Towner, Villard, Wallace, Ward, Wells and Wynn. Indexed in North Dakota 1885 Census Index, Ronald Vern Jackson, editor, published by Accelerated Indexing Systems, Bountiful, UT, 1982, 61 pages. FHL book 978.4 X22j.

■ *1885 Dakota Territory Census,* microfilm of original records (for southern Dakota Territory counties) at the South Dakota State Historical Society in Pierre, South Dakota. Most of the 1895 Census has been lost or destroyed. The only known county schedules are for Beadle, Brule, Charles Mix, Edmunds, Fall River, Faulk, Hand, Hanson, Hutchinson, Hyde, Lake, Lincoln, Marshall, McPherson, Moody, Roberts, Sanborn, Spink, Stanley, and Turner counties. Filmed by the SDSHS in 1971, 2 rolls at the FHL, beginning with FHL film #1405268. See also *South Dakota 1885 Census Index,* compiled by Ronald Vern Jackson, Scott D. Rosenkilde, and W. David Samuelsen, published by Accelerated Indexing Systems, 1984, 296 pages. FHL book 978.3 X22j.

■ *Compiled Service Records of Volunteer Union Soldiers Who Served in Organizations from the Territory of Dakota,* microfilm of original records at the National Archives, Washington, D.C. "Contains the compiled military service records of volunteer Union soldiers belonging to the 1st Battalion Dakota Cavalry. Company A, 1st Battalion Dakota Cavalry was organized at Yankton, Dakota Territory, in April 1862 and was mustered out of service on May 9, 1865. Company B was organized at Sioux City, Iowa, on March 31, 1863 and was mustered out on November 15, 1865. The battalion was assigned to duty in the District of Iowa and Dakota, Department of the Northwest, where it defended the frontier and operated against hostile Indians." Filmed by the National Archives, series M1960, 1996, 3 rolls. FHL has entire series, beginning with FHL film #2229930 (Military Service Records, Alderson, Richard – Goodfellow, William R.).

■ *Index to Compiled Service Records of Volunteer Union Soldiers Who Served in Organizations from the Territory of Dakota,* microfilm of original records at the National Archives, Washington, D.C. Contains an alphabetical card index to the service records of soldiers belonging to the First Battalion of Dakota Cavalry. Filmed by the National Archives, series M536, 1964, 1 roll, available as FHL film #881616. This is the source for the list of Dakota names now online at the National Park Service website at: **www.civilwar.nps.gov/cwss/.**

■ *The Leading Business Men of Dakota Cities: Accompanying the Map of Dakota Territory, Name and Address.* microfilm of original published by Warner & Foote, Minneapolis, MM.1883, 105 pages. Filmed by the Library of Congress, 1984. LOC Call number of original: F655.W27. FHL has 1 roll, FHL film #14640114.

■ *Pensioners on the Roll as of January 1, 1883 (Living in Dakota Territory),* abstracted and published by Park Genealogical Books, Roseville, MN, 1996, 26 pages. Information includes military pensioners living in North and South Dakota counties. FHL book 978 M2pr.

■ *Index of North Dakota 1890 Special Census [Veterans],* compiled by Edith Helmer, Mary Ann Quring, and Lily B. Zwolle, published by the Lewistown Genealogy Society, Lewistown, MT, 1986, 49 pages. FHL book 978.4 X22n. Also on 2 microfiche, FHL fiche #6100564.

■ *South Dakota Graves Registration Service; Field Data – Veterans,* microfilm of field forms done by the WPA ca.1940-1941, now at the Veterans Memorial Building, Pierre, SD. Records arranged alphabetically by county, then by name of veteran. Filmed by the Genealogical Society of Utah, 1980, 12 rolls, beginning with FHL film #1295768.

■ *Grand Army of the Republic (South Dakota) Collection,* microfilm of original records at the South Dakota State Historical Society in Pierre, SD. Contains records of Dakota (Territory) and South Dakota Departments, G. A. R. posts including membership rosters, attendance registration books of various encampments (some include Women's Relief Corps.), post descriptive books, member deaths, adjutant reports and muster rolls, lists of officers, applications to form a post, reunion rosters, etc. Filmed by the Genealogical Society of Utah, 2006, 7 rolls, beginning with FHL film #2400586.

■ *1890 Federal Census, Population Schedules, Jefferson Township, Union County, South Dakota,* microfilm of original records at the National Archives at Washington, D.C. Most of the 1890 population schedules were so badly damaged by fire in the Commerce Department Building in January 1921 that they were later disposed of. Only a few fragments of the census schedules are extant. Included on the microfilm are the surviving names from Jefferson Township, Union County, South Dakota on FHL film #926499.

■ *1895 South Dakota State Census,* microfilm of originals located at the South Dakota State Historical Society in Pierre, South Dakota, filmed by the society, 1971, 1 roll. Most of the 1895 schedules were destroyed. Surviving counties: Beadle, Brule, Pratt, Presho, Campbell and Charles Mix counties. See FHL film #1405183.

■ *1905 South Dakota State Census,* microfilm of original records at the South Dakota State Historical Society in Pierre, South Dakota. Consists of cards containing statistical data for all individuals enumerated in the state. The cards are arranged alphabetically by surname. Information given includes the individual's name, address, age, sex, color, nationality, occupation, ability to read and write, whether blind, deaf and dumb, idiotic or insane, place of birth, years in South Dakota, years in United States, birthplace of father and birthplace

of mother. Filmed by the Genealogical Society of Utah, 2002, 125 rolls, beginning with FHL film #2139869 (Aaberg, Albert – Aldous, William).

■ *1915 South Dakota State Census,* microfilm of original records at the South Dakota Historical Society in Pierre. Consists of cards containing statistical data for all individuals enumerated in the state. The cards are arranged in alphabetical order. Each person's card includes: county; post office where person received mail; township name; if in a city, city name; ward; age; occupation; owner or renter of residence; place of birth; ancestry; years living in SD; years living in US; birthplace of father and birthplace of mother; extent of education and whether a graduate; military service, including wars fought, state of service, company, regiment; marital status; maiden name of wife; year married; church affiliation; sex; ethnicity (color); marital status; whether the person could read and write; whether blind, deaf, idiotic, or insane; and naturalization info, if foreign born. Filmed by the Genealogical Society of Utah, 2002, 182 rolls, beginning with FHL film #2283045 (Aaberg, Agnes – Akre, Emma).

■ *1925 South Dakota State Census,* microfilm of original records at the South Dakota State Historical Society in Pierre. Consists of cards containing statistical data for all individuals enumerated in the state. The cards are arranged alphabetically by surname. Each card contains: name of person, county, post office where person received mail; town or township name (if in a town, ward number); person's age, occupation, whether owner or renter, place of birth, years living in SD, years living in US; if foreign born, whether naturalized; birthplace of father and birthplace of mother; extent of education; military service, including wars fought, state, company, regiment, and division; marital status, maiden name of wife, year married, church affiliation; sex, ethnicity (color); and Misc. (read, write, blind, deaf, idiotic, insane. Filmed by the Genealogical Society of Utah, 2003, 213 rolls, beginning with FHL film #2368063 (Aabelson, Magnus – Afrank, Mollie).

■ *1935 South Dakota State Census,* microfilm of original records at the South Dakota State Historical Society in Pierre. Consists of cards containing statistical data for all individuals enumerated in the state. The cards are arranged alphabetically by surname. Each card contains: name of person, county, post office where person received mail; town or township name (if in a town, ward number); person's age, occupation, whether owner or renter, place of birth, years living in SD, years living in US; if foreign born, whether naturalized; birthplace of father and birthplace of mother; extent of education; military service, including wars fought, state, company, regiment, and division; marital status, maiden name of wife, year married, church affiliation; sex, ethnicity (color); and Misc. (read, write, blind, deaf, idiotic, insane. Filmed by the Genealogical Society of Utah, 2003, 733 rolls, beginning with FHL film #2369161 (Aaberg – Adolph, Ina).

■ *1945 South Dakota State Census,* microfilm of original records located at the South Dakota State Historical Society, Pierre, SD. Consists of cards containing statistical data for all individuals enumerated in the state. The cards are arranged alphabetically by surname. Each card contains: name of person, county, post office where person received mail; town or township name (if in a town, ward number); person's age, occupation, whether owner or renter, place of birth, years living in SD, years living in US; if foreign born, whether naturalized; birthplace of father and birthplace of mother; extent of education; military service, including wars fought, state, company, regiment, and division; marital status, maiden name of wife, year married, church affiliation; sex, ethnicity (color); and Misc. (read, write, blind, deaf, idiotic, insane). Filmed by the Genealogical Society of Utah, 2004, 193 rolls, beginning with FHL film #2370848.

DELAWARE

Online Delaware Resources

State Archives. Delaware Public Archives, Dover, DE.

■ **DE Public Archives. Sample Records Relating to the Civil War in Delaware.** Go to: **http://archives.delaware.gov/exhibits/document/.** Click on Records related to Delaware's involvement in the American Civil War.

■ **Delaware GenWeb Archives, Civil War Databases. www.rootsweb.com/~usgenweb/de/.**

■ **Delaware in the Civil War Website.** Go to: **http://home.comcast.net/~33dny/torbert.htm.** "Some bits and pieces of Delaware's Civil War History." Includes a list of Delaware's Civil War Regiments, and Delaware Department, Grand Army of the Republic.

■ **Delaware Civil War Websites.** Use keywords "Delaware Civil War" in a Google search.

Published Delaware Resources

■ *Compiled Military Service Records of Volunteer Union Soldiers Who Served in Organizations from the State of Delaware,* microfilm of original records at the National Archives, Washington, D.C. Filmed by the national Archives, series M1961, 117 rolls. FHL has a pamphlet describing the series (FHL book 973 J53m no. 1961) but does not have the film.

■ *Index to Compiled Service Records of Volunteer Union Soldiers Who Served in Organizations from the State of Delaware,* microfilm of original records at the National Archives, Washington, D.C. Filmed by the Archives, 1964, series M537, 4 rolls. FHL has entire series, beginning with FHL film #881617 (Index, A – D, 1861-1865). The Delaware entries are incorporated into the national index at the National Park Service website at: **www.itd.nps.gov/cwss/.**

■ *1859-1860 Boyd's Delaware State Directory, Containing the Names of all Persons in Business on Their Own Account, Also the Censers, Manufacturing Statistics, and Names of the Inhabitants of Wilmington City,* microfiche of original directory by William H. Wilmington and Andrew Boyd, on 2 fiche, FHL fiche #6043859.

■ *Enrollment Lists for Delaware, 1863-1865,* microfilm of original records at the National Archives, Washington, D.C. Filmed by the Archives, 1973, 4 rolls. FHL has entire series, beginning with FHL film #2310935 (Delaware original enrollment, Classes 1-3, Persons subject for military duty in Sussex, Kent and New Castle Counties, June-July 1863).

■ *Delaware Volunteer Units, Regimental Books, 1862-1865,* microfilm of original records at the National Archives, Washington, D.C. The descriptive roll of each company gives name, age, height, complexion, color of eyes and hair, birthplace, occupation, when, where and by whom enlisted, term, and remarks. Filmed by the Archives, 1974, 2 rolls. FHL has the following:

- Regiments 1-8, commissioned and non-commissioned officers, transfers, discharges, deaths, deserters and descriptive roll of each company, 1862-1865 (with some additions made in 1894), FHL film #2310939.
- Regiments 8 (cont.) -9, commissioned and non-commissioned officers, transfers, discharges, deaths, deserters and descriptive roll of each company, 1862-1865 (with some additions made in 1894), FHL film #2310940.

■ *1862-1866 Internal Revenue Assessment Lists for Delaware,* microfilm of original records at the National Archives, Washington, D.C. Filmed by the Archives, series M759, 8 rolls. FHL has entire series, beginning with FHL film #1578436 (Annual lists 1862 Monthly lists Sep 1862-Apr 1863).

■ *1865-1867 Amnesty Papers: Name Index to Pardon Application Files. Group 2, Pardon applications submitted by persons from Delaware.* Refer to the National Confederate Lists for a detailed description of the records. FHL has entire series, described for all states in RG8 (page 24), applications from Delaware residents on FHL film #1578811.

■ **1862-1872 Delaware Income & Manufacturers Tax.** Name lists in *Delaware History,* Vol. 14, No. 4 (Oct 1971), a publication of the Historical Society of Delaware, Wilmington, DE.

■ *1795-1932 Naturalization Records,* microfilm of original records at the Philadelphia Branch, National Archives. Some volumes include their own indexes. Declarations are also sometimes included. Filmed by the Genealogical Society of Utah, 1990, 27 rolls, beginning with FHL film #1704294 (Indexes).

■ *Deaths from the Delaware Gazette, 1854-1859, 1861-1864 (1860 not Available),* edited by Mary Fallons Richards, published by the Delaware Genealogical Society, Wilmington, DE, 1995, 311

pages. This work is intended to supplement and authenticate census records and Delaware vital records sources prior to 1913. Sources include: death and marriage notices, "local intelligence" columns, estate references by the Register's office, and executor/trustee sales. FHL book 975.1 V28d.

DISTRICT OF COLUMBIA

Online DC Resources

■ **Historical Society of the District of Columbia.** The Kiplinger Research Library of the society holds a large collection of books, pamphlets, photographs, maps, prints, archives and manuscripts in the Gibson reading room on the second floor of the Carnegie building. Use the online catalog to search for keywords such as "Civil War District of Columbia." Go to: **www.historydc.org/Do_ Research/research.asp**.

■ **District of Columbia in the Civil War.** Start at the Civil War Homepage and find links to "Washington, DC" Go to: **www.civil-war.net/**.

Published DC Resources

■ *Selected Final Pension Payment Vouchers, 1818-1864, District of Columbia,* abstracted by Alycon Trubey Pierce, published by Willow Bend Books, Leesburg, VA, 1998, 235 pages. Arranged alphabetically by name of individual applying with a name index. FHL book 975.3 M28p.

■ *Index to Compiled Service Records of Volunteer Union Soldiers Who Served in Organizations from the District of Columbia,* microfilm of original records at the National Archives, Washington, D.C. Filmed by the Archives, 1964, series M538, 3 rolls. FHL has series, beginning with FHL film #881964 (Index, A-G, 1861-1865). The DC entries are incorporated into the national index at the National Park Service website at: **www.itd.nps.gov/cwss/**.

■ *1862-1866 Internal Revenue Assessment Lists for the District of Columbia,* microfilm of originals at the National Archives in Washington, D.C. Records indicate a name and place of residence for each person subject to the tax. (generally, land owners, but occasionally those with personal property only). Filmed by the Archives, 1969, series M760, 8 rolls, beginning with FHL film # 1578491 (Annual tax lists, divisions 1-8, 1863-1864).

■ *1865-1867 Amnesty Papers: Name Index to Pardon Application Files. Group 2, Pardon applications submitted by persons from the District of Columbia.* Refer to the National Confederate Lists for a detailed description of the records. FHL has entire series, described for all states in RG8 (page 24), applications from DC residents on FHL film #1578811.

FLORIDA

Online Florida Resources

State Library & Archives. Tallahassee, FL. Website: **http://dlis.dos.state.fl.us/index_ researchers.cfm**.

■ **Online Civil War Databases at the FL State Archives Website:**
  • Florida Memory Project
  • Florida Confederate Pension Application Files
  • Civil War Guide

■ **Civil War Florida (Private Website).** **www.civilwarflorida.com/site/news/**.

Published Florida Resources

■ *Compiled Service Records of Confederate Soldiers Who Served in Organizations from the State of Florida,* microfilm of original records at The National Archives, Washington, D.C. Filmed by the Archives, 1957, series M251, 104 rolls, beginning with FHL film #191679 (Index, A – Bru) and FHL film #191688 (1st Cavalry, A – E).

■ *Index to Compiled Service Records of Confederate Soldiers Who Served in Organizations from the State of Florida,* microfilm of original records at the National Archives. Filmed by the National Archives, series M225, 9 rolls, beginning with FHL film #191679.

■ *Compiled Service Records of Volunteer Union Soldiers Who Served in Organizations from the State of Florida,* microfilm of original records at the National Archives, Washington, D.C. Filmed by the Archives, 1962, 11 rolls. FHL has entire set, beginning with FHL film #1299987 (1st Cavalry, A – C). The Florida entries are incorporated into the national index at the National Park Service website at: **www.itd.nps.gov/cwss/**.

■ *Index to Compiled Service Records of Volunteer Union Soldiers Who Served in Organizations from the State of Florida,* microfilm of original records at the National Archives. Filmed by the National Archives, series M264, 1 roll, FHL film #821767. The Florida entries are incorporated into the national index at the National Park Service website at: **www.itd.nps.gov/cwss/**.

■ *Records of the War Department, War Department Collection of Confederate Records: Compiled Military Service Records of General and Staff Officers from the State of Florida,* microfilm of original records at the Central Plains Region, National Archives. Filmed by the Archives, 1958, 3 rolls. The names are arranged alphabetically. FHL has this series, beginning with FHL film #191674 (FL General and Staff Officers: A – Col).

■ *Confederate Service Records* (for Florida soldiers who served in Alabama units), microfilm of original records compiled by the ADAH, filmed by the Genealogical Society of Utah, 1987, 1 roll, FHL film #1411532 (Item 2, Florida soldiers).

■ *Index of Floridians Serving in War Between States,* microfilm of typescript (carbon copy, 210 pages) at the Pension Department, State Capitol Building, Tallahassee, FL (1956). Indexes the Civil War section of *Soldiers of Florida in the Seminole Indian, Civil, and Spanish American Wars.* Filmed by the Genealogical Society of Utah, 1956, 1 roll, FHL film #6887.

■ *Biographical Rosters of Florida's Confederate and Union Soldiers, 1861-1865,* by David W. Hartman, compiler; Davis Coles, associate compiler, published by Broadfoot Publishing, Wilmington, NC, 1995, 6 vols. From preface: "Compiled from service records, pension records, diaries, family and local histories, descendants' letters, wartime newspapers and diaries etc. to create a biographical record for as many Confederate and Union soldiers as possible who have been identified as having served in Florida units." Arranged alphabetically by surname within each company. Bibliography: p. 2356-2386 (in vol. 6). Contents: vol. 1: Histories of Florida Infantry Regiments: First (old and new), companies A-K; Second, companies A-M; Third-Fourth, companies A-K; vol. 2: Histories of Florida Infantry Regiments: Fifth-Eighth, companies A-K; vol. 3. Histories of Florida Infantry Regiments: Ninth-Tenth, companies A-K; Eleventh, companies A-L; Second Florida Battalion, companies A-F; History of the First Florida Reserve Regiment, companies A-L; vol. 4: Histories of the First and Second Florida Cavalry Regiment; the Third Battalion Florida Cavalry; the Fifth Florida Cavalry Battalion; the Fifteenth Confederate Cavalry Regiment; First East Florida (US) Cavalry; and the First Florida (US) Cavalry; vol. 5: 2nd Florida Cavalry (US), and Home Guard and miscellaneous units;' vol. 6: Miscellaneous, bibliography, footnotes, index. Includes staff members for each company. FHL book 975.9 M28h v.1-6.

■ *1865-1867 Amnesty Papers: Name Index to Pardon Application Files. Group 1, Pardon applications submitted by persons from Florida.* Refer to the National Confederate Lists for a detailed description of the records. FHL has entire series, described for all states in RG8 (page 24), applications from Florida on FHL film #1578753.

■ *Pension Claims of Confederate Veterans and Their Widows Beginning 1885-1955,* (with Index), microfilm of transcript (hand and typewritten) at the Florida State Archives, Tallahassee, FL. Includes index. Filmed by the Genealogical Society of Utah, 1955, 169 rolls, beginning with FHL film #6717 (Index of pensioners, widows of pensioners, and denied claims) and FHL film #6718 (pension claims No. 1-100). See also *Register of Florida CSA Pension Applications,* transcribed by Virgil D. White, published by National Historical Pub. Co., Waynesboro, TN, 1989, 278 pages. FHL book 975.9 M2w.

■ *Florida Territorial and State Election Records, 1826-1865,* by Florida Division of Elections. Originals and microfilm located at state archives,

Tallahassee, Florida. Election records arranged alphabetically by county, then chronologically (by date of election) within each county. Includes returns of elections for county, state and national offices, amnesty oaths, poll books, lists of registered voters, original ballots, etc. Filmed by the Genealogical Society of Utah, 1990. See FHL film #1673224-1673232.

■ **1864 Florida Military Census.** See *Department for the South, November 1864, for Jacksonville, Fernandina and St. Augustine, Florida, Ordered by the Department of the South, Hilton Head, South Carolina,* by the Florida State Genealogical Society, Tallahassee, FL, published by Heritage Books, Bowie, MD, 2002, 280 pages. Includes index. From the forward: "One of the forgotten legacies... was a special census of eastern Florida conducted on the orders of Federal military authorities. Its motivation is to this day unclear, but it seems likely to have been part of the work done to help register voters under Lincoln's '10 percent' reconstruction plan. African-Americans living in the region were also enumerated despite the fact that they did not yet have the legal right to vote." Includes name, height, color of eyes, complexion, age, where born or contraband [slave], last residence, where registered for draft or name of owner, date moved into the South, oath of allegiance, and remarks. See FHL book 975.91 X2f.

■ *1864 Florida Military Census, Fernandina County,* name list published serially in the *Nassau County Genealogist,* Vol. 1, No. 1 (Winter 1994), thru Vol. 2, No. 1 (Fall 1994), a periodical of the Amelia Island Genealogical Society, Fernandina Beach, FL.

■ *Internal Revenue Assessment Lists for Florida, 1865-1866,* microfilm of original records at the National Archives, Washington, D.C. Filmed by the Archives, 1968, series M761, 1 roll. See FHL film #1578499 (Annual lists, 1865-66; monthly and special lists, Mar.-Dec. 1866).

■ *1867-1905 Florida Voter Registration Rolls, Florida Secretary of State,* microfilm of records at Bureau of Archives and Records Management, Tallahassee, Florida, filmed by the Genealogical Society of Utah, 1990. From the introduction: "Congress passed an act on March 23, 1867 calling for a registration of qualified voters. These voters would then elect delegates to a convention for the purpose of establishing a constitution and civil government. A qualified voter had to be male, twenty-one years of age, a resident of the county, and had to take an oath of allegiance to the United States government. A Board of Registration composed of three loyal officers or persons was set up to make, complete, and witness the registration. This was the first time that Blacks were allowed to register to vote. Most volumes list voter's name, race, time of residence in county and state, native (of what state), naturalization (where, when, and how) and date of registration." See FHL film #1672578 and 1672579.

■ *Register of Deceased Veterans, Florida,* microfilm of a 67-volume report of the Veterans' Graves Registration Project, Division of Professional and Service Projects, Work Projects Administration, 1940-1941; original published by The Project, St. Augustine, FL, 1941. This WPA project was cosponsored by the Military Department, State of Florida, and the American Legion, Florida Department. Cemeteries in most Florida counties were canvassed to identify graves of Florida veterans. In most cases, the information about each veteran was limited to the tombstone inscription, which usually gives a name, year of birth and death, unit of service, war, and rank. Added information from a cemetery sexton may have been added, or information gained from local funeral homes, local histories, or local sources. Not all Florida counties participated, the contents of the volumes includes the following counties: Alachua, Baker, Bay, Bradford, Brevard, Broward, Calhoun, Charlotte, Citrus, Clay, Collier, Dade, De Soto, Dixie, Duval, Flagler, Glades Gulf, Hamilton, Hardee, Hernando, Hillsborough, Holmes, Indian River, Jackson, Lafayette, Lake, Lee, Liberty Manatee, Martin, Monroe, Nassau, Okaloosa, Okeechobee, Orange, Osceola, Palm Beach, Pasco, Polk, St. Lucie, Santa Rosa, Sarasota, Seminole, Sumter, Suwannee, Taylor, Union, Volusia, Wakulla, and Washington. Filmed by the Genealogical Society of Utah, 1953, 1 roll, FHL film #6716.

GEORGIA

Online Georgia Resources

■ **Georgia Department of Archives and History,** (GDAH) Atlanta, GA. Go to the Home Page for the Georgia Archives: **www.sos.state.ga.us/archives/**.

■ **Online Databases at the GDAH Website:**
  • Index to Georgia Confederate Pension Applications
  • Georgia Death Certificates, 1919-1927

■ **"The Civil War in Georgia" Website.** **www.cviog.uga.edu/Projects/gainfo/civilwar.htm**.

Published Georgia Resources

■ *Compiled Service Records of Confederate Soldiers Who Served in Organizations from the State of Georgia,* microfilm of original records in the National Archives, Washington, D.C. From intro: "The compiled service records consist of a jacket-envelope for each soldier, labeled with his name, his rank, and the unit in which he served. The jacket-envelope typically contains card abstracts of entries relating to the soldier as found in original muster rolls, returns, rosters, payrolls, appointment books, hospital registers, Union prison registers and rolls, parole rolls, and inspection reports; and the originals of any papers relating solely to the particular soldier. There are cross-reference cards and jacket- envelopes for soldiers' names that appear in the records under more than one spelling. Filmed by the Archives, 1959, series M266, 607 rolls. FHL has entire series, beginning with FHL film #821700 (A – All). The Georgia entries are incorporated into the national index at the National Park Service website at: **www.itd.nps.gov/cwss/**.

■ *Index to Compiled Service Records of Confederate Soldiers Who Served in Organizations from the State of Georgia,* microfilm of original records at the National Archives, Washington, D.C. Filmed by the National

Archives, 1956, series M226, 67 rolls, beginning with FHL film #821700 (A – All). The Georgia entries are incorporated into the national index at the National Park Service website at: **www.itd.nps.gov/cwss/.**

■ *Compiled Service Records of Volunteer Union Soldiers Who Served in Organizations from the State of Georgia,* microfilm of original records in the National Archives, Washington, District of Columbia. Contains alphabetical records of the First Battalion, Infantry, as well as miscellaneous card abstracts and personal papers. Filmed by the Archives, 1962, series M403, 1 roll. FHL film #1276608.

■ *Index to Compiled Service Records of Volunteer Union Soldiers Who Served in Organizations from the State of Georgia,* microfilm of original records at the National Archives, Washington, D.C. Filmed by the National Archives, 1962, series M385, 1 roll, FHL film #881394. The Georgia entries are incorporated into the national index at the National Park Service website at: **www.itd.nps.gov/cwss/.**

■ *Confederate Service Records* (for Georgia soldiers who served in Alabama units), microfilm of original records compiled by the ADAH, filmed by the Genealogical Society of Utah, 1987, 1 roll, FHL film #1411532 (Item 3, Georgia soldiers).

■ *Roster of the Confederate Soldiers of Georgia, 1861-1865,* microfiche of original volumes compiled by Lillian Henderson, director, Georgia State Division of Confederate Pensions and Records, originally published by Longina & Porter, Hapeville, GA, 1959-1964, six vols., filmed by University Publications of America, Bethesda, MD, 1990, 64 fiche. FHL has entire series, beginning with FHL fiche #6082336.

■ An index to the six volumes cited above is in *Roster of the Confederate Soldiers of Georgia, 1861-1865, (Index)* compiled for the Lake Blackshear Regional Library, Americus, GA, by Juanita S. Brightwell, Eunice S. Lee, and Elsie C. Fulghum. This is an 80,000 name index to *Roster of the Confederate Soldiers of Georgia, 1861-1865,* six volumes, by Lillian Henderson. Index reprinted

by The Reprint Company, Spartanburg, SC, 1982, 513 pages. FHL book 975.8 M22h.

■ *1865-1867 Amnesty Papers: Name Index to Pardon Application Files. Group 1, Pardon applications submitted by persons from Georgia.* Refer to the National Confederate Lists for a detailed description of the records. FHL has entire series, described for all states in RG8, applications from Georgia residents:
- Georgia surnames, Ab – By, FHL film #1578754.
- Georgia surnames, Ca – De, FHL film #1578755.
- Georgia surnames, Di – Gra, FHL film #1578756.
- Georgia surnames, Gre – Hy, FHL film #1578757.
- Georgia surnames, Il – Li, FHL film #1578758.
- Georgia surnames, Lo – Ny, FHL film #1578759.
- Georgia surnames, Oa – Sa, FHL film #1578760.
- Georgia surnames, Sc – Tr, FHL film #1578761.
- Georgia surnames, Tu – Ze; Two-or-More Name File; Miscellaneous File, FHL film #1578762.

■ *Internal Revenue Assessment Lists for Georgia, 1865-1866,* microfilm of original records at the National Archives, Washington, D.C. Filmed by the Archives, 1988, series M762, 8 rolls. The name lists are organized by the federal districts established for collecting the tax, then by the county, and then by the type of assessment, then the names of the taxpayers. To locate a county, the following is provided on the first roll: DISTRICT 1 contains Appling, Berrien, Brooks, Bryan, Bulloch, Camden, Charlton, Chatham, Clinch, Coffee, Colquitt, Echols, Effingham, Emanuel, Glynn, Irwin, Johnson, Laurens, Liberty, Lowndes, McIntosh, Montgomery, Pierce, Tattnall, Telfair, Thomas, Ware, Wayne, and Wilcox counties. DISTRICT 2 contains Baker, Bibb, Butts, Calhoun, Chattahoochee, Clay, Crawford, Decatur, Dooly, Dougherty, Early, Harris, Houston, Lee, Macon, Marion, Miller, Mitchell, Monroe, Muscogee, Pike, Pulaski, Quitman, Randolph, Schley [sic], Spalding, Stewart, Sumter, Talbot, Taylor, Terrell, Upson, Webster, and Worth counties. DISTRICT 3 contains Baldwin, Burke, Columbia, Elbert, Glascock, Greene, Hancock, Jasper, Jefferson, Jones, Lincoln, Morgan, Newton, Oglethorpe, Putnam, Richmond, Screven, Taliaferro, Twiggs, Warren, Washington, Wilkes, and Wilkinson counties. DISTRICT 4 contains Banks, Campbell, Carroll, Cass, Catoosa, Chattooga, Cherokee, Clarke, Clayton, Cobb, Coweta, Dade, Dawson, De Kalb, Fannin, Fayette, Floyd, Forsyth, Franklin,

Fulton, Gilmer, Gordon, Gwinnett, Habersham, Hall, Haralson, Hart, heard, Henry, Jackson, Lumpkin, Madison, Meriwether, Milton, Murray, Paulding, Pickens, Polk, Rabun, Towns, Troup, Union, Walker Walton, White, Whitfield. FHL has this series, beginning with FHL film #1578459 (DISTRICT 1 Annual lists 1865-1866, Monthly and special lists Aug. 1865-Dec. 1866).

■ *Returns of Qualified Voters, 1867-1868,* microfilm of originals at the GDAH, Atlanta, GA. Filmed by the GDAH, 1991, 22 rolls. FHL has entire series, beginning with FHL film #1843918 (Returns of qualified voters dist. 1, v. 1-3, 1867-1868 Counties: Bryan, Chatham, City of Savannah).

■ *Reconstruction Registration Oath Books, 1867-1868,* microfilm of originals at the GDAH, Atlanta, GA. Filmed by the GDAH, 1991, 23 rolls. FHL has entire series, beginning with FHL film #1843848 (Reconstruction Registration Oath Books 1867-1868 dist. 1, v. 1-3, Bryan County no. 1, Chatham County no. 1-2).

■ The *Returns of Qualified Voters* and *Registration Oaths* were indexed in *Index to Georgia's 1867-1868 Returns of Qualified Voters and Registration Oath Books, White,* compiled by John David Brandenburg and Rita Binkley Worthy, published by J.D. Brandenburg, Atlanta, GA, 1995, 532 pages. FHL book 975.8 N42b.

■ *Confederate Pension Rolls,* microfilm of manuscripts at GDAH, Atlanta, Georgia. Confederate soldiers received pensions for military service beginning in 1879. The law establishing pension payment was changed in 1891 to include widows of soldiers. There are cards in this record for the witnesses of these soldiers and widows attesting to the service of each soldier. The arrangement is alphabetical by the name of the pensioner and included on the card are: notations concerning the county of residence, unit designation, and husband's name in the case of widow cards. Filmed GDAH, 1963, 634 rolls. FHL has entire series, beginning with FHL film #315678 (Confederate pension rolls: Appling County: Abbott, J. H. – Johnson, Obadiah).

■ For a statewide combined index to the above pension rolls, see *Index to Georgia Civil War Confederate Pension Files,* transcribed by Virgil

D. White, published by National Historical, Waynesboro, TN, 1966, 1,063 pages. FHL book 975.8 M22w.

■ See also *Index to Georgia's Confederate Pension Supplements,* by Ted O. Brooke and Linda Woodward Geiger, published by T. Brooke, Cumming, GA, 1999, 210 pages. FHL book 975.8 M22b.

■ *Georgia Veterans & Their Widows Who Applied For Government Pensions in Alabama,* compiled by F.W. Weatherbee, Jr., published by Pioneer Pub. Co., Carrollton, MS, 1991, 206 pages. FHL book 975.8 M2wf.

■ *Georgia Pension List of All Wars from the Revolution Down to 1883,* compiled by Lucy Kate McGhee, publisher and place of publication not known. FHL book 975.8 M24m.

■ *Militia Enrollment Lists; Re-organizing the Militia, ca. 1864; Pension Enrollments Lists, 1920-1940, ca. 1864; 1920-1940,* microfilm of originals at the GDAH, Atlanta, GA. Militia lists are arranged alphabetically by county. Filmed by the Genealogical Society of Utah, 1963, 7 rolls, beginning with FHL film #351787 (Lists of men enrolled in the Georgia Militia by militia districts as required by the Act of 14th December 1863 for re-organizing the militia of the State. Also included within each county are typed copies of the enrollment lists which were prepared by the Georgia Pensions and Records Department between 1920 and 1940. Appling County – Carlton County).

■ *1864 Census for Re-Organizing the Georgia Militia,* compiled by Nancy J. Cornell, published by Genealogical Publishing Co. Inc., Baltimore, 2000, 843 pages. From preface: "From originals at GDAH, this is an extraction and index of a special statewide census during the Civil War of all white males between the ages of 16 and 60 who were not at the time in the service of the Confederate States of America, it is a list of some 42,000 men – many of them exempt from service – who were able to serve in local militia. Each one of the persons enrolled was listed by his full name, age, occupation, place of birth, and reason (if any) for his exemption from service. Sometime between 1920 and 1940 the Georgia Pension and Record Department typed up copies of these lists. Names on the typed lists, unlike most of the originals, are in alphabetical order." See FHL book 975.8 X22.

■ *Georgia Military Roster, Index, 1869,* microfilm of originals at the GDAH, Atlanta, GA. Filmed by the GDAH, 1965, 1 roll, available from the FHL as FHL film #465190.

■ *Tax Digests and Compilation, 1854-1877,* microfilm of originals of the Georgia State Tax Commissioner, now located at the GDAH, Atlanta, GA. County name lists filmed by the Genealogical Society of Utah, 1957, 13 rolls, with counties and years of tax lists as follows:

- Appling, 1877; Burke, 1863; Berrien, 1867; Baldwin, 1871; Bryan, 1871; Bibb, 1871; Dade, 1864, 1871; Effingham, 1866, 1870-1871, FHL film #159195.
- Cherokee, 1871; Colquitt, 1869; Charlton, 1871; Clay, 1855, 1864; Chattahoochee, 1871; Crawford, 1868, 1871; Coffee, 1869, 1871-1872, FHL film #159196.
- Gilmer, 1866; Gwinnett, 1866; Glascock, 1868-1872; Fannin, 1863, 1866; Fayette, 1872, FHL film #159197.
- Hart, 1867; Heard, 1871-1872; Irwin, 1870; Jones, 1869; Jasper, 1866, 1868; Jackson, 1866; Johnson, 1864, 1866, 1872, FHL film #159198.
- Lincoln, 1868, 1869; Lowndes, 1870; Lumpkin, 1866; Laurnes, 1866, 1871, 1872, FHL film #159199.
- Morgan, 1863, 1871; Murray, 1868-1869; McDuffie, 1871; Marion, 1871; Meriweather, 1863; Muscogee, 1867, FHL film #159200.
- Milton, 1866, 1868; Miller, 1871-1872; Monroe, 1868-1869, 1871; Pierce, 1864, 1868, 1869-1870, FHL film #159201.
- Pickens, 1867; Pulaski, 1869; Polk, 1870; Paulding, 1868-1869; Pike, 1866, 1871-1872; Oglethorpe, 1871, FHL film #159202.
- Sumter, 1864; Schley, 1858, 1866, 1870; Spalding, 1866, 1871-1872; Stewart, 1864, 1868; Rockdale, 1871; Richmond, 1866, FHL film #159203.
- Terrell, 1870; Taylor, 1870; Taliaferro, 1869; Twiggs, 1863, 1870; Upson, 1869, 1871, FHL film #159204.
- Troup, 1861, 1866-1867; Thomas, 1854, 1870-1871; Towns, 1869-1870, FHL film #159205.
- Webster, 1861, 1864; Warren, 1867, 1870; Wayne, 1866, 1868-1871; Washington, 1869-1870, FHL film #159206.
- Ware, 1862, 1867-1869; White, 1863, 1864, 1866-1870; Wilcox, 1870, FHL film #159207.

■ *War Tax Digest for Marion, Schley and Other Counties of Georgia, No Dates,* microfilm of original records of the Marion County Court of Ordinary, filmed by the Genealogical Society of Utah, 1966, 1 roll, FHL film #422236.

■ *Roster of Confederate Graves,* compiled and published by the United Daughters of the Confederacy. Georgia Division, Atlanta, GA, 1997, 8 vols. Contents: vol. 1: Georgia: Appling County – Crawford County; vol. 2: Georgia: Crisp County – Gordon County; vol. 3: Georgia: Grady County – McDuffie County; vol. 4: Georgia: McIntosh County – Terrell County; vol. 5: Georgia: Thomas County – Worth County: vol. 6: Alabama – West Virginia; vol. 7: First supplemental volume; vol. 8:. Second supplemental volume, Alabama – West Virginia, Index (Vol. 8 includes listings from the following states: Alabama, Arizona, Arkansas, California, Delaware, District of Columbia, Florida, Georgia, Illinois, Indiana, Kentucky, Louisiana, Maryland, Mississippi, New York, North Carolina, Ohio, Pennsylvania, South Carolina, Tennessee, Texas, Virginia, and West Virginia.). FHL book 975.8 V3r vol. 1-8.

HAWAII TERRITORY

Annexed to the United States in 1898, Territory of Hawaii, 1900-1959; State of Hawaii, 1959. Although it was not part of the United States during the Civil War, veterans migrated to Hawaii after the war. The best sources for locating such veterans in Hawaii are the following:

■ *1878, 1890 & 1896 Hawaii Census Records,* microfilm of originals from the Hawaiian Bureau of Customs, now located at the Archives of Hawaii, Honolulu. Filmed by the Genealogical Society of Utah, 1977, 8 rolls, beginning with FHL film #1010681 (1878 census records, island of Hawaii: town of Hilo).

■ *1884-1936 Honolulu and Hawaii Territory Directories,* microfilm of originals by various publishers in various libraries and societies, filmed by Research Publications, Woodbridge, CT, 1980-1995. FHL has 18 rolls, beginning with FHL film #2156544 (1884 city directory of Honolulu and island of Oahu; 1890 directory, Kingdom of Hawaii; 1892 directory and hand-book of Honolulu and the Hawaiian Islands).

IDAHO TERRITORY

Idaho Territory was created during the Civil War, in March 1863. There were no Union regiments formed in Idaho Territory, but many Idaho residents joined the Union Army from surrounding territories.

■ **The Idaho State Historical Society** has several databases online at: **www.idahohistory.net/library. collections.html#anchor**. From this webpage, you will be led to several On-line Name Indexes, including, *Civil War Veterans of Idaho,* an index in a downloadable *Excel* database with over 4,500 entries.

■ *Internal Revenue Assessment Lists for Idaho Territory, 1865-1866; 1867-1874,* original records filmed by the National Archives, series M763 (1865-66); and series T1209 (1867-74). No film at the FHL.

ILLINOIS

Online Illinois Resources

Illinois State Archives (ISA), Springfield, IL. Website (Home): **www.cyberdriveillinois.com/ departments/archives/archives.html**. Go to: "Search our online databases."

■ **"Genealogy in the ISA."** Visit this site directly at: **www.cyberdriveillinois.com/departments/ archives/services.html**.

■ **Online Searchable Illinois Veterans Databases at the ISA Website:**
  • Database of Illinois War of 1812 Veterans
  • Database of Illinois Winnebago War Veterans
  • Database of Illinois Black Hawk War Veterans
  • Database of Illinois Mexican War Veterans
  • Illinois Civil War Muster and Descriptive Rolls
  • Database of Illinois Civil War Veterans Serving in the U.S. Navy
  • Database of Illinois Civil War Veterans of Missouri Units
  • Database of Illinois Spanish–American War Veterans
  • Database of the 1929 Illinois Roll of Honor
  • Database of Illinois Soldiers' and Sailors' Home Residents

■ **Illinois in the Civil War Website.** A Project to put Illinois Civil War Rosters and History on the Internet. Go to: **www.illinoiscivilwar.org/**.

■ **Online 1883 Pensioners, Illinois. www.arealdomain.com/illinois1883.html**.

Published Illinois Resources

■ *Illinois Military Units in the Civil War,* photocopy of original published by the Civil War Centennial Commission of Illinois, Springfield, IL, 1962, 53 pages. Includes military units by county & by infantry, cavalry, & artillery regiments. Also includes independent artillery. Includes popular names of Illinois military organizations along with their official names. FHL book 977.3 M2im. Also on microfiche, FHL fiche #6334558.

■ *Index to Compiled Service Records of Volunteer Union Soldiers Who Served in Organizations from the State of Illinois,* microfilm of original records at the National Archives, Washington, D.C. Filmed by the Archives, 1964, series M539, 101 rolls. FHL has entire series, beginning with FHL film #881621 (A – Alle). The Illinois entries are incorporated into the national index at the National Park Service website at: **www.itd.nps.gov/cwss/**.

■ *Confederate Service Records* (for Illinois soldiers who served in Alabama units), microfilm of original records compiled by the ADAH, filmed by the Genealogical Society of Utah, 1987, 1 roll, FHL film #1411532 (Item 4, Illinois soldiers).

■ *1861-1862 Illinois Military Census,* microfilm of original records at the office of Secretary of State, Springfield, IL. A list, by county, of able-bodied male citizens between the ages of eighteen and forty-five in pursuance of General Orders No. 99 of the War Department and instructions from the Adjutant General of the state of Illinois. Includes Adams, Cook, Jo Daviess, and Lake counties. FHL film #2209347 (Illinois military census, 1861-1862).

■ *Militia Rolls, 1862-1863,* microfilm of original records at the Illinois State Archives, Springfield, IL. Name lists are organized by county. Filmed by the Genealogical Society of Utah, 1977, 19 rolls, beginning with FHL film #1012406 (Adams – Champaign counties).

■ *Roster of Illinois Soldiers and Sailors in Nebraska,* by G.E. Whitman, photocopy of original 1892 roster. These Civil War vets were known to be living in Nebraska in 1891 but were originally recruited from Illinois counties. FHL book 973 M2wg. Also on microfilm, FHL film #1425496.

■ *1865-1867 Amnesty Papers: Name Index to Pardon Application Files. Group 2, Pardon applications submitted by persons from Illinois.* Refer to the National Confederate Lists for a detailed description of the records. FHL has entire series, described for all states in RG8 (page 24), applications from Illinois residents on FHL film #1578811.

■ *Grand Army of the Republic, Department of Illinois: Transcription of the Death Rolls, 1879-1947,* by Dennis Northcott and Thomas Brooks, published by D. Northcott, St. Louis, MO, 2003, 537 pages. Names are in alphabetical order. Page headings: Name; Rank; Company, Regiment or Ship; Post; Death date; Proceedings. From intro: "To compile these death rolls, the department requested each of the local chapters, known as 'posts,' to submit a death roll of its members. Compliance with this request varied from post to post and year to year; some posts submitted incomplete rolls or none at all. This transcription, compiled primarily from 'Proceedings' in the holdings of the Illinois State Historical Library, contains records of more than 32,000 comrades, who served in Civil War units from thirty-six states." FHL book 977.3 M2n.

■ *Roster of Men from Illinois Who Served in the United States Navy During the War of the Rebellion, 1861-1866,* microfilm of original manuscript at the Illinois State Archives. Filmed by the Genealogical Society of Utah, 1974, 2 rolls, FHL film #1001182 (Index to Roster of men) and FHL film #978491 (Roster of men).

■ *Report of the Adjutant General of the State of Illinois,* revised by J.N. Reece, Illinois. Adjutant General's Office, microfilm of original published by Phillips Bros., Springfield, IL, 1900-02, 9 vols. Includes index. Alphabetical indexes of men, rosters, and records of officers and men in the Mexican War, Indian Wars, Civil War and the Spanish-American War. FHL book 977.3 M23iL v.1-9. Also on microfilm, beginning with FHL film #1001124 & 1001125 (Index, Mexican War: Index, Indian Wars: A-Z Index, Civil War: A– Allen, A.).

■ *Biographical Sketches of Illinois Officers Engaged in the War Against the Rebellion of 1861,* by James Grant Wilson, published by J. Barnet, Chicago, IL, 1862, 106 pages. FHL book 977.3 D3w. Also on microfiche, FHL fiche #6049393.

■ *Internal Revenue Assessment Lists for Illinois, 1862-1866,* microfilm of originals at the National Archives. Includes a locality index (filmed at the beginning of each roll of film) that references counties to districts and film roll numbers. From intro: "The lists were created in the offices of assessors and assistant assessors of Internal Revenue during the period 1862-1866. The lists are arranged by collection district and thereunder by division. They are filmed in the order in which they are bound in the volumes." Filmed by the Archives, 1968, series M764, 63 rolls. FHL has entire series, beginning with FHL film #1534562 (District 1, 1862-1863).

■ *1865 Illinois State Census,* microfilm of original records at the Illinois State Archives, Springfield, IL. At the time of filming, the state was missing the 1865 census schedules for Gallatin, Mason & Monroe counties. Only Elm Grove Township is included for Tazewell County. From IL State Archives description: "Each county return includes for each household name of head of household; numbers of free white males and females in each decennial age group (e.g., ages 0-9, 10-19, 20-29); numbers of male and female Negroes; total number of inhabitants in household; number of males eligible for duty in state militia; type (e.g., blacksmith shop, wheelwright shop) and valuation of products of manufacturing establishments; valuations of livestock, grain products, and other agricultural products; tons of coal produced annually; pounds of wool products; and numbers of flour and gristmills, sawmills, and distilleries. Also included in each return are numbers of universities, academies, grammar schools, and common schools and number of pupils enrolled in each. Each return also includes the signature of a census commissioner certifying the return, date certified, and occasional recapitulations of totals. Legal subdivisions also are indicated such as cities, towns, and townships and recapitulations frequently are given for them." Filmed by the Genealogical Society of Utah, 1964, 1977, 25 rolls, as follows:

- Adams, Bureau, Edwards, Ford, and Effingham counties, FHL film #972746.
- Fayette, Franklin, Grundy, Henderson, and Fulton counties, FHL film #972747.
- Jo Daviess, Pulaski, Alexander, Bond, and Boone counties, FHL film # 972748.
- Clinton, Champaign, Clark, Cumberland, and Christian counties, FHL film #972749.
- Crawford, Carroll, DeWitt, DeKalb, Douglas, DuPage, and Brown counties, FHL film #972750.
- Coles, Calhoun, Cass, Clay, and Greene counties, FHL film #972751.
- Edgar, Jasper, Pike, Hardin, and Jefferson counties, FHL film #972752.
- Jackson, Johnson, Henry, and Hancock counties, FHL film #972753.
- Hamilton, Iroquois, Kankakee, and Knox counties, FHL film #972754.
- Jersey County, FHL film #972755.
- Kane, Kendall, and Logan counties, FHL film #972756.
- Lake, Lawrence, Lee, and Livingston counties, FHL film #972757.
- McHenry, Montgomery, Macoupin, and Ogle counties, FHL film #1012404.
- Madison and Macon counties, FHL film #972758.
- Menard, Morgan, Pope, and Richland counties, FHL film #972759.
- Cook Co. (Chicago wards 1-12), FHL film #972760.
- Cook Co. (Chicago wards 12-16; other towns), FHL film #972761.
- Randolph, Saline, Mercer, McDonough, and McLean counties, FHL film #972762.
- Marshall, Peoria, Piatt, Perry, and Putnam counties, FHL film #972763.
- Rock Island Co., FHL film #972764.
- Sangamon, St. Clair, and Tazewell (Elm Grove Township only) counties, FHL film #972765.
- Vermilion, Will, and La Salle counties, FHL film #972766.
- Marion, Massac, Moultrie, Shelby, Stephenson, Schuyler, and Stark counties, FHL film #972767.
- Scott, Union, Wayne, White, Woodford, and Washington counties, FHL film #972768.
- Williamson, Winnebago, Wabash, and Warren counties, FHL film #972769.

INDIANA

Online Indiana Resources

■ **Indiana State Library,** Indianapolis, IN. The Databases page at: **www.in.gov/library/ databases.htm**. Includes links to Civil War era searchable databases online:
- Indiana Biography Index
- Indiana Cemetery Index
- Indianapolis Newspaper Index, 1848-1888
- New databases added from time to time

■ **Indiana State Archives,** Indianapolis, IN. The Online Indexes page at: **www.in.gov/icpr/2355.htm**, has links to these Civil War era searchable databases online:
- Indiana Soldiers/Sailors Children's Home Database
- Indiana Naturalizations

■ **1883 Indiana Pensioners Online.** (Carroll, Cass, Clinton, Grant, Howard, Miami, Tipton, Tippecanoe, Vermillion, and Wabash counties: **www.arealdomain.com/indiana1883.html**.

■ **"Civil War – Indiana" Website.** **http://civilwarindiana.com/**. Includes Web pages for the following topics:
- Indiana's Role in the Civil War
- Soldier Search
- Photograph Archives (Searchable)
- Other Indiana Civil War
- Photographic Resources
- New Indiana Civil War Books For Sale
- Indiana's Prominent Civil War Personalities
- Indiana Regimental Histories
- Indiana Civil War Speakers Bureau
- Links to other Civil War websites
- Indiana Bibliography
- Researching An Indiana Soldier
- Discuss Indiana in the Civil War
- Indiana Men on the Sultana
- Indiana Men at Andersonville
- Indiana Medal of Honor Awards & Citations
- Black Soldiers from Indiana
- A Jewish Colonel from Indiana
- Summary of Troops Furnished by States &Territories

- Indiana Civil War Museums & Historical Sites
- Your Help Is Needed
- Friends of Civil War Indiana

■ **"Indiana in the Civil War" Website. www.indianainthecivilwar.com/.** Includes Web pages for the following topics:
- Indiana Regiments
- Hoosiers of Note
- Letters/Diaries/Stories
- List of Engagements
- Bibliography
- Reading About Indiana in the Civil War
- Confederate POW Burials
- Announcements & Want Ads
- Indiana War Memorial Battle Flag Photos
- Hoosier Cemetery Project
- Civil War Links

Published Indiana Resources

■ *1859-1861 Indiana State Directories,* microfiche of originals published by various publishers. Filmed by Research Publications, Woodbridge, CT, 1980-1984. FHL has the following:
- 1858-1859 G. W. Hawes' Indiana state gazetteer and business directory (10 fiche), FHL Fiche #6043990.
- 1860-1861 Second edition of George W. Hawes Indiana state gazetteer and business directory (on 12 fiche), FHL fiche #6043991.

■ *Index, Indiana Source Books*, compiled by Dorothy Riker, published by the Family History Section, Indiana Historical Society, Indianapolis, 1983, 3 vols., 406 pages. Contains an index to marriages, wills and naturalizations that appeared in the *Hoosier Genealogist* (1961-1979), compiled into three volumes, including more than 115,000 names. FHL book 977.2 D29h.

■ *Index to Compiled Service Records of Volunteer Union Soldiers Who Served in Organizations from the State of Indiana,* microfilm of original records at the National Archives, Washington, D.C. Consists of alphabetically arranged General Index Cards for Indiana, with over 277,220 entries. Filmed by the National Archives, series M540, 86 rolls. FHL has entire series, beginning with FHL film #881722 (Index, A-Al). The Indiana entries are incorporated into the national index at the National

Park Service website at: **www.itd.nps.gov/cwss/.**

■ *The Soldier of Indiana in the War for the Union,* published anonymously (but believed to be by Catherine Merrill, second female college professor in the U.S.). Published Indianapolis, 1869, 815 pages. Includes index. Also on microfilm. FHL film #1307612.

■ *Report of the Adjutant General of the State of Indiana,* microfilm of original, State Printer, Indianapolis, 1867-1869. 8 vols. Contents: vol. 1: Indiana in the War of the Rebellion, and statistics and documents; vol. 2: Governor's military staff; Indiana officers commissioned by the president; Officers and historical memoranda of Indiana regiments, numbered from the Sixth to the Seventy-fourth inclusive; vol. 3: Officers and historical memoranda of Indiana regiments, numbered from the Seventy-fifth to the One hundred and fifty-sixth inclusive; of the Twenty-fourth regiment of U.S. colored troops, and of Indiana batteries of light artillery, numbered from the First to the Twenty-sixth, inclusive; also, Rosters of officers of the U.S. Navy appointed from Indiana; and of officers of the Indiana Legion; also an alphabetical list of all officers; vol. 4: Rosters of enlisted men of Indiana regiments numbered from the sixth to the Twenty-ninth inclusive; vol. 5: Rosters of enlisted men of Indiana regiments numbered from the Thirtieth to the Fifty-ninth inclusive; vol. 6: Rosters of enlisted men of Indiana regiments numbered from the Sixtieth to the One hundred and ninth inclusive; vol. 7: Rosters of enlisted men of Indiana regiments numbered from the One hundred and eleventh to the One hundred and fifty-sixth inclusive; Colored troops; and Batteries light artillery, numbered from the First to the Twenty-sixth inclusive; vol. 8: Additional information and corrections of previous volumes; A list of officers and men who lost their lives in the service, and a list of dissenters. Filmed for the FHL by the Library of Congress Photoduplication Service, 1989, 3 rolls, FHL film #1703857 (vols. 1-3); FHL film #1703856 (vols. 4-6); and FHL film #1703855 (vols. 7-8). See also *Index to the Report of the Adjutant General of the State of Indiana: An Every Name Index to Volumes I, II and III,* by Glenda K. Trapp, published by Trapp Publishing,

Evansville, IN, 1986, 213 pages. FHL book 977.2 M22t.

■ *Indiana Legion, 1861-1865, Index of Soldiers,* microfilm of original index cards prepared by the Indiana Commission on Public Records, now located at the Indiana State Archives. Index cards include name of soldier, regiment, company, duration of enlistment, dates of enrollment and when mustered, county, age, physical description, occupation, where discharged or mustered out, and date. For historical information on the Indiana Legion see *Report of the Adjutant General of the State of Indiana,* vol. 1, pages 106 through 136 found on FHL film #1703857. Indiana Legion index cards filmed by the Genealogical Society of Utah, 1988, 5 rolls, as follows:
- Abberger, Simon – Dooley, Wm. H., FHL film #1571078.
- Dooley, Wm. H – Haven, Joseph, FHL film #1556707.
- Haven, Joseph – Miller, Oliver P., FHL film #1556708.
- Miller, Oliver P – Steward, Blackburn, FHL film #1556872.
- Steward, Blackburn – Zurstadt, George C., FHL film #1556873.

■ *Indiana Substitutes Hired for the Civil War,* microfilm of index cards located at the Indiana State Library, Indianapolis. Contains name of man hiring a substitute and a reference to a service record card for the substitute. Filmed by the Genealogical Society of Utah, 1988, 1 roll, FHL film #1556875.

■ *Confederate Service Records* (for Indiana soldiers who served in Alabama units), microfilm of original records compiled by the ADAH, filmed by the Genealogical Society of Utah, 1987, 1 roll, FHL film #1411532 (Item 5, Indiana soldiers).

■ *Internal Revenue Assessment Lists for Indiana, 1862-1866,* microfilm of original manuscripts at the National Archives, Washington, D.C. Lists are arranged alphabetically by surname (within Internal Revenue divisions) of those being assessed for each period, and provide a good representation of heads of households of Indiana during the Civil War era. Both personal and property owners are named, but are not indexed and not easily accessible. The lists are organized by tax year, type of list, Internal

Revenue districts, and sub-divisions of the districts. Filmed by the National Archives, 1971, series M765, 42 rolls, beginning with FHL film #1491004 (District 1, division 9, special lists 1864, annual lists 1862-1864; and Divisions 9 and 11, monthly and special lists, Dec. 1862-Dec. 1866). To see which Indiana counties/townships are in which district/division, refer to *Internal Revenue Assessment Lists for Indiana, 1862-1866: National Archives Microfilm Publications, Pamphlet Describing M765,* 11 pages, available as FHL book 973 J53m No. 765.

■ *1865-1867 Amnesty Papers: Name Index to Pardon Application Files. Group 2, Pardon Applications Submitted by Persons from Indiana.* Refer to the National Confederate Lists for a detailed description of the records. FHL has entire series, including applications from Indiana residents on FHL film #1578811.

■ *Enrollment of the Late Soldiers, Their Widows and Orphans of the Late Armies of the United States, Residing in the State of Indiana [for the years 1886, 1890, & 1894],* microfilm of records located at the Indiana State Archives, Indianapolis. This is the primary source for locating a veteran (or widow) living in Indiana from 1886-1894. From intro: "Contains an enrollment of persons employed in the late armies of the United States, i.e., the War of 1812; the War of the United States with Mexico; the Civil War of 1861-1865; and of all wars of the United States with Indian tribes. By enactment of the General Assembly of the state of Indiana, each township assessor at the time of taking lists of property for taxation, was to list all persons who served in the United States armies (regardless of the state from which they served), as well as their widows and orphans. Assessors were to return their listings to the County Clerks who in turn sent them to the Adjutant General for the State to be put on permanent file in his office." (Duplicate records may still be located at the Circuit Court for an Indiana county). Separate assessor lists were done in 1886, 1890, and 1894. The records are arranged by county, then township, and within each township, alphabetically by the name of the veteran; and identifies for each veteran, a company and regiment, residence (post office address), and number of children under 16. Additional information may be given on wounds suffered, imprisonment, and current physical condition. For deceased veterans, death date, and name of widow and any orphans are given. Filmed by the Genealogical Society of Utah, 1988-1990, 89 rolls, as follows:

1886 Listings:
- Adams, Bartholomew counties, FHL film #1605057.
- Benton, Blackford, Boone, Brown counties, FHL film #1605058.
- Clark, Clay, Clinton counties, FHL film #1605059.
- Clinton, Daviess, Crawford, Decatur counties, FHL film #1605179.
- DeKalb, Delaware, Dubois counties, FHL film #1605180.
- Elkhart, Fayette, Floyd, Fountain counties, FHL film #1605181.
- Fulton, Gibson, Greene counties, FHL film #1605322.
- Hamilton, Hancock, Harrison, Hendricks counties, FHL film #1605323.
- Hendricks, Henry, Huntington, Jackson counties, FHL film #1605324.
- Jasper, Jay, Jefferson counties, FHL film #1605325.
- Jennings, Johnson, Knox counties, FHL film #1605326.
- Knox, Kosciusko, La Grange counties, FHL film #1605665.
- La Porte, Lawrence, Madison counties, FHL film #1605666.
- Madison, Marshall, Martin, Miami counties, FHL film #1605667.
- Monroe, Morgan, Newton, Noble counties, FHL film #1605668.
- Noble, Parke, Perry, Pike counties, FHL film #1605669.
- Porter, Posey, Pulaski counties, FHL film #1605682.
- Putnam, Randolph, Ripley counties, FHL film #1605683.
- Rush, St. Joseph, Scott counties FHL Film #1498457.
- Shelby, Spencer, Starke counties, FHL film #1498458.
- Sullivan, Switzerland, Tippecanoe, Tipton counties, FHL film #1498459.
- Vanderburgh, Vermillion, Wabash, Warrick counties, FHL film #1498460.
- Washington, Wells, White counties, FHL film #1498461.
- Whitley county, FHL film #1498462.

1890 Listings:
- Bartholomew, Benton, Boone counties, FHL film #1639000.
- Brown, Carroll, Cass, Clark counties, FHL film #1639001.
- Clark, Clay, Clinton counties, FHL film #1639002.
- Clinton, Daviess, Decatur counties, FHL film #1639003.
- DeKalb, Delaware, Dubois counties, FHL film #1639004.
- Elkhart, Fayette, Floyd counties, FHL film #1651066.
- Fountain, Franklin, Fulton, Gibson counties, FHL film #1651067.
- Grant, Greene, Hamilton counties, FHL film #1651068.
- Hancock, Harrison, Hendricks, Henry counties, FHL film #1651069.
- Henry, Howard, Huntington counties, FHL film #1651070.
- Jackson, Jasper, Jay, Jefferson counties, FHL film #1651071.
- Johnson, Knox counties, FHL film #1651095.
- Kosciusko, LaGrange, Lake counties, FHL film #1651096.
- LaPorte, Lawrence, Marshall counties, FHL film #1651097.
- Martin, Miami, Monroe counties, FHL film #1651098.
- Monroe, Montgomery, Morgan, Newton counties, FHL film #1651099.
- Noble, Ohio, Orange counties, FHL film #1705534.
- Orange, Owen, Parke, Perry counties, FHL film #1705535.
- Pike, Porter counties, FHL film #1705536.
- Posey, Pulaski, Putnam counties, FHL film #1705537.
- Putnam, Randolph, Ripley counties, FHL film #1705538.
- Rush, St. Joseph, Scott counties, FHL film #1705539.
- Shelby, Spencer, Starke counties, FHL film #1705540.
- Steuben, Sullivan, Switzerland, FHL film #1710571.
- Tippecanoe, Tipton, Union counties, FHL film #1710572.
- Vanderburgh, Vermillion, Vigo counties, FHL film #1710573.
- Wabash, Warren, Warrick, Washington counties, FHL film #1710574.
- Washington, Wayne, Wells counties, FHL film #1710575.
- White, Whitley, Jennings, Franklin counties, FHL film #1710576.

1894 Listings:
- Adams, Allen counties, FHL film #1710577.
- Allen, Bartholomew, Benton, Blackford counties, FHL film #1710578.
- Boone, Brown, Carroll counties, FHL film #1710579.
- Cass, Clark counties, FHL film #1710580.
- Clay, Clinton counties, FHL film #1710581.

- Clinton, Crawford, Daviess counties, FHL film #1710582.
- Decatur, DeKalb counties, FHL film #1710838.
- Delaware, Dubois counties, FHL film #1710827.
- Elkhart, Fayette counties, FHL film #1710828.
- Floyd, Fountain, Franklin counties, FHL film #1710829.
- Fulton, Gibson, Grant counties, FHL film #1710830.
- Grant, Greene counties, FHL film #1710831.
- Hamilton, Hancock, Harrison counties, FHL film #1710832.
- Harrison, Hendricks, Howard counties, FHL film #1710833.
- Huntington, Jackson counties, FHL film # 1710834.
- Jasper, Jay counties, FHL film #1710835.
- Jefferson, Jennings counties, FHL film #1710836.
- Johnson, Kosciusko counties, FHL film #1710837.
- LaGrange, Lake counties, FHL film #1710854.
- La Porte, Lawrence, Marshall counties, FHL film #1710855.
- Marshall, Martin, Miami counties, FHL film #1710856.
- Miami, Monroe, Montgomery counties, FHL film #1710857.
- Morgan, Newton, Noble counties, FHL film #1710858.
- Noble, Ohio, Orange counties, FHL film #1710859.
- Owen, Parke, Perry counties, FHL film #1710860.
- Perry, Pike, Porter counties, FHL film #1710861.
- Posey, Pulaski, Putnam counties, FHL film #1710862.
- Putnam, Ripley, St. Joseph counties, FHL film #1710863.
- St. Joseph, Scott, Shelby counties, FHL film #1710864.
- Spencer, Starke, Steuben counties, FHL film #1710868.
- Sullivan, Switzerland, Tipton, Union counties, FHL film #1710869.
- Vanderburgh, Vermillion, Vigo counties, FHL film #1710870.
- Wabash, Warren, Warrick counties, FHL film #1711004.
- Warrick, Washington, Wayne counties, FHL film #1711005.
- Wells, White counties, FHL film #1711006.
- Whitley county, FHL film #1711007.

■ *Index to Indiana Enrollments of Soldiers, Their Widows, and Orphans [1886 listings only, with 1890 and 1894 substitutes for missing 1886 listings],* microfilm of a card file index to the original enrollment books in the Indiana State Archives; only the 1886 listings are indexed; an 1890 or 1894 book was substituted for a missing 1886 listing. In some cases, the particular township or town enumeration for 1886 or 1890 might have been missing, requiring an index card to be made from the 1894 enumeration. If an enumeration was missing at the Indiana State Archives, an attempt was made to find the Circuit Court Clerk's copy and film it for the Family History Library. Filmed by the Genealogical Society of Utah, 1988, 13 rolls, names in alphabetical order, as follows:

- Aarbaugh, William – Blake, Josephus, FHL film #1556996.
- Blake, Josephus – Cemer, Abraham, FHL film #1556997.
- Cemer, Abraham – Deits, John, FHL film #1557010.
- Deits, John – Fribarger, A. J., FHL film #1557011.
- Fribarger, A. J. – Hatch, Mary D., FHL film #1557012.
- Hatch, Mary D. – Johnson, Wells, FHL film #1558386.
- Johnson, Wells – Lowe, Charles C., FHL film #1558490.
- Lowe, Charles C. – Mizener, Levi J., FHL film #1558610.
- Mizener, Levi J. – Place, Allen T., FHL film #1558611.
- Place, Allen T. – Schneider, Anthony, FHL film #1558612.
- Schneider, Anthony – Stoops, Jasper, FHL film #1452074.
- Stoops, Jasper – Waugh, Joseph, FHL film #1452075.
- Waugh, Joseph – Zwyers, Thomas, FHL film #1452076.

■ *Indiana Civil War Veterans: Transcription of the Death Rolls of the Department of Indiana, Grand Army of the Republic, 1882-1948,* by Dennis Northcott, published D. Northcott, St. Louis, MO, 2005, 411 pages. Names are listed alphabetically. FHL book 977.2 M2n.

■ *Civil War Veteran Obituaries Copied from the South Bend [Indiana] Tribune, 1816-1928,* microfilm of original manuscript by the South Bend Tribune. Includes birth as well as death information. Filmed by the Genealogical Society of Utah, 1990, 1 roll, FHL film #1673045.

■ *Indiana and Indianans: A History of Aboriginal and Territorial Indiana and the Century of Statehood,* by Jacob Piatt Dunn, published by the American Historical Society, Chicago, 1919, 5 vols., 2,291 pages. FHL book 977. H2d v.1-5. Indexed in *Indiana and Indianans by Jacob Piatt Dunn, An Index,* prepared by the Works Progress

Administration, published by the Indianapolis Public Library, 1939, 197 pages. FHL book 977.2 H2d index. Also on microfilm, FHL film #1000526. See also, *An Every Name Index for Indiana and Indianans, Volume IV,* compiled by Cynthia Cochran Scheuer, published C.C Scheuer, 1987, 36 pages. Indexes vol. 4 only. FHL book 977.2 H2d vol. 4 index.

IOWA

Online Iowa Resources

■ **State Archives:** The **State Historical Society of Iowa** (SHSI) has two major facilities, one at Des Moines, the other at Iowa City. There is some overlap of resources, and the two facilities have excellent collections of Iowa county records, vital records, state censuses, and a myriad of materials of value to genealogists. Materials related to Iowa's involvement in the Civil War are not together in one place, so a search of the online catalog is required. Both facilities share the same website at **www.state.ia.us/government/dca/shsi.** Iowa has taken more state censuses than any other state, dating from 1846 to 1925, but unfortunately, the census name lists taken during the Civil War era have not survived. State censuses were taken in Iowa in 1862, 1867, and 1869, but only the published statistical summaries of these censuses are available. Complete, every-name statewide censuses really begin with the 1885, continuing every ten years thereafter until the last one in 1925.

■ **Iowa in the Civil War Websites.**
 ● American Civil War – Iowa: **www.archaeolink.com/civil_war_iowa.htm**.
 ● Iowa in the Civil War Project: **http://iagenweb.org/civilwar**.

■ **Civil War Soldiers and 1861-1869 Tax Lists** from the various Iowa counties are found at county sites on the Internet. To see what is available for Scott County, for example, use your browser and search for the keywords "Scott County Iowa Genealogy."

Published Iowa Resources

■ *Iowa and the Civil War: A Reference Guide*, by James I. Robertson, Jr., a 45-page article reprinted from the April 1961 issue of the *Iowa Journal of History* (Iowa City, Iowa: State Historical Society of Iowa, 1995). Contains a bibliography of over six hundred entries of record sources pertaining to the involvement of the state of Iowa and its people in the Civil War. See FHL book 977.7 M23r.

■ *Discovering Your Iowa Civil War Ancestry,* by Steve Meyer, published by Meyer Publishing, Garrison, Iowa, 1993, 63 pages. See FHL book 977.7 M2ms.

■ *Iowa in War Times,* by Samuel Hawkins Marshall, published by W. D Condit & Co., Des Moines, 1888, 615 pages. Includes index. FHL has microfiche copy, FHL fiche #6084435.

■ *Roster and Record of Iowa Soldiers in the War of the Rebellion: Together with Historical Sketches of Volunteer Organizations, 1861-1866,* prepared by the Iowa Adjutant General's office, published by authority of the General Assembly, Des Moines, Iowa: E. H. English, 1908-1911, 6 vols. FHL book 977.7 M2i vol. 1-6. See also *Index to Iowa Soldiers,* an index to the *Roster and Record of Iowa Soldiers in the War of Rebellion*, a project of the Idaho State Historical Society Genealogical Library, FHL book 977.7 M2i v. 1-7: vol. 1: A-C; vol. 2: D-G; vol. 3: H-K; vol. 4: L-Mc; vol. 5: N-R; vol. 6: S-T; vol. 7: U-Z.

■ *Grand Army of the Republic Records, Iowa Posts: Indexes to Veterans; Post Membership Records,* microfilm of original records of the Grand Army of the Republic, Department of Iowa, with indexes made by members of the Daughters of the American Revolution chapters in Iowa, giving names of soldiers, birth dates and places, death dates (if available) and cemeteries where buried, and the G.A.R. posts which veterans belonged to, as well as their membership records. The membership records are arranged by county and then by posts within each county. They include veteran's name, residence, occupation, date and place of birth, date and place of death, cemetery where buried, war record, dates of enlistment and discharge, names of parents, spouse, children (if given), and sources of information. The alphabetical index to veterans of the Civil War was filmed twice. It appears to have been compiled from cemetery surveys and other records. Filmed by the Genealogical Society of Utah, 1978, 1987, 69 rolls, beginning with FHL film #1570121 (Index: Aarons, Andrew – Barker, Francis C.).

■ *Iowa, Kansas and Nebraska Civil War Veterans: Compilation of the Death Rolls of the Departments of Iowa, Kansas and Nebraska, Grand Army of the Republic, 1883-1948,* by Dennis Northcott, published D. Northcott, St. Louis, MO, 2007, 688 pages. Names are listed alphabetically. FHL book 973 M2nde.

■ *Index to Compiled Service Records of Volunteer Union Soldiers Who Served in Organizations from the State of Iowa,* microfilm of original records at the National Archives, Washington, D.C. Consists of alphabetically arranged General Index Cards for Iowa, with over 97,165 entries. Filmed by the National Archives, 1964, series M541, 29 rolls. FHL has entire set, beginning with FHL film #881808 (Index, A-Bam). The Iowa entries are incorporated into the national index at the National Park Service website at: **www.itd.nps.gov/cwss/**.

■ *Internal Revenue Assessment Lists for Iowa, 1862-1866,* microfilm of original manuscripts at the National Archives, Washington, D.C. Lists are arranged alphabetically by surname (within Internal Revenue divisions) of those being assessed for each period, and provide a good representation of heads of households of Iowa during the Civil War era. Both personal and property owners are named, but are not indexed and not easily accessible. The lists are organized by tax year, type of list, Internal Revenue districts, and sub-divisions of the districts. Filmed by the National Archives, 1971, series M766, 16 rolls, beginning with FHL film #15634648 (District/county list; District 1, division 1-11 Annual 1862). To see which Indiana counties/townships are in which district/division, refer to *Internal Revenue Assessment Lists for Indiana, 1862-1866: National Archives Microfilm*

Publications, Pamphlet Describing M765, 8 pages, FHL book 973 J53m no. 766.

■ *1865-1867 Amnesty Papers: Name Index to Pardon Application Files. Group 2, Pardon Applications Submitted by Persons from Iowa.* FHL has entire series, described for all states in RG8 (page 24), applications from Iowa residents.

■ *Persons Subject to Military Duty, ca. 1862-1910,* microfilm of original records of the Iowa Adjutant General's Office, located at the Iowa State Historical Society, Des Moines, Iowa. Names organized by county, filmed by the Genealogical Society of Utah, 1978, 94 rolls, beginning with FHL film #1024847 (Adair County).

■ *1865 Iowa State Gazetteer (and Directory),* compiled by James T. Hair, published Chicago, Bailey & Hair, 722 pages, FHL book 977.7 E4h. Also on microfilm, FHL film #982200. Another filming, FHL film #1024846.

■ *1885 Iowa State Census,* microfilm of original records at the Iowa State Historical Society, Des Moines, Iowa. The census schedules provide detailed information for all members of a family, including relationship to head of house, an exact property description, whether a street address in a town or an indication of a Range / Township / Section for a farm; age, birthplace by county for a person born in Iowa, or the state/country of birth; whether first papers filed for aliens; occupation; and military information, including an indication of Civil War service. This state census may be the best way to locate a Civil War veteran living in Iowa in 1885. Filmed by the Genealogical Society of Utah, 1977, 95 rolls, beginning with FHL film #1021316 (Adair County). An index to the *1885 Iowa State Census* is included at the **www.ancestry.com** site.

■ *1895 Iowa State Census,* microfilm of original records at the Iowa State Historical Society, Des Moines, Iowa. The census schedules provide detailed information for all members of a family, similar to the 1885, but adding questions relating to "Religious Belief" and the exact company and regiment of service in the Civil War, if applicable. Filmed by the Genealogical Society of Utah, 1977, on 121 rolls, beginning with FHL film #1021706.

■ *1925 Iowa State Census,* microfilm of original records at the Iowa State Historical Society, Des Moines, Iowa. If your ancestor fought in the Civil War while in his 20s, survived the war, and was living in Iowa in 1925 (and probably over 80 years old), the *1925 Iowa State Census* provides more information about a person than any other census ever taken in America. In addition to the standard vitals, all members of a family were asked for the full name of their father and maiden name of their mother. The place of marriage was also a question for each married couple, and military information for each person was included. Filmed by the Genealogical Society of Utah, 1976, 434 rolls, beginning with FHL film #1429191 (Adair County). An SHSI *1925 Iowa State Census Index* exists for these cities: Boone, Cedar Falls, Centerville, Cedar Rapids, Clinton, Council Bluffs, Dubuque, Ottumwa, Sioux City, Waterloo, Davenport, and Des Moines. 29 rolls, beginning with FHL film #1430705.

■ **Countywide Name Lists for Civil War Veterans** from tax lists, voter lists, pensions, discharge papers, or other military name lists exist for virtually all Iowa counties, and are mostly still maintained at a county courthouse. To see what is available on microfilm at the Family History Library, go to: **www.familysearch.org** / FHL Library / Catalog / Place Search: "Iowa." At the state listing of categories, click on "View Related Places" for a list of all Iowa counties.

KANSAS

Online Kansas Resources

■ **State Archives.** Genealogical researchers with Kansas ancestors will find one of the most important resources online is at the **Kansas State Historical Society** (KSHS) website. The KSHS "Genealogists" page at: **www.kshs.org/ genealogists/index.htm** is the starting point to learn what types of records are stored at the KSHS in Topeka. This is one of America's best state archives. The records of most value to genealogists have all been microfilmed, and there are numerous indexes and guides.

■ **Military Records: Civil War (1861–1865).** Online resources available at the KSHS site are described at: **www.kshs.org/genealogists/ military/recscivil.htm**, with links to these searchable databases:
  ● Kansas in the Civil War (a brief history)
  ● Kansas Adjutant General's Report, 1861-1865
  ● Civil War Veterans in Kansas Database
  ● Published Genealogical Materials on the Civil War
  ● State Archives Resources
  ● Civil War Manuscript Resources
  ● Civil War in Kansas and the West: Bibliography
  ● Regimental histories
  ● Grand Army of the Republic (G.A.R.)

■ **Kansas Civil War Websites.**
  ● Kansas in the Civil War: **http://skyways.lib.ks. us/kansas/genweb/civilwar**. A good array of resources, links to relevant sites, and related military information.
  ● Kansas in the Civil War Message Board: **http://history-sites.net/mb/cw/kscwmb/index.cgi** A place to leave a message relating to a Kansas ancestor who served in the Civil War.

■ **County Name Lists Online.** A few name lists of Civil War soldiers; 1861-1869 tax lists; or later pensioner records from the various Kansas counties are found at county sites on the Internet. To see what is available for Bourbon County, for example, use your browser and search for the keywords "Bourbon County Kansas Genealogy."

■ **1861-1869 City Directories (Online), Various Kansas Cities.** A large database of searchable city directories is at the KSHS webpage at: **www.kshs.org/genealogists/directories/ directories.php**. The database includes names of residents from these cities during the Civil War era:
  ● 1860-1861 Leavenworth
  ● 1860-1861 Atchison city directory
  ● 1860-1861 Elwood city directory
  ● 1862-1863 Leavenworth city directory
  ● 1863-1864 Leavenworth city directory
  ● 1865 Atchison city directory
  ● 1865-1866 Leavenworth city directory
  ● 1865-1866 Fort Scott city directory
  ● 1866 Lawrence city directory
  ● 1866 Leavenworth city directory
  ● 1868 Topeka city directory
  ● 1868-1869 Doniphan County directory
  ● 1868-1869 Leavenworth city directory
  ● 1869-1870 Fort Scott city directory

■ **1883 Pensioners on the Roll (Kansas).** For name lists from most of the Kansas counties, see the KS GenWeb site at: **http://skyways.lib.ks.us/ genweb/archives/pensions.htm**.

Published Kansas Resources

■ *A Selected, Annotated Bibliography of Sources in the Kansas State Historical Society Pertaining to Kansas in the Civil War,* by Donald Eugene Decker, published by Kansas State Teachers College, Emporia, KS, 1961, 95 pages, FHL book 978.1 A1 No. 13. Also on microfilm, FHL film #896829.

■ *Index to Compiled Service Records of Volunteer Union Soldiers Who Served in Organizations from the State of Kansas,* microfilm of original records at the National Archives, Washington, D.C. Consists of alphabetically arranged General Index Cards for Kansas, with over 40,280 entries. Filmed by the National Archives, 1964, series M542, 10 rolls, filmed by surname in alphabetical order, beginning with FHL film #881837 (A-Br). The Kansas entries are incorporated into the national index at the National Park Service website at **www.itd.nps.gov/cwss/**.

■ *Report of the Adjutant General of the State of Kansas, 1861-65,* microfiche of original published by the state printer, Topeka, KS, 1896, 2 vols., 948 pages. Also known as *Official Military History of Kansas Regiments During the War for the Suppression of the Great Rebellion.* Filmed by University Publications of America, 1993, 11 microfiche. FHL has entire set, beginning with FHL fiche #6084552.

■ *Index to the Kansas Militia in the Civil War,* compiled by John Haupt Chapter, Daughters of the American Revolution, published by the chapter, Topeka, KS, 1979, 219 pages. FHL book 978.1 M22i. Also on 3 microfiche, FHL fiche #6007705.

■ *1862-1866 Internal Revenue Lists for Kansas,* microfilm of original records at the National Archives, Washington, D.C. Lists are arranged alphabetically by surname (within Internal Revenue divisions) of those being assessed for each period, and provide a good representation of heads of

households of Kansas during the Civil War era. Both personal and property owners are named, but are not indexed and not easily accessible. The lists are organized by tax year, type of list, Internal Revenue districts, and sub-divisions of the districts. Filmed by the National Archives, 1965, series M767, 3 rolls, FHL has the following:

- Annual lists, 1863-1864; Monthly lists, 1862-1864; Special lists Aug.-Dec. 1864, FHL film #1578484.
- Annual lists, 1865; Monthly lists, 1865; Special lists, 1865, FHL film #1578485.
- Annual lists, 1866; Monthly lists, 1866, FHL film #1578486.

To see which Kansas counties/townships are in which federal district/divisions, refer to *Internal Revenue Assessment Lists for Kansas, 1862-1866: National Archives Microfilm Publications, Pamphlet Describing M767,* 4 pages, FHL book 973 J53m no. 767.

■ *1865 Kansas State Census,* microfilm of original records at the Kansas State Historical Society, Topeka, KS. The 1865 state census lists all members of household by name, including age, sex, race or color, and state or country of birth. A description of the 1865 KS state census and information about several county indexes in print or online can be found at the KSHS webpage: **www.kshs.org/genealogists/ census/kansas/census1865ks.htm**.

The originals were microfilmed by KSHS, 1951, 9 rolls. KSHS has interlibrary loan of all their census microfilms, and the FHL has the complete 1865 set, as follows:

- Allen – Atchison counties, FHL film #570189.
- Bourbon – Coffey counties, FHL film #570190.
- Davis – Doniphan counties, FHL film #570191.
- Douglas County, FHL film # 570192.
- Franklin – Johnson counties, FHL film #570193.
- Leavenworth County, FHL film #570194.
- Linn – Morris counties, FHL film #570195.
- Nemaha – Wyandotte counties, FHL film #570196.
- Compendium of social statistics reported to the legislature, FHL film #570197.

■ *Kansas Biographical Index: County Histories: More Than 69,000 Citations from 183 Volumes of Kansas County Histories,* compiled by Patricia Douglass Smith, published Garden City, Kansas by P.D. Smith and S.C. Smith, 2001, 2 vols. Index lists personal name, county name, number of source (refers to bibliography at beginning of book) and page number. Contents: vol. 1: Surnames A-K; vol. 2: Surnames L-Z. FHL has bound volumes one and two as one volume, FHL book 978.1 D32sm.

■ *1885 Kansas State Census,* microfilm of original records at the Kansas State Historical Society, Topeka. The 1885 census lists all members of household by name, including age, sex, race or color, and state or country of birth. Also listed: where from to Kansas (state or country) and military record (condition of discharge, state of enlistment, letter or name of company or command, number of regiment or other organization to which attached, arm of the service, and name of military prison if confined in one). The *1885 KS State Census* may be the best place to find a Civil War veteran living in Kansas 20 years after the war. A description of the 1885 KS state census and information about several county indexes in print or online can be found at the KSHS webpage: **www.kshs.org/genealogists/ census/kansas/census1885ks.htm**. The originals were microfilmed by KSHS, 1969-70, 151 rolls. KSHS has interlibrary loan of all of their census microfilms, and FHL has complete 1885 set, beginning with FHL film #975699 (Allen County, Humboldt city and twp.; Iola Twp.)

■ *1895 Kansas State Census,* microfilm of original records at the Kansas State Historical Society, Topeka. The 1895 repeats the same information as the 1885, including detailed military information for Civil War veterans. More details and information about microfilmed indexes can be found at the 1895 webpage at: **www.kshs.org/genealogists/census/ kansas/census1895ks.htm**. KSHS has interlibrary loan for all of their census microfilms, and the FHL has all 202 microfilm rolls, beginning with FHL film #570221 (Allen Co. Townships C-S). The 1895 KS state census index (previously only on microfilm) is going online in stages. Go to this page for the searchable database, list of completed counties, and counties in work: **www.kshs.org/genealogists/census/kansas/ census1895ks.htm#indexes**.

■ *Iowa, Kansas and Nebraska Civil War Veterans: Compilation of the Death Rolls of the Departments of Iowa, Kansas and Nebraska, Grand Army of the Republic, 1883-1948,* by Dennis Northcott, published D. Northcott, St. Louis, MO, 2007, 688

pages. Names are listed alphabetically. FHL book 973 M2nde.

KENTUCKY

Online Kentucky Resources

■ **Kentucky Department for Libraries and Archives.** A good overview of resources is located at: **www.kdla.ky.gov/**. The state archives in Frankfurt holds significant original resources for Kentucky during the Civil War era, including Kentucky military records for both Union and Confederate troops; Confederate pension records, and numerous tax lists from various Kentucky counties taken during that time. Kentucky vital records are also well represented. However, this state agency has not chosen to place any databases online for the public. Instead, they have produced CD-ROMs of various records that they sell to the public; and they have a comprehensive request for research system online at this site. Kentucky residents pay $6.00 per request; out-of-state people must pay $15.00 per request. One non-refundable request can be submitted at a time and you must wait for the response before you can submit another. The categories within each request form indicates the types of records available for searching: Birth Record, Death Record, Divorce Record, Marriage Record, Military Record, Census Records 1790-1930, Civil Case Request, Criminal Case Request, Deed Record, Tax Record, and Will/Estate Records. Visit the **Researching Your Civil War Ancestor** webpage at: **www.kdla.ky.gov/resources/ KYCivilWarResearch3.htm** for the types of records available through the search program.

■ **Kentucky Historical Society**, a state agency, includes research facilities in and around the Old State Capitol campus site in Frankfurt. At the Search The Collections webpage found at: **http://history.ky.gov/sub. php?pageid=94%A7ionid=14**, these databases are accessible:
  ● Kentucky Historical Society Library Catalog
  ● KHS Digital Collections
  ● Civil Rights Movement in Kentucky Online Digital Media Database
  ● Kentucky Historical Marker Database

- Guide to Kentucky Oral History Collections
- Kentucky Cemetery Records Database
- Kentucky Virtual Library
- Kentuckiana Digital Library

■ Kentucky Civil War Websites.
- Kentucky Civil War Rosters: **www. rootsweb.com/~kymercer/CivilWar/Union/**.
- Kentucky in the American Civil War: **www. earthstation9.com/index.html?kentuck3.htm**.
- The American Civil War Homepage: **http://sunsite.utk.edu/civil-war/warweb.html**.
- The Kentucky Civil War Research Series: **www.kycivilwarbooks.netfirms.com/**.

■ *1861-1865 Kentucky Confederate Volunteers,* an online database at **www.ancestry.com**. Original data: *Report of the Adjutant General of the State of Kentucky. Confederate Kentucky Volunteers. War 1861-1865.* Frankfort, KY: State Journal Company Printers, 1915. This database lists the Confederate volunteers enlisted in the various Kentucky military organizations during the Civil War. In addition to providing the names of the volunteers this record also lists rank, when enlisted, where enlisted, and remarks.

■ *1861-1865 Kentucky Union Volunteers,* an online database at **www.ancestry.com**. Original data: *Report of the Adjutant General of the State of Kentucky. Vol. I-II. 1861-1866.* Frankfort, KY: John H. Harney, Public Printer, 1866. Printed by Authority of the Legislature of Kentucky.

Published Kentucky Resources

■ *Compiled Service Records of Confederate Soldiers Who Served in Organizations from the State of Kentucky,* microfilm of original records at the National Archives, Washington, D.C. Filmed by the National Archives, 1960, series M319, 130 rolls. FHL has complete series, beginning with FHL film #881380 (A-Bi).

■ *Index to Compiled Service Records of Confederate Soldiers Who Served in Organizations from the State of Kentucky,* microfilm of original records at the National Archives, Washington, D.C. Consists of alphabetically arranged General Index Cards for Kentucky, with over 51,600 entries. Filmed by the National Archives, series M319, 14 rolls, beginning with FHL film #881380 (Index, A-Bi 1861-1865). The Kentucky Confederate entries are incorporated into the national index at the National Park Service website at: **www.itd.nps.gov/cwss/**.

■ *Confederate Service Records* (for Kentucky soldiers who served in Alabama units), microfilm of original records compiled by the ADAH, filmed by the Genealogical Society of Utah, 1987, 1 roll, FHL film #1411532 (Item 6, Kentucky soldiers).

■ *Compiled Service Records of Volunteer Union Soldiers Who Served in Organizations from the State of Kentucky,* microfilm of original records at the National Archives, Washington, D.C. Filmed by the National Archives, 1962, series M307, 515 rolls. FHL has complete series, beginning with FHL film #881492 (A-).

■ *Index to Compiled Service Records of Volunteer Union Soldiers Who Served in Organizations from the State of Kentucky,* microfilm of original records at the National Archives, Washington, D.C. Consists of alphabetically arranged General Index Cards for Kentucky, with over 108,000 entries. Series M386, 30 rolls, beginning with FHL film #881492 (Index, A, 1861-1865). The Kentucky Union entries are incorporated into the national index at the National Park Service website at **www.itd.nps.gov/cwss/**.

■ *Report of the Adjutant General of the State of Kentucky, Confederate Kentucky Volunteers, War 1861-1865,* published by Authority of the Legislature of Kentucky, Frankfort, KY, 1910?, 511 pages. FHL has a reprint by McDowell Publications, published 1980, Utica, KY, which includes a name index prepared by Glenda K. Trapp. FHL book 976.9 M2rc. See also *Confederate Soldiers of Kentucky: A Roster of the Veterans, 1861-1865,* edited by Stephen Douglas Lynn, published by Thomson-Shore, Dexter, MI, 2000, 386 pages. Names extracted from the *Report of the Adjutant General...*, FHL book 976.9 M28Ls. See also *Index to Report of the Adjutant General of the State of Kentucky: Confederate Kentucky Volunteers,* indexed by Michael L. Cook, published by McDowell Publications, Utica, KY, 1979, 97 pages, FHL book 976.9 M2rc v. 1 index.

■ *1862-1866 Internal Revenue Assessment Lists for Kentucky,* microfilm of originals at the National Archives, Washington, D.C. Names of taxpayers within each Internal Revenue Division are generally in alphabetical order. Which rolls have which county on them are noted at the front of each roll. National Archives microfilm, series M768, 24 rolls, beginning with FHL film #1491176.

■ *1865-1867 Amnesty Papers: Name Index to Pardon Application Files. Group 2, Pardon Applications Submitted by Persons from Kentucky.* Refer to the National Confederate Lists for a detailed description of the records. FHL has entire microfilmed series, including applications from Kentucky residents.

■ *Kentucky Index of Biographical Sketches in State, Regional and County Histories,* by Michael L. Cook, published Cook Publications, Evansville, IN, 1986, 179 pages. Indexes 65 various state, regional and county histories. FHL book 976.9 D32c.

■ *1890 Federal Census, Special Schedules Enumerating Union Veterans and Widows of Union Veterans,* microfilm of original records at the National Archives, Washington, D.C. Virtually all of the schedules for the states Alabama through Kansas and approximately half of those for Kentucky appear to have been destroyed before the transfer of the remaining schedules from the Census Bureau to the National Archives in 1943. Each schedule lists the name of the veteran (or if he did not survive, the names of both the widow and her deceased husband); the veteran's rank, company, regiment or vessel, date of enlistment, date of discharge, and length of service in years, months, and days; post office and address of each person listed; disability incurred by the veteran; and remarks. Filmed by the National Archives, 1948, series M123, 118 rolls. FHL has entire series, with Kentucky veterans and widows found on 3 rolls of film, organized by the following surviving counties: FHL film #338160: Boone, Bourbon, Bracken, Campbell, Clark, Fayette, Franklin, Gallatin, Grant, Harrison, Jessamine, Kenton, Owen, Pendleton, Scott, and Woodford Counties; FHL film #338161: Bath, Boyd, Carter, Elliott, Fleming, Floyd, Greenup, Johnson, Lawrence, Lewis, Magoffin,

Martin, Mason, Menifee, Montgomery, Morgan, Nicholas, Pike, Powell, Robertson, Rowan, and Wolfe Counties; & FHL film #338162: Adair, Bell, Boyle, Breathitt, Casey, Clay, Clinton, Cumberland, Estill, Garrard, Harlan, Jackson, Knott, Knox, Laurel, Lee, Leslie, Letcher, Lincoln, Madison, Owsley, Perry, Pulaski, Rockcastle, Russell, Wayne, and Whitley Counties; and certain Federal, State, & local institutions throughout Kentucky.

■ *1890 Kentucky Veterans Census Index,* compiled by Bryan Lee Dilts, published 1984, Index Publishing, Salt Lake City, UT, 125 pages. FHL book 976.9 X22d 1890. Also on microfiche, FHL fiche #6331355. See also *1890 Kentucky Census Index, Special Schedule of the Eleventh Census (1890) Enumerating Union Veterans and of Widows of Union Veterans of the Civil War,* compiled by Ronald Vern Jackson, published 1984, Accelerated Indexing Systems, 266 pages, FHL book 976.9 X22j 1890. See also *1890 Veterans' Schedules, Selected States,* a CD-ROM publication by Genealogy.com, CD131, 1998. This CD contains an index of approximately 385,000 war veterans and veterans' widows who were enumerated on the special veterans' schedule of the 1890 United States census, including those residing in Kentucky.

■ *Civil War Pension Applications,* microfilm of original records of the Kentucky Confederate Pension Board at the Kentucky Historical Society, Frankfort. Includes: Index to Confederate pension papers in the Kentucky Historical Society – List of persons receiving pensions under Confederate pension act, state of Kentucky. Both are by the Historical Society. The law under which these pensions were made was passed by the state legislature in 1912. Filmed by the KHS, 50 rolls, the first roll has the name index to the papers. FHL has entire series, beginning with FHL film #1670795 (Index).

■ See also, *Index of Confederate Pension Applications, Commonwealth of Kentucky,* compiled by Alicia Simpson (archivist), published by the Kentucky Department of Library and Archives, 1981, 207 pages. From intro: "...index is arranged alphabetically and lists the applicant's name, county of residence at the time the application was made, the date the application was received in the Confederate pensions office, and the application number. The listings for the widow's applications provide maiden names if stated on the application. The veteran husbands' names are listed in parentheses." FHL book 976.9 M2k. See also *Inventory of Confederate Pension Applications, Commonwealth of Kentucky,* compiled by Alicia Simpson (archivist), published by the Kentucky Department of Library and Archives, 1981, 10 pages. FHL book 976.9 A1 No. 294. See also *Confederate Pensioners of Kentucky: Pension Applications of the Veterans & Widows, 1912-1946,* abstracted by Stephen Douglas Lynn, published by Gateway Press, Baltimore, MD, 2000, 322 pages. Includes an index of pensioners by county. FHL book 976.9 M28L. Also on microfilm, FHL film #1425435.

■ *Old Confederate Soldier's Homes, 1902; Confederate Pension Payroll, November 1948,* by Commonwealth of Kentucky, Department of Military Affairs, Military Records and Research Branch, Frankfurt, KY, 48 pages. Includes a list of Old Confederate Soldier's Homes from 1902, a list of cards of widows residing in Kentucky, a list of soldiers and their company (mostly for Kentucky with a few for the other southern states), and a Confederate pension payroll for the November quarter of 1948 for widows residing in Kentucky. FHL book 976.9M2o.

LOUISIANA

Online Louisiana Resources

■ **Louisiana State Archives – Research Library.** This Baton Rouge facility is the starting point for research in Louisiana Genealogy; Confederate Pension Applications Index Database; New Orleans Ship Passenger List Online Index; Louisiana History; Reference; Vital Records and more. Click on Research Library at the LSA Home Page: **www.sos.louisiana.gov/archives/archives/archives -library.htm.**

■ **Confederate Pension Applications Index.** At the Research Library page, click on Confederate Pension Applications. The online searchable index contains over 49,000 names that were included in pension applications submitted to the Board of Pension Commissioners. The Confederate Pension Applications Collection consists of alphabetically arranged pension applications for pensions that were granted to veterans and widows beginning in 1898, and are recorded on 152 reels of microfilm. The pension applications may include service information, occupation, place of residence, and number of children. Other materials that may have been included with applications are letters, notes, copies of checks, newspaper clippings, court papers of various types, obituaries, and other miscellaneous papers.

■ **The Civil War in Louisiana. www.researchonline.net/lacw/index.htm.** Categories include Research Online, Announcements of new stuff, Military Units of Louisiana, Confederate Military History, Official Records Citations, Biographical Sketches, Photo Gallery, Postlude to the War, Catalog, and Order Form.

■ **Civil War Rosters – Louisiana Links. www.geocities.com/Area51/Lair/3680/cw/cw-la.html.** This is a directory of Civil War Rosters/Muster   Rolls that have been found on the Internet. Over   half of the Louisiana regiments are represented   with direct links from this site.

■ Google search for **"Confederate Soldiers and Sailors Buried in Louisiana"** (and some Louisiana Confederates buried in other States). Website may be obsolete, but available elsewhere. This is a searchable online database containing over 15,000 names in 2,087 cemeteries.

Published Louisiana Resources

■ *Internal Revenue Assessment Lists for Louisiana, 1863-1866,* microfilm of original records at the National Archives, Washington, D.C. Names of taxpayers are grouped by year and Internal Revenue district, organized as follows: DISTRICT 1 contains Ascension, Jefferson, Lafourche, Livingston, Orleans, Plaquemines, St. Bernard, St. Charles, St. Helena, St. James, St. John the Baptist, St. Tammany, Terrebonne, Washington parishes. DISTRICT 2 contains Assumption,

Avoyelles, Calcasieu, East Baton Rouge, East Feliciana, Iberville, Lafayette, Natchitoches, Pointe Coupee, Rapides, Sabine, St. Landry, St. Martin, St. Mary, Vermilion, West Baton Rouge, West Felilciana parishes. DISTRICT 3 contains Bienville, Bossier, Caddo, Caldwell, Carroll, Catahoula, Claiborne, Concordia, De Soto, Franklin, Jackson, Madison, Morehouse, Ouachita, Tensas, Union, Winn parishes. Filmed by the National Archives, Central Plains Region, 1985. FHL has all 10 rolls, beginning with FHL #1578469 (DISTRICT 1 Annual and special lists 1863-1864). See also *Register of Direct Tax Payers,* microfilm of original records located at the Louisiana State Archives, Baton Rouge, LA. Does not include Acadia, Calcasieu, Cameron, Grant, Iberia, Lincoln, Red River, Richland, Tangipahoa, Union, Vermilion, Vernon, or Webster parishes. Filmed by the Genealogical Society of Utah, 1985, 5 rolls, beginning with FHL film #1412744.

■ See also *List of Names of Citizens of Louisiana from Whom the United States Direct Tax Was Collected in 1865, Together with the Amounts Paid by Each,* originally published by Advocate Printing Office, Baton Rouge, 1892. FHL has reprint with the title, *The Civil War Tax in Louisiana, 1865: Based on Direct Tax Assessments of Louisianians,* reprint by Polyanthos, Inc., New Orleans, 1975, 356 pages, FHL book 976.3 R4c. Reprint also on 5 microfiche, FHL fiche #6051324.

■ *Military Record of Louisiana: Including Biographical and Historical Papers Relating to the Military Organizations of the State: A Soldier's Story of the Late War, Muster Rolls, Lists of Casualities in the Various Regiments (so far as now known), Cemeteries Where Buried, Company Journals, Personal Narratives of Prominent Actors, etc.,* by Napier Bartlett, originally published by L. Graham Printers, New Orleans, 1875, part of the series *Civil War Unit Histories. Part 1, The Confederate States of America and Border States: LA 005.* FHL has microfiche copy, published by University Publications of America, Bethesda, MD, 1990, on 5 fiche. FHL fiche #6082423. See also *Records of Louisiana Confederate Soldiers and Louisiana Confederate Commands,* compiled by Andrew B. Booth, published New Orleans, 1920, 3 vols.

Names arranged in alphabetical order. FHL has copy on microfilm, 5 rolls, beginning with FHL film #1305383.

■ *Compiled Service Records of Confederate Soldiers Who Served in Organizations from the State of Louisiana,* microfilm of original records at the National Archives, Washington, DC. Organized first by unit/regiment, the compiled service records consist of a jacket-envelope for each soldier, labeled with his name, rank, and the unit in which he served. The jacket-envelope typically contains card abstracts of entries relating to the soldier as found in original muster rolls, returns, rosters, payrolls, appointment books, hospital registers, Union prison registers and rolls, parole rolls, and inspection reports; and the originals of any papers relating solely to a particular soldier. Filmed by the National Archives, 1960, series M320, 386 rolls. FHL has complete set, service records beginning with FHL film #1447604 (1st Cavalry, A – Gi).

■ *Index to Compiled Service Records of Confederate Soldiers Who Served in Organizations from the State of Louisiana,* microfilm of original records at the National Archives, Washington, D.C. Consists of alphabetically arranged General Index Cards for Louisiana, with over 128,250 entries. Each index card gives the name of the soldier, his rank, and the unit in which he served. Filmed by the National Archives, 1962, series M378, 31 rolls. FHL has complete set, beginning with FHL film #881457 (Index, surnames beginning with A). The Louisiana Confederate entries are incorporated into the national index at the National Park Service website at: **www.itd.nps.gov/cwss/.**

■ *Compiled Service Records of Volunteer Union Soldiers Who Served in Organizations from the State of Louisiana,* microfilm of original records at the National Archives, Washington, D.C. Filmed by the National Archives, 1960, series M320, 46 rolls. FHL has complete set, service records beginning with FHL film #1380930 (1st Cavalry, A – Bi).

■ *Index to Compiled Service Records of Volunteer Union Soldiers Who Served in Organizations from the State of Louisiana,* microfilm of original records at the National Archives, Washington, D.C. Consists of alphabetically arranged General Index Cards for

Louisiana, with over 14,680 entries. Each index card gives the name of the soldier, his rank, and the unit in which he served. Filmed by the National Archives, 1962, series M387, 4 rolls. FHL has complete set, beginning with FHL film #821926 (Index, A-E, 1861-1865). The Louisiana Union entries are incorporated into the national index at the National Park Service website at: **www.itd.nps.gov/cwss/**.

■ *Confederate Service Records* (for Louisiana soldiers who served in Alabama units), microfilm of original records compiled by the ADAH, filmed by the Genealogical Society of Utah, 1987, 1 roll, FHL film #1411532 (Item 7, Louisiana soldiers).

■ *Index to Prisoners of War Compiled from Various Union Prisons,* microfilm of original records at the Jackson Barracks Military Library, New Orleans. Filmed by the Genealogical Society of Utah, 1990, 1 roll, FHL film #1685402.

■ *1890 Louisiana Census Index: Special Schedule of the Eleventh Census (1890) Enumerating Union Veterans and Widows of Union Veterans of the Civil War,* edited by Ronald Vern Jackson, published by Accelerated Indexing Systems, Salt Lake City, UT, 1984, 125 pages, FHL book 973.3 X22L. See also *1890 Louisiana Census Index of Civil War Veterans or Their Widows,* compiled by Bryan Lee Dilts, published by Index Publishing, Salt Lake City, UT, 1984, 68 pages, FHL book 976.3 X2d. Also on microfiche, FHL fiche #6331358.

■ *1911 Enumeration of Ex-Confederate Soldiers and Widows of Deceased Soldiers of Louisiana,* microfilm of original records located at the Louisiana State Archives, Baton Rouge, LA. In 1908 the General Assembly of the State of Louisiana passed Act No. 71 to provide for the enumeration of ex-Confederate soldiers and widows of deceased soldiers residing in the state, and to fix compensation from the State for the veterans' educatable children. Filmed by the Genealogical Society of Utah, 1985, 1 roll, FHL film #1412742. See also *An index to the Census of 1911 of Confederate Veterans or Their Widows, Pursuant to Act 71 of 1908,* compiled by Houston C. Jenks, published by the author, Baton Rouge, LA, 1989, 115 pages. This index lists, alphabetically, names of soldiers or their widows, and includes their parish (county) of residence, age, state where he enlisted for service, his regiment and company in which he served, an assessment and a valuation of property, any infirmities the soldier or widow might have, the date of their marriage, and the reel number where the data was found at the Louisiana State Archives. The compiler lists the following parishes as not being accounted for among the records: Assumption, Caldwell, East Baton Rouge, East Carroll, Franklin, Iberia, Jackson, Pointe Coupee, Richland, Saint James, Saint John the Baptist, Terrebonne, Vernon, West Carroll. Vermilion Parish was also not found when looked for by the library. The following parishes were not created by 1911, so the parent parishes (in parentheses) must be consulted: Allen (Calcasieu); Beauregard (Calcasieu); Evangeline (St. Landry); Jefferson Davis (Calcasieu). FHL book 976.3 M22j. Also on microfilm, FHL film #1822969.

■ *1898-1929 Records of Pensioners of the State of Louisiana,* microfilm of original records located at the Louisiana State Archives, Baton Rouge, LA. Includes name, residence, company or regiment, date, place and nature of wound received, disability, where and when paroled or discharged, if discharged where remaining until surrender, cause of death of widow's husband, where and when died, date of granting pension, monthly amount, and date of application. Filmed by the Genealogical Society of Utah, 1985, 2 rolls, FHL film #1412742 (1898-1910, and 1910-1929); and FHL film #1412743 (1910-1929).

■ *1898-1944 Applications for Pensions,* microfilm of original records located at the Louisiana State Archives, Baton Rouge, LA. Includes names, address, company or command, disposition of claim, and date. Filmed by the Genealogical Society of Utah, 1985, 2 rolls, FHL film #1412743 (vol. 1-3, 1898-1942; and vol. 4, A-C, 1911-1944) and FHL film #1412744 (vol. 4, D-Z, 1911-1944).

■ *1912-1936 Louisiana Confederate Veterans Pensions,* microfilm of original records at the Jackson Barracks Military Library, New Orleans, LA. Filmed by the Genealogical Society of Utah, 1990, 1 roll, FHL film #1704156.

■ *Civil War Pensions in Louisiana, 1924 & 1933: Veterans & Widows,* compiled by Winston DeVille, published by Provincial Press, Lafayette, LA, 2000,150 pages. Names are in alphabetical order by parish. FHL book 976.3 M2dw.

MAINE

Online Maine Resources

■ **Maine State Archives.** This Augusta facility is located in the Cultural Building, which also houses the Maine State Library and the Maine State Museum. The archives' Research Room provides access to original records from the Legislature, Governor's Executive Orders, Election Returns, Deeds to and from the State of Maine, Maps from the Land Office, Vital Statistics, Federal Census records from Maine up to 1920, County Court Records dating back to the 1600's, Military records through World War I, Attorney General and State Supreme Court opinions, to name only a few. Computer indexes to many of these records are available in the Research Room and online at "Archives Interactive" at:
 www.informe.org/sos_archives where keyword searches can be done within these categories:
  ● General Search (all categories)
  ● Photographs
  ● Maps
  ● Legislation Proposed or Enacted 1820-1860
  ● Executive Council papers
  ● Early Court Cases from York, Washington and Kennebec Counties
  ● Miscellaneous Municipal Records Filed with the State
  ● Town and City Microfilm Collection
  ● Moving Images, Motion Pictures
  ● Maine Towns Legal Histories, dates of incorporation, name and boundaries changes

■ **Maine State Archives – Civil War Page.** www.maine.gov/sos/arc/archives/military/civilwar/ civilwar.htm. Background information, stories, Maine people involved in the Civil War, links to regimental sites, and more.

■ **URSUS,** the shared online catalog of the University of Maine System, Bangor Public Library, Maine State Archives, Maine State Library, and Maine State Law and Legislative Reference Library at: **http://ursus.maine.edu**. This is a very useful resource for locating a reference to a Maine ancestor, place of residence, or subject.

■ **Maine in the American Civil War.** www.earthstation9.com/index.html?maine2.htm. General resources: Civil War Records, Maine State Archives; Civil War Rosters; Regimental Histories, Maine in the Civil War site, Maine State Archives Civil War page; Paul's Civil War page – History of Maine Soldiers and Sailors.

■ **Civil War Rosters – Maine Links.** www.geocities.com/area51/lair/3680/cw/cw-me.html. This is a directory of Civil War Rosters/Muster Rolls that have been found on the Internet. Since only 50-60% of all rosters are on the Internet, some units will not be listed.

■ **Maine in the Civil War Home Page.** www.rootsweb.com/~mecivilw/mecivilw.htm. Under construction is a database of personnel with military and biographical notes. This is a major project based on a multitude of records, gravestone recordings, and contributions from many persons interested in preserving the Civil War data on veterans and has a long way to go. The files are arranged alphabetically.

Published Maine Resources

■ *Maine in the War for the Union: A History of the Part Borne by Maine Troops in the Suppression of the American Rebellion,* by William E.S. Whitman and Charles H. True, published by Nelson Dingley, Jr., Lewiston, ME, 1865, 637 pages, FHL book 974.1 M2. Also on microfilm, FHL film #1597664.

■ **1861 Business Directory.** See *Maine at Work in 1861: A Directory to 17,000 Maine Residents and Their Occupations & Businesses,* by Robert Moseley Jackson, Jr., published by Higginson Books, Salem, MA, 1999, 334 pages, FHL book 974.1 E4j.

■ *1862-1866 Internal Revenue Assessment Lists for Maine,* microfilm of original records at the National Archives, Washington, D.C. Names of taxpayers within each Internal Revenue Division are generally in alphabetical order. Which rolls have which county on them are noted at the front of each roll. Filmed by the National Archives, 1970,series M770, 15 rolls. FHL has entire set, beginning with FHL film #1534403.

■ *1861-1866 Annual Reports of the Adjutant General of the State of Maine,* published by Stevens & Sayward, Augusta, ME, 1862-1867. Annual reports which include rosters of civil war soldiers, 7 vols., Vol. 1 (1861) as FHL fiche #6082970. Vol. 2-7 as FHL book 974.1 M2mag. See also *Supplement to the Annual Reports of the Adjutant General of the State of Maine for the Years 1861, '62, '63, '64, '65 and 1866,* same publisher, 1867, 1,210 pages. This later version is the most complete, and contains alphabetical lists of Union Volunteers in all Maine organizations, as well as U.S. Army Regulars drawn from Maine. FHL book 974.1 M2 mag. supp. 1861-1865. Also on 14 microfiche, FHL fiche #6046926.

■ *Index to Compiled Service Records of Volunteer Union Soldiers Who Served in Organizations from the State of Maine,* microfilm of original records of the U.S. Adjutant General at the National Archives, Washington, D.C. Consists of alphabetically arranged General Index Cards for Maine, with over 83,000 entries. Filmed by the National Archives, 1964, series M543, 23 rolls. FHL has entire set, beginning with FHL film #881847 (Index, surnames A-Ba). The Maine entries are incorporated into the national index at the National Park Service website at: www.itd.nps.gov/cwss/.

■ *1890 Maine Census Index of Civil War Veterans or Their Widows,* compiled by Bryan Lee Dilts, published by Index Publishing, Salt Lake City, 1984, 156 pages, FHL book 974.1 X22d. Also on microfiche, FHL fiche #6331400.

■ *Cemetery Index of Veterans,* microfilm of card file at the Maine State Archives, which indexes veterans buried in cemeteries in Maine. Records are arranged alphabetically by name of county, town and cemetery. Filmed by Photographic Sciences Corp. for the archives, 1975. FHL has 11 rolls, beginning with FHL film #1001841 (Androscoggin – Aroostook counties).

MARYLAND·

Online Maryland Resources

■ **Maryland State Archives (MSA),** Annapolis, MD. **www.msa.md.gov/msa/homepage/html/ homepage.html**. The 39 miles of shelving at this facility are surpassed in the U.S. only by those at the Library of Congress. Aside from being America's leading state archives in terms of quantity, quality, preservation, or access to original records, it is also one of the most user-friendly facilities for genealogists. The online resources at the MSA Home Page includes links to Family History Research, Maryland Manual On-Line, Order Digital Images from Archives' Collections, Study of the Legacy of Slavery in Maryland, and Vital Records (Births, Deaths, Marriages & Divorces).

■ **MSA Genealogy/Family History. www.msa.md. gov/msa/refserv/genealogy/html/genstart.html**. Includes links to Court Records, Birth and Death Records, Other Genealogy Web Sites, Ethnic Groups, Land Records, Libraries and Archives; help in finding maiden names, places of residence, and names of parents of an individual; plus Military Records, Missing Records, Naturalizations and Immigration, Probate Records, and Published Sources.

■ **MSA Archives of Maryland Online. http://aomol.net/html/index.html**. From this large collection of the published archival documents of Maryland dating from 1636, over 140 volumes have been digitized and made available online. The index is huge, and provides access via searches by keywords, surnames, places, subjects, etc. (A keyword search for "Civil War Rosters" brought up over 80 different references). Because of the combined Archives of Maryland series, many of the statewide Civil War name lists were published here first, unlike other states, where many publications (such as Adjutant General rosters and related lists) were published separately. As a result, most of Maryland published civil war records and other Civil War era name lists are together, accessible from the same index search. Other name lists from a myriad of original document sources are here, including countywide tax lists, militia lists, legislative actions with names of people, and more; and every name within a list is included in the main online index lookup. It should be noted that the Archives of Maryland series is also online at **www.ancestry.com**, but the MD archives site is more complete and with a better index (and its free).

■ **MSA Guide to Civil War Research in Maryland.** **www.msa.md.gov/msa/refserv/ genealogy/html/civilwar.html**. References to essential starting sources at the state archives, including publications, documents, rosters, and more.

■ **Maryland Units in the Civil War.** **www.2ndmdinfantryus.org/sites.html**. Includes Confederate Unit Histories & Reenacting Links; List of Basic Research Sources on Maryland CSA Units; Union Unit Histories & Reenacting Links; How To Research a Maryland Civil War Unit or Ancestor; Unit Research 101; Other Maryland in the Civil War Topics (Monuments, The Winans Steam Gun).

■ **Civil War Rosters – Maryland Links.** **www.geocities.com/Area51/Lair/3680/cw-md.html**.

■ **American Civil War – Maryland.** **www.archaeolink.com/american_civil_war_ maryland.htm**.

Published Maryland Resources

■ *Compiled Service Records of Volunteer Union Soldiers Who Served in Organizations from the State of Maryland,* microfilm of original records at the National Archives, Washington, D.C. Organized first by unit/regiment, the compiled service records consist of a jacket-envelope for each soldier, labeled with his name, rank, and the unit in which he served. The jacket-envelope typically contains card abstracts of entries relating to the soldier as found in original muster rolls, returns, rosters, payrolls, appointment books, hospital registers, Union prison registers and rolls, parole rolls, and inspection reports; and the originals of any papers relating solely to a particular soldier. Filmed by the National Archives, 1962, series M384, 238 rolls. FHL has complete set, beginning with FHL film #881522.

■ *Index to Compiled Service Records of Volunteer Union Soldiers Who Served in Organizations from the State of Maryland,* microfilm of original records of the U.S. Adjutant General at the National Archives, Washington, D.C. Consists of alphabetically arranged General Index Cards for Maryland Union soldiers, with over 53,500 entries. Filmed by the National Archives, 1964, series M388, 13 rolls. FHL has entire set, beginning with FHL film #881522 (Index, surnames A – Bo). The Maryland Union entries are incorporated into the national index at the National Park Service website at: **www.itd.nps.gov/cwss/**.

■ *Compiled Service Records of Confederate Soldiers Who Served in Organizations from the State of Maryland,* microfilm of original records at the National Archives, Washington, D.C. Filmed by the National Archives, 1960, series M321, 22 rolls. FHL has entire set, beginning with FHL film #1292663 (1st Cavalry, A – C).

■ *Index to Compiled Service Records of Confederate Soldiers Who Served in Organizations from the State of Maryland,* microfilm of original records at the National Archives. Consists of alphabetically arranged General Index Cards for Maryland Confederate soldiers, with over 6,080 entries. Filmed by the National Archives, 1962, series M379, 2 rolls. FHL has set, FHL #821887 (Index, A-K) and FHL film #821888 (Index, L-Z). The Maryland Confederate entries are incorporated into the national index at the National Park Service website at: **www.itd.nps.gov/cwss/**.

■ *History and Roster of Maryland Volunteers, War of 1861-1865,* prepared by L. Allison Wilmer, et al, published for the MD General Assembly by Guggenheimer, Weil & Co., Baltimore, 1898-1899, 2 vols. Reprinted by Family Line Publications, Silver Spring, MD, 1967. MSA Library call no.

09850-L26179-1/2. FHL has a microfilmed copy of the original 2 vols. obtained through the Library of Congress, FHL film #1466002.

■ *Index to The Maryland Line in the Confederate Army: 1861-1865,* compiled by Mrs. Charles Lee Lewis, published by the Maryland Hall of Records Commission, Annapolis, MD, 1946, 74 pages. FHL book 975.2 B4ma No. 3.

■ *Confederate Service Records* (for Maryland soldiers who served in Alabama units), microfilm of original records compiled by the ADAH, filmed by the Genealogical Society of Utah, 1987, 1 roll, FHL film #1411532 (Item 8, Maryland soldiers).

■ *Internal Revenue Assessment Lists for Maryland, 1862-1866,* microfilm of original records at the National Archives, Washington, D.C. Names of taxpayers within each Internal Revenue Division are generally in alphabetical order, by the following districts: DISTRICT 1 includes, Caroline, Cecil, Dorchester, Kent, Queen Annes, Somerset, Talbot, and Worcester counties; DISTRICT 2 includes Baltimore city (wards 1-7) and Baltimore (districts 5-7, 9-12) and Harford counties; DISTRICT 3 includes Baltimore city (wards 8-20); DISTRICT 4 includes Allegany, Carroll, Frederick, and Washington counties; and DISTRICT 5 includes Anne Arundel, Baltimore (districts 1-4, 8, 13), Calvert, Charles, Howard, Montgomery, Prince Georges, and St. Marys counties. Filmed by the National Archives, 1970, series M771, 21 rolls. FHL has entire set, beginning with FHL film #1534367 (District 1, Annual Lists).

■ *The Civil War Enrollment and Draft of 1862 in Howard County, Maryland*, by Joseph H. Nichols, Jr. and Richard W. Bush, published by the Howard County Genealogical Society, Columbia, MD, 2001, 85 pages. Includes full name index. FHL book 975.281 M2n.

■ *Roll Call, the Civil War in Kent County, Maryland,* by Walter J. Kirby; text by Lanetta W. Parks, published by Family Line Publications, Silver Spring, MD, 1985, 181 pages. Includes index. FHL book 975.236 M2k.

■ *1865 List of Qualified Votes & 1862 Union Draft List, Somerset County, Maryland,* compiled by Rebecca F. Miller, published by Miller's Choice, Princess Anne, MD, 1991, 15 pages. FHL book 975.2 A1 No. 188.

■ *1863-1869 City Directories, Baltimore, Maryland,* microfilm of originals produced by various publishers, filmed by Research Publication, Woodbridge, CT, 1980-1984. From the entire 192 roll series (1752-1923), the directories of the Civil War era are as follows:
  • 1863/64 E. M. Cross & Co.'s Baltimore city business Directory... by E. M. Cross & Co., FHL film #1376528.
  • 1864 Woods' Baltimore city directory... by John W. Woods, FHL film #1376528.
  • 1865/66 Woods' Baltimore city directory... by John W. Woods, FHL #1376528.
  • 1867/68 Woods' Baltimore city directory... by John W. Woods, FHL film #1376529.
  • 1868/69 Woods' Baltimore city directory... by John W. Woods, FHL film #1376530.

■ *1890 Maryland Census Index of Civil War Veterans or Their Widows,* compiled by Bryan Lee Dilts, published by Index Publishing, Salt Lake City, 1985, 90 pages, FHL book 975.2 X22d.

MASSACHUSETTS

Online Massachusetts Resources

Massachusetts Archives, Boston, MA. **www.sec.state.ma.us/arc/**. At the Home Page, click on "Researching Your Family's History at the Massachusetts Archives" for a good review of genealogical resources, including this one: "Civil War records held by the Archives include a variety of muster, clothing and descriptive rolls, lists of assignments of recruits to particular town quotas, materials documenting the use of substitutes for draftees, and records of Massachusetts bounty payments to southern African-Americans who were recruited into the U.S. Army. Additional archival materials from this period include the records of the State Military Agent and the letters of Governor John Andrew, an early and strong supporter of the war effort." There is no online catalog or index to archives holdings, but locations and guides to the Civil War materials can be found using the site search. Several of the collections during the Civil War era have been published, either in print or as microfilm publications, and those available through the Family History Library are itemized below under Published Resources. In addition, there are searchable databases now online, accessible at the Home Page under "Our Collections":

- Massachusetts Archives Collection Database (1629-1799): **www.sec.state.ma.us/arc/arcsrch/ RevolutionarySearchContects.html**.
- Index to Passenger Manifests (1848-1891): **www.sec.state.ma.us/arc/arcsrch/Passenger ManifestSearchContents.html**.
- Index to Vital Records (1841-1910): **www.sec.state.ma.us/arc/arcsrch/ VitalRecordsSearchContents.html**.

■ **"Massachusetts Civil War Web Sites."** **www.masshome.com/histcwar.html**. This is a very useful listing of dozens of websites with a connection to the Civil War in Massachusetts. There are many regimental sites. Unit listings are numerical by unit name within a branch of service, within the categories of Artillery, Cavalry, Infantry, Reenactment Units, Information Resources, Web Rings, Historic Sites, and Historical Societies. there are also links to national sites, historic sites, National Park Service sites, and regional National Archives sites. The Civil War page is just one of many informative pages relating to Massachusetts, as part of "MassHome™ – Your Online Guide to Massachusetts."

Published Massachusetts Resources

■ *Lists of Persons Whose Names Have Been Changed in Massachusetts, 1780-1892,* microfilm of published court records, 119 pages. Filmed by the Massachusetts Archives, Boston. FHL book 974.4 E6m, and FHL film # 865449.

■ *Massachusetts Soldiers, Sailors and Marines in the Civil War: Index to Army Records,* compiled and published by the adjutant general, Charles H. Cole, printed by Wright & Potter Printing, Boston, 1937, 634 pages. This is most complete listing of Massachusetts participants in the Civil War. There were over a dozen reports published by the Adjutant General of Massachusetts from 1861 forward. This title is the culmination of the many volumes produced earlier. FHL book 974.4 M2ma. Also on microfilm, FHL film #238370.

■ *Index to Compiled Service Records of Volunteer Union Soldiers Who Served in Organizations from the State of Massachusetts,* microfilm of original records at the National Archives, Washington, D.C. Filmed by the National Archives, series M544, 1965, 44 rolls. FHL has complete set, beginning with FHL film #881870 (surnames beginning with A). The Massachusetts entries are incorporated into the national index at the National Park Service website at: **www.itd.nps.gov/cwss/**.

■ *Massachusetts Military Records 1817-1915,* microfilm of originals at the National Guard Supply Depot, Natick, Massachusetts. Contents: **Massachusetts Volunteers** includes the brigades N.G.S., Ambulance Corps, 1st Battalion Cavalry and Company F, 1st Battery Artillery and Battery B, 1st and 2nd Corps Cadets, Naval Brigade N.G.S., and the Signal Corps. **Spanish American War** records are arranged alphabetically by town name. Within each town are cards for the Army, Navy, and Marines (in that order). The names on the cards are in alphabetical order within each branch of service. The Navy is the only one with a mark of identification, there is an 'N' in the upper right hand corner of the card. Another word of caution: some of the towns are out of order, so please be sure to check all films to see where they might be listed. Also some cards may go as early as 1861 up to and including 1921; some also include residency from elsewhere in the United States. **Spanish War – Philippines** includes enlistment information, physical description, age, birthplace, occupation, residence, death date, discharge, etc. Each card contains at least part of the information listed above. The cards are arranged alphabetically by name of person serving, not by town as stated on the title boards. Includes information on persons enlisted in Massachusetts but which have residency in other states. **Miscellaneous Massachusetts Infantry Records** includes Civil War lists of Massachusetts soldiers wounded or killed, or taken prisoner with death or parole dates, applications for furloughs, enlistees entitled to bounty, surgeons lists, lists of officers killed in service, deserters, prisoners, certificates of exemption, and other papers. Records include enlistments, enrollments, medical examinations, detachments, oaths, rosters, election returns, discharges, desertions, and resignations. Some lists include name, rank, company, regiment, enlistment, and discharge dates. Filmed by the Genealogical Society of Utah, 1988-1991, 148 rolls, beginning with FHL film #1562394 (Enlistments and Enrollments – General service – Regular Army and Cavalry 1863-1864).

■ *Military Records, 1861-1917,* microfilm of original records at the Massachusetts Archives, Boston, MA. Filmed by the Genealogical Society of Utah, 1997-1998, 7 rolls, as follows:
- Certificates of naval enlistments, 1862-1864, FHL film #2108352.
- Certificates of naval enlistments (cont.), 1864-1865 Naval enlistment rolls: vol. 1, 1862 vol. 2, 1863 vol. 3, 1864 vol. 4, 1865 Lists of entitlements to prize money, 1884-1886; Enrollment reports from cities and towns, 1862-1864, FHL film #2108353.
- Enrollment reports from cities/towns, (cont.), 1862-1864 Naval enlistments by town, v. 1, 1861-1870, FHL film #2108354.
- Naval enlistments by town, v. 2, 1861-1870; Index to naval personnel from Massachusetts, 1885-1889; Returns of naval enlistments for municipalities (v. 1 for towns starting with letter A-G is missing) v. 2 for towns starting with letter H-P, 1864-1867 v. 3 for towns starting with letter Q-Y (to town of Somerset), 1864-1867, FHL film #2108379.
- Returns of naval enlistments for municipalities v. 3 (cont.), 1864-1867; Index to Mass. volunteers in the U.S. Navy, 1861-1865; Enlistment and elective rolls for the U.S. Marine Corps, 1861-1864; Index to naval bounty payments, 1864; List of naval credits, v. 1, towns A-B, 1861-1865; List of naval credits, v. 2, towns C-M, 1861-1865 (to town of Canton), FHL film #2108452.
- List of naval credits, v. 2 (cont.), towns C-M, 1861-1865; List of naval credits, v. 3, towns N-Y, 1861-1865; Index to transfers from army to navy, 1861-1917; Lists of recruits enrolled at Washington, D.C., 1863-1865 (volume unbound, damaged; pages out of order), FHL US/CAN Film #2108453.
- List of seamen and officers from Boston in the U.S. Navy (only surnames beginning with H-Y), FHL film #2108520.

■ *Massachusetts in the Army and Navy During the War of 1861-65,* prepared under the authority of the state by Thomas Wentworth Higginson, published Wright & Potter Printing, 1896, in 2 vols. Includes indexes; also, includes (in v. 2) Officers from Massachusetts in United States Navy, 1861 to 1865, by Captain Charles W. Wilson; and, Massachusetts women in the Civil War, by Mary A. Livermore. FHL book 974.4 M2ht. Also on microfilm, FHL film #238371.

■ *Massachusetts Soldiers, Sailors, and Marines in the Civil War,* prepared by Charles H. Cole, adjutant General, published by Norwood Printing, Norwood, MA, 1931-1935, 9 vols., FHL book 974.43 M2ma.

■ *Massachusetts in the War, 1861-1865,* by James L. Bowen, published by Clark W. Bryan, Springfield, MA, 1989, 1,029 pages. FHL has copy microfilmed for them by the Library of Congress Photoduplication Service, 1989, 1 roll, FHL film #1482275.

■ *Massachusetts in the Rebellion: A Record of the Historical Position of the Commonwealth, and the Services of the Leading Statesmen, the Military, the Colleges, and the People, in the Civil War of 1861-65,* by Phineas Camp Headley, published Walker, Fuller & Co., Boston, 1886, 688 pages. Includes index. FHL has microfiche copy by University Publications of America, Bethesda, MD, 1991, on 8 fiche, FHL fiche #6083029.

■ *Returns of Municipal Bounties, 1863-1864,* microfilm of original records at the Massachusetts Archives, Boston. Includes name lists of various town allotments for Civil War soldiers. Filmed by the Genealogical Society of Utah, 1998, on 3 rolls, beginning with FHL film #2110249.

■ *Civil War Correspondence, Diaries, and Journals at the Massachusetts Historical Society, 1842-1885, Bulk 1861-1865: Guide to the Microfilm Edition, 29 Reels,* published by the Massachusetts Historical Society, Boston, MA, includes indexes. From introduction: "This publication presents 28 individual collections arranged in 16 parts, with some of the smaller collections being grouped in one part. Some collections record the experiences of individuals who served successively in more than one military unit, and some collections record pre- and post-war material." See FHL book 974.A1 No.207.

■ *1865 Massachusetts State Census,* microfilm of originals at the Massachusetts State Archives, Boston, MA. The 1865 census schedules are complete for all Massachusetts counties and towns. For each member of a family, the data includes the full name of the person, age, birthplace (town in MA, or state/country), occupation, and any disabilities. The 1855 and 1865 MA state censuses were filmed together as one series by the Genealogical Society of Utah, 1974, 68 rolls. 1865 schedules begin with FHL film #953966 (Barnstable County – Towns of Barnstable to Yarmouth).

■ *History and Complete Roster of the Massachusetts Regiments: Minute Men of '61 Who Responded to the First Call of President Abraham Lincoln, April 15, 1861, to Defend the Flag and Constitution of the United States Together with Photographs and Biographical Sketches of Minute Men of Massachusetts,* by George W. Nason, published by Simon & McCance, c1904, 413 pages. FHL book 974.M2n. Also on microfilm, FHL film #1425662.

■ *1890 Massachusetts Census Index of Civil War Veterans or Their Widows,* compiled by Bryan Lee Dilts, published by Index Publishing, Salt Lake City, 1985, 222 pages. FHL book 974.4 X22d.

■ *Grand Army of the Republic: Civil War Veterans, Department of Massachusetts 1866 to 1947,* compiled by A. Dean Sargent, published by Heritage Books, Bowie, MD, 2002, 518 pages. FHL book 974.4 M2sa. Also available on CD-ROM, FHL CD No. 1660.

■ *Index to Genealogical and Personal Memoirs Relating to the Families of the State of Massachusetts,* originally compiled by William Richard Cutter (1847-1918) from various Massachusetts state, county, and town histories. As a 1980 project of LDS Church service volunteers, Salt Lake City, the work was typed and indexed in three volumes, FHL book 974.4 D2c v.1-3. Also on microfilm, FHL film #1033839.

■ *A Surname Guide to Massachusetts Town Histories,* by Phyllis O. Longver & Pauline J. Oesterlin, published by Heritage Books, Bowie, MD, 1993, 425 pages. This is a master guide to the surnames to be found in 128 volumes of Massachusetts town histories. FHL book 974.4 H22Lp.

MICHIGAN

Online Michigan Resources

■ **The Archives of Michigan, Genealogy/Military Sources.** Go to the History, Arts and Libraries home page at: **www.michigan.gov/hal/**. At the main page, select Genealogy – Military Sources. The Archives of Michigan contains primary material on Michigan's wars from territorial days to World War II and beyond. Sources include records of the Michigan Executive Office and Department of Military and Veterans Affairs, as well as county and municipal government records and private papers. Genealogists, scholars, military history buffs and casual researchers can all discover useful information. With the recent support of the Abrams Foundation, the Archives of Michigan will improve access to its military collections of genealogical value. More database name indexes will be created and uploaded onto the web. The most recent – The Civil War Principals and Substitutes Index – is already uploaded and available. Also of use is a new joint project with the Michigan Department, Sons of the Union Veterans of the Civil War (SUVCW) to create the most complete grave listing for Michigan.

Current Online Searchable Military Databases:
- SUVCW Graves Database.
- Civil War Principals and Substitutes Index
- Civil War Soldier Images Database
- Guest Register of World War I Michigan Clubroom (located in New York City)
- World War II Honor List of Dead and Missing: State of Michigan

Databases Coming Soon:
- Grand Army of the Republic Indexes - Michigan Posts #1-50

Archives of Michigan Circulars (PDF):
- Archives of Michigan - Military Records (Archives Circular #4)
- Archives of Michigan - Military Records (Archives Circular #7)
- Archives of Michigan - Military Records (Archives Circular #27)
- Archives of Michigan - Civil War Manuscripts (Archives Circular #20)

Links to Resources Outside the Archives of Michigan.
- Michigan Department of Military and Veterans Affairs - Veterans Information
- U.S. National Archives and Records Center (Pre-World War I Military records)
- U.S. National Military Personnel Records Center
- Civil War Soldiers and Sailors Database, National Park Service

■ **The Library of Michigan, Genealogy Research.** Go to the History, Arts and Libraries home page at: **www.michigan.gov/hal/**. Click on Family History. Online searchable databases that may have Civil War era names include the following:
- **ANSWER Library Catalog.** Search the holdings of the Library of Michigan and the Archives of Michigan.
- **Michigan 1870 Census: www.michigan.gov/1870census**. The 1870 Federal Census for Michigan provides a list of the family names in each household in every county and township in Michigan in 1870. View and download images of the census pages.
- **Michigan Cemetery Sources: www.michigan.gov/cemeteries**. Michigan Cemetery Sources represents a compilation of published cemetery transcriptions located at the Library of Michigan. It also identifies the location of more than 3,700 cemeteries in Michigan. It is not intended to include personal names.
- **Michigan Naturalization Record Indexes.** Indexes to the naturalization records for 29 Michigan counties are online in PDF format. Researchers may request copies of naturalization records from the Archives of Michigan.
- **Michigan Newspapers.** A list of Michigan newspapers on microfilm at the Library of Michigan. The list is organized by county, and a date range is given for each newspaper.

■ **Michigan in the Civil War 1861-1865. www.michiganinthewar.org/cwmireg.htm**. From the Home Page introduction: "During the war, Michigan fielded thirty-one regiments of infantry, eleven regiments of cavalry, fourteen batteries of artillery, one regiment of sharpshooters, and one regiment of engineers. As the men who volunteered exceeded Michigan's quotas, many men joined Units in Other States (link to site). Of these 90,000 Michigan men who left their homes, farms, businesses and loved ones many were to become one of 359,755 Deaths by States (link to site)

statistics of the Union deaths in the Civil War. Thousands were to return maimed and disabled, 14,434 never to return at all, most of whom rest beneath a stone marked, 'Unknown;' except, to the rest of their comrades, when they arrived at the final Bivouac of the Dead (link to site). Also included is a chronological list of every Battles of the Civil War (link to site) including casualties, and the Order of Battle for The Army of the Potomac (link to site) and The Army of Northern Virginia (link to site)."

Other Searchable Databases at this site:
- Michigan Regimental Histories. The histories of all of the fielded Michigan Regiments.
- Michigan Regimental Rosters. Over 88,500 men listed by regiment and company.
- Regimental Organization Locations, to locate a Regiment that was organized in a particular soldier's area of enlistment.
- Michigan Wartime Deaths. An alphabetical listing of all the 14,749 deaths.
- Michigan Soldier Gravesites.
- Faces from the Past. A collection of soldier photographs.
- Officers of the War. 145 copies of woodcuts of officers from both North and South that appeared in *Harpers Weekly* during the war years.
- Photos of Michigan Monuments at Gettysburg.

Links to other sites:
- 4th Michigan Infantry Information
- Civil War Signal Corps
- Andersonville Prison
- Don Troiani's Historical Art Prints
- The Florence Stockade
- Gettysburg Discussion Group
- Illinois in the War
- Illinois Roster Database
- Iowa in the War
- 20th Massachusetts Infantry
- 24th Michigan Infantry
- New York in the War
- Ohio in the War
- 103rd Pennsylvania
- Salisbury Prison
- Soldiers and Sailors System (National Park Service)
- United States Civil War Center
- Vermont in the War
- Unknown CW soldiers photos

■ **1894 Michigan Veterans Census – Online Database. www.mifamilyhistory.org/civilwar/ 1894VetsCensus/**. This is an online searchable database of the full extraction of the printed *Census of the State of Michigan 1894: Soldiers, Sailors and Marines, Volume III,* compiled by Washington Gardner, Secretary of State, published by Robert Smith & Co., State Printers, Lansing, MI, 1896. From the website: "In June of 1894 census enumerators recorded the names of U.S. soldiers of the Civil War living in Michigan. 42,544 soldiers were enumerated. 34,946 were native and 7,598 were foreign born. 148 Confederate soldiers resided in the state at that time. 102 were native and 46 were foreign-born. The average age was 55.41 years. Washington Gardner, Secretary of State, recognized that it was not possible to determine with any degree of accuracy some of the names as enumerated. In March of 1896 after a completed list was in type, the list was sent to each enumerator for verification and to the Grand Army of the Republic Posts in each county. The request was made to correct spelling errors and add those not enumerated. Names of those individuals not included in the original census enumeration, but returned by correction from either the enumerator or the G.A.R. (Grand Army of the Republic) appear with brackets around their names. It was found that 172 individuals from the original list were not soldiers. Those names remain on the listing without designation. The brackets had to be removed from the database to make it searchable. A field was added called Correction and shows the word 'yes' to mark those veterans later added."

Published Michigan Resources

■ *Michigan Surname Index,* microfiche of original card file at the Library of Michigan, Lansing, MI. Card file is alphabetically arranged. Contains genealogical data, addresses, names of the contributors and the societies. Filmed by Microform Systems, Inc., 1985, on 136 microfiche. FHL has entire set, FHL fiche #6334367.

■ *The Flags of Michigan,* compiled by John Robertson, Adjutant General, published by the Adjutant General's Office, Lansing, MI, 1877, 119 pages. Contains unit histories for all Michigan regiments of the Civil War. FHL has microfiche reproduction by University Publications of America, 1993, 2 fiche, FHL fiche #6084589.

■ *Michigan in the War,* compiled by John Robertson, Adjutant General, printed by W. S. George & Co., Lansing, MI, 1882, 1,039 pages. Contents: part 1, In the State; part 2, In the Field;

Part 3, Register of Commissioned Officers; Appendix. FHL has microfiche reproduction by University Publications of America, 1993, 11 fiche, FHL fiche #6084587. See also *Index to John Robertson's Michigan in the War, Revised Edition, Lansing, Michigan,* compiled by Helen H. Ellis, typescript, 250 pages, microfiche reproduction by University Microfilms, Ann Arbor, MI, 1989. FHL has the 5-fiche set, FHL fiche #6078584.

■ *Index to Compiled Service Records of Volunteer Union Soldiers Who Served in Organizations from the State of Michigan,* microfilm of original records at the National Archives, Washington, D.C. The General Index Cards, filed in alphabetical order by name of solder/sailor, Filmed by the National Archives, series M545, 48 rolls. FHL has complete set, beginning with FHL film #881914 (A – Aur). Michigan entries are incorporated into the national index at the National Park Service website at: **www.itd.nps.gov/cwss/**.

■ *Record of Service of Michigan Volunteers in the Civil War, 1861-1865,* official report of the Michigan Adjutant General, 46 volumes, organized by Michigan regiments of the Civil War. This is the most complete listing of Michigan participants of the Civil War. Original volumes printed by Ihling Bros. & Everard, Kalamazoo, MI, ca 1915; FHL has a reprint (of most volumes) by Detroit Free Press, ca. 1985. All 46 volumes are indexed in *Alphabetical General Index to Public Library Sets of 85,271 Names of Michigan Soldiers and Sailors Individual Records,* originally published by the Michigan Adjutant General's Office, Lansing, MI, 1915, 1,097 pages. FHL has a reprint by Michael A. Hogle, Military Bookseller, Okemos, MI, 1984. See FHL book 977.4 M2r. Also on microfilm, FHL film #915948.

■ *GAR (Grand Army of the Republic) Cemetery Index [Michigan], ca. 1800's-1900s,* microfilm of card file in possession of the Grand Rapids Public Library, Grand Rapids, MI. Covers primarily Civil War soldiers but includes some from other wars as well… an index with over 2,400 cards containing names of soldiers buried in Michigan. Veterans facilities (or Soldiers Home Cemeteries) included with names of sections to which they belong.

Filmed by the Genealogical Society of Utah, 2004, 7 rolls, beginning with FHL film #2372316 (Burlison, Eli – Ely, Ralph).

■ *Michigan Volunteers Descriptive Rolls, 1861-1866; Index to Michigan Volunteers, 1861-1865,* microfilm of original records at the Michigan Adjutant General's office, Lansing (1972). Filmed by the Genealogical Society of Utah, 1972, 16 rolls, beginning with FHL film #915346 (Index, A – O) and FHL film #915347 (Index, P – Z).

■ *Internal Revenue Assessment Lists for Michigan, 1862-1866,* microfilm of original records at the National Archives, Washington, D.C. From introduction: "On the 15 rolls of this microfilm publication are reproduced records of tax assessment lists for six collection districts established in the state of Michigan by Executive order of September 17, 1862. The lists were created in the offices of assessors and assistant assessors of Internal Revenue during the period 1862-1866... The Internal Revenue Act of July 1, 1862 (12 Stat. 432), was intended to 'provide Internal Revenue to support the Government and to pay interest on the public debt. Monthly specific and ad valorem duties were placed on manufactures, articles, and products ranging from ale to zinc. Monthly taxes were levied on gross receipts of transportation companies, on interest paid on bonds, on surplus funds accumulated by financial institutions and insurance companies, on gross receipts from auction sales, and on sales of slaughtered cattle, hogs, and sheep. Gross receipts from newspaper advertisements were subject to a quarterly tax. Annual licenses were required for trades and occupations, and annual duties were placed on carriages, yachts, billiard tables, and gold and silver plate.... The lists are arranged by collection district and thereunder by division. They are filmed in the order in which they are bound in the volumes. There are no annual lists for Divisions 1, 13, and 14 of District 1 for 1865; Division 2 of District 4 for 1864-65; Districts 2, 4, and 6 for 1862; and District 5 for 1864. Monthly and special lists are not included for every division for every month. An index that lists county names in each collection district is filmed after this introduction.... The assessment lists are divided into three categories: annual, monthly, and special. Entries in the annual and monthly lists are for taxes assessed or collected in those specific periods. The special lists augment incomplete annual and monthly lists, and include special taxes; for example, the special income tax of October 1864." Filmed by the National Archives, series M773, 15 rolls, FHL has complete set, beginning with FHL film #1534388 (District 1 annual, monthly and special lists, Sept. 1862 – Dec. 1863; annual lists, May 1864).

■ *Civil War Graves Registration Index Cards, ca. 1861-1930,* microfilm of original records at the Archives of Michigan, Lansing, MI. Contains names, regiments, and counties. Filmed by the Genealogical Society of Utah, 1994, 22 rolls, beginning with FHL film #1955405 (A – Barnes).

■ *Abstract of Drafted Men and Their Substitutes, 1863,* microfilm of 94-page transcript at the Archives of Michigan. Includes records for Allegan, Macomb, Cass, Genesee, Monroe, Oakland, Tuscola, Calhoun, Hillsdale, St. Clair, Saginaw, Barry, Clinton, St. Joseph, Ingham, Lapeer, Jackson, Shiawasee, and Livingston counties. Includes date, name of draftee/substitute, and place of residence. Filmed by the Genealogical Society of Utah, 1 roll, FHL film #2194772.

■ *Confederate Service Records* (for Michigan soldiers who served in Alabama units), microfilm of original records compiled by the ADAH, filmed by the Genealogical Society of Utah, 1987, 1 roll, FHL film #1411532 (Item 9, Michigan soldiers).

■ **1864 Michigan State Census.** Name lists from three Michigan counties only have survived:
  ● *1864 Michigan State Census, Clinton County,* microfilm of originals at the Michigan State Archives, Lansing, MI, filmed by the Genealogical Society of Utah, 1972, 1 roll, FHL film #915297.
  ● *1864 Michigan State Census, Eaton County,* microfilm of original records at the Michigan State Archives, Lansing, MI. Filmed by the Genealogical Society of Utah, 1972, 1 roll, FHL film #915302.
  ● *1864 Michigan State Census, Houghton County,* microfilm of original records at the Michigan State Archives, Lansing, MI. Filmed by the Genealogical Society of Utah, 1972, 1 roll, FHL film #915276.

■ *1890 Michigan Census Index of Civil War Veterans or Their Widows,* compiled by Bryan Lee Dilts, published by Index Publishing, Salt Lake City, UT, 1985, 236 pages. FHL book 977.4 X22d.

MINNESOTA

Online Minnesota Resources

■ **Minnesota Historical Society (MHS) – Family History.** **www.mnhs.org/genealogy/**. Accessible from this page are featured online searchable databases, including those which may give reference to a Civil War era resident of Minnesota:

- Birth Certificates Index – currently covers the years 1900-1934.
- Death Certificates Index – currently covers the years 1904-2001.
- Veteran Graves Registration Index – currently covers the reports from 1857 to 1975.
- Search MHS Library Catalog – keyword searching for names, places, and Civil War subjects.
- Minnesota State Census Index. Search the MN State Censuses from 1865, 1875, 1885, 1895, and 1905.

■ **Minnesota Civil War Soldiers** (database online at **www.Ancestry.com**). An index to over 26,000 soldiers mustered from Minnesota during the Civil War.

■ **Civil War Rosters – Minnesota Links.** **www.geocities.com/Area51/Lair/3680/cw/. cw-mn.html**. This is a directory of Civil War Rosters/Muster Rolls available on the Internet.

■ **Minnesota Infantry Regiments.** **www.mosocco.com/minnesota.html**. This site has links to any MN regimental websites, and brief regimental histories for all MN units serving during the Civil War.

Published Minnesota Resources

State Censuses in Minnesota began in 1849, 1853, then 1855 and every ten years thereafter until the last one taken in 1905. The original census schedules (and microfilmed copies) are located at the Minnesota Historical Society in St. Paul, MN; with microfilm copies at the Family History Library, Salt Lake City, UT. An index to the names and the scanned images of all of the MN state censuses, 1849-1905, are now online at **www.ancestry.com**. For a review of MN counties by year and microfilm numbers, see *A Guide to*

the Minnesota State Census Microfilm, by Mary Bakeman, published by Park Genealogical Books, Brooklyn Park, MN, 1992, 14 pages, FHL book 977.6 A1 Nol. 157. The MN state censuses that may identify a Civil War veteran by name are the 1865, 1885, 1895, and 1905 name lists:

■ *1865 Minnesota State Census,* microfilm of original records at the Minnesota Historical Society, St. Paul, MN. Names listed for head of households (without ages, occupations, or nativity); with just indicators for male, female, race, etc., but the final column is for "Soldiers & Sailors in Federal Service as of June 1, 1865." Filmed by the MN State Library, 1969, 3 rolls, as follows:

- Counties of Blue Earth, Brown, Carlton, Lake, St. Louis, Carver, Cass, Chisago, Clay, Crow Wing, Dakota, Dodge, Faribault, Fillmore, Freeborn, and Goodhue, FHL film #565714.
- Counties of Hennepin, Houston, Isanti, Kanabec, Le Sueur, McLeod, Mahnomen, Martin, Meeker, Morrison, Mower, Nicollet, Olmsted, Pine, Ramsey, and Rice, FHL film #565715.
- Counties of Scott, Sherburne, Sibley, Stearns, Steele, Todd, Wabasha, Waseca, Washington, Watonwan, Winona, and Wright, FHL film #565716.

■ *1885 Minnesota State Census,* microfilm of original records at the Minnesota Historical Society, St. Paul, MN. Includes names of all members of a household (without relationships), with an age, sex, race, nativity, parentage (whether father or mother of foreign birth), condition (deaf, dumb, blind, insane or idiotic); and "Served as a soldier in Federal army during the rebellion." Filmed by the MN State Library, 1969, 28 rolls. FHL has entire set, beginning with FHL film #565733 (Aitkin – Benton counties).

■ *1895 Minnesota State Census,* microfilm of original records at the Minnesota Historical Society, St. Paul, MN. Includes names of all members of a household (without relationships), with an age, sex, race, nativity, parentage (whether father or mother of foreign birth), and a column, "Soldier or Sailor in War of Rebellion." Added for males over 23 are years & months in the state, and years & months in the enumeration district. Filmed by the MN State Library, 1969, 59 rolls. FHL has entire set, beginning with FHL film #565761 (Aitkin, Anoka, Becker counties).

■ *1905 Minnesota State Census*, microfilm of original records at the Minnesota Historical Society, St. Paul, MN. Includes names of all members of a household (without relationships), with each person's age, sex, race, nativity (person, father of person, mother of person), period of residence (years & months in state, and years & months in the enumeration district), regular occupation, and two final columns for "**Army Service**" and "**Wars**" (Civil, Spanish, etc.). Filmed by the MN Historical Society, 1977, 58 rolls. FHL has entire set, beginning with FHL film #928767 (Aitkin, Anoka, Becker counties).

■ *Minnesota in the Civil and Indian Wars, 1861-1865*, prepared and published by the Board of Commissioners on Publication of History of Minnesota in Civil and Indian Wars, 1889, Pioneer Press Co., St. Paul, 2 volumes, FHL book 977.6 H2bc. See also, *Minnesotans in the Civil and Indian Wars: An Index to the Rosters in Minnesota in the Civil and Indian Wars, 1861-1865*, compiled as a WPA project for the Minnesota Historical Society, under the direction of Irene B. Warming. FHL has this index on microfiche, FHL fiche #6361456.

■ *Minnesota in the Civil War*, by Kenneth Carley, published by Ross & Haines, Minneapolis, 1961, 168 pages. Includes roster of Minnesota troops and some of the battles they fought in. includes index. FHL book 977.6 M2ca.

■ *Index to Compiled Service Records of Volunteer Union Soldiers Who Served in Organizations from the State of Minnesota*, microfilm of original records at the National Archives, Washington, D.C. Filmed by the National Archives, 1965, series M546, 10 rolls. FHL has entire set, beginning with FHL film #821930 (Index, A – Br, 1861-1865). Minnesota entries are incorporated into the national index at the National Park Service website at: **www.itd.nps.gov/cwss/**.

■ *Civil War Unit Histories: Regimental Histories and Personal Narratives: Part 4: The Union – Midwest and West*, 5 vols., with vol. 4 containing the official 1861-1866 Adjutant General Reports for Minnesota. See *Guide to the Microfiche*

Edition of Civil War Unit Histories, compiled by Robert E. Lester, published by University Publications of America, Bethesda, MD, 1993, FHL book 973. M2cwu pt. 4.

■ *1862-1866 Internal Revenue Assessment Lists for Minnesota*, microfilm of original records at the National Archives, Washington, D.C. Filmed by the National Archives, 1984, series M774, 3 rolls. FHL has the set cataloged under the title, *Bound Tax Revenue Assessment Lists for Minnesota, 1862-1865*, FHL film #1602225-1602227. A pamphlet describing M774 identifies the federal tax divisions and the Minnesota counties within each. See FHL book 973 J53m No. 774. The pamphlet was microfilmed at the beginning of the first roll (FHL film #1602225).

■ *Minnesota Adjutant General's Report of 1866*, a reproduction of the original report, published by Park Genealogical Books, Roseville, MN, 1997, 464 pages. Includes soldier's name, age, birthplace, rank, regiment, company, date and place mustered in, date and place mustered out, and other information. FHL book 977.6 M2ma.

■ *List of Pensioners on the Roll, January 1, 1883: Giving the Name of Each Pensioner, The Cause for Which Pensioned, The Post-Office Address, The Rate of Pension Per Month, and the Date of Original Allowance, as Called for by Senate Resolution of December 8, 1882*, originally published as United States Government Document, Serial numbers 2078-2082, Senate Executive Document 84, parts 1-5, 47th Congress, 2nd Session. Minnesota pensioners from volume 4 reprinted by Ancestor Publishing, Arvada, CO, 1990. FHL has microfiche copy, FHL fiche #6334560. See also, *Pensioners on the Roll (Living in Minnesota) as of 1 January 1883: With Every Name Index*, a reproduction of the original report, published by Park Genealogical Books, Roseville, MN, 1994, 82 pages. FHL book 977.6 M2po.

■ *1890 Minnesota Census Index of Civil War Veterans or Their Widows*, compiled by Bryan Lee Dilts, published by Index Publishing, Salt Lake City, 1985, 96 pages. FHL book 977.6 X22d.

MISSISSIPPI

Online Mississippi Resources

■ **Mississippi Department of Archives & History – Archives & Library Online Catalog.** **http://zed.mdah.state.ms.us/F?func=find-b-0.** Online databases at MDAH are limited to a few resources in the Online Archives (Jefferson Davis Estate Papers, Oral History Interviews with Sam H. Bowers, Jr., and Sovereignty Commission, 1956-1973). The main online resource at MDAH is a very comprehensive Online Catalog, searchable by keywords, title, author, subject, etc., Added to the Basic Catalog Search are **Additional Research Tools** with Browse Specific Collections, Tools, and Quick Searches. Catalog searching within categories include Biographical Index, Cemetery Index, County Court Case Files, County Records on Microfilm, Family Coat of Arms, Freedmen's Bureau Record Index, Manuscript Collections, Newspaper Holdings, Photograph Collection, and Subject Files. A search for names of residents, soldiers, and any other subject relating to Mississippi during the Civil War era can be accomplished here. For example, a keyword search in this database for "civil war" brings up many county record titles, e.g., soldier lists, mustering rolls, burials, induction rolls, and more.

■ **The Civil War in Mississippi.** **www.researchonline.net/mscw/msstart.htm.** This website devoted to Mississippi includes:
- For the Cause (1865 address of Mississippi Governor Humphreys)
- Confederate Military History – Mississippi
- Timeline of the War in Mississippi
- Military Units of Mississippi
- Mississippi Citations in the Official Records
- Biographical Sketches

■ **Civil War Battle Summaries.** **www.nps.gov/ history/hps/abpp/battles/MSmap.htm.** An interactive map showing all Mississippi battle sites. Click on Battle name for more information. This site sponsored by the National Parks Service's American Battlefield Protection Program.

■ **Civil War Rosters – Mississippi Links.** **www.geocities.com/area51/lair/3680/cw/cw-ms.html.** This is a directory of Civil War Rosters/Muster Rolls that have been found on the Internet.

Published Mississippi Resources

■ *Compiled Service Records of Confederate Soldiers Who Served in Organizations from the State of Mississippi,* microfilm of original records at the National Archives, Washington, D.C. Organized first by unit/regiment, the compiled service records consist of a jacket-envelope for each soldier, labeled with his name, rank, and the unit in which he served. The jacket-envelope typically contains card abstracts of entries relating to the soldier as found in original muster rolls, returns, rosters, payrolls, appointment books, hospital registers, Union prison registers and rolls, parole rolls, and inspection reports; and the originals of any papers relating solely to a particular soldier. Filmed by the National Archives, 1959, series M269, 386 rolls. FHL has complete set, service records beginning with FHL film #1488026 (1st Cavalry, A – D).

■ *Index to Compiled Service Records of Confederate Soldiers Who Served in Organizations from the State of Mississippi,* microfilm of original records at the National Archives, Washington, DC. Filmed by the National Archives, series M253, 1956, 45 rolls. FHL has entire set, beginning with FHL film #821838 (A – Ar). Mississippi Confederate entries are incorporated into the national index at the National Park Service website at: **www.itd.nps.gov/cwss/.**

■ *Compiled Service Records of Union Soldiers Who Served in Organizations from the State of Mississippi,* microfilm of original records at the National Archives, Washington, D.C. Filmed by the National Archives, series M404, 1962, 4 rolls. FHL has entire set, beginning with FHL film #1292659 (1st Battalion, Mounted Rifles, A – F).

■ *Index to Compiled Service Records of Union Soldiers Who Served in Organizations from the State of Mississippi, 1861-1865,* microfilm of original records at the National Archives, Washington, DC. Filmed by the National Archives, series M389, 1962, 1 roll. FHL film #881535. Mississippi Union entries are incorporated into the national index at the National Park Service website at: **www.itd.nps.gov/cwss/**.

■ *1866 Mississippi State Census.* Originals located at MDAH, Jackson, MS. Search requests can be made at the MDAH website noted above. Microfilm of MS state censuses available at the Family History Library under the title, **State Census Records, 1792-1866,** 3 rolls, FHL film #899868-899870. An index to the 1866 MS state census is online at **www.ancestry.com** as part of the series, **Mississippi Census, 1805-1890** (no images). Like all of Ancestry's databases, a search for a name can be conducted within just the 1866 census listings. Ancestry's 1866 state census database was originally published as **Mississippi 1866 State Census Index,** edited by Ronald Vern Jackson, published by Accelerated Indexing Systems, North Salt Lake, UT, 1988, 158 pages, FHL book 876.2 X22m.

■ *1865-1866 Internal Revenue Lists for Mississippi,* microfilm of originals at the National Archives, Washington, D.C. Filmed by the National Archives, series M775, 3 rolls, FHL films #1578481-1578483.

■ *Military Annals of Mississippi: Military Organizations Which Entered Service of the Confederate States of America from the State of Mississippi,* compiled by J. C. Rietti, original published 1895, reproduced by University Publications of America, Bethesda, MD, 1990, on 3 microfiche. FHL fiche #6082482.

■ *Confederate Soldiers & Sailors, Widows Pension Applications,* microfilm of original records at the Mississippi Auditor's Office (now at the MDAH). Names are filed in alphabetical order. Filmed by the Genealogical Society of Utah, 1972, 94 rolls, beginning with FHL film #902556 (Aa – Allen).

■ *Mississippi Confederate Pension Applications,* compiled by Betty Couch Wiltshire, published by Pioneer Publishing, Carrollton, MS, 1995, 3 vols. Lists name, application date, service unit, county of residence. Vol. 1. A-G, Vol. 2. H-O, Vol. 3. Po-Z.

See FHL book 976.2 M2wb Vol. 1-3.

■ *Enumeration of Confederate Soldiers and Widows from Montgomery County, Mississippi 1907,* compiled by Evelyn Bell Crouch and Christie Crouch Genola, published by Pioneer Pub. Co., Carrollton, MS, 2004, 151 pages. FHL book 976.2642 M2c.

■ *North West Mississippi Confederate Soldiers and Widows Pension and Enumeration Records of the Civil War,* compiled and published by Betty Arnold Loftiss, Coldwater, MS, 1994, 82 pages. Includes Tallahatchie County, Mississippi pension rolls; enumeration of Tallahatchie County soldiers; Marshall County, Mississippi pension roll; Tunica County, Mississippi enumeration of soldiers and widows; and Quitman Light Artillery and Infantry. FHL book 976.2 M2Lb.

■ *Pension Record Reports (1902-1942) of Confederate Soldiers and Widows Living in Newton County, Mississippi,* photocopy of original records at the Lauderdale County Department of Archives& History, 2003, 284 pages, FHL book 976.2672 M2p.

■ *Confederate Dead and Other Confederate Records,* compiled by Marie Haven Carlton, published by the Tate County Genealogical and Historical Society, Senatobia, MS, 1997, 120 pages. Includes surname index. FHL book 976.2 M2c.

■ *1861-1865, 1907 Confederate Military Records, Claiborne County, Mississippi,* microfilm of original records at the Claiborne County Courthouse, Port Gibson, MS. Filmed by the Genealogical Society of Utah, 1993, 2 rolls, FHL film #1887836 (1907 Enumeration of Confederate Soldiers & Widows), and FHL film #1887840 (Record of Confederate Soldiers, 1861-1865).

■ *Confederate Service Records* (for Mississippi soldiers who served in Alabama units), microfilm of original records compiled by the ADAH, filmed by the Genealogical Society of Utah, 1987, 1 roll, FHL film #1411532 (Item 10, Mississippi soldiers).

■ *Lauderdale County Confederate Induction Records,* abstracted by William L. Blanks & James T. Dawson, published by the Lauderdale County Dept. of Archives & History, Meridian, MS, 1987, 235 pages. Records give place of birth, county and state, age, height, complexion, color of eyes, color of hair, occupation, place of residence at time of induction, plus information on assignments, exemption, furloughs, etc. FHL book 976.2 M2b.

■ *Mississippi Confederate Grave Registrations,* compiled by Betty Couch Wiltshire, published by Heritage Books, Bowie, MD, 1991, 2 vols. Information, when known, includes the soldier's names, their service units, the years of birth and death, the county or state where they were buried. Most of these soldiers were from Mississippi. FHL book 976.2 M2w.

■ *Mississippi Confederate Pardon Applications,* compiled by Anne Webster, published by Pioneer Pub. Co., Carrollton, MS, 2004, 148 pages. FHL book 976.2 M2wm.

■ *1890 Mississippi Census Index of Civil War Veterans or Their Widows,* compiled by Bryan Lee Dilts, published by Index Publishing, 1985, 50 pages, FHL book 976.2 X22d.

MISSOURI

Online Missouri Resources

■ **Missouri State Archives.** **www.sos.mo.gov/archives/.** Online searchable databases include the Missouri Death Certificate Database (1910-1956), with many digitized images of the actual certificates. Missouri is the national leader in indexing and scanning death certificates for online viewing. Another online resource is the Missouri Judicial Records Database.

■ **The State Historical Society of Missouri – Newspaper Search.** **www.shsofmissouri.org/.** **cgi/store/0065.html.** This site is for searching for a specific newspaper reference to a person for an exact date. If you know the exact date of death for a person, for example, use this search screen to submit a request for a copy of a death notice,

obituary, burial, etc. The same screen can be used to search for birth announcements, wedding announcements, or other events. The newspaper images are not online – this search box is for submitting a request for a search in Missouri newspapers for a fee.

■ **Index of the Civil War in Missouri – Links and Resources available on the Internet.** **http://home.usmo.com/~momollus/Mocwlink.htm.** Categories include the following:
  ● Listing of Battles in MO (906), Maps and links of other interests (2)
  ● History of Battles, Battlefields, Parks, Museums, Historical Sites, and Cemeteries (106)
  ● Index to the Officers of Missouri Volunteers and Missouri State Militia
  ● Online Database Searches
  ● MO Volunteer Forces in the Civil War (447)
  ● The Grand Army of the Republic (GAR) in MO
  ● Confederate Troops in Missouri
  ● Descendant Organizations (64)(Includes Additional Union and Confederate Links)
  ● Civil War Round Tables (9)
  ● Living Historians (2)
  ● Reenactor Organizations (69)
  ● Libraries with notable Collections on the Civil War in MO (42) and MO Genealogical Societies
  ● Special Interest/Research Topic Links (116)
  ● Surrounding States Civil War Resources (AR, IA, IL, KS, KY, MO, OK, NE, & TN) (31)
  ● Selected National Civil War Resources and Links (19)
  ● Calendar of Civil War Events in the Missouri Area (Full Year 2000!)
  ● MO Civil War Bookstore

■ **Missouri in the Civil War.** **http://mocivwar.mogenweb.org/.** Includes these categories (and more):
  ● Veterans Buried in Missouri
  ● Missouri Veterans Buried in Other States
  ● Missouri Only Links for Civil War Research
  ● Missouri Civil War Reunions and Other Events
  ● Missouri in the Civil War Query Pages
  ● Confederate Troops in Missouri
  ● The German Regiment, Missouri Volunteers (Benton County Home Guard)
  ● Battle Sites in Missouri with Map

Published Missouri Resources

■ *Military Records, 1812-1904,* microfilm of original records of the Missouri Adjutant General's Office, now located at the Missouri State Archives,

Jefferson City, MO. Includes records related to: (1) the Seminole War of 1837; (2) Mexican War; (3) War of 1812; (4) Mormon War; (5) Civil War; (6) Iowa War; (7) Heatherly War; and (8) Black Hawk War. Records alphabetical by surname, but not always in strict alphabetical order within each letter. Filmed by the Genealogical Society of Utah, 1977-1978, 214 rolls, beginning with FHL film #1204650 (General index, 1837-1865), and FHL film #1204651 (And – Bad).

■ *Compiled Service Records of Union Soldiers Who Served in Organizations from the State of Missouri,* microfilm of original records at the National Archives, Washington, D.C. Organized first by unit/regiment, the compiled service records consist of a jacket-envelope for each soldier, labeled with his name, rank, and the unit in which he served. The jacket-envelope typically contains card abstracts of entries relating to the soldier as found in original muster rolls, returns, rosters, payrolls, appointment books, hospital registers, Union prison registers and rolls, parole rolls, and inspection reports; and the originals of any papers relating solely to a particular soldier. Filmed by the National Archives, series M405, 1962, 796 rolls. FHL has entire set, beginning with FHL film #1500223 (1st Cavalry, A – Ba).

■ *Index to Compiled Service Records of Volunteer Union Soldiers Who Served in Organizations from the State of Missouri,* microfilm of original records at the National Archives, Washington, D.C. Filmed by the National Archives, series M390, 1962, 54 rolls. FHL has entire set, beginning with FHL film #881536 (Index, A – Ar). Missouri Union entries are incorporated into the national index at the National Park Service website at: **www.itd.nps.gov/cwss/**.

■ *Compiled Service Records of Confederate Soldiers Who Served in Organizations from the State of Missouri,* microfilm of original records at the National Archives, Washington, D.C. Organized first by unit/regiment, the compiled service records consist of a jacket-envelope for each soldier, labeled with his name, rank, and the unit in which he served. The jacket-envelope typically contains card abstracts of entries relating to the soldier as found in original muster rolls, returns, rosters, payrolls, appointment books,

hospital registers, Union prison registers and rolls, parole rolls, and inspection reports; and the originals of any papers relating solely to a particular soldier. Filmed by the National Archives, 1960, series M322, 177 rolls. FHL has complete set, service records beginning with FHL film # (1st Cavalry, A – D).

■ *Index to Compiled Service Records of Confederate Soldiers Who Served in Organizations from the State of Missouri,* microfilm of original records at the National Archives, Washington, D.C. Filmed by the National Archives, series M380, 1962, 16 rolls. FHL has entire set, beginning with FHL film #882002 (A – Bi). Missouri Confederate entries are incorporated into the national index at the National Park Service website at: **www.itd.nps.gov/cwss/**.

■ *Confederate Service Records* (for Missouri soldiers who served in Alabama units), microfilm of original records compiled by the ADAH, filmed by the Genealogical Society of Utah, 1987, 1 roll, FHL film #1411532 (Item 11, Missouri soldiers).

■ *Confederate Hospital Register, 1861-1862,* compiled by Mary Neblett Beck, published by Mid-Missouri Genealogical Society, Jefferson City, MO, 1995, 140 pages, FHL book 977.8 J4b.

■ *1862-1866 Internal Revenue Assessment Lists for the State of Missouri,* microfilm of original records at the National Archives, Washington, D.C. The federal taxing districts are identified by counties within each, and listed for each roll of film. Filmed by the National Archives, series M776, 22 rolls. FHL has complete set, beginning with FHL film #1695299 (District 1, St. Louis Co, 1862).

■ *Confederate Roll of Honor, Missouri,* compiled by Leslie Anders, published by the West Central Missouri Genealogical Society and Library, 1989, 162 pages. From intro: "This register of 6,519 Confederate fatalities is the result of the most intensive statistical research ever carried out on the subject." See FHL book 977.8 M2a.

■ *Selected Union Burials, Missouri Units,* compiled by Edward Parker, Published by the State Historical Society of Missouri, Columbia, MO,

1988, 1993, 2 vols. From Intro: "This index was gleaned from the U.S. Quartermaster's Dept. 'Roll of Honor.' It lists the names of soldiers who died while serving with Missouri units, and where they are buried. Each volume contains a different alphabetical list of Union burials." See FHL book 977.8 M22p v.1-2.

■ *Confederate Pension Applications and Soldiers' Home Admission Applications,* microfilm of original records at the Missouri State Archives, Jefferson City, MO. Filmed by the Genealogical Society of Utah, 1977, 27 rolls, beginning with FHL film #1021101 (Confederate pension applications, approved, A – Ba). See also, *Missouri Confederate Pensions and Confederate Home Applications Index,* compiled by Peggy Barnes Fox, published by Hill College Press, Hillsboro, TX,1996, 51 pages, FHL book 977.8 M2fp.

■ *Index of Residents State Federal Soldiers' Home of Missouri, St. James, Missouri, 1899-1946,* by Marie C. Concannon, published by the State Historical Society of Missouri, Columbia, MO, 1998. Includes records of veterans and widows of veterans who were residents in the Federal Soldiers' Home. The home was established in 1897 in St. James to house indigent Union veterans of the Civil War, their wives, widows, and army nurses. See FHL book 977.8 M22i.

■ *1862-1877 Court-Martial Papers,* microfilm of Record Group No. 133, Missouri State Archives, Jefferson City, MO. Arranged in alphabetical order by surname of prisoner. A list of the contents of each box and folder is at the beginning of the first film. From intro: "This collection consists of handwritten military correspondence, printed and handwritten courts-martial records, special orders, rolls of sentenced prisoners, prisoners' referral letters, prisoners' statements regarding their crimes, military pardons and commutations, and numerous papers concerning the transfers of prisoners between the Alton (Illinois) and other military prisons and the Missouri State Penitentiary at Jefferson City." Filmed by the Genealogical Society of Utah, 2006, 4 rolls, beginning with FHL film #2407222 (Index to register of military prisoners, June 1864 – June 1875).

■ *1864 Missouri State Census, Gasconade County, Missouri,* photocopies of original documents at the Gasconade County courthouse, Hermann, MO, reproduced and indexed by Robert E. Parkin, published by Genealogical Research and Productions, 1980, 64 pages. FHL book 977.861 X2e and FHL film #6075652.

■ *1868 Missouri State Census, Cape Girardeau County, Missouri,* microfilm of original records at the Cape Girardeau County courthouse, Jackson, Missouri. Filmed (with 1876 census) by the Genealogical Society of Utah, 1976, 1 roll, FHL film #1006668.

■ *1868 Missouri State Census, St. Charles County, Missouri,* transcribed from originals at the County Clerk of St. Charles County by Carrol Geerling, published by Lineage Press, Bridgeton, MO, 1988, 212 pages. FHL book 977.839 X2g.

■ *1869 Census of Carondelet (now part of St. Louis, Missouri),* microfilm of originals by Carondelet city assessor, Filmed by the City of St. Louis, 1963, FHL film #981654.

■ *Grand Army of the Republic, Missouri Division, Index to Death Rolls 1882-1940: Taken from the Proceedings of the Annual Encampments,* project organized by Marie Concannon; transcribed by Josiah Parkinson, published by the State Historical Society of Missouri,1995, 184 pages. The GAR was a patriotic organization open to Union veterans of the Civil War. The organization provided fraternity, commemoration and assistance to its members, primarily by establishing soldiers' homes for caring for war orphans. Each post was supposed to submit lists of members who had died during the previous year. These rolls were included in the minutes of each encampment. See FHL book 977.8 M22c.

■ *1890 Missouri Census Index of Civil War Veterans or Their Widows,* compiled by Bryan Lee Dilts, published by Index Publishing, Salt Lake City, UT, 1985, 304 pages. The 1890 special schedules of surviving soldiers, sailors, and marines, and their widows, were only intended to be for Union veterans and spouses. But many

Confederates must have been listed by accident Arranged in alphabetical order by surname. See FHL book 977.8 X2d.

MONTANA TERRITORY

At the onset of the Civil War, the Bitterroot area of Washington Territory, and the mining camps of Dakota Territory supplied a number of Union troops to the war effort. These areas became part of Idaho Territory in 1863, and Montana Territory in 1864. Neither Idaho or Montana territories supplied troops to the war in their own names. In May 1864, Montana Territory was established, with the same bounds as the present state of Montana, admitted in November 1889.

Online Montana Resources

■ **Montana Historical Society – Shared Online Catalog.** http://mtscprod.msl.mt.gov/uhtbin/ cgisirsi/1uv2sGMz7I/MT-IST/285050006/60/1180/X. Through the Montana Historical Society/State Archives, this online catalog lists the holdings of virtually all libraries in the state of Montana. Keyword searching on any name, place, or subject reveals resources in locations all over the state.

■ **The Civil War in Montana.** www.archaeolink.com/civil_war_montana.htm. This is a thirty-page essay by Tom Sargent of Virginia City, Montana, giving some historical details regarding Montana's involvement with the Civil War. During the 1860s, Virginia City and Nevada City were the two most populated mining communities of Montana Territory, and both communities were dominated by vigilante Confederate sympathizers.

Published Montana Resources

■ *1864-1872 Internal Revenue Assessments for the Territory of Montana,* microfilm of originals at the National Archives in Washington, D.C. Includes annually, monthly and special lists of assessments for 1864-1872. Filmed by the National Archives, 1980, Series M0777, 1 roll, FHL film #1578505.

■ **1868-1869 and 1879-1880 Montana Histories and Directories.** See *Montana (Territory) Directories,* microfilm of originals published by various publishers, by Research Publications, Woodbridge, CT, 1980-1984, 1 roll, FHL film #1377090, includes *1868-1869 Historical Sketch and Essay on the Resources of Montana...* by Herald Book and Job Printing Office.

■ *First Families of Montana and Early Settlers,* a project of the Montana State Genealogical Society to collect profiles of early pioneers, called the First Families of Montana, published by the society, 2000. The profiles were submitted by descendants. Al Stoner, project chairman. Includes lists of submitters. Contents: Part 1: To MT before 8 Nov 1889; and part 2: Early settlers of Montana 9 Nov 1889-31 Dec 1929. FHL book 978.6 D2s. Also on microfilm, FHL film #1440428.

■ *Montana, its Story and Biography: A History of Aboriginal and Territorial Montana and Three Decades of Statehood,* edited by Tom Stout, published by American Historical Society, Chicago, IL, 1921, 3 vols. (Biographies in Vol. 2 & 3). FHL book 978.6 H2s. Indexed in *Every-Name Index to Stout's Montana: Its Story and Biography,* by Hamilton Computer Service, Park City, UT, ca1985, 433 pages. Index includes names, birthdates, and birthplaces. FHL book 978.6 H2s index. Also on microfilm, FHL film #1320700.

NEBRASKA TERRITORY

Online Nebraska Resources

■ **Nebraska State Historical Society (NSHS) – Currently Available Searches.** Go to: www.nebraskahistory.org/databases/index.html. This NSHS webpage is a portal to many special databases available online. From this webpage, access a search box at a NSHS webpage or a link to another website. Most searches can begin with just a surname. Indexes to the records are extensive, organized as follows:

- **Library / Archives Home Page.** Learn the many ways to search for your information in the Library and Archives.
- **Archival Collection Search.** The Archival Collection Database provides access to basic information on the Society's collections of manuscripts (papers of families and individuals,

and records of businesses and organizations), photographs, moving images, and sound recordings.

- **Library Catalog Search.** The library collection (books, maps, serials, and newspapers) includes over 50,000 titles of which over 40,000 are represented in this online catalog.
- **Gazetteer Index, 1890 and 1911.** A statewide place/name directory. Includes communities, businesses, and farmers directory.
- **Nebraska Atlases / Plat Books.** The NSHS library has a collection of over 500 county atlases or plat books and about 150 have been microfilmed. The approximate time period of these atlases and plat books is 1885 to the present. This database gives an accurate account of our holdings and helps researchers verify the existence of atlases/plat books for their years of interest.
- **Nebraska Atlases / Plat Books Name Index.** This database allows researchers to locate name references within the various Nebraska county atlases that are on microfilm.
- **Nebraska City / County Directories.** The NSHS library collects all available city/county directories for all communities and counties in the state. The coverage is from territorial days to within the last two years. This database gives an accurate account of our holdings and helps researchers verify the existence of these directories for town/county and years of interest.
- **Nebraska Civil War Veterans** (NEGenWeb). This database allows researchers to locate name references within the Civil War Veterans Indexes. The researcher may input a Last Name, First Name, Unit Served, GAR Unit Number, GAR Unit City, and/or GAR Unit County and will be given a listing of all the matching name index entries.
- **Nebraska Department of Public Instruction Reports, 1861-1960.** This database allows researchers to locate references within the reports.
- **Nebraska History Index Search. Nebraska: Name Index to Cancelled, Rejected, and Relinquished Land Entry Files** (National Archives website). The National Archives' Central Plains Region (Kansas City) has a variety of guides, reference information papers, lists, and other finding aids. Those available online for Nebraska are listed.
- **Nebraska Newspaper Indexes.** Most of these newspaper indexes are card indexes or privately produced volumes at the Society Library. This database has grown to include indexes found in published material, other libraries within the state, as well as the worldwide web. It is an index of indexes. You can NOT look up a family name here.
- **Nebraska . . . Our Towns (University of Nebraska database).** Historic information for over 600 Nebraska cities. Compiled by Jane Graff.
- **Nebraska Government Records.** By law, government records are public records. This

database indexes federal, state, county, municipal, and special district records held in the Society Archives.

- **Nebraska Prison Records, 1870-1990.** This database allows researchers to locate name references within the Prison Records.
- **Nebraska State Newspaper Project.** This database has over 200,000 names indexed from Nebraska newspapers and is available at the NEGenWeb website.
- **Nebraska Telephone Directories.** The NSHS library is the only library in the state that collects old phonebooks from towns, cities, or regions in Nebraska. The coverage is from the early 1900s to near the present. This database gives an accurate account of our holdings and helps researchers verify the existence of phonebooks for towns/cities and years of interest.
- **Nebraska U.S. General Land Office Tract Books.** Search homestead applications, proofs, final certificates, and supplemental information.
- **Nebraska Statewide Cemetery Registry.** This database needs your help! Scheduled to go online in 2007, your assistance will enhance this valuable tool.
- **Sherard's Nebraska Place Names.** Find Nebraska Place Names researched by Jerry Sherard. From more than 25 sources and contains more than 3500 entries.
- **WWI Draft Registration Cards: 1917-1918, Nebraska.** Over 276,000 records, arranged by county.

■ **Nebraska in the Civil War.   www.archaeolink. com/american_civil_war_nebraska.htm.**   Includes links to websites with references to important civil war resources related to Nebraska.

■ **Civil War Rosters – Nebraska Links. www.geocities.com/area51/lair/3680/cw/cw-ne.html**. This is a directory of Civil War Rosters/Muster Rolls that have been found on the Internet.

Published Nebraska Resources

■ *Civil War Unit Histories, Part 4, The Union-Midwest and West* is a compendium of military information from all states of the Civil War era. The Nebraska sections include 1) the 28-page military section from *History of the State of Nebraska...* available on fiche from University Publications of America, 1993 (FHL fiche #6118452); and 2) a 236- page section, *Roster of*

Nebraska Volunteers, from 1861 to 1869: Compiled from Books, Records, and Documents on File in the Office of Adjutant General of State, FHL fiche #6118454. FHL also has microfilm of the original book, published by Wigton & Evans, Hasting, NE, 1888. See FHL film #164034.

■ *Roster of Nebraska Soldiers,* originally published by Klopp, Bartlett & Co., Omaha, 1888, filmed by the Genealogical Society of Utah, 1958, 1 roll, FHL film #164034.

■ *Roster of Illinois Soldiers and Sailors in Nebraska,* by G.E. Whitman, photocopy of original 1892 roster. These Civil War vets were known to be living in Nebraska in 1891 but were originally recruited from Illinois counties. FHL book 973 M2wg. Also on microfilm, FHL film #1425496.

■ *Roster of Soldiers, Sailors and Marines of the War of 1812, the Mexican War, and the War of the Rebellion, Residing in Nebraska as of June 1, 1891, Who Enlisted from the State of Illinois,* published by John C. Allen, Secretary of State, printed by State Journal, Lincoln, NE, 1892, 354 pages, FHL book 978.2 M2n. Reprinted by the Nebraska State Genealogical Society, Lincoln, NE, 2000, FHL book 978.M2ro.

■ *Roster and Indexes of Soldiers, 1911,* microfilm of original records of the Grand Army of the Republic (GAR), Department of Nebraska, now located at the Nebraska State Historical Society (NSHS), Lincoln, NE. Filmed by the NSHS, 1974, 2 rolls. FHL has film #1705170 (Indexes, Roster, v. 1-2), and FHL film #1705171 (Roster, v. 3-4).

■ *Iowa, Kansas and Nebraska Civil War Veterans: Compilation of the Death Rolls of the Departments of Iowa, Kansas and Nebraska, Grand Army of the Republic, 1883-1948,* compiled and published by Dennis Northcott, St. Louis, MO, 2007, 658 pages, FHL book 973 M2nde.

■ *Nebraska Born Veterans Buried in Colorado, 1862-1949,* by Gerald E. Sherard, published by G. E. Sherard, Lakewood, CO, 1997, 10 pages, FHL book 978.8 A1 No. 125.

■ *Index to Compiled Service Records of Volunteer Union Soldiers Who Served in Organizations from the Territory of Nebraska,* microfilm of original records at the National Archives, Washington, D.C. Filmed by the National Archives, series M547, 2 rolls, FHL film #821905 (Index, A-La), and FHL film #821906 (Index, Le-Z). Nebraska entries are incorporated into the national index at the National Park Service website at: **www.itd.nps.gov/cwss/**.

■ *Compiled Service Records of Volunteer Union Soldiers Who Served in Organizations from the Territory of Nebraska,* microfilm of original records at the National Archives, Washington, D.C. Filmed by the National Archives, series M1787, 43 rolls. FHL has a pamphlet describing this series (FHL book 973 J53m no. 1787) but does not have the film.

■ *Nebraska, 1890 Special Census of Veterans,* edited by Ronald Vern Jackson, published by Accelerated Indexing Systems, North Salt Lake, UT, 1987, 351 pages.

NEVADA

In March 1861, a month before the first shots of the Civil War, Nevada Territory was established by the U.S. Congress, mainly as a means of securing Nevada's rich gold and silver deposits for the Union. Nevada Territory supplied a number of troops to Union units early in 1861. Three years later, President Lincoln saw statehood for Nevada as a means of obtaining the necessary votes for his upcoming election for a second term. In a matter of a days, a rush constitution was prepared, voted on, telegraphed to Washington, and ratified in October 1864, just days before the election day.

Online Nevada Resources

■ **Nevada State Library and Archives – Genealogical Resources. http://dmla.clan.lib.nv.us/docs/nsla/services/gene alres.htm#Biographical**.
This webpage is a portal to the various categories of records available, many with indexes online:
  ● Nevada State Library Biographical Clipping File – Biographical files on important Nevadans
  ● Russell McDonald Collection Index - Biographical Files for Legislators, Judges, Lt. Governors and

others. Compiled by Darrell L. Muckleroy. Located at the Nevada Historical Society, Reno.

- Nevada Census Online – 1860, 1870, 1880, 1900, 1910 and 1920 Nevada Census. from the Nevada State Historic Preservation Office.
- Native American Census Rolls (1885-1940) from the National Archives and Records Series M595.
- Churchill County Cemetery Database (Fallon Cemetery).
- Mineral County Death Index (includes records from Esmeralda and Nye counties).
- Nevada Appeal [Carson City] Obituary Index.
- Nevada Cemetery Transcriptions – From Access Genealogy, this is the most complete online index to Nevada cemeteries.
- Obituaries from the Las Vegas Review-Journal
- Obituaries from the Reno Gazette Journal
- California Vital Records - Search California's Death Records for 1940-1997. Offered through RootsWeb.com.
- Genealogical Resources in U.S. Federal Depository Libraries – Compiled by Kevin D. Motes, Oklahoma Department of Libraries. "This guide is intended to give those interested in genealogical research some idea of the kinds of materials available… through the Federal Depository Library System."
- National Cemetery Administration
- Social Security Death Index – RootsWeb.com
- Clark County Marriage Inquiry System
- Western States Historical Marriage Record Index
- Carson Appeal Newspaper Index – 1865-66, 1879-80, 1881 and 1885-86
- Nevada Newspaper Indexes. Some Nevada newspapers have been indexed. This is a list of those papers indexed, the dates covered, and location of the indexing.
- Nevada State Library Vertical File Index and Nevada State Library Biographical File Index – Newspaper clipping files on Nevada-related subjects.
- Humboldt County Newspapers (Rootsweb.com)
- Birth/Death/Marriage/Divorce Records in Nevada
- Naturalization Records
- Nevada County and State Agencies
- Nevada State Prison Inmate Case Files - name index, 1863 to 1972
- Yearbooks – list of school yearbooks from around Nevada. Located at the Nevada Historical Society, Reno.

■ **American Civil War – Nevada.**
www.archaeolink.com/nevada_in_the_civil_war.htm. Links to *The Civil War Period in Nevada* (an excellent essay), and **Union Regimental Index – Nevada**, giving background information about the 1st Battalion Cavalry and 1st Battalion Infantry

■ **Nevada's Historical Myths.**
www.nevadaweb.com/nevadaca/rocha-2.html. This webpage presents an essay, "Why Did Nevada Become A State?" by Guy Rocha, Nevada State Archivist. Debunking the long-held opinions of why Nevada became a state, this essay sets the record straight, and should be mandatory reading by anyone interested in Nevada's history during the Civil War era.

Published Nevada Resources

■ *An Inventory & Index to the Records of Carson County, Utah & Nevada Territories, 1855-1861,* compiled by Marion Ellison for the Carson Valley Historical Society in cooperation with the Nevada State Division of Archives & Records. Published by the Grace Dangberg Foundation, 1984, 438 pages. Includes index. Includes history of early Utah and Nevada Territories. Consists chiefly of land records. Contains probate records. FHL book 979.3 R2e.

■ *Compiled Service Records of Volunteer Union Soldiers Who Served in Organizations from the Territory and State of Nevada,* microfilm of original records at the National Archives, Washington, D.C. Organized first by unit/regiment, the compiled service records consist of a jacket-envelope for each soldier, labeled with his name, rank, and the unit in which he served. The jacket-envelope typically contains card abstracts of entries relating to the soldier as found in original muster rolls, returns, rosters, payrolls, appointment books, hospital registers, Union prison registers and rolls, parole rolls, and inspection reports; and the originals of any papers relating solely to a particular soldier. Filmed by the National Archives, series M1789, 1996, 16 rolls. FHL has entire set, beginning with FHL film #2155471 (1st Battalion, Nevada Cavalry).

■ *Index to Compiled Service Records of Volunteer Union Soldiers Who Served in Organizations from the State of Nevada, 1861-1865,* microfilm of original records at the National Archives, Washington, D.C. Filmed by the National Archives, series M0548, 1 roll, FHL film #821939. Nevada Union entries are incorporated into the national index at the National Park Service website at: **www.itd.nps.gov/cwss/**.

■ *Nevada Territory Manuscript Census, 1861-1864; and Nevada State Manuscript Census for Washoe County, 1875,* microfilm of records located at Nevada State Library and Archives, Division of Archives and Records, Carson City, Nevada. Includes partial index to 1862 census for Storey and Ormsby Counties, Nevada Territory; census report of Henry DeGroot, 1861 (summaries only); Churchill County census report, 1862 (summaries only); Douglas County, 1862; Humboldt County, Buena Vista, 1862; Humboldt County, Echo township, 1862; Humboldt County, Humboldt township, 1862; Humboldt County, Prince Royal township, 1862; Humboldt County, Santa Clara township, 1862; Humboldt County, Star township, 1862; Lander County, 1863; Lyon County, Dayton, El Dorado Canyon, Palmyra, 1862; Lyon County, Silver City, 1862; Lyon and Churchill Counties, census report, 1863 (summaries only); Ormsby County, 1862; Storey County, Flowery District, 1862; Storey County, Gold Hill, 1862; Storey County, Virginia City, 1862; Washoe County, 1862; Washoe County, 1875. Filmed by the Nevada Division of Printing and Micrographics, 1991, FHL has 1 roll, FHL film #1689341.

■ *1862 Census of Washoe County, Territory of Nevada,* microfilm of original records at the Nevada State Library, Division of Archives, Carson City, Nevada. Filmed 1983, 1 roll, FHL film #1705177.

■ **1862 State Directory.** See *First Directory of Nevada Territory: Containing the Names of Residents in the Principal Towns,* compiled by J. Wells Kelly, published by Valentine, San Francisco, 1862. FHL book 979.3 E4v 1862. See also *An Alphabetical Listing of the First Directory of Nevada Territory*, compiled by J. Wells Kelly, circa 1861-1862, for the Towns of Aurora, Carson City, Dayton, Empire, Genoa, Gold Hill, Jack's Valley, Silver City, Virginia City, Washoe, microfilm of typescript, dated 1995, 120 pages. Filmed by the Genealogical Society of Utah, 1995, 1 roll, FHL film #1598348.

■ *1862 Nevada Territorial Census,* name lists by towns, published in *Name Tracer,* a periodical of the Las Vegas Branch Library, Las Vegas, NV. For Empire City, Genoa, and Washoe, see Vol. 1, No. 1 (Jul 1997). Aurora, see Vol. 1, No. 3 (Sep 1967) and Vol. 1, No. 4 (Nov 1967); Dayton, see Vol. 1, No. 2 (Jul 1967) and Vol. 1, No. 3 (Sep 1967); Virginia City, see Vol. 2, No. 2 (Mar 1968) and Vol. 2, No. 3 (May 1968).

■ **1862-1869 Nevada Territory & State Directories,** microfilm of originals published by various publishers. Filmed by Research Publications, Inc., Woodbridge, CT, 1980-1984. First roll in this series includes *1862 First directory of Nevada Territory*; *1863 Second directory of Nevada Territory; 1864-1865, Mercantile guide and directory for Virginia City, Gold Hill, Silver City and American City; 1866 Harrington's directory of the city of Austin;* and *1868-1869, The Nevada directory,* FHL film #1377106.

■ *Lander County, Nevada 1863 Census,* compiled by J.S. Thompson. Microfilm of typescript, 62 pages (made in 1995). Contents: part 1: Every-name index giving age (when known) and town; part 2: Alphabetical listing by surname in each town. Filmed by the Genealogical Society of Utah, 1995, 1 roll, FHL film #1598348.

■ *1863-1866 Internal Revenue Assessment Lists for the Territory and State of Nevada,* microfilm of original records at the National Archives, Washington, D.C. Filmed by the National Archives, 1980, series M779, 2 rolls, FHL film #1578506 (District 1 Feb. 1863-Nov. 1865), and FHL film #1578506 (District 1, Jan. – Dec. 1866).

■ **1881 History.** See Reproduction of Thompson and West's *History of Nevada, 1881: With Illustrations and Biographical Sketches of its Prominent Men and Pioneers,* with introduction by David F. Myrick. Includes history of Nevada and biographical sketches of some of the prominent men and pioneers and a patrons directory. Original published by Thompson & West, Oakland, CA, 1881, 680 pages. Reprint published by Howell-North, Berkeley, CA, 1958. FHL book 979.3 H2t. Indexed in *Index to History of Nevada,* by Helen J. Poulton and Myron Angel, published by the University of Nevada Press, Reno, NV, 1966, 148 pages. This index can be used with the original 1881 edition published by Thompson and West, or the 1958 reprint. FHL book 979.3 B4u v. 6.

■ *Nevada Veterans, Civil War,* microfilm of cards compiled by Eleanor Slagle for the Reno Family History Center, Reno, Nevada. Cards arranged in alphabetical order by surname of Nevada veterans of Civil War, companies A-F. Filmed by the Genealogical Society of Utah, 1994, 1 roll, FHL film #1307686.

■ *1890 Nevada Census Index: Special Schedule of the Eleventh Census (1890) Enumerating Union Veterans [and Widows] of the Civil War,* edited by Ronald Vern Jackson, published by Accelerated Indexing Systems, Salt Lake City, UT, 1983, 9 pages.

NEW HAMPSHIRE

Online New Hampshire Resources

■ **New Hampshire State Archives – Genealogical and Family History Information. www.sos.nh.gov/archives/genealogy.html**. This webpage presents an outline of the NH Archives' collections from probate, deeds, military, census, town records, and more. Under the "Military Indices" category, the following items are listed

- C. E. Potter's Military History of New Hampshire, 1623 – 1861
- S. Lanzerdorf's New Hampshire Militia Officers, 1820 – 1850
- Revolutionary War Rolls (N.H. State & Provincial Papers)
- War of 1812 Soldiers Index (21st Regiment)
- A. D. Ayling's Civil War Register Index
- Civil War Pension Index
- Civil War Enlistment Cards and Papers
- Civil War Cemetery Records
- Civil War Death Rolls
- Civil War Muster Rolls, Descriptive Rolls, & Returns
- "Military Miscellaneous" V64 (Revolutionary to recent publications)

■ **New Hampshire State Library (NHSL) – Genealogy & NH History. www.nh.gov/nhsl/services/public/genealogy.html**. The NHSL has over 2,400 titles of published family histories for New Hampshire and New England. This collection is enhanced by the unique name index to early town records on microfilm (sometimes referred to as the "Sargent" Name Index). The town records, ranging in years for each town but falling roughly between the years 1640 to 1830/40, can provide birth and marriage dates, as well as listings of such items as tax inventories. Other major resources available include:

- Town reports and county histories (Index to towns and inventory online)
- NH newspapers on microfilm (Index to citations online)
- Federal census records for NH (1790-1930)
- Genealogical columns of the "Boston Transcript"
- Legislative biographies (1890 +)
- City and county directories
- Military indexes to 1900

■ **New Hampshire Historical Society – Tuck Library. www.nhhistory.org/library.html**. This webpage has links to descriptions of the Printed Collection and Special Collections (Images, Manuscripts, Maps, Broadsides, and Ephemera), and a link to the Online Catalog of the New Hampshire Historical Society Library and Museum Collections. A search for "civil war" in the catalog reveals 310 references.

■ **New Hampshire Civil War History and Genealogy Project. www.usgennet.org/usa/nh/topic/civilwar/**. This site is a place for anyone to submit information about a New Hampshire Civil War participant, with emphasis on copies of rosters, photos, diaries, letters or papers that refer to NH people who served in the Civil War. There are regimental histories, and links to related subjects.

■ **New Hampshire Heritage, 1861-1865. www.geocities.com/nh_heritage/**. This site is an ongoing project to list the service rosters of all New Hampshire units during the Civil War.

■ **Union Regiments – New Hampshire. www.civilwararchive.com/unionnh.htm**. Histories of all New Hampshire regiments of the Civil War are shown.

Published New Hampshire Resources

■ *Index to Compiled Service Records of Volunteer Union Soldiers Who Served in Organizations from the State of New Hampshire,* microfilm of original records at the National Archives, Washington, D.C. New Hampshire supplied 17 regiments to the Union Army, with over 30,000 volunteers, and some 8,000 draftees and/or substitutes. This index refers to over 46,600 individual soldier records (including multiple entries for variant name spellings, or those soldiers who served in more than one regiment). Filmed by the National Archives, series M549, 1964, 13 rolls. FHL has complete series, beginning with FHL film #882018 (surnames A – Bo). This is the same list of names now online at the National Park Service website at: **www.civilwar.nps.gov/cwss/**. At the NPS site, all of New Hampshire's military units are identified, with a name list of participants in each unit.

■ *Civil War Service Record, Card File Index, 1860-1865,* microfilm of original card file at the New Hampshire Historical Society, Concord, NH. This name list is another resource for identifying New Hampshire's Civil War soldiers from their service records, plus records of principals and substitutes not included in the official Compiled Service Records at the National Archives. Filmed by the Genealogical Society of Utah, 1975, 13 rolls, FHL film #1001781 (service record, A – Buel, James W.).

■ *Revised Register of the Soldiers and Sailors of New Hampshire in the War of the Rebellion, 1861-1866,* prepared and published by authority of the Legislature, by Augustus D. Ayling, Adjutant General. Printed by Ira C. Evans, Concord, NH, 1895, 2 vols., 1,347 pages. FHL has bound together both volumes in one, FHL book 974.2 M23nh (large Q book). Also on microfilm, FHL film #1697872.

■ *1862-1866 Internal Revenue Assessment Lists for New Hampshire.* Microfilm of original records at the National Archives, Washington, D.C. District 1 includes Belknap, Carroll, Rockingham, and Strafford counties; district 2, Hillsborough and Merrimack counties; and district 3, Cheshire, Coos, Grafton, and Sullivan counties. National Archives publication M780, 10 rolls. FHL films #1534780-1534789.

■ *Civil War Enlistment Papers, Muster In and Out Rolls, 1861-1865 and Indexes 1861-1866, New Hampshire,* microfilm of original records at the New Hampshire State Archives, Concord, NH. Filmed by the Genealogical Society of Utah, 2001, 48 rolls, beginning with FHL film #2317642 (Index).

■ *Honor Roll of New Hampshire Union Soldiers Who Died During the Civil War, With Their Original Burial Locations,* compiled by Sherman Lee Pompey, a manuscript prepared for publication as a book but never published. Includes names of soldiers, companies/regiments to which they belonged, and the places where they were buried. Manuscript microfilmed by the Genealogical Society of Utah, 1972, 1 roll, FHL film #928041.

■ *New Hampshire in the Great Rebellion: Containing Histories of the Several New Hampshire Regiments, and Biographical Notices of the Prominent Actors in the Civil War of 1861-1865,* by Major Otis F. R. Waite, published by Tracy, Chase & Co., Claremont, NH, 1870, 608 pages. FHL book 974.2 M2w.

■ *Pension Records Indexes and Pension Records by Town, 1861-1865 New Hampshire,* microfilm of original records at the New Hampshire State Archives. Filmed by the Genealogical Society of Utah, 2001, 4 rolls, beginning with FHL film #2257745 (index by names).

■ *1855 and 1865 Massachusetts State Census (New Hampshire People),* published serially in *New Hampshire Genealogical Record,* (New Hampshire Society of Genealogists, Concord, NH), beginning with Vol. 10, No. 4 (Oct 1993). This extraction and index of names is based on the place of birth data from the MA state censuses. The 1855 and 1865 MA state censuses at the FHL were microfilmed as one series (68 rolls, beginning with FHL film #953965). The contents of the 1855 state census includes names of all members of a household, age, sex, color, occupation, place of birth, and whether a person was deaf, dumb, blind, insane, idiotic, pauper, or convict. The 1865 state census adds marital status for each person, plus an indication if a male were over the age of 16 and owned enough land to be taxed, and whether the person were of legal age, or a naturalized citizen.

■ *Non-Resident Tax Lists, 1849-1874,* microfilm of original records at the New Hampshire Historical Society, Concord, NH. Filmed by the Genealogical Society of Utah, 1975, 9 rolls, with tax lists 1861-1863 on FHL film #980944; 1864-1866, FHL film #980945; and 1867-1870, FHL film #98094.

■ **1640-1900 New Hampshire Vital Records Indexes,** microfilm of original card files of the Register of Vital Statistics, Department of Health, Concord, NH, filmed by the Genealogical Society of Utah, 1974, with the following FHL film titles:
- *Index to Births, Early to 1900,* 98 rolls, beginning with FHL film #1000480 (Abair – Aldrich).
- *Index to Deaths, Early to 1900,* 60 rolls, beginning with FHL film #1001058 (Ash – Blake).
- *Bride's Index, 1640-1900,* 17 rolls, beginning with FHL film #975678 (A – Baker).

■ *Card File Index to Publishments of Marriage Intention Prior to 1900,* microfilm of original records at the New Hampshire Historical Society, Concord, NH. Cards arranged alphabetically by first letter of last name of groom. Filmed by the Genealogical Society of Utah, 1975, 1 roll, FHL film #1001439.

■ *Index to Divorces and Annulments Prior to 1938,* microfilm of original records at the New Hampshire State Archives. The records are indexed by surname. Filmed by the Genealogical Society of Utah, 1975, 8 rolls, beginning with FHL film #1001323 (Index to divorces, Abare – Browne).

■ *Register of Convicts Committed to the State Prison in Concord, New Hampshire, 1812-1883,* microfilm of original records at the New Hampshire State Archives. Includes names, ages, birthplaces, when convicted, crime, when committed, term of confinement, when discharged. Filmed by the Genealogical Society of Utah, 1975, 1 roll, FHL film #980930.

■ *New Hampshire Name Changes, 1768-1923,* compiled by Richard P. Roberts, published by Heritage Books, Bowie, MD, 1996, 333 pages, FHL book 974.2 D4r. Contains a list of name changes in the state of New Hampshire taken from state court records. The names were originally extracted as *New Hampshire Name Changes: Taken from Section Records,* compiled by Robert E. Marsh, and filmed by the Genealogical Society of Utah, 1993, on 3 rolls, FHL films #1598106-8. The microfilmed series includes an index of

individuals mentioned in the Laws of New Hampshire.

■ *Card Index to Genealogies, Published and Manuscript,* microfilm of original card file at the New Hampshire Historical Society, Concord, NH. Filmed by the Genealogical Society of Utah, 1975, 2 rolls, FHL film #1001440 (surnames A-M); and FHL film #1001441 (surnames N-Z).

■ *Index to Genealogies in New Hampshire Town Histories,* compiled by William Copeley, published by the New Hampshire Historical Society, Concord, NH, 1988, 103 pages, FHL book 974.2 D22c. Also on microfiche, FHL fiche #6010808.

■ *1890 New Hampshire Census Index: Special Schedule of the Eleventh Census (1890) Enumerating Union Veterans and of Union Veterans of the Civil War,* edited by Ronald Vern Jackson, published by Accelerated Indexing Systems, North Salt Lake, UT, 1985, 169 pages.

NEW JERSEY

Online New Jersey Resources

■ **New Jersey State Archives.** www.state.nj.us/state/darm/links/archives.html. This is the NJ State Archives Home Page, with links to the online catalog, searchable databases, and imaged collections. At the "Catalogued Holdings" page, a list of pre-established catalog searches is presented, including "Genealogical Holdings" and "Other Research Topics," both areas with numerous links to vital records, 1865 state census records, county records, and military records of the Civil War era. Online searchable databases include Supreme Court Case Files, 1704-1844; Marriage Records, 1666-1799; and Index to Marriages, 1848-1867. Noted as databases that will be available online in the near future are Civil War Payment Vouchers, 1861-1866; East Jersey Proprietors Loose Surveys, 1786-1951; and Name-Change Judgments, 1876-1947. Start at the "Catalog Holdings" page, then click on "Genealogical Holdings" for an excellent review of what types of records are available at the NJ State Archives. In addition, the archives'

"Imaged Collections" contains several groups of documents and photographs related to the Civil War period in New Jersey, including Portraits of Soldiers, Military Activities and Monuments, and Military Service Records of NJ Colored Troops.

■ **New Jersey State Library – Genealogy and Local History Collection.** www.njstatelib.org/ Collections_and_Services/Genealogy/index.php. Visit this webpage for a review of the types of resources available at the NJ State Library in Trenton, NJ. This site also provides links to Categories, Periodicals, Geography and Ethnic Groups, WWI Draft Registrations, New Jersey Locations, Family Histories, Censuses, Local Libraries around the state, State Archives, and the NJ Office of Vital Statistics. An online catalog search for "civil war" reveals 162 titles.

■ **New Jersey Historical Society – Genealogists' Guide.** www.jerseyhistory.org/genealogy.html. Go to this webpage for an excellent review of resources available at the NJ Historical Society in Newark, NJ, with categories under Cemetery Transcriptions, Census and Tax Records, City Directories, Compiled Genealogical Material, Genealogical Card Indices, Histories of Towns, Cities and Counties, Maps and Cartographic Records, Military Records, Newspapers, Vital Records, and Other Record Sources. Any keyword search in the Jerseyhistory.org search box presents a categorized results list, with a very useful breakdown of areas, databases, or titles. Search for a placename, subject, or family surname here and the results lists will include any reference to the keyword from across the entire collection. Go to any referenced item and the manuscript, document, or photograph will be identified as in a catalog search. Online database searches include the **Browse Manuscript Collections**, **Browse Church Records**, **Browse Estate Papers**, and the very large **New Jersey Historical Society Biography Index.**

■ **American Civil War – New Jersey.** www. archaeolink.com/new_jersey_in_the_civil_war.htm. This site provides a portal to websites related to New Jersey in the Civil War, including these links:

- **New Jersey in the American Civil War.** www.earthstation9.com/index.html? new_jer2.htm. A good list of resources about New Jersey and the Civil War, with an emphasis on infantry, light artillery, and militia regiments.
- **New Jersey in the Civil War.** Subtopics organized as Horrors of War, Opposing Viewpoints, Patriotic Contributions from New Jersey People; battles; Ellis' Letters; and NJ Women and the War.
- **New Jersey And The Civil War 1861-1865.** http://49njrvs.tripod.com/. A history of the era.
- **New Jersey Volunteer Regiments.** http://home. att.net/~geneology/15thNJVI/15thform.html. Regimental histories and rosters.
- **New Jersey's Civil War History Page 1860-1865.** www.newjersey1861.com/. Rosters and cemetery information. A work in progress.
- **Union Regiments – New Jersey.** www.civilwararchive.com/unionnj.htm. Organization and service history of New Jersey military units (cavalry, artillery, infantry).

Published New Jersey Resources

■ *Index to Compiled Service Records of Volunteer Union Soldiers Who Served in Organizations from the State of New Jersey,* microfilm of original records at the National Archives, Washington, D.C. Filmed by the National Archives, 1964, series M550, 26 rolls. FHL has entire set, beginning with FHL film #882031 (surnames A-Bar). This is the same list of names now online at the National Park Service, website at: www.civilwar.nps.gov/cwss/. At the NPS site, all of New Jersey's military units are identified, with a name list of participants in each unit.

■ *Record of Officers and Men of New Jersey in the Civil War, 1861-1865,* compiled by the office of William S. Stryker, Adjutant General, published 1876 by authority of the Legislature, printed by John L. Murphy, Steam Book and Job Printer, Trenton, NJ., 2 vols., FHL book 974.9 M25nr v.1-2. Also on microfilm, which includes additional notes and a full name index, 5 rolls, beginning with FHL #579866 (Index).

■ *Register of the Commissioned Officers and Privates of the New Jersey Volunteers: in the Service of the United States,* published 1863, New Jersey Legislature, Jersey City, NJ, 584 pages, FHL book 974.M2e. See also *Alphabetical Roll of New Jersey Volunteers in the Civil War,* microfilm of original records at the NJ State Archives, Trenton, NJ. Filmed by the Genealogical Society of Utah, 1969, 3 rolls, FHL films #579863 (A-H), #579864 (L-P), and #579865 (Q-W).

■ *New Jersey Civil War Records, Books 1-829,* microfilm of original typescript and manuscript at the NJ State Archives. Trenton, NJ. Indexed by names of civil war participants, and organized again by county. Filmed by the archives, 1969, 121 rolls. FHL has entire series, beginning with FHL film #579866 (Index).

■ *Clothing Books, New Jersey Infantry, 1861-1865,* microfilm of original records at the NJ State Archives, Trenton, NJ. The clothing books record the disbursement of uniforms and accessories to NJ soldiers. They are organized by regiment, company, and the name of the soldier. Filmed by the Genealogical Society of Utah, 1973, 36 rolls, beginning with FHL film #944719 (4th Regiment, companies A – C). See also, *Clothing Books, New Jersey Cavalry, 1861-1865,* 8 rolls, beginning with FHL film #944711 (1st Regiment, Company A - D).

■ *Card Index to Civil War Soldiers' Graves,* microfilm of original card file at the New Jersey Historical Society, Newark, NJ. This index to Civil War soldiers' graves provides access to New Jersey regiment volunteers who are buried in the state. Filmed by the Genealogical Society of Utah, 2000, 2 rolls, FHL film #2137754 (Aaronson, Benjamin – Parkhurst, Andrew L.), and FHL film #2137755 (Parkhurst, John S. – Zoble, Henry). See also *New Jersey Civil War Burial Records, 1800s-1900s,* FHL film #2195517 (different title, but may be the same set of records).

■ *Internal Revenue Assessment Lists for New York and New Jersey, 1862-1865,* microfilm of original records at the National Archives, Washington, D.C. The Federal Bureau of Internal Revenue established districts within each state, comprised of one or more counties. The microfilm is organized by district, with the counties listed at the beginning of each roll. Filmed by the National Archives, series M603, 1965, 218 rolls. New Jersey districts begin with FHL film #1534790.

■ *1865 New Jersey State Census,* microfilm of original records of the NJ Board of Assessors, now at the NJ State Archives. The contents of this state census includes a name of each household member, age, sex, race, and whether native or foreign born, or at school. Of New Jersey's 21 counties, bound volumes of original census returns are extant for 15 counties. Completely missing counties: Cape May, Mercer, Morris, Ocean, Somerset, and Warren. Partial name lists exist for Essex (part of Newark only), and Sussex (Belleville and Caldwell only). Filmed by the NJ archives in 1962. Although the FHL in Salt Lake City has a set of the film, there are differences comparing the reel contents with those listed at the NJ archives website. It appears that the NJ archives added certain partial county name lists, e.g., cities and areas in Essex County, after the initial filming, and the later filming has never been acquired by the FHL. To access the film from the NJ State Archives, visit their website shown above. For the FHL set, the 1855 and 1865 state censuses were filmed together as one 8-roll series, 1865 rolls starting with FHL film #802947. Another series for 1865 in 4 rolls begins with FHL film #865495. Included on the first roll of this latter series are name lists for Hudson County, where the FHL catalog notes, "the census for Hudson County is for 1860, not 1865."

■ *New Jersey Prerogative Court Registers, 1776-1877,* microfilm of original records at the NJ State Archives. Prerogative (probate) courts were responsible for the probates and administrations of property of deceased persons. A Register acts as an index to the probate papers, and includes at least the name of the deceased property owner, but may also mention administrators, heirs, witnesses, etc. The records are organized in chronological order, beginning with 1776. Filmed by the Genealogical Society of Utah, 1978, 19 rolls, records from the Civil War era beginning with FHL film #1028321.

■ *Civil War Pension Claims, New Jersey Soldiers (Alphabetical),* microfilm of original records at the NJ State Archives. Filmed by the Genealogical Society of Utah, 1969, 1 roll, FHL film #579866.

■ *Records of Births, Marriages, and Deaths of New Jersey, 1848-1900,* microfilm of original records from all New Jersey counties at the NJ State Archives, Trenton, NJ. Filmed by the

Genealogical Society of Utah, 1969, 290 rolls, beginning with FHL film #493686 (Index, Births, A – Bo, 1848-1878). See also *New Jersey W.P.A. Birth and Death Records, Early to 1900,* microfilm of a card index at the NJ State Archives. Filmed by the Genealogical Society of Utah, 1969, 12 rolls, beginning with FHL film #820014 (Births, Aa – Eu).

■ *Records of Admission to Soldier's Children Home, Trenton, NJ, Mar. 23, 1865 – Apr. 6, 1876,* microfilm of original records at the NJ State Archives, Trenton, NJ. Filmed by the Genealogical Society of Utah, 1969, 1 roll, FHL film #579871.

■ **1890 New Jersey Census Index: Special Schedule of the Eleventh Census (1890) Enumerating Union Veterans of the Civil War,** FHL title, *New Jersey, 1890,* edited by Ronald Vern Jackson, published by Accelerated Indexing Systems, Salt Lake City, UT, 1990, 397 pages.

NEW MEXICO TERRITORY

Early in 1861, Confederate forces from Texas invaded New Mexico Territory, taking military control of the Rio Grande valley from El Paso to Santa Fe. Soon after, a Territory of Arizona was established and recognized by the Confederate States of America. This short-lived Confederate territory was defined as the southern half of pre-Civil War New Mexico Territory, which at the time stretched from Texas to California, included all of present Arizona. By July 1862, Union forces had recaptured the area, which was returned to the jurisdiction of New Mexico Territory. New Mexico supplied troops to the Union army, before and after the Confederate occupation. The Confederate Territory of Arizona supplied Confederate troops, and the U.S. Arizona Territory, created in February 1863 supplied Union Troops.

Online New Mexico Resources

■ **New Mexico State Records Center and Archives (NMSRCA). www.nmcpr.state.nm.us/.** The NM State Archives in Santa Fe includes original records from the Spanish Period (1621-1821), Mexican Period (1821-1846), Territorial Period (1846-1912), and Statehood Period (1912-). There has been extensive microfilming of New Mexico's public records, but since the NM State Archives does not participate in the national inter-library loan system, there is still a need to identify original records available at this facility. Some of the microfilm is available at libraries outside of the archives, particularly, the New Mexico State Library in Santa Fe, the Special Collections Library in Albuquerque, or the FHL in Salt Lake City. At the NMSRCA website, a very thorough online catalog is the preferred method to access the titles and descriptions of materials within the various collections. The catalog contains descriptive information and some digital facsimiles for archival materials, plus many photographic images. For example, a catalog search for "civil war" revealed over 40 items, including such original documents as the NM Adjutant General's reports, muster rolls, claims, certificates for payments for military service, and several more references to manuscripts, maps, correspondence, and other collections on the subject of the civil war in New Mexico. After viewing a hit list of titles/descriptions, a selected item will have an "online finding aid" option, where further information about the history and contents of the record series is well presented.

■ **Special Collections Library, Albuquerque-Bernalillo County Library System. www.cabq. gov/library/specol.html.** Located in Albuquerque, this separate facility is home to the largest genealogical collection in the state. The Special Collections Library has a comprehensive collection on New Mexico genealogy, including the Spanish Archives of New Mexico, the Mexican Archives of New Mexico, Land Grant Records, and the Territorial Archives on microfilm. DAR Lineage books, federal census records, Civil War pension records for New Mexico, and county records for the Territorial period are also available. All publications of the New Mexico Genealogical Society are here, as are the works of Fray Angelico Chavez. The Dreesen files provide information on the original settlers of the Rio Abajo prior to 1900. There are newspapers from the Territorial period, and Albuquerque city directories dating back to the 1880s. A collection of 16th century Spanish passenger lists, Pasajeros a las Indias, is available on microfilm. The library also has a complete collection of the Archives of the Archdiocese of Santa Fe. These records extend as far back as 1678 and as recent as 1956 for some areas. Local researchers have extracted many of these records and published them in book format. The beautifully organized online catalog to the county-wide library holdings is a real treasure. A search for "civil war in New Mexico" brought up 31 published items, many with photos of the book covers.

■ **The Civil War in New Mexico, 1861-1862.** **www.nmculturenet.org/heritage/civil_war/.** This site is sponsored by the Museum of New Mexico in Santa Fe. The Home Page briefly describes the civil war history for New Mexico, and provides links to Solders & Weapons, Maps & Documents, Photos & Sketches, Artifacts & Remains, Essays & Letters, Links, and a Timeline. Use this webpage to find links to other websites specific to the soldiers, battles, and miscellany related to the civil war in New Mexico and elsewhere.

Published New Mexico Resources

■ *Compiled Service Records of Volunteer Union Soldiers Who Served in Organizations from the Territory of New Mexico,* microfilm of original records at the National Archives, Washington, D.C. The compiled service records consist of a jacket-envelope for each soldier, labeled with his name, his rank, and the unit in which he served and typically containing card abstracts of entries relating to the soldier as found in original muster rolls, returns, hospital rolls, descriptive books, and lists of deserters; and the originals of any papers relating solely to the particular soldiers. There are cross-references for soldiers' names that appeared in the records under more than one spelling. The records are arranged according to an organizational breakdown ending with the regiment or the independent battalion or company. Under each unit the service records are arranged alphabetically by soldiers' surnames. Preceding the jacket-envelopes for the individual soldiers in most of the organizational units are envelopes containing record-of-events cards giving the stations, movements, or activities of the unit or a part of it, and sometimes information relating to its organization or composition. In addition, there sometimes are envelopes containing general

notation cards giving information relating to the entire organizational unit that was not stamped on or filed with the card abstracts. Filmed by the National Archives, series M427, 1963, 42 rolls. FHL has entire series, beginning with FHL film #471538 (1st Cavalry, surnames A-Aq).

■ *Index to Compiled Service Records of Volunteer Union Soldiers Who Serviced in Organizations from the Territory of New Mexico,* microfilm of original records at the National Archives, Washington, D.C. Filmed by the National Archives, series M242, 1958, 4 rolls. FHL has series, beginning with FHL film #821883 (surnames A-D). Nearly 13,000 New Mexico volunteers are identified here. This is the same list of names now online at the National Park Service website at: **www.civilwar.nps.gov/cwss/.**

■ *Compiled Service Records of Confederate Soldiers Who Served in Organizations from the [Confederate] Territory of Arizona,* microfilm of original records at the National Archives, Washington, D.C. Filmed by the archives, 1961, series M318, 1 roll, FHL film #536241.

■ *The Confederate Army of New Mexico,* by Martin Hardwick Hall, with the assistance of Sam Long, published by Presidial Press, Austin, TX, 1978, 422 pages. Contains New Mexico and Texas Civil War military records, U.S. military records, and a history of the Civil War in New Mexico. FHL book 978.9 M2ha.

■ *When the Texans Came: Missing Records from the Civil War in the Southwest, 1861-1862,* by John P. Wilson, published by University of New Mexico Press, Albuquerque, NM, 2001, 364 pages. Includes index. FHL book 978.M2w.

■ *Internal Revenue Assessment Lists for the Territory of New Mexico, 1862-1874,* microfilm of original records at the National Archives, Washington, D.C. The Federal Bureau of Internal Revenue established districts within each state, comprised of one or more counties. The microfilm is organized by district, with the counties listed at the beginning of each roll. New Mexico's name lists filmed by the National Archives, series M782, 1988, 1 roll, FHL film #1578508.

■ *1844-1933 Parish Registers, Diocese of Santa Fe, New Mexico,* microfilm of original Catholic church records now at the New Mexico State Records Center and Archives, Santa Fe, NM. Includes parish registers from Socorro-San Miguel, Santa Cruz, San Lldefonso, San Jose de Chama, St. Gertrudis, Ocate, Guadalupita, Mora, Mauelitas, Alamos, Joya Larga, Las Vegas, San Geronimo, San Miguel, and others. Records may be general indexes, baptisms, burials, church censuses, marriages, or confirmations. Filmed by the Archdiocese of Santa Fe, 1992, 7 rolls, beginning with FHL film #1930433.

■ *Official Army Register of the Volunteer Force of the United States for the Years, 1861, '62, '63, '64, '65,* part of the series, *Civil War Unit Histories. Part 4, The Union-Midwest and West: WT 084,* microfiche of original published by U.S. Printing Office, Washington, D.C., 1867, 15 pages (Part VIII New Mexico only). FHL fiche #6118461. **Note:** various publications of the New Mexico Adjutant General (in their original form), including rosters, pay records, and miscellaneous papers related to the Civil War era in New Mexico, are located at the New Mexico State Records Center and Archives in Santa Fe.

■ *New Mexico's Buffalo Soldiers, 1866-1900,* by Monroe Lee Billington, published by University Press of Colorado, 1991, 258 pages. Buffalo soldiers were black soldiers who served in the U.S. Army. Approximately 4,000 served in New Mexico Territory. FHL book 978.9 F2b.

■ *Pre-1895 Newspapers, Index of Various Newspaper Microfilm Holdings at the Albuquerque Special Collections Library, Albuquerque, New Mexico: An Index of the Following Newspapers on Microfilm: The Acorn, The Albuquerque Advance, The Albuquerque Weekly Review, The Evening Review, The Gallup Gleaner, The New Mexico press, The Rio Abajo Weekly press,* compiled by Howard W. Henry, published by Albuquerque Genealogical Society, 2004, 42 pages. Arranged in alphabetical order by surname. FHL book 978.9 B32h.

■ *Soldiers and Settlers: Military Supply in the Southwest, 1861-1885,* by Darlis A. Miller, published by University of New Mexico Press, Albuquerque, NM, 1989, 506 pages. Includes index. From preface: "This book... focuses upon the economic interaction between the military and civilians. Its intent is to document the intricacies of military contracting and to assess the army's economic impact on civilian society. The focus therefore is as much on civilians as it is on military personnel. Since the Army was the single largest purchasing and employment agency in the Southwest, it benefited a wide assortment of civilians, including poorer residents who on occasion sold burro loads of hay and wood to the Army. By carefully sifting through military documents, it has been possible to recover important history of a segment of society usually neglected in regional studies. In addition, the study underscores the prominence of the frontier army in western society. In the years from the Civil War to the arrival of railroads in the 1880s, the United States Army was the mainstay of the economy of the Southwest. The military paid tens of millions of dollars to local farmers and ranchers for most of the supplies needed to maintain troops and garrisons. The money encouraged expansion of agriculture and commerce, which in turn transformed frontier regions in Arizona, New Mexico, southern Colorado, and west Texas into homesteads and communities. The Southwest developed a mixed economy in an era when laissez-faire capitalism dominated. The army's demand for bread and beef, for instance, created the flour-milling and cattle industries of the Southwest. Moreover, the frontier army was the single largest employer of civilians and relied on them for much of the skilled labor needed in everything from building forts to shoeing horses." See FHL book 973 H2miL.

■ *New Mexico 1890 Special Census of Veterans,* edited by Ronald Vern Jackson, published by Accelerated Indexing Systems, North Salt Lake, UT, 1986, 34 pages, FHL book 978.9 X22jv.

■ *1890 New Mexico Tax Assessments: A Territorial Census Substitute,* compiled by Karen Stein Daniel, published by New Mexico

Genealogical Society, Albuquerque, NM, 2003, 204 pages, includes index. Name lists gathered from all New Mexico counties around the 1890 time period. A comparison of names of veterans in the *1890 Special Census* index may add details about a particular New Mexico Civil War veteran. See FHL book 978.9 R4d.

NEW YORK

Online New York Resources

■ **New York State Archives/New York State Library – Research Room**. **www.archives. nysed.gov/a/research/res_services_nysa.shtml**. This is an information webpage for **Research Services at the New York State Archives**. The Research Room is located within the Cultural Education Center, Empire State Plaza, Albany, New York, and is shared with the NY State Library's Manuscripts and Special Collections Unit, providing a one-stop access point to New York's historical documents located at either the state archives or state library. At this webpage there are links to published guides by topic, lists of archives publications, and the online catalog – the Excelsior system.

Go to the **Topics** list to review the types of records available at the NY State Archives as well as Statewide resources. Topics include Digital Collections, Genealogy, Local History, Military, People, Groups & Cultures and much more. Subtopics under "Genealogy" include Introduction, Access to Records in the State Archives, Vital Records Indexes, Census Records, Indian Records, Real Property Transfer Records, Real Property Tax Records, Court Records, Naturalization and Related Records, Marriage Records, Prison and Reformatory Records, Poorhouse Censuses, Cartographic Records, Local Records on Microfilm, and Bibliography.

Go to **Excelsior** to search the online catalog. Excelsior combines and identifies resources at the NY State Archives, NY State Library, and archival facilities across the state. For anyone interested in New York genealogy, an Excelsior catalog search has become the most important tool for locating the name of any person mentioned in historic records of New York. Excelsior includes an Historical

Document Inventory of archival collections across the state, providing in one place the ability to locate obscure genealogical references in city and county libraries, historical society collections, county and town historian archives, county and town museums, as well as the state library and state archives.

As the state with the largest population, and the state that supplied the largest number of regiments and troops during the Civil War, there were more records of the Civil War era generated by New York than any other state. Accordingly, there are more Civil War era resources identified in Excelsior than any other state. You can specify the facilities you want to search in Excelsior, including All, Historic Document Inventory, Manuscripts and Special Collections, New York State Archives, or New York State Library. A search for the keywords "civil war" in Excelsior (state archives only) reveals 175 original document series. But within the Historical Document Inventory, there are over 1,100 items. Using the same keywords for all facilities, the hit list includes over 13,000 books, articles, and reference materials containing the words, "civil war," with nearly 11,000 items at the state library alone.

■ **New York State Archives – The Digital Collections**. **www.archives.nysed.gov/d/**. The Digital Collections provide a gateway to a variety of primary source materials held by the State Archives, State Library, and State Museum. Through this collection, you can access photographs, textual materials, artifacts, government documents, manuscripts, and other materials. In addition, some of these resources have been developed as part of special projects or initiatives, thereby bringing together the resources around a topical theme. These collections include the Conservation Department Records, Environmental History Collection, Factory Investigating Committee, Fairchild Aerial Surveys, Native American Collection, Harlem Hellfighters Collection, New York Chamber of Commerce Portraits, and the New York Lantern Slides Collection. There are over 500,000 photographic images alone in this collection. From this webpage, go to Search All Images, or Browse by Collection to search for a keyword, name, place, or subject. A search for "civil war" will reveal many photographs, personal letters, and memorabilia. For an example of a search for a name, a search for

"William Smith" brought up four images of Muster Roll Abstracts, with very good photographic resolution of the original printed forms filled-in by hand.

■ **New York State Archives – Civil War Soldiers Database.** **http://iarchives.nysed.gov/ CivilWarWeb/search.jsp.** This online database is an index to the Civil War Service Records for all New York soldiers, sailors, and marines. At this webpage, there is a search box for finding a person by first name, last name, regiment, or name and regiment. For example, a search for William Smith brought up 692 matching records. Click on the **Click to Order** box to see more details, number of entries, microfilm roll number, and details on how to order a copy of the original service record document.

■ **The New-York Historical Society – Civil War Treasures.** **www.archives.nysed.gov/a/research/ res_topics_mi_civilwar_dbintro.shtml.** This website is part of the American Memory (digital photograph collection) sponsored by the Library of Congress. The images in this digital collection are drawn from the New-York Historical Society's archival collections that document the Civil War. They include recruiting posters for New York City regiments of volunteers; stereographic views documenting the mustering of soldiers and of popular support for the Union in New York City; photography showing the war's impact, both in the North and the South; and drawings and writings by ordinary soldiers on both sides. Search the database by keyword, or browse by subjects, names, or within specific archival collections.

■ **New York State and the Civil War.** **http://library.morrisville.edu/local_history/sites/.** This site is a portal to many Internet resources relating to New York's Civil War soldiers, regiments, history, and miscellany, including links to these websites:
- New York State G.A.R. Posts
- Regional Resources in N.Y.S.
- Civil War Soldiers in Madison County
- Miscellaneous New Yorkers in the Civil War
- Miscellaneous New York Sites
- Biographical Web Pages - The New York Connection
- New York Civil War Regiments Online
- NY's Civil War Flags

- New York State's Civil War U.S. Colored Troops
- New York City Harbor Defenses
- Civil War Prison Camps & Prisoners
- Civil War Resources – Gateways on the WWW
- Medal of Honor Winners from New York State
- Civil War Round Tables in New York State
- Index of N.Y. Soldiers' Images
- Military Disasters
- Civil War Monuments in New York State
- New York at Antietam
- New York at Gettysburg – author R.L. Murray's site
- New York at Gettysburg
- The Civil War in Other States
- The New York Connection, a work in progress

Published New York Resources

■ *The Union Preserved: A Guide to the Civil War Records in the New York State Archives,* edited by Harold Holzer; compiled by Daniel Lorello; introduction by Harold Holzer & Hans L. Trefousse; foreword by James M. McPherson; published by the New York State Archives Partnership Trust and Fordham University Press, New York, NY, 1999, 172 pages. Includes index. Includes collection titles and a description of the records within the collection. See FHL book 974.7 J53h.

■ *Reports of the Adjutant General, 1895-1906,* Argus, State Printer, Albany, NY, 43 vols., Available in individual volumes at NYSL, NYPL, et al. Filmed by University Publications of America, Bethesda, MD. FHL has several volumes under call no. 974.7 M2n.

■ *New York in the War of the Rebellion, 1861 to 1865,* compiled by Frederick Phisterer (Adjutant General), published by J. B. Lyon Co., State Printer, Albany, NY, 1912, 6 vols. Filmed as part of the series *Civil War Unit Histories. Part 3, The Union-Mid-Atlantic,* filmed by University Publications of America, Bethesda, MD, 1992, 64 microfiche, beginning with FHL fiche #6083559.

■ *New York Soldiers in the Civil War: A Roster of Military Officers and Soldiers Who Served in New York Regiments in the Civil War as Listed in the Annual Reports of the Adjutant General of the State of New York,* by Richard A. Wilt, published by Heritage Books, Bowie, MD, 1999, 2 vols. Lists name and unit of service, vol. 1: A-K; vol. 2: L-Z. See FHL book 974.7 M2wil.

■ *Index to Compiled Service Records of Volunteer Union Soldiers Who Served in Organizations from the State of New York,* microfilm of original records in the National Archives, Washington, D.C., series M0551, 157 rolls. FHL film begins with #882057 (surnames A – Alc). This is the same list of names now online at the National Park Service website at: **www.civilwar.nps.gov/cwss/**.

■ *New York State Censuses & Substitutes: An Annotated Bibliography of State Censuses, Census Substitutes, and Selected Name Lists in Print, on Microform, or Online; with County Boundary Maps, 1682-1915; and State Census Examples and Extraction Forms, 1825-1925,* by William Dollarhide, originally published by Heritage Creations, Bountiful, UT, 2005, 250 pages. Reprinted with updates by Genealogical Publishing Co., Inc., Baltimore, MD, 2006, 2007. Most of the originals of NY state censuses taken from 1825-1905 are still in the hands of the county wherein the census was taken. The original censuses may be at a county courthouse, county historian's office, museum, or a local library. Originally, the state census office received an original copy, while the county retained a duplicate original copy. A fire in 1911 destroyed the state's duplicate originals located at the NY state library, and the only sets remaining are the county copies for 1825-1905. (State duplicate originals for 1915-1925 are at the NY state archives in Albany). Onsite microfilming of the surviving county census records was done by the Genealogical Society of Utah, which began in the early 1950s, and was completed in the early 1970s. This book provides a comprehensive guide to the location of the state censuses of New York for each of its 62 counties, including the original copies, microfilm versions, published versions (in both books and periodicals), and online indexes. County-by-county bibliographic references specific to the Civil War era are extensive. See FHL book 974.7 X23d.

■ *1865 New York State Census.* Of importance to locating ancestors during the Civil War era, the *1865 New York State Census* is a powerful resource. Original 1865 NY census schedules exist for 52 of the 62 New York counties. Missing/lost schedules: Clinton, Franklin, Genesee, Hamilton, New York, Putnam, Queens, Seneca, Westchester, and Wyoming counties. In addition to the 1865 population schedules, there were several pages of data related to New York's recent Civil War soldiers and sailors. The 1865 had eight tables spread over twelve pages, with a total of 259 columns, the most comprehensive census ever taken in the United States. 1865 contents: Dwelling numbered in order of visitation; material of which dwelling is built; value; family numbered in order of visitation; every name (including that of anyone absent in army or navy); age, sex, and color (white, black or mulatto); relation to head of family; place of birth (county of New York State, other state, or foreign country); parent of how many children; number of times married; whether now married, widowed or single; profession, trade or occupation; usual place of employment; native and naturalized voters; aliens; colored not taxed; owners of land; over 21 who cannot read and write; deaf and dumb, blind, insane or idiotic; servicemen (those now or formerly in the army or navy of the United States), plus tables for marriages and deaths within the previous year; civil war statistics (soldiers name, regiment, company, status, health, death, and more); detailed industry and manufacturing statistics, and comprehensive agricultural statistics. Locate the 1865 NY census schedules on microfilm using the FHL catalog. Use the Place search for New York, then "View Related Places" to search within the countywide topic lists. For example, search Albany County, New York, to find the title, "New York, Albany - Census – 1865." The 4 rolls of FHL film for Albany begin with FHL film #521927.

■ *Internal Revenue Assessment Lists for New York and New Jersey, 1862-1865,* microfilm of original records at the National Archives, Washington, D.C. The Federal Bureau of Internal Revenue established districts within each state, comprised of one or more counties. The microfilm is organized by district, with the counties listed at the beginning of each roll. Filmed by the National Archives, series M603, 1965, 218 rolls. New York districts begin with FHL film #1534827.

■ *The New York State Biographical, Genealogical, and Portrait Index,* a private card index to over 750,000 names from more than 6,000 histories, biographical compendia, periodicals, atlases, and other sources, compiled by Gunther Pohl, former head, Local History and Genealogy, New York Public Library, New York City. There are numerous state, regional, and county histories with biographical information, but there is no comprehensive index to these other than Pohl's list. Gunther Pohl will check the index for a fee. Address: 134 Lowry Lane, Wilmore, KY 40390. In the initial letter enclose particulars about the ancestor, and send a self-addressed stamped envelope.

■ *Town Clerks' Registers of Men Who Served in the Civil War, ca. 1865-1867,* microfilm of original records at the New York State Archives, Albany, New York. Since microfilming, the State Archives has re-titled this series as *Town and City Registers...* because they contain at least partial data on soldiers and sailors in a few of New York's cities (Albany, Buffalo, Oswego, and Syracuse). Records consist of bound registers containing printed questionnaires, handwritten by town clerks throughout New York State of all soldiers and officers representing the town quotas of the troops furnished to the United States during the Civil War. Registers are arranged alphabetically by name of county, then alphabetically by name of town. Includes index at beginning of each volume. Questionnaire includes individual's full name, residence, date and place of birth, present rank, regiment and company, date of enlistment, date of muster and rank, length of enlistment, place of enlistment, race, amount of bounty paid by town or county if disbursed by supervisor, marital status, previous occupation, parents' names, dates of promotions, resignations, discharges, and death. Although some of the questionnaires were not answered fully, this series of registers is far more revealing than the federal compiled service records kept by the National Archives. Filmed by the State Archives, 1991. FHL has 37 rolls, beginning with FHL film #1993401 (Albany – Allegany Co.).

■ *Membership Records and Rosters, ca. 1882-1986,* microfilm of records compiled by various authors and editors, collected by Ernest L. Snider for the Sons of Union Veterans. Records include membership applications and rosters for society rolls from various New York county chapters of the Sons of Union Veterans of the Civil War; the Grand Army of the Republic; and the Daughters of Union Veterans of the Civil War. Filmed by the Genealogical Society of Utah, 1987, 2 rolls, FHL #1421789 & 1421790.

■ *1890 New York Census Index of Civil War Veterans or Their Widows,* compiled by Bryan Lee Dilts, published by Index Publishing, Salt Lake City, 1984, 451 pages.

NORTH CAROLINA

Online North Carolina Resources

■ **North Carolina State Archives – MARS Catalog Search.** Start at Home Page: **www.ah.dcr. state.nc.us/Archives/**. Go to Links – MARS Catalog. One of America's great archives, the NC State Archives in Raleigh holds over 50,000 linear feet of original materials containing millions of individual items. Collections from the Civil War era are extensive, as are county records transferred to the archives, vital records, and colonial and state records dating to the early 1600s. Although the archives contains by far the most extensive assembly of manuscript records and North Caroliniana, a researcher must visit the archives in person to view any records included in the huge collection – the NC State Archives has virtually no digitized databases available via the Internet. But, one online service that is very useful is the **Manuscript and Archives Reference System** (MARS), the descriptive catalog of their holdings. The categories are well organized for locating certain types of records, for example, the category, "Civil War Collection," includes the following subheadings:

- Bounty Payrolls
- Claims for Bounty Pay and Allowance Due Deceased Officers and Soldiers of North Carolina
- Disabled Veterans' Claims and Correspondence Pertaining to Artificial Limb Companies
- Miscellaneous Records
- Paymaster Department
- Petitions for Pardon
- Quartermaster Department
- Regimental and Unit Records
- Subsistence and Ordnance Departments

■ **North Carolina State Library – Online Library Catalog.** Genealogical Research Page: **http://statelibrary.dcr.state.nc.us/iss/gr/ genealog.htm**. At this page, go to the link for the State Library Catalog. The State Library of North Carolina in Raleigh is located in the same building as the NC State Archives, and together, these facilities represent the largest collection of published and manuscript materials for all periods of North Carolina's history. A program to include digitized documents at the state library's website is just getting organized, so the main online service at this state facility is the very fine **State Library Catalog.** Searching the catalog allows many different routines, including those within subject categories such as "genealogy." As an example, a search for "Winslow Family" brought up 8,837 entries, with results included from any reference to the keywords from the title, author, subject listing, plus any descriptive wording attached to a particular title. A search can also be specific to a title, for example, a search for any title containing the words "civil war," revealed 1,306 entries.

■ **The North Carolina Civil War Home Page. http://members.aol.com/jweaver303/nc/nccwhp. htm.**
Categories organized as follows:
The North Carolina Civil War Home Page Message Board - General Resources
- Statistical Abstract from the 1860 North Carolina Census
- Results of the 1856 and 1860 North Carolina Gubernatorial Election - By County
- Results of the 1860 Presidential Election in North Carolina - By County
- Results of the 1862 and 1864 North Carolina Gubernatorial Election - By County
- The 1861 Secession Convention Vote - By County
- Delegates to the 1861 North Carolina Secession Convention - By County
- North Carolina Civil War Military Conscription Pool - By County
- Proceedings of the North Carolina Secession Convention
- North Carolina Ordinances 1861-1862
  - The Civil War in North Carolina

Confederate Resources
- Information by Unit
- Information by County or City
- Engagements and Significant Sites
- Biographies of North Carolina Military and Civilian Personalities
- Civil War Naval Forces Index from Ken Jones.
- Civil War Genealogy FAQ

Union Unit Resources
- Links to other useful Civil War sites
- Links to Similar Collections for Other States
  - The Virginia Civil War Home Page
  - The Tennessee Civil War Home Page
  - Ashe and Alleghany County, North Carolina in the Civil War
  - Kentucky State Guard
  - New River Notes

Medical Items
- Virginia Confederate Hospitals
- Civil War Medical Terminology
- Glossary of Medical Terms (Modern usage)

Occupational Terminology

Descendant Organizations
- Sons of Confederate Veterans
- North Carolina Division Sons of Confederate Veterans
- United Daughters of the Confederacy
- North Carolina Division UDC
- Order of Southern Gray
- Children of the Confederacy
- North Carolina Civil War Genealogy

Booksellers
- Looking for out of print books, try Bibliofind or Alibris

■ **The Civil War in North Carolina – Civil War Soldiers Index. www.researchonline.net/nccw/mastindx.htm**. The index appears to be complete for the nearly 200,000 soldiers supplied by North Carolina to Civil War regiments. Find a name from the main alpha list to see the soldier's name, regiment, and company. Click on a name to see a description of the regiment, history, battles, number killed/wounded, etc., and a link to any website dedicated to a particular regiment. Compare this name list with those found at the National Park Service website at: **www.civilwar.nps.gov/cwss/**. Confederate unit histories are not complete at the NPS website, so this North Carolina site provides that service very nicely.

Published North Carolina Resources

■ *Roster of North Carolina Troops in the War Between the States,* prepared by John W. Moore by order of the NC Legislature in 1881, published by Broughton & Co., Raleigh, NC, 1882, 4 vols. Original printed volumes at NC State Library, NC State Archives, and larger U.S. libraries. Filmed by the Genealogical Society of Utah, 1941, 4 rolls (1 vol. per roll), FHL film #18075-18078. This is the official roster of all Confederate regiments and units formed in North Carolina. Indexed in *Roster (Index) of North Carolina Troops in the War Between the States*, compiled by the WPA Historical Records Survey, original record filmed by the North Carolina State Archives, 1958, 15 rolls, in alphabetical order for the soldier names. FHL film organized as follows:

- Aaron – Blalock, L. C., FHL film #194214.
- Blalock, M. – Byrd, Lemuel, FHL film #194215.
- Byrd, L. – Creaman, J., FHL film #194216.
- Creaman, J. – Elroy G., FHL film #194217.
- Elrod, W. – Granger, FHL film #194218.
- Grant – Hicks, A., FHL film #194219.
- Hicks, A. – Johnston, J. A., FHL film #194220.
- Johnston, W. C. – Lloyd, W. J., FHL film #194221.
- Lloyd, W. R. – Messor, E., FHL film #194222.
- Metcalf – Painter, E. B., FHL film #194223.
- Painter, E. M. – Reece, Larkin, FHL film #194224.
- Reece, Leonard – Settle, H. C., FHL film #194225.
- Settle, R. J. – Stuman, FHL film #194226.
- Stumper – Waters, James R., FHL film #194227.
- Waters, Jesse – Zollicoffer, FHL film #194228.

■ *North Carolina Troops, 1861-1865: A Roster,* compiled by the North Carolina Department of Archives of History, edited by Louis H. Manarin, published by Broadfoot Pub. Co., 1966, 16 vols., FHL book 975.6 M2nc and 15 supplement volumes. See also *North Carolina Confederate Soldiers, 1861-1865,* edited by Janet B. Hewett; arranged by Joyce Lawrence, published by Broadfoot Pub., 1999, 3 vols. From intro: "These are names of North Carolina Confederate soldiers that are listed in the 16-volume Broadfoot Publishing Company set, *The Roster of Confederate Soldiers, 1861-1865.* The name roster lists the soldiers alphabetically by name. The unit roster lists the soldiers sequentially by units in the order of cavalry, artillery, and infantry and miscellaneous. These rosters may be used as an index for accessing individual compiled service records." Contents: vol. 1: Name roster: A-O; vol. 2: Name roster P-Z, unit roster, Cav., 6th Sr. Res.; vol. 3: Unit roster, 7th. Inf.-Misc., FHL book 975.6M2nccv.1-3.

■ *Compiled Service Records of Confederate Soldiers Who Served in Organizations from the State of North Carolina,* microfilm of original records at the National Archives, Washington, D.C. The compiled service records consist of a jacket-envelope for each soldier, labeled with his name, his rank, and the unit in which he served. The jacket-envelope typically contains the card abstracts of entries relating to the soldier as found in original muster rolls, returns, rosters, payrolls, appointment books, hospital registers, Union prison registers and rolls, parole rolls, and inspection reports; and the originals of any papers relating solely to the particular soldier. There are cross-reference cards and jacket-envelopes for soldiers' names that appear in the records under more than one spelling... Preceding the jacket-envelope for the individual soldiers in each organizational unit there are empty envelopes on which are listed the officers of that unit. Following these are jacket-envelopes containing (1) caption cards for muster-in and muster-out rolls showing the exact caption of the rolls that were copied and the certificate of the mustering officer verifying the accuracy of the rolls; and (2) record-of-events cards, indicating the activities in which any portion of the unit had been engaged. Filmed by the National Archives, series M270, 580 rolls. FHL has complete set, beginning with FHL film #821768. See also *Confederate Soldiers Service Records,* a register compiled by Beth B. Workman for the Family History Library, 1969, filmed on 1 roll, FHL film #599499. Another filming, FHL film #908646.

■ *Index to Compiled Service Records of Confederate Soldiers Who Served in Organizations from the State of North Carolina,* microfilm of original records at the National Archives, Washington, D.C. North Carolina supplied over 197,000 soldiers to Confederate units during the Civil War. This index is a list of the names as prepared on the General Index Cards. Filmed by the National Archives, series M2770, 43 rolls. FHL has complete set, beginning with FHL film #821768 (surnames A – At). This is the same list of names now online at the National Park Service website at: **www.civilwar.nps.gov/cwss/**.

■ *Compiled Service Records of Volunteer Union Soldiers Who Served in Organizations from the State of North Carolina,* microfilm of original records at the National Archives, Washington, D.C. Filmed by the National Archives, series M401, 25 rolls. FHL has complete set, beginning with FHL film #1473248 (1st Infantry, A – Bl).

■ *Index to Compiled Service Records of Volunteer Union Soldiers Who Served in Organizations from the State of North Carolina,* microfilm of original records at the National Archives, Washington, D.C. Over 5,000 Union soldiers were drawn from North Carolina. Filmed by the National Archives, series M391, 2 rolls. FHL has both rolls as FHL film #881590 (Index, A-L) and FHL film #881591 (Index, Le – Z). This is the same list of names now online at the National Park Service website at: **www.civilwar.nps.gov/cwss/**.

■ **Histories** *of the Several Regiments and Battalions from North Carolina in the Great War 1861-1865,* written by members of the respective commands; edited by Walter Clark, published by the state, 1901, 5 vols. Filmed by Microfilming Corp. of America, Sanford, NC, 1983, on 48 microfiche. FHL has series cataloged as FHL fiche #6052205. All five volumes are indexed in *Clark's Regiments, an Extended Index: to the Histories of the Several Regiments and Battalions from North Carolina in the Great War, 1861-1865,* by Charles C. Davis, published by Pelican Pub., Gretna, LA, 2001, 506 pages. FHL book 975.6 M2hs.

■ *Confederate Service Records* (for North Carolina soldiers who served in Alabama units), microfilm of original records compiled by the ADAH, filmed by the Genealogical Society of Utah, 1987, 1 roll, FHL film #1411532 (Item 12, North Carolina soldiers).

■ *Muster rolls and Lists of Confederate Troops Paroled in North Carolina, 1862-1865,* introduction compiled by Claire Prechtel-Kluskens and Karen Martinson, microfilm of original records at the National Archives in Washington, D.C. May include name, rank, unit, witness, place of parole, and other remarks. Includes list of military units for each parole locality. Filmed by the National Archives, 1995, 7 rolls. FHL has entire series, beginning with FHL film #2155455 (Places of parole: Albemarle, Bunn's House, Charlotte, Ft. Macon, Goldsboro).

■ **North Carolina, Civil War Amnesty Papers,** compiled by Sandra Lee Almasy, published by Kensington Glen Pub., Middleton, WI, 1999, 12 vols. Includes indexes to amnesty files, general, location and ship & troops, extracted from the

North Carolina section of the records at the National Archives (filmed on 72 rolls, see Part 1, National Confederate Lists). Contents: vol. 1: Beaufort, Bertie, Camden, Carteret, Chowan, Craven, Currituck, Dare, Gates, Hertford, Hyde, Martin, Northampton, Pamlico, Pasquotank, Perquimans, Tyrrell, and Washington counties; vol. 2: Brunswick, Columbus, Duplin, Jones, Lenoir, New Hanover, Onslow, Pender counties; vol. 3: Edgecombe, Greene, Halifax, Nash, Pitt, Wilson counties; vol. 4: Bladen, Cumberland, Hoke, Johnston, Robeson, Sampson, Wayne counties; vol. 5: Durham, Orange, Wake counties; vol. 6. Caswell, Franklin, Granville, Person, Vance, Warren counties; vol. 7: Alamance, Chatham, Harnett, Lee, Montgomery, Moore, Richmond, Scotland counties; vol. 8: Forsyth, Guilford, Randolph, Rockingham, Stokes counties; vol. 9: Alexander, Alleghany, Ashe, Catawba, Davie, Iredell, Surry, Wilkes, Yadkin counties; vol. 10: Anson, Cabarrus, Davidson, Rowan, Stanly, Union counties; vol. 11: Burke, Caldwell, Cleveland, Gaston, Lincoln, Mecklenburg, Watauga counties; vol. 12: Avery, Buncombe, Cherokee, Clay, Graham, Haywood, Henderson, Jackson, Macon, Madison, McDowell, Mitchell, Polk, Rutherford, Swain, Transylvania, Yancey counties. FHL book 975.6 M2as v. 1-12.

■ *North Carolina Petitions for Presidential Pardon 1865-1868 (an index),* compiled by Russell S. Koonts, published 1996, 76 pages. An index to the petitions from some 2,000 North Carolinians who were excluded from the general amnesty proclamations of May 29, 1865. FHL book 975.6 M2kr.

■ *Applications for Confederate Soldier's and Widow's Pensions, 1885-1953,* microfilm of original records at the North Carolina State Archives, Raleigh, NC. The names found in the various files and indexes are in alphabetical order by the veterans' last name. The pension applications are in three files: (1) 1885-1901; (2) after 1901; and, (3) some "after 1901" material that belongs in the 1885-1901 file. he dates indicated for each item are not always reliable. For this reason, the archive staff has been removing "After 1901" material that belongs in the earlier file. Also, the earlier file contains a small amount of material created prior to 1885. Indexes for each of the file sets are found on the first roll in the series (FHL film #175779); and the last roll (FHL film #1547723). Filmed by the Genealogical Society of Utah, 1958, 1988, 105 rolls, applications beginning with FHL film #1535033 (Abbott, Macon – Blackwood, John).

■ *Internal Revenue Assessment List for North Carolina, 1864-1866,* microfilm of original records at the National Archives, Washington, D.C. Contains information for the following districts: DISTRICT 1: Beaufort, Bertie, Camden, Chowan, Currituck, Gates, Halifax, Hertford, Hyde, Martin, Northampton, Pasquotank, Perquimans, Tyrrell, and Washington counties; DISTRICT 2: Carteret, Craven, Duplin, Edgecombe, Greene, Jones, Lenoir, New Hanover, Onslow, Pitt, Wayne, and Wilson counties; DISTRICT 3: Anson, Bladen, Brunswick, Columbus, Cumberland, Harnett, Montgomery, Moore, Richmond, Robeson, Sampson, and Stanly counties; DISTRICT 4: Chatham, Franklin, Granville, Johnston, Nash, Orange, Wake, and Warren counties; DISTRICT 5: Alamance, Caswell, Davidson, Forsyth, Guilford, Person, Randolph, Rockingham, Stokes, and Surry counties; DISTRICT 6: Alexander, Cabarrus, Catawba, Davie, Gaston, Iredell, Lincoln, Mecklenburg, Rowan, Union, Wilkes, and Yadkin counties; DISTRICT 7: Alleghany, Ashe, Buncombe, Burke, Caldwell, Cherokee, Clay, Cleveland, Haywood, Henderson, Jackson, Macon, Madison, McDowell, Mitchell, Polk, Rutherford, Transylvania, Watauga, and Yancey counties. Filmed by the Genealogical Society of Utah, 1988, 2 rolls, FHL film #1578467-1578468.

■ *North Carolina Extant Voter Registrations of 1867,* compiled by Frances Holloway Wynne, published by Heritage Books, Bowie, MD, 1992, 278 pages. Includes index. "All known voter lists for 1867.... The counties are: Carteret, Chowan, Clay, Cleveland, Craven, Cumberland, Currituck, Davidson, Duplin, Edgecombe, Franklin, Gaston, Granville, Guilford, Hyde, Onslow, and Wake. All males twenty-one years old or older, who had been in the precinct a year or more were to register; each was to sign an oath of allegiance and assure that he had not given aid to the enemy, i.e., the Confederate government. Blacks, many of whom were former slaves, were included in these lists. Names are alphabetically arranged by surnames.

Data includes acceptance or rejection (and if so, why), county and township, and color. Appendices cover such items as a listing of counties and voting precincts, and population comparisons of free blacks and whites from the 1860 and 1870 Federal Censuses" – back cover. FHL book 975.6 N4w.

■ **1886 Regional Directory.** See *Chas. Emerson's North Carolina Tobacco Belt Directory: Embracing the Counties of Alamance, Durham, Forsyth, Granville, Guilford, Orange, Rockingham, Vance and Wake Giving the Location of all Business and Professional Men, a Complete List of all Land-owners, Number of Acres Owned, and P.O. Address of Each, Post-office... Directory of North Carolina... City, County and State Governments...,* microfilm of original published by Emerson, Greensboro, NC, 1886, 764 pages. Filmed by Microfilming Corporation of America, Sanford, NC, 1979. FHL has 9 microfiche, FHL fiche #6014477-6014485.

■ *North Carolina, 1890, Civil War Veterans Census,* by Sandra L. Almasy, published by Kensington Glen Pub., 1990, 316 pages. Includes index. A census of veterans of the Union armed forces and their widows, containing also information on other U.S. veterans and many Confederate veterans. FHL book 975.6 M2a.

■ *Confederate Gravestone Records,* microfilm of index giving volume and page numbers in the original references at the NC State Archives, Raleigh, filmed by the NC archives, 1972, 1 roll, FHL film #882970.

■ *Pre-1914 Cemetery Inscription Card Index,* microfilm of original records prepared by the Historical Records Survey, Works Projects Administration. Surname index cards list county, name of cemetery, town, person, date of birth, death date, age, spouse or parents, location of grave, military information. Cemetery cards are organized alphabetically by county, alphabetically by town and then alphabetically by cemetery name. Filmed by the NC State Archives, 1972, 23 rolls. FHL has entire set, beginning with FHL film #882944 (surname index, Aa – At). See also *Post-1914 Cemetery Inscription Card Index,* 5 rolls, beginning with FHL film #882965 (surnames A-C).

OHIO

Online Ohio Resources

■ **The Ohio Historical Society Archives/Library – Online Collection Catalog.** www.ohiohistory.org/occ/menu.htm.
The Ohio Historical Society's Online Collection Catalog allows you to search the records of more than 230,000 items in the Society's library, newspaper, manuscript, audiovisual, state archives, history, natural history, and archaeology collections; organized as follows:

- **All Society Collections:** This choice offers several searches that will bring back both Archives/Library and Museum records.
- **The Archives/Library Collections:** These collections include the majority of OHS books, pamphlets and newspapers, a large portions of the state archives holdings, and significant numbers of manuscripts and audiovisual materials.
- **The Museum Collections:** These collections include all of the natural history items, the vast majority of history objects and a sampling of archaeology artifacts.
- **The Newspaper Database:** The Newspaper Database searches OHS' hardcopy and microfilm newspaper holdings which are all Ohio titles.
- **Local Government Records Database.** Keyword searching is possible to locate records transferred from the various Ohio counties to the OH Historical Society Archives/Library.
- **Online Documents – Civil War.** Search Adjutant General documents, including abstracts of almost 4,000 letters from Series 147, *Correspondence to the Governor and Adjutant General, 1861-1866*; *Index to [Ohio] Prisoners at Andersonville and Salisbury Prisons, 1864-1865*; and also from the *Civil War Guide Project, Guide to Primary Resource Collections at OHS.*
- **Online Documents – Fundamental Documents.** Search the full text of the early Ohio Constitutions, the Ordinance of the Northwest Territory, Executive Journal of the Northwest Territory, War of 1812 in the Northwest documents, biographical sketches of Ohio governors (1803-1971), Early Ohio Political Leaders finding aid.
- **Online Documents – Military Rosters.** Search the full text of the *Roster of Ohio Soldiers in the War of 1812* from the Adjutant General records. Ohio furnished 1759 Officers and 24,521 enlisted men.

■ **American Civil War – Ohio.** www.archaeolink.com/ohio_civil_war_page.htm.
This site features direct links to webpages related to Ohio's involvement in the Civil War.

■ **Civil War Documents – Ohio Historical Society.** www.ohiohistory.org/resource/database/civilwar.html. A searchable base for information ranging from personal letters to an "Index to [Ohio] Prisoners at Andersonville, Georgia, and Salisbury, North Carolina Prisons, 1864-1865" The letters alone are an excellent resource. "The letters came from throughout Ohio and outside of the state, and were written by county military committees, local officials, military commanders, politicians, recruiters, etc. Battles, border defense, camps, county military committees, disloyalty, the draft, ethnic companies and regiments, Morgan's Raid, the pay of soldiers, prisoners of war, promotions, recruiting, and subsistence (supplies) for the soldiers, are some of the topics covered in the letters.

■ **Civil War Websites:**
- **Civil War Ohio: A Special Collection.** This Civil War Ohio special collection consists mostly of primary source materials written about Ohio's vast contribution to the Civil War. It is a comprehensive research-oriented collection that includes documents from the following categories: official documents; military histories; military organizations; speeches, addresses, and sermons; and manuscripts. Go to: **www.libraries.wright.edu/special/collections/local/civwar.html.**
- **Ohio in the Civil War.** You will find history, rosters, units, photos and a general overview of Ohio in the war along with a searchable database. Go to: **www.ohiocivilwar.com/.**
- **Ohio Civil War Map of Battles.** You will find click-to-read histories, locations of battles, flags and more. Go to: **http://americancivilwar.com/statepic/oh.html.**
- **Union Regiments – Ohio.** Organization and service history of Ohio's military units (cavalry, artillery, infantry). Go to: **www.civilwararchive.com/unionoh.htm.**

Published Ohio Resources

■ *Index to Compiled Service Records of Volunteer Union Soldiers Who Served in Organizations from the State of Ohio,* microfilm of original Card Indexes at the National Archives, Washington, D.C. Indexes the names of over 460,000 Ohio soldiers/sailors/marines. Filmed by the National Archives, series M552, 122 rolls. FHL has entire set, beginning with FHL film #882214 (Index, A – Alk). This is the same list of names now online at the National Park Service website at: **www.civilwar.nps.gov/cwss/**.

■ *Official Roster of the Soldiers of the State of Ohio in the War of the Rebellion: Original Muster In & Muster Out rolls of Ohio Military Organization in the Civil War, 1-3 year Enlistments, 1861-1866,* microfilm of the original records from the Adjutant Generals Office in Columbus, Ohio. Some regiments have indexes. Filmed by the Genealogical Society of Utah, 1959-1960, 365 rolls, beginning with FHL film #212908 (Regiment 1). The original records were indexed in an 1938 WPA project as *Official Roster of the Soldiers of the State of Ohio in the War of the Rebellion, 1861-1866,* microfilmed by the Genealogical Society of Utah, 1959, 17 rolls, beginning with FHL film #195467 (Index, A-C, books 1-2, pages 1-672).

■ *Ohio Military Records, 1863-1903,* microfilm of original records at the Ohio Historical Society, Columbus, Ohio. Record may contain name, age, date of enlistment, discharged by whom, description, nativity, occupation, residence, marital status, when enrolled, where enrolled, date of discharge, cause of discharge, date of approval, date of election and ranks, date of commission issued, field and staff, township or ward, remarks, company of assignment, date of leave, and date of leave expires. Filmed by the Genealogical Society of Utah, 2005, 7 rolls, beginning with FHL film #2396273 (Rosters and enrollments, 1st to 16th Battalion).

■ *Ohio in the War: Her Statesmen, Her generals, and Soldiers,* by Whitelaw Reid, published by Wilstach & Baldwin, Cincinnati, OH, 1868, 2 vols. Includes index. Contents, vol. 1: History of the state during the war, and the lives of her generals; vol. 2: The history of her regiments, and other military organizations. FHL has a photocopy, FHL book 977. H2re vol. 1-2. Also on microfiche, FHL fiche #6051205.

■ *Grave Registrations of Soldiers Buried in Ohio,* microfilm of grave files, originals housed at the Office of the Ohio Adjutant General in Columbus, Ohio. Filmed by the Genealogical Society of Utah,

1958, 92 rolls, beginning with FHL film #182702 (A – Alderman, Francis R.).

■ *Ohio Veteran's Home Death Records, January 3, 1889 Through December 31, 1983,* compiled and published by the Erie County Chapter, Ohio Genealogical Society, Sandusky, OH, 1984, 295 pages. FHL book 977.1 V4o. Also on microfiche, FHL fiche #6105079.

■ *A List of Ohioan's Killed During the Civil War: Buried at National Cemetery, Andersonville, Georgia; Antietam Cemetery, Maryland, and Miscellaneous Cemeteries,* microfilm of card file (repository not noted), filmed by the Genealogical Society of Utah, 1962, 1 roll, FHL film #285059.

■ *Records of Abstracts of Soldiers Who Applied for Pensions While Residing in Ohio,* a 100-page typescript compiled by Annie W. B. Bell, filmed by the Genealogical Society of Utah, 1985, 1 roll, FHL film #1321014.

■ **Index to Ohio Pensioners of 1883,** by W. Louis Phillips, published by Heritage Books, Bowie, MD, 1987, 367 pages. Contains an index to Civil War, and War of 1812 veterans and their widows who received federal pensions. FHL book 977.1 M2ph. Also on microfiche, FHL fiche #6087608.

■ *Confederate Service Records* (for Ohio soldiers who served in Alabama units), microfilm of original records compiled by the ADAH, filmed by the Genealogical Society of Utah, 1987, 1 roll, FHL film #1411532 (Item 13, Ohio soldiers).

■ *Army & Navy Post no. 187 Records, 1861-1865, 1913-1920, Grand Army of the Republic (GAR),* microfilm of the original records at the Western Reserve Historical Society Library in Cleveland, Ohio. Includes list of members who served in the Civil War with information concerning their births, deaths, & military service; minutes of meetings, 1913-1920; & a memorial volume to Louis Black, Company A, 150th Ohio Infantry. Filmed by the Genealogical Society of Utah, 1974, 1 roll, FHL film #960615.

OKLAHOMA & INDIAN TERRITORY

During the era of the Civil War, most of the area of present Oklahoma was under the control of the five civilized tribes, i.e., the Choctaw, Cherokee, Chickasaw, Creek, and Seminole Nations. The region was commonly described as "Indian Territory," but that term did not become part of official government treaty records until 1872. All five of the slave-holding Nations supported the southern cause with troops to the Confederate Army. After the Civil War, the U.S. Government voided the treaties with the five civilized tribes, wrote new ones, and began a process of allotments of land to individual tribal members. After various acts involving the sale of lands in the Indian Territory, in 1890 the area was divided into Indian Territory and Oklahoma Territory. The two territories were joined in 1907 to become the state of Oklahoma. One of the early acts of the new state was to provide pensions to surviving Confederate veterans of the Civil War living in Oklahoma.

Online Oklahoma & Indian Territory Resources

■ **The Civil War in Indian Territory – Site Index. www.civilwaralbum.com/indian/site_index. htm.** Includes categories for the following:
- Battles/Skirmishes
- Forts
- Museums
- Misc.
- CWSAC Battle Summaries (Indian Territory)
- Links

■ **Oklahoma Historical Society – The Research Center. www.okhistory.org/research/index.html.** The OK Historical Society is the official state archives and also holds the American Indian Archives. The new Oklahoma History Center, located across from the state capitol in Oklahoma City, is home to the Oklahoma Museum of History, Research Center, and Historic Preservation Office. The Research Center is the most important place for genealogical research in Oklahoma. A catalog

search for titles, authors, subjects, and keywords, such as "Civil War in Oklahoma," here brought up a unique list of resources. Many of these OHS resources are not found at the Family History Library in Salt Lake City, and a combined list of the important published items follows, below.

Published Oklahoma & Indian Territory Resources

Important Civil War resources available at either the Oklahoma Historical Society (OHS) in Oklahoma City, or the Family History Library (FHL) in Salt Lake City:

■ *Compiled Service Records of Confederate Soldiers Who Served in Organizations Raised Directly by the Confederate Government (1861-1865),* microfilm of original records at the National Archives, Washington, D.C. Contains records of Confederate soldiers who served in military organizations formed by the Confederate Government and therefore not identified with any one state. Includes units of the Confederate Regular Army, several units raised among residents of Indian Territory, and one for foreigners recruited among Union prisoners of war. Filmed by the National Archives, series M258, 123 rolls. FHL has entire series, beginning with FHL film #880207 (First Confederate Cavalry, A – C).

■ *Bourland in North Texas and Indian Territory During the Civil War: Fort Cobb, Fort Arbuckle, & the Wichita Mountains,* by Patricia Adkins Rochette, published Broken Arrow, OK, 2005, 2 vols. OHS call no. E470.9 A35 2005.

■ *Papers & Certificates, 1931-1959,* Oklahoma Confederate Home, Ardmore, OK, compiled by Anne Ault, Ardmore, United Daughters of the Confederacy. OHS call no. UP00024.

■ *Big War / Little war: Oklahoma Indians in the Civil War, 1861-1865,* by Center of the American Indian, Oklahoma City, 1985. OHS call no. E 585 I3 C4.

■ *Civil War in Indian Territory,* OK Historical Society, OHS call no. E 470.9 5558.

■ *Turmoil in Indian Territory: The Civil War Experience of the Five Nations,* by Clarissa Woelfer Confer, published by University of Oklahoma Press, Norman, OK, 1939, 1982, 241 pages. OHS call no. F 698 C63.

■ *The Prairie Was on Fire: Eyewitness Accounts of the Civil War in the Indian Territory,* by Whit Edwards, published by the Oklahoma Historical Society, 2001, 180 pages. OHS call no. E 505.95 E39.

■ *Quantrill's Civil War Operations in Indian Territory,* by LeRoy H. Fischer and Lary C. Rampp, published by the Oklahoma Historical Society, 1968, 27 pages, OHS call no. E 470.9 F5.

■ *The Civil War in the Western Choctaw Nation, 1861-1865,* by Raymond L. Holcomb, published by the Atoka County Historical Society, 1990, 94 pages, OHS call no. E 470.9 H8.

■ *Kepis and Turkey calls: An Anthology of the War Between the States in Indian territory,* edited by Mark Lea (Beau) Cantrell and Mac Harris, published Western Heritage Books, Oklahoma City, 1982, OHS call no. E 470.9 C3.

■ *Names of the Civil War Veterans in the Purcell Cemetery, McCain County,* typescript, 5 pages, in OHS Reading Room, OHS call no. F 704 P8.

■ *Tribal and Civil War Battlefield Sites in Oklahoma,* prepared by Bob L. Blackburn, Mary Jane Warde, and Tom Franzmann., published by Oklahoma Battlefield Preservation Commission, 1996, 5 pages, OHS call F 695 O453 1996.

■ *Civil War in Indian Territory,* published by the Oklahoma Civil War Centennial Commission, 4 pages, OSH call no. E 505.95 O4.

■ *An Index to the 1890 United States Census of Union Veterans and Their Widows in Oklahoma and Indian Territories (including old Greer County) and Soldiers Stationed at Military Installations in the Territories (Section I); Also An index to Records from the Oklahoma Union*

Soldiers' Home Including Civil War Veterans and Their Dependents, Veterans of Wars with Spain and Mexico, Army Nurses, and Certain Members of the National Guard of Oklahoma, and the Union Soldiers' Cemetery Record (Section II), published by the Oklahoma Projects Committee, Oklahoma City, OK, 1970, 53 pages, OHS call no. F 691 O41s no.3.

■ *Civil War Union Soldiers Buried in Oklahoma,* by N. Dale Talkington and Deone K. Pearcy, draft copy, by the authors, 1992, 262 pages. OHS call no. F 693 T3.

■ *Tributes of Blue: Obituaries of Civil War Union Soldiers and Sailors Buried in Oklahoma,* by N. Dale Talkington and Deone K. Pearcy, published by T.P. Productions, Tehachapi, CA, 1996, 722 pages, OHS call no. F 693 T146. See also *The Long Blue Line: Civil War Union Soldiers and Sailors Buried in Oklahoma,* by N. Dale Talkington, published by the author, Houston, TX, 1999, 754 pages, FHL book 976.6 V3tn.

■ *Civil War Sites in Oklahoma,* by Muriel H. Wright and LeRoy H. Fischer, published by Oklahoma Historical Society, 1967, 61 pages, OHS call no. F 697 W952.

■ *Confederate Pension Applications for Soldiers and Sailors,* Microfilm of original records at the Oklahoma Historical Society, Oklahoma City, OK. Filmed by the society, 1975, 22 rolls. FHL has complete set, beginning with FHL film #1001531 (1915-1919 applications).

■ *Veteran Burials in the State of Oklahoma,* compiled by the members of the Oklahoma Genealogical Society, edited by Linda Chandler, Special Publications, Oklahoma Genealogical Society, Oklahoma City, 1998, 2 vols. This book was compiled from submissions to an on-going project to compile records of veterans buried in Oklahoma. Information was taken from tombstones, cemetery records, newspaper obituaries, American Legion records, and family records. The letters and papers used to compile this book are in the Veteran Burials Vertical File in the Oklahoma Historical Society Library in Oklahoma City, Oklahoma. Contents: vol. 1. pt. 1. A-K; vol. 2. L-Z. Names of veterans are listed in alphabetical order. Information given for each veteran may include name; dates of birth, death, and burial; war in which veteran served; name of cemetery where buried; rank, branch, and service group in military; and supplemental information about medals, American Legion or VFW affiliation, etc. FHL Library has bound Vols. 1 & 2 as one volume, FHL book 976.6 V3.

■ *Alabama Confederate Veterans, Residing in Indian Territory,* typescript compiled by MariLee Beatty Hageness, filmed by the Genealogical Society of Utah, 1994, 1 roll, FHL film #1750773.

■ *Genealogical Records on the Confederate Indian Troops,* by Sherman Lee Pompey, published Albany, OR, 1984, 13 pages. Indian soldiers were mustered in Indian Territory from the Five Civilized Tribes including Cherokee, Creek, Choctaw, and Chickasaw and then fought in engagements elsewhere in the United States. Contains muster lists, complete and partial, for John Miller's Cherokee Regiment, Captain George Washington's Squadron of Indians, the 2nd Creek Volunteers, Major James W. Cooper's Battalion 1st Indian Brigade, Captain John Williams' Company Choctaw Infantry, Colonel J. McCurtin's 1st Battalion Choctaw Cavalry, 2nd and 3rd Choctaw Cavalry, 2nd Choctaw Infantry, Captain Edmund Pickins' Company Mounted Choctaws, Major Solomon Jones' Creek Nation Regiment, 1st Battalion Chickasaw Cavalry and Colonel Martin Shecoe's Chickasaw Battalion Mounted Volunteers. FHL book 970.1 A1 no. 106. Also on microfiche, FHL fiche #6049323.

■ *Confederate Veterans in Oklahoma: Tennessee,* compiled by Joe L. Todd, published by the OK Historical Society, 1996, 32 pages. This is a list of Confederate veterans living in Oklahoma (ca. 1910-1913) who served in Tennessee units during the Civil War. Arranged in alphabetical order by surname, the list gives name, rank unit, county of residence in Oklahoma, birth and death dates (if given) and the source of the information. The list is compiled from records of the United Confederate Veterans in the Archives Division of the Oklahoma Historical Society. FHL book 976.6 M2.

■ *1890 Oklahoma Census Index: Special Schedule of the Eleventh Census (1890) Enumerating Union Veterans and Widows of Union Veterans of the Civil War,* edited by Ronald Vern Jackson, et al., published by Accelerated Indexing Systems, North Salt Lake, UT, 1984, 37 pages. FHL book 976.6 X22jv.

OREGON

Online Oregon Resources

■ **Oregon State Archives – Historical Records Index.** **http://genealogy.state.or.us/**. Although a work-in-progress, representing only a fraction of the resources available at the Oregon State Archives, the online **Oregon Historical Records Index** is a starting point for finding the name of a person, place, or subject from Oregon's archival records. Included are many original county records, military records, census records, and much more. Use this webpage to search the index by name, year, record type, county, or for Portland births. Go to the "Genealogy Records" page for a good review of the types of records available.

■ **Oregon Civil War Genealogy.** **www.geocities.com/Heartland/woods/3099/.** General information about Oregon's role in the Civil War, and a list of some of the participants, with vitals as found in various sources. Includes many soldiers who served from other places, but were buried in Oregon.

■ **Civil War Veterans Buried in Oregon Pioneer Cemetery, Bandon, OR.** **http://skyways.lib.ks. us/genweb/civilwar/oregonvets.html**. Over 60 veteran burials in this cemetery, a rather large number for a community of under 3,000 people on the south coast of Oregon.

■ **Oregon Blue Book – Civil War in Oregon.** **http://bluebook.state.or.us/cultural/history/history 16.htm**. A short history of Oregon's role in the Civil War.

■ **The Civil War Archive – Union Regimental Histories (Oregon).** www.civilwararchive.com/Unreghst/unortr.htm. Oregon supplied one Infantry Regiment (1st) and one Cavalry Regiment (1st) to the Civil War. The histories of these regiments are reproduced here from Frederick H. Dyer's *A Compendium of the War of the Rebellion.*

Published Oregon Resources

■ *1837-1933 Oregon State Archives Combined Military Alphabetical Index,* microfilm of original computer-generated index at the Oregon State Archives in Salem, Oregon. This 12,000-page index was compiled by the State Archives staff and includes Oregon military and other names extracted from 1) Provisional and Territorial Government Documents, 1837-1859; 2) Supreme Court Case Files, 1855-1904; 3) Oregon Soldiers Home Patient Histories, 1894-1933; 4) State Treasurer Quarterly Reports of Estates, 1903-1913; and 5) Defense Council Personal Military Service Records, 1917-1918. Includes name, state archives number, and description of record. Arranged in alphabetical order by surname. Filmed by the Genealogical Society of Utah, 2000, 37 rolls, beginning with FHL film #2194727 (Aandahl – Austin, Henry R.).

■ *Compiled Service Records of Volunteer Union Soldiers Who Served in Organizations from the State of Oregon,* microfilm of original records at the National Archives, Washington, D.C. Under each organizational unit, the compiled service records consist of a jacket-envelope for each soldier, labeled with his name, his rank, and the unit in which he served and typically containing card abstracts of entries relating to the soldier as found in original muster rolls, returns, hospital rolls, descriptive books, and lists of deserters; and the originals of any papers relating solely to the particular soldiers. Filmed by National Archives, series M1816, 34 rolls. FHL has entire series, beginning with FHL film #2155494 (1st Oregon Cavalry, Abend – Bond).

■ *Index to Compiled Service Records of Volunteer Union Soldiers Who Served in Organizations from the State of Oregon,* microfilm of original records in the National Archives, Washington, D.C. Filmed by National Archives, series M553, 1 roll, FHL film #821947. This is the same list of names now online at the National Park Service website at: www.civilwar.nps.gov/cwss/.

■ *Grand Army of the Republic Descriptive Books and Index, [1870-1930],* microfilm of original records at the Oregon Historical Society in Portland, OR. Part of manuscript #1378 of the Oregon Historical Society. Index is arranged in alphabetical order by surname. Descriptive books are arranged by Post name and number. Lists item number, name, post name and number. Descriptive books may list name, age, state of birth, residence in Oregon, occupation, date-rank-company-regiment of service and final discharge, cause of discharge, when mustered into G.A.R., status, and date of death. Filmed by the Genealogical Society of Utah, 1999, 1 roll, FHL film #2167206. Also indexed separately in *G.A.R. Descriptive Books,* a 1998 copy of manuscript, arranged in alphabetical order by surname. Lists name of member of the Grand Army of the Republic (G.A.R.), number, post name and number. FHL book 979.5 C42g.

■ *Civil War Veterans Who Were Residents of Oregon,* microfilm of original records at the Genealogical Forum of Oregon, Portland, OR. Arranged in alphabetical order by surname. "Information was collected by Spencer Leonard from DAR rosters given to the Genealogical Forum of Portland, Oregon in May 1971" – first card. Includes information on index cards listing name of veteran, personal information, and reference information. Filmed by the Genealogical Society of Utah, 2003, 4 rolls, as follows:
- Abbey, Peter M. – Downs, Samuel, FHL film #2367711.
- Doxy, Charles L. – Kinman, Martin V., FHL film #2367712.
- Kinmont, William F. – Robey, Cyrus A., FHL film #2367713.
- Robins, David A. – Zwickie, W. F., FHL film #2367765.

■ *Genealogical Notes on the 1st Oregon Cavalry, Union Volume One, Field and Staff and Company A,* by Sherman Lee Pompey, published by the author, Albany, OR, 1984, 38 pages. FHL book 979.5 M2pg.

■ *Honor roll of Oregon Grand Army of the Republic, 1881-1935: Deaths Reported in Oregon of Members of the GAR, Extracted from*

Proceedings of the Annual Encampments of the Department of Oregon, Grand Army of the Republic, compiled by Jane Myers, published by the Cottage Grove Genealogical Society, Cottage Grove, OR, 1980, 96 pages. Arranged in alphabetical order by surname. Lists name, military organization, date of death, age, and post number if known. FHL book 979.5 M2m.

■ ***Soldiers Who Served in The Oregon Volunteers: Civil War Period, Infantry and Cavalry,*** compiled by Mrs. M. A. Pekar and Miss Edna Mingus for Chemeketa Chapter, Daughters of the American Revolution, published by the Genealogical Forum of Oregon, Portland, OR, 1961, 78 pages, FHL book 979.5 M2pm.

■ ***Card Index from Post 7 Eugene [Oregon] Minutes,*** compiled by Spencer Leonard, Grand Army of the Republic, Post 7, Eugene, OR. Microfilm of original records at the Genealogical Forum of Oregon in Portland, Oregon. Title from first card. Arranged in alphabetical order by surname. Filmed by the Genealogical Society of Utah, 2003, 1 roll, FHL film #2367847.

■ ***Oregon Soldiers Home Applications, 1894-1933,*** microfilm of original records at the Oregon State Archives, Salem, OR. From intro: "This series documents the application of veterans for admission to the Oregon Soldiers Home, a care facility for indigent veterans located in Roseburg, Oregon. Applications show application date, periods of service, enlistment and discharge dates, units served, applicant's signature, affidavits, and personal information. Supporting records include correspondence, pension check receipts, pension and service certificates, and home record cards." Arranged in alphabetical order by surname. Filmed by the Genealogical Society of Utah, 2000, 16 rolls, beginning with FHL film #2231519 (Boyles, David – Carter, Andrew B.).

■ ***1863-1935 City Directories, Portland, Oregon,*** microfilm of originals published by various publishers. Filmed by Research Publications, Inc., Woodbridge, CT, 1980-1984. FHL has 34 rolls, with a complete run of directories, 1863-1935, beginning with FHL film #1377327 (1863 Portland Directory) through FHL film #1611935 (1935 Portland Directory).

■ ***Oregon Pioneers Card Index at the Multnomah County Library, Portland, Oregon.*** (not the official title, but the library staff will know what you are talking about). Contains thousands of references to people of early Oregon from newspaper articles, books, and various public records. For more information, visit the library's genealogy webpage at **www.multcolib.org/ ref/gene.html#oregon**. Or, get a copy of ***Guide to Genealogical Material in the Multnomah County Library, Portland, Oregon,*** compiled by members of the Genealogical Forum of Portland, with the assistance and cooperation of the staff of Multnomah County Library, published 1967, 215 pages. FHL book 979.549 A3g. Also on microfilm, FHL film #1321456.

■ ***Oregon Biography Index,*** edited by Patricia Brandt and Nancy Guilford, published as Bibliographic Series No. 11, Oregon State University, Corvallis, OR, 1976, 131 pages. Indexes subjects of biographical sketches from many histories of early Oregon. FHL book 979.5 D3b.

■ ***Genealogical Notes on the Oregon Territory and State of Oregon, 1810-1910,*** by Sherman Lee Pompey, an unpublished manuscript. Includes some indexes. Contains miscellaneous genealogical notes compiled from census, marriage, territorial, military, and business directory records of Oregon Territory and State. Also includes information copied from the 1850, 1860, and 1870 census records of Oregon Territory and State, and an index to the 1865 state census. Filmed by the Genealogical Society of Utah, 1986, 1 roll, FHL film #1421678.

■ ***1865, 1870, 1875, and 1885 Agricultural and Property Assessment and Census for Umatilla County, Oregon,*** microfilm of original records at the Oregon State Archives in Salem, Oregon. Includes name, number of acres, lots, and blocks, value of land, amount of state and county taxes, number of females and males and age groups, amount of bushels of various products, amount of various farm animals, amount of seafood, and remarks from the state 1865 and 1875 census. Filmed by the Genealogical Society of Utah, 2002, 2 rolls, FHL film #2319765 (Oregon state census 1865; 1870 Federal Census; Oregon state census

1875 (p. 1-30); and FHL film #2319766 (Oregon state census 1875 (p. 31-end); Oregon state census 1885).

■ *1867-1873 Internal Revenue Assessment Lists, Oregon,* microfilm of originals in the National Archives Branch in Seattle, Washington. Some years missing. There are no volume numbers on books. Filmed by the Genealogical Society of Utah, 1989, 2 rolls, FHL film #1639854 (Assessment lists 1867-1870) and FHL film #1639855 (Assessment lists 1871-1873).

■ *Oregon State 1890 Special Federal Census of Union Veterans and Their Widows: Eleventh Census of the United States,* compiled by Jane A. Myers, published by Cottage Grove Genealogical Society, 1993, 460 pages. Extracted by county, enumeration district, and enumerator. Includes index of veterans and index of enumerators. FHL book 979.5 X28m. See also *Oregon 1890 Census Index: Special Schedule of the Eleventh Census (1890) Enumerating Union Veterans and of Union Veterans of the Civil War,* compiled by Ronald Vern Jackson, et al., published by Accelerated Indexing Systems, North Salt Lake, UT, 1985, 87 pages. FHL book 979.5 X2j.

■ *Oregon Statewide Delayed Filings of Births, 1842-1902,* microfilm of original records at the Oregon State Archives in Salem, Oregon. Arranged in chronological order by the year of birth (of the person filing a delayed birth record) and then alphabetical by county wherein the delayed birth was filed. (The place of birth could be anywhere, including out-of-state locations). Oregon is one of only a few states with statewide delayed birth records available to the public. These records are powerful genealogical sources. The delayed birth certificates were originally filed with the county circuit courts with copies going to the State Division of Vital Statistics. This series is the state's copy. (Another copy of the filing may be located at the county courthouse in which it was originally filed.). Most of these records were filed by individuals needing proof of birth prior to receiving Social Security benefits, which began in 1935. But there may be filings earlier than that (exact range of dates of filing not noted on the microfilm series). The first two rolls in the series contain an alpha index to the names of persons filing a delayed birth

record, which includes the name, date of birth, and place of filing; allowing a researcher to find the roll of film containing the microfilmed image of the delayed birth record. The delayed birth record itself is more revealing than a standard birth certificate because it includes affidavits of relatives and acquaintances, and supporting documents such as Bible pages, identification papers, etc. The films are not in strict numerical order, but following the 2-roll index are 72 rolls of birth records, filmed by the Genealogical Society of Utah, 2001, 2003, beginning with FHL film #2363225 (Statewide delayed birth index, Aamold, Walter – Hood, Helen Owsley) and FHL film #2363226 (Statewide delayed birth index, Holzmeyer, Selma Elsie Johanna – Zysett, Lawrence Albert); followed by FHL film #2230783 (Delayed birth filings, 1842-1868, Deschutes County).

PENNSYLVANIA

Online Pennsylvania Resources

■ **Pennsylvania State Archives – Civil War Webpage.** www.phmc.state.pa.us/BAH/DAM/ militarycivilwar.htm. Officially, the Division of Archives and Manuscripts of the Pennsylvania Historical and Museum Commission, the **Pennsylvania State Archives** holds many records relating to the Civil War. A detailed 97-page guide to these records is available as a PDF download at this site, and describes the records in hundreds of titles, categories, record groups, etc., and whether a record is available on microfilm. This webpage features detailed descriptions for all archival holdings related to the Civil War.

Generally, only Pennsylvania veterans are referenced in their collections. Even though the historic battle of Gettysburg was fought on Pennsylvania soil, the State Archives does not have the records of non-Pennsylvanians who saw action in that battle. The State Archives holds Civil War regimental records for Pennsylvania units, including those regiments of U.S. colored troops formed in Pennsylvania. Muster rolls, descriptive rolls, deserter lists, orders and correspondence are available for most units. The PA Archives has Civil War draft records only for 1862. Beginning in May 1863, the Provost Marshal's General Bureau administered the draft from Washington, D.C., and pertinent records will be found in Record Group 110 at the National Archives. The PA holdings are identified as follows:

Holdings Listing Pennsylvania Veterans:
- Civil War Veteran's Card File, 1861-1866
- Register of Pennsylvania Volunteers
- List of Sick and Wounded Soldiers, Pennsylvania Volunteers, 1861-1864
- Civil War Muster Rolls
- Military Claims File

Holdings for a PA Civil War Unit:
- Civil War Muster Rolls and Related records, 1861-1864
- Descriptive Books (Regimental and Company), 1861-1864
- Registers of Pennsylvania Volunteers
- Diaries and Journals Collection, 1763-1938
- Military Manuscripts Collection, 1758-1931
- Samuel Penniman Bates Papers, 1853-95
- Battery B, First Pennsylvania Light Artillery papers, 1861 (1861-65)-1924
- Ruben S. Gardner Papers, 1861-66
- Wilmer C. Hall Papers, 1860-79
- McCormick Family Papers, 1818 (1861-1864)- 1881
- Hugh W. McNeil Collection, 1866 (1861-62)-1916
- Richard A. Oakford Papers, 1861-62
- Weiser Family Collection, 1742-1927
- John F. Hartranft Papers, 1853-97
- John Anderson Papers, 1684-1904
- Samuel P. Glass Collection, 1861-1865
- Francis W. Reed Collection, 1861-65
- L.M. Anderson Collection, 1860-65
- Christian Geisel Collection, 1862-68
- Forty-Second Regiment ("Bucktails"), Pennsylvania Volunteers, Records, 1861-64
- Records of the First City Zouaves; Company A, 127th Pennsylvania Volunteer Infantry; Harrisburg City Grays; and Company D, 8th Regiment, N.G.P., 1862-1917

Holdings for Civil War Draft Records:
- Conscientious Objector Depositions, 1862
- Discharge Orders and Letters of Notice of Alien Status of Individuals serving in Military, 1862-1863
- Substitute Depositions

■ **Pennsylvania State Archives – Archives Records Information Access System (ARIAS).** www.digitalarchives.state.pa.us/. This resource offers images from digitized microfilm that index and summarize the military service of Pennsylvania soldiers during several wars and time periods, including:
- **PA National Guard Veterans' Card File, 1867-1921.** Arranged alphabetically by surname of veteran.

Names generally read from left to right: Last, Middle, First. Consists of 4" x 6" cards originally maintained by the Office of the Adjutant General. Data generally shown about each veteran includes name, rank, age, physical description (height, complexion, hair and eye color), occupation and residence; the date and place of enlistment; the date and reason for discharge; and the unit (company and regiment) to which assigned. Information about federal service rendered by the veteran and the date of death or first appearance in the military records also routinely appears.
- **Civil War Veterans' Card File, 1861-1866.** Arranged alphabetically by surname of soldier. These 3" x 5" cards were initially prepared to serve as an index to Samuel Penniman Bates' "History of Pennsylvania Volunteers, 1861-1865," (Harrisburg, 1869-1871). The Office of the Adjutant General later expanded the scope of the cards by transcribing onto them data found on the original Civil War Muster Rolls and Related Records, 1861-1866 {series #19.11}. The information generally includes the soldiers' names, military units, Bates' citations (volume and page), ages at enrollment, descriptions (complexion, height, color of hair and eyes), residences and birthplaces; the dates and places where enrolled; the dates and places where mustered in; and the dates of discharge.
All of the above databases are accessed by clicking on the title, then selecting a letter of the alphabet for the surname of the subject. The full text reproductions from the microfilmed index cards are clear and well imaged.

■ **State Library of Pennsylvania Catalog.** http://pilot.passhe.edu:8020/cgi-bin/Pwebrecon.cgi?DB=local&PAGE=First. A keyword search for "Civil War Pennsylvania" will reveal over 1,100 titles of published books, manuscripts, films, videos, maps, and more. This is the place to locate that obscure book published about the soldiers of Pennsylvania, the regiments, county muster rolls, burials, pensions, and memories of civil war veterans.

■ **Pennsylvania in the Civil War.** www.pa-roots.com/~pacw/. This is a private website with many links to civil war databases, including complete rosters of soldiers for all Pennsylvania units. The site is organized within the following categories:
- Andrew G. Curtin, Governor, 1861-1867
- The Coming Storm
- Artillery
- Cavalry

- Infantry Independent Company C (Infantry) Muster Roll
- Engineers
- Pennsylvania Reserves
- U. S. Colored Troops
- Militia of 1861
- Militia of 1862
- Militia of 1863
- Militia of 1864
- Pennsylvanians in 5th West Virginia Cavalry
- Pennsylvanians in the U. S. Navy
- Veteran Reserve Corps
- U. S. Veteran Volunteers
- County Units
- Jefferson County Draft
- Regimental Histories
- Medal of Honor
- PA MOH Recipients
- Camp Parole, Annapolis, MD
- Survivors of Salisbury Prison Camp
- Pennsylvanians who died at the Salisbury Prison Camp
- Prisoners of War Troops Captured at Reams Station, August 25, 1864
- Death Statistics
- National and Other Cemeteries
- Battlefield National Cemetery
- Burial Index
- Pennsylvania Veterans Who Died in Illinois
- U. S. Veterans Affairs, Cemetery Administration: U. S. Veterans Affairs Cemeteries Burial Location Assistance
- Headstones and Markers
- Soldiers' Orphans Schools
- Gettysburg
- Battles, Skirmishes in Pennsylvania
- PA Civil War Flags Searchable Data Base
- National Archives Records
- Bates' History of PA Volunteers
- PA Digital Archives - Index Cards to the PA Volunteers
- Bates' Martial Deeds of Pennsylvania
- Hospitals and Medicine
- Campaign Medal
- Grand Army of the Republic Museum
- GAR Posts in PA (PDF File)
- GAR Badges
- Queries
- Search Tool

■ **Pennsylvania Volunteers of the Civil War.** www.pacivilwar.com/. At this site, you are encouraged to look for your ancestors in the PA genealogy database of American Civil War soldiers - infantry, cavalry & artillery rosters, histories, biographies, draft, journals, letters, medal of honor

recipients, prisoners of war & pensions of Pennsylvania military ancestors.

Published Pennsylvania Resources

■ *Index to Compiled Service Records of Volunteer Union Soldiers Who Served in Organizations from the State of Pennsylvania,* microfilm of original records at the National Archives, Washington, D.C. Filmed by the National Archives, series M554, 136 rolls, 1964. FHL has entire series, beginning with FHL film #882336 (surnames A – Alld). This is the same list of names now online at the National Park Service website at: **www.civilwar.nps.gov/cwss/**.

■ *History of Pennsylvania Volunteers, 1861-65,* prepared in compliance with acts of the legislature by Samuel P. Bates, published by B. Singerly, Harrisburg, PA, 1869-1871, 5 vols. FHL has microfilm copies, FHL films #824366 (vol. 1), #824367 (vol. 2), #824401 (vol. 3), #963340 (vol. 4), and #963341 (vol. 5). All five volumes are indexed in the online ARIAS online database, "Civil War Veterans Card File, 1861-1865," with reproductions of the index cards as digital images.

■ *List of Soldiers, (Prisoners of War), Belonging to Pennsylvania Regiments, Who Died at the Military Prison, at Andersonville, Georgia: from February 26, 1864, to March 24, 1865,* microfilm of original records compiled by the Pennsylvania Surveyor General's Office, Harrisburg, PA, originally published by Singerly & Myers, State Printers, Harrisburg, 1865, 24 page. FHL microfiche #6083894.

■ *Bucktail Regiment: Index to Muster Roll Names,* by Herbert R. Welch and Margaret E. Welch, published 1993, 58 pages. An index to the 42nd PA Infantry Regiment of the Civil War, also called the "First Rifles" and "Bucktails." FHL book 974.8 M22we. Also on microfilm, FHL film #1698163.

■ *History of Pennsylvania Volunteers 1861-65; Index,* compiled by Rickie Broadfoot, et al, published by Broadfoot Publishing Co., 1994, 4 vols., FHL book 974.8 M2b index A-D, E-K, L-R, and S-Z.

■ *Gopsill's Directory of Lancaster, Harrisburg, Lebanon and York, 1863-1864,* microfilm of original published by James Gopsill, 1863, 379 pages. Filmed by W.C. Cox Co., Tucson, AZ, 1974, FHL film #1000559.

■ *Internal Revenue Assessment Lists for Pennsylvania, 1862-1865,* microfilm of original records (and finding aid) at the National Archives, Washington, D.C. Districts are divided into divisions and lists are generally alphabetical by first letter of last name within the division. No records were received for District 16 (Adams, Bedford, Franklin, Fulton, and Somerset counties). There is no 1863 annual list for District 22. Other miscellaneous lists which are missing for various divisions are noted in the finding aids on each film. Includes an index of counties and cities arranged alphabetically with the associated collection districts. Filmed by the National Archives, Series M787, 107 rolls. FHL has entire series, beginning with FHL film #1549103 (District 1 [Philadelphia, Wards 2-6 and 11] Annual, monthly and special lists Sept. 1862-Aug. 1863).

■ *Pennsylvania Civil War Veteran Burials,* edited by Marion F. Egge, published by the Pennsylvania Genealogical Magazine, Monograph Series No. 6, Philadelphia, 2000, Contents: Adams County, Perry County. From preface: "In an attempt to further its mission of making available genealogical information about Pennsylvania and Pennsylvanians, the Genealogical Society of Pennsylvania has embarked on a project to preserve and disseminate the records held by county departments of veterans' affairs.... As with any work, this volume has limitations; it is not claimed that the burials recorded by the county consist of every Civil War soldier, merely those on file at the county office. In addition, these are transcriptions of the records from the veterans' departments and some errors may lie in those original records. It is hoped that this volume is the beginning of series that will cover the entire state." FHL book 974.8 V3e v.1.

■ *Proceedings of the 41st Annual Encampment, Department of Pennsylvania, Grand Army of the Republic, Easton, June 5 and 6, 1907,* printed by the state printer, Harrisburg Pub. Co., 1907, 290 pages. FHL book 974.C4g. Also on microfilm, FHL film #1697886.

■ *Record of Eligibility of Ladies of the Grand Army of the Republic; Department of Pennsylvania; 1938-1993,* by GAR, Dept. of PA, microfilm of original records at Ellwood City, PA. Information includes name of circle and city where organized; name of applicants and residence; name of veteran and how applicant is related to him, rank of veteran, company, regiment, dates of enlistment, branch of service. Filmed by the Genealogical Society of Utah, 1993, 2 rolls, FHL films #1888615 and #1888616.

■ *Mother's Pension Accounts, 1913-1917,* microfilm of original records at the Pennsylvania State Archives, Harrisburg, PA. Counties are listed alphabetically. Record contains names of mothers receiving pensions and the names and ages of their children. Filmed by the Genealogical Society of Utah, 1979, 1 roll, FHL film #1032344.

■ **County Records Related to the Civil War Era.** For each of Pennsylvania's counties, the Family History Library has a wealth of published and microfilmed local records, including many related to the era of the Civil War, 1861-1869. As an example of one county, visit the Family Search website (**www.familysearch.org**) / Family History Library Catalog / place search: Pennsylvania / view related places / Adams County. Click on any of the categories, but note that one category is for "Pennsylvania, Adams – Military Records – Civil War, 1861-1865," where a specific item is listed: *1862 Adams County, Pennsylvania: Indexed Civil War Draft Lists,* by Sherry Bailey, published by Renaissance Market Press, Bellefonte, PA, 2004, 63 pages, FHL book 974.842 M2b. Repeat this exercise for all PA counties of interest.

RHODE ISLAND

Online Rhode Island Resources

Online Library Catalog Searching – Civil War Era Resources.

■ The **Rhode Island State Archives** in Providence holds the state's largest array of original resource materials related to Rhode Island's history, including the original state census returns for Rhode Island, 1865-1935; statewide birth and marriage records for the years 1853-1897; statewide deaths for the years 1853-1947; state military records relating to the Civil War era; and a myriad of records from state departments, agencies, boards, and commissions. Yet, this archives has virtually no presence on the Internet, except a page at the Secretary of State's website giving a brief description, address, and directions on how to get there – the RI archives wants you to visit the facility in person and any access to any of the state's archival records via the Internet is apparently well into the future. As a result, genealogists must visit other Internet websites to access catalog information or find what resources may be available on microfilm. Fortunately, many of the microfilmed resources are available at the Family History Library in Salt Lake City, and those of great value for the Civil War era are shown below under the Published Resources section.

■ The **Rhode Island State Library** in Providence is operated in a similar manner as the RI archives, except the library does have an online catalog – perhaps the worst online catalog for any state library in the country. It is cumbersome, restrictive, and difficult to sort through titles, authors, or subjects. A search for the keywords "civil war Rhode Island" brought up zero entries, and a search for just "civil war" brought up 61 entries, most of which were related to civil wars in other countries, not the American Civil War of 1861-1865. Clearly, the RI state library has the desired civil war references, but keyword searching at the online catalog does not reveal them.

■ Genealogists may find more success using the **Brown University Library Catalog** (Josiah), which is a state-of-the art Internet catalog listing for one of New England's best libraries in terms of holdings related to genealogical research. Go to: **http://dl.lib.brown.edu/libweb/index.php**, the Brown University Library Home Page, and search the "Josiah" catalog using keywords such as "civil war Rhode Island." That will bring up 293 results, including Annual Reports of the Adjutant General during the war years with complete rosters of troops, regimental histories, and many other resources directly related to the civil war in Rhode Island. The Brown University Library in Providence is also a great source for published New England family histories, county and town histories, and many, many other historical references for Rhode Island. For example, many of the huge databases of family and local histories digitized by Quintin Publications came from this library. The Quintin website identifies the thousands of titles, go to: **www.quintinpublications.com/**. It should be noted that over 10,000 Quintin databases are now going online at the World Vital Records site, a subscription genealogy look-up service at: **www.worldvitalrecords.com**.

■ **Rhode Island Historical Records Advisory Repositories Directory – State and Local Government Agencies.** **www.state.ri.us/rihrab/Statelocal.html**. This is a list of the agencies in Rhode Island holding historical records. Beginning with the state archives, Department of Health, Division of Vital Records, and Judicial Records Center, the list then identifies all Town and City Clerk Offices, with an address and phone number. With the exact name of each Town or City, a Google search should reveal whether there is a website specific to that Rhode Island location.

■ **Rhode Island Civil War Round Table.** **http://www.ricwrt.com/**. The Rhode Island Civil War Round Table, founded in 1992, is for those who share an interest in this area and Civil War research. This private website has been useful, mainly as a place to find links to related Civil War sites, including: ● The Department of Rhode Island, Sons of Union Veterans of the Civil War; ● The Rhode Island Re-enactors Association; ● First Rhode Island Volunteer Infantry; ● Battery B, First Regiment, Rhode Island Light Artillery; ● Battery F, 1st Rhode Island Light Artillery; ● Sons of Union Veterans of the Civil War, Elisha, Dyer Camp No. 7; ● The United States Civil War Center; ● The American Civil War Homepage.

Joining the RICWRT

To join the Rhode Island Civil War Round Table, you must fill in an application form (available at the website) and submit it with a check for $25 (made out to RICWRT) to cover a one-time-only initiation fee of $10 and $15 annual dues.

For more information about RICWRT, email Mark Dunkelman at: NYVI154th@aol.com.

Published Rhode Island Resources

■ *Index to Compiled Service Records of Volunteer Union Soldiers Who Served in Organizations from the State of Rhode Island,* microfilm of original records at the National Archives, Series M555, 7 rolls, beginning with FHL film #821940. This is the same list of names now online at the National Park Service website at: **www.civilwar.nps.gov/cwss/**.

■ *Official Register of Rhode Island Soldiers and Sailors, Who Served in the United States Army and Navy, from 1861 to 1865,* microfiche of original published by the State Printer, Providence, RI, 1866, 830 pages. Filmed by University Publications of America, Bethesda, MD, 1991, on 9 microfiche. FHL has this title cataloged as FHL fiche #6118831. See also *Military Records, 1847-1900,* microfilm of original records at the Rhode Island State Archives. Consists of descriptive books (mostly muster rolls) in the RI Adjutant General's office for various Rhode Island military units. Years span 1847-1848; 1861-1864; 1866, and 1879-1900. Filmed by the Genealogical Society of Utah, 1994, 7 rolls, beginning with FHL film #1976214 (1st Regt., A – K).

■ *Civil War Enlistment Papers for Various Rhode Island Military Units, 1862 and 1864,* microfilm of original records at the Rhode Island State Archives. Filmed by the Genealogical Society of Utah, 1996, 5 rolls, beginning with FHL film #2033187 (Enlistment papers, 11th Regiment, Abbot – Ryder). See also *List of Persons Drafted in the U.S. Army, 1863,* microfilm of originals at the Rhode Island State Archives, filmed by the Genealogical Society of Utah, 1974, 1 roll, FHL film #954935.

■ *Honor Roll of Rhode Island Soldiers Who Died During the Civil War: With Their Original Burial Locations,* a typescript by Sherman Lee Pompey, filmed by the Genealogical Society of Utah, 1975, 1 roll, FHL film #928044.

■ *1855 & 1865 Massachusetts State Census (Rhode Island People),* name lists for people born in Rhode Island, published serially in *Rhode Island Roots,* a periodical of the Rhode Island Genealogical Society, Greenville, RI, Vol. 19, No. 1 (Mar 1993) through Vol. 20, No. 4 (Dec 1994).

■ *1862-1866 Internal Revenue Tax Assessment Lists for Rhode Island,* microfilm of original records at the National Archives, Washington, D.C. Series M788, 1974, 7 rolls. FHL film #1299309-1299315.

■ *Providence (Rhode Island) City Directories,* microfilm of annual city directories published 1824-1933, by various publishers, collected and microfilmed by Research Publications, Woodbridge, CT, 1980-1984. Directories for the Civil War era included in this series are for the years 1861, 1862, 1863, 1864, 1865, 1866, 1867, 1868, and 1869. FHL has entire series, beginning with FHL film #6044349 (1824). For the 1861-1865 directories, see FHL film #1377340; the 1866-1869 directories, FHL film #1377341.

■ *1865 Rhode Island State Census and Index,* Microfilm of original records at the Rhode Island State Archives, Providence, RI. The census schedules and a card index compiled by the archives were filmed together in one series by the Genealogical Society of Utah, 1998, 29 rolls, beginning with FHL film #2135474 (Index, Baillayon – Boardman) through #2115175 (Index, Wood – Zuel); followed by the census schedules, Vol. 1 (#2130153) through Vol. 23 (#2130267). Contents of schedules: name of all members of a household, age, sex, color, place of birth, nativity of parents, whether a person over 15 could read or write, occupation, naturalization info, if attended school, deaf and dumb, blind, insane, or idiotic; employment in military or navy since 1860. It should be noted that for those persons born in Rhode Island, this census listing gives their exact Rhode Island Town of birth!

■ *1875 Rhode Island State Census Schedules,* microfilm of original records at the Rhode Island State Archives, Providence, RI. Filmed by the Genealogical Society of Utah, 1973, 9 rolls, FHL film #947361-947369. Refer also to *Rhode Island 1875 State Census Index Cards,* microfilm of original index cards prepared by the RI State Archives, filmed by the Genealogical Society of Utah, 2000, 48 rolls, beginning with FHL film #2223509. Contents of census schedules: name of each member of a household, marital status, nativity of parents, read/write, occupation, voter info, number of months in school (whether Public, Select, or Catholic School). NOTE: The 1875 state census did not ask questions about military service, but civil war veterans (or their widows) might be identified by using their 1865 location, or from the 1870 Federal census.

■ *1885 Rhode Island State Census*, microfilm of original records at the Rhode Island State Archives, Providence, RI. Filmed by the Genealogical Society of Utah, 1975, 13 rolls, beginning with FHL film #953910. In addition, the 1885 census was published in book form as *Rhode Island State Census, 1885,* published by E. L. Freeman, Printers to the State, Providence, RI, 1887, 660 pages. Includes a name index for each town, one for males, another for females. See FHL book 974.5 X2. Contents of census schedules: name of each family member of a household, sex, relationship to head of household, color/race, age, marital status, place of birth, nativity of parents, occupation, read/write, number of months in school, whether blind, deaf and dumb, idiotic, or insane; voting info for males over 21, and naturalization info. NOTE: The 1885 state census did not ask questions about military service, but civil war veterans (or their widows) might be identified by using their 1865/1875 location, or from the 1880 Federal Census.

■ *Rhode Island 1890 Special Census of Veterans,* by Ronald Vern Jackson, et al., published by Accelerated Indexing Systems, North Salt Lake, UT, 1986, 164 pages, FHL book 974.5 X22j.

■ *1905 Rhode Island State Census,* microfilm of original records at the Rhode Island State Archives, Providence, RI. Filmed by the Genealogical Society of Utah, 1997-1999, 445 rolls, beginning with FHL film #2070397. The name lists are organized by town, with separate alphabetized listing of males and females. Contents: name of all members of a household, relationship to head of household, color/race, age, marital status, date of birth, number of children, place of birth, read/write, year of immigration to the U.S., number of years in the U.S., number of years a resident of Rhode Island, number of months (of the census year) a resident of the Town, birthplace of father and mother, occupation, number of months unemployed, whether a Union soldier, sailor or marine during Civil War or service in the Spanish American War; pension information; and religion. NOTE: Rhode Island did not conduct a state census in 1895, but following 1905, three more state censuses were taken for 1915, 1925, and 1935/6, all available on microfilm at the Family History Library in Salt Lake City.

■ *Rhode Island Returns of Birth (1893-1898), Certificates of Death (1946-1948), Out of State Deaths (1946-1947, 1954-1955), Out of State Death Index (1900-1948, 1951-1954), and Miscellaneous 1954-1955,* microfilm of original records at the Rhode Island State Archives. Filmed by the Genealogical Society of Utah, 1999-2007, 25 rolls, beginning with FHL film #2167968 (Returns of Birth, 1893-1898).

■ *Rhode Island Vital Records: Deaths 1951-1955, Out of State Deaths Index, 1900-1905; Delayed Birth Index, 1846-1900; Birth Records & Index, 1902-1905; Marriage Records & Index, 1901-1905, and B, M, D Corrections 1800s-1919,* microfilm of original records at the Rhode Island State Archives. Filmed by the Genealogical Society of Utah, 2004-2007, 35 rolls, beginning with FHL film #2203568 (Deaths, 1951, Barrington – East Providence).

■ *Rhode Island Death indexes: 1921-1930, 1931-1935, 1936-1940, 1941-1945,* microfiche of the original records at the Rhode Island State Archives. Filmed by the archives, (no date), complete series at the FHL, fiche #6082179 (201 fiche).

■ *Rhode Island Index to Death Records on Microfiche, 1946-1950,* microfiche of the originals at the Rhode Island State Archives. Filmed by the archives, 2001. FHL has entire series, FHL fiche #6360213 (40 fiche).

■ *Delayed Births, 1846-1892, 1896-1898, 1901-1905; Index 1846-1898,* microfilm of originals at the Rhode Island State Archives. Filmed by the Genealogical Society of Utah, 1994-2007, 6 rolls, beginning with FHL film #1927508 (1846-1880).

■ *Arnold's Vital Records of Rhode Island: Contents of 21 Volumes,* microfilm of typescript in the Berkshire Athenaeum, Pittsfield, Massachusetts, 5 pages. Filmed by the Genealogical Society of Utah, 1961, 1 roll, FHL film #234583.

■ *Genealogical Index Rhode Island Records,* compiled by Frank T. Calef, a listing of names found in the vital records from Rhode Island with some dates and other information including the title of the vital record in which the person can be found. Filmed by the Genealogical Society of Utah, 1950, 42 rolls, FHL film #22431 (Aaron – Allen).

■ *Rhode Island Biographical and Genealogical Sketch Index,* compiled by J. Carlyle Parker, published by Marietta Publishing Co., 1991, 272 pages. This is an index to the biographies in 214 state, regional, county, and city histories; periodical articles, newspaper articles, and biographical directories published between 1827 and 1989. See FHL book 974.5 D32p.

SOUTH CAROLINA

Online South Carolina Resources

■ **South Carolina Archives Digital Collections.** **www.state.sc.us/scdah/pilotintro.htm.** The South Carolina Department of Archives and History (SCDAH) in Columbia is a pioneer in providing Internet access to its historical documents. The first collections made available online, however, were not the documents themselves, but indexes to them. For example, a combined index to the name lists began with the following collections:

- Confederate Pension Applications 1919-1938 (10,242 items)
- Criminal Journals 1769-1776 (2,087 items)
- Index to Multiple Record Series ca. 1675 -1929 (172,763 items)
- Legislative Papers 1782-1866 (52,951 items)
- National Register of Historic Places (494 items)
- Plats for State Land Grants 1784-1868 (51,809 items)
- School Insurance Photographs 1935-1952 (2,662 items)
- Will Transcripts 1782-1855 (11,059 items)

However, the SCDAH has now begun digitizing selected portions of its holdings for online access. The following materials have been scanned and are now linked within the index:

- Confederate Pension Applications, 1919-1938
- Insurance file photographs of public schools, 1935-1952
- Grand Jury Presentments to the General Assembly, 1783-1877
- National Register of Historic Places files
- Collection Curiosities
- Colonial Plats

A hit on a particular name in the index will indicate if an image is available. The index is powerful. You can search for all databases or select a specific database; then a name of an individual, location, document type, or time period; add a second individual; and even "and" "or" Boolean options. With these search options, you can be very specific to one or two names, two counties, and/or a specific range of years. And, even for a common surname such as Jones, the simple search is quick and rewarding.

■ **South Carolina State Library – WebLION Catalog Search.** The South Carolina State Library has an outstanding collection of materials related to the civil war era. A WebLION catalog search for just the keywords, "civil war" brought up over 2,000 entries, and adding "civil war South Carolina" brought up 232 titles, most with a thumb of the book cover.

■ **South Carolina in the Civil War Homepage.** **http://members.tripod.com/mwyckoff/.** This is a private website featuring links to South Carolina units of the civil war, battles, research, soldiers, and miscellaneous. **Section One – South Carolina Units** has links to unit histories and rosters for Artillery Units, Cavalry Units, and Infantry Units.

Section Two – Battles has links to Battles in South Carolina, Battles in Other States in which South Carolina Soldiers Fought, Official Reports, and Naval Actions in South Carolina. **Section three – Civil War Research** has links and addresses for archives, historical societies, and museums around the state that have information about the Civil War. **Section Four – South Carolina Soldiers** has links to biographical information and photos of South Carolina soldiers; lists of cemeteries around the state, and other states where South Carolina soldiers are buried; and links to dozens of sources of information on genealogy. **Section Five – Miscellaneous** has links to sites with history, regiments, and people; Civil War bookstores; other South Carolina Civil War Organizations; Crisis Fort Sumter; and Columbia Prisoner of War Camp.

■ **Civil War Rosters – South Carolina Links.** www.geocities.com/Area51/Lair/3680/cw/cw-sc.html. This is a list of 169 websites where lists of South Carolina's Civil War soldiers can be found. The rosters may be regimental lists, lists from censuses; and include lists of South Carolina soldiers found in other state lists, such as pensioners in Alabama, North Carolina, etc. Also included are maps, court records, and photographs.

Published South Carolina Resources

■ *1695-1925 Combined Alphabetical Index,* microfilm of original manuscript at the South Carolina Department of Archives and History, Columbia, SC. This is a computer-generated, microfilm finding aid to thirty early record series held either in the original or on microfilm. Reference numbers are given for each entry in the consolidated index so that patrons may order photocopies of the original documents. The index is on 19 rolls of microfilm, beginning with FHL #1690457 (A.C. Tuxberry Land & Timber Co. – Berkeley County).

■ *South Carolina Name Index to Genealogical Records Collected by South Carolina Daughters of the American Revolution (DAR)*, 25,666 pages filmed by the Genealogical Society of Utah, 1988. An alphabetical list of surnames, vol./page number of records collection, on 102 microfiche, FHL fiche #6052835 (fiche #1: A., Pearl – Abbott, Moses S.).

■ *1784-1883 South Carolina Land Grants,* microfilm of original records at the Secretary of State's Office in Columbia, SC. Includes partial general index. Also, some volumes individually indexed. Filmed by the Genealogical Society of Utah, 1950-1951, 50 rolls, beginning with FHL film #22531 (Index to grants, A-Z, 1790-1821).

■ *1864-1866 Internal Revenue Assessment Lists for South Carolina,* microfilm of originals at the National Archives, Washington, D.C. Includes index that references counties to districts and indicates whether the county is represented on reel 1, reel 2, or, both reels. This index is found at the beginning of each reel of film. Film by the National Archives, series M789, 2 rolls, FHL film 1578451 (Districts 1-2, 1865-1866); and FHL film #1578452 (District 2-3, 1864-1866).

■ *Charleston (South Carolina) City Directories,* microfilm of annual city directories published 1782-1934, by various publishers, collected and microfilmed by Research Publications, Woodbridge, CT, 1980-1984, 22 rolls. Directories for the Civil War era included in this series are for the years 1867/68 and 1869/70, FHL film #1376645.

■ *1890 South Carolina Census Index,* by Ronald Vern Jackson, et al., published by Accelerated Indexing Systems, North Salt Lake, UT, 1984, 32 pages. This is the name list of the special schedules of Union veteran soldiers and widows living in South Carolina, the only part of the 1890 Federal Census that survived the fire of 1921. There may be a few Confederate veterans listed, but they were not supposed to be included. Since the only troops supplied by South Carolina to the Union Army during the Civil War was one company of 67 colored troops, the names of people in this 1890 special census listing would most likely include U.S. veterans with service after the Civil War, or Civil War veterans who happened to be living in South Carolina in 1890. See FHL book 975.7 X28j.

■ *Records of the Assistant Commissioner for the State of South Carolina, Bureau of Refugees, Freedmen, and Abandoned Lands, 1865-1870,* microfilm of original records at the National Archives, Washington, D.C. The Bureau of Refugees, Freedmen, and Abandoned lands, often referred to as the Freedmen's Bureau, was established within the War Department by an act of March 3, 1865. In addition to supervising the disposition of abandoned or confiscated lands and property, Bureau officers issued rations, clothing, and medicine to destitute refugees and freedmen; established hospitals...schools; listened to complaints of the freedmen...helped black soldiers and sailors to file and collect claims for bounties, pensions, and pay arrearages. Includes indexes, and many of the records are arranged alphabetically by the surnames of the persons involved. Filmed by the National Archives, 1972, Series M869, 44 rolls. FHL has entire series, beginning with FHL film #1579188.

■ *Compiled Service Records of Confederate Soldiers Who Served in Organizations from the State of South Carolina,* microfilm of original index cards at the National Archives, Washington, D.C. Under each organizational unit, the compiled service records consist of a jacket-envelope for each soldier, labeled with his name, his rank, and the unit in which he served and typically containing card abstracts of entries relating to the soldier as found in original muster rolls, returns, hospital rolls, descriptive books, and lists of deserters; and the originals of any papers relating solely to the particular soldiers. Filmed by the National Archives, 1959, Series M267, 357 rolls. FHL has entire series, beginning with FHL film #1380691 (1st Cavalry A-B).

■ *Index to Compiled Service Records of Confederate Soldiers Who Served in Organizations from the State of South Carolina,* microfilm of original index cards at the National Archives, Washington, D.C. Filmed by the National Archives, 1962, Series M253, 35 rolls. FHL has entire series, beginning with FHL film #881967. This is the same list of names now online at the National Park Service website at: **www.civilwar.nps.gov/cwss/**.

■ *South Carolina Troops in Confederate Service,* compiled by A.S. Salley, published by R.L. Bryan, State Printer, Columbia, SC, 1913-1930, 3 vols. FHL has a microfilm copy, filmed by the Genealogical Society of Utah, 1977, 1 roll, FHL film #982339.

■ *South Carolina Civil War Pension Applications, 1888-1906,* microfilm of original records at the SCDAH, Columbia, SC. Information is in typed, alphabetical order, 1888-1906. It includes name, county, unit & year. Filmed by the Genealogical Society of Utah, 2000, 2 rolls, FHL film #2209910 and 1 application file on film #2210399. See also South Carolina Pension Rolls & Some Applications for Pension, 1888-1894, 1898, 1903, microfilm of original records at the SCDAH, Columbia, SC. Filmed by the Genealogical Society of Utah, 2000, 1 roll, FHL film #2209910.

■ *South Carolina's Confederate Pensioners in 1901,* by Brent H. Holcomb, published by SCMAR, Columbia, SC, 2001, 181 pages, FHL book975.7 M2hb.

■ *South Carolina State Pension List of Confederate Veterans for 1921,* microfilm of original published by Gonzales and Bryan, State Printers, Columbia, SC, 1922, 251 pages. Filmed by the Genealogical Society of Utah, 1960, 1 roll, FHL film #206856.

■ *Applications for the Home for Confederate Veterans, Columbia, South Carolina, ca. 1909-1958,* microfilm of original manuscripts at the SCDAH, Columbia. Filmed by the Genealogical Society of Utah, 2000, 4 rolls, beginning with FHL film #2194841.

■ *Artificial Limb Vouchers for Confederate Service (South Carolina), 1867-1869, 1880-1887,* microfilm of original records at the SCDAH, Columbia, SC. Includes index at the beginning of the film. Filmed by the Genealogical Society of Utah, 2005, 1 roll, FHL film #1574395. See also *Artificial Limbs for Confederate Soldiers,* by Patrick J. McCawley, published by Alexia J. Helsley, South Carolina, 1992, 40 pages. See FHL book 975.7 A1 No. 109.

■ *Broken Fortunes: South Carolina Soldiers, Sailors and Citizens Who Died in the Service of Their Country and State in the War for Southern Independence, 1861-1865,* by Randolph W. Kirkland, Jr., published by the South Carolina Historical Society, Charleston, 1995, 413 pages. Names are in alphabetical order. From Intro: "The organization of the individual records in this register of South Carolina dead generally follows that used in Professor [William J.] Rivers' "Roll of Honor" [Roll of the Dead] with the addition of burial location data and the inclusion of codes indentifying the information sources." See FHL book 975.7 M2k. See also, ***Roll of the Dead, South Carolina Troops, Confederate States Service,*** by William J. Rivers, published by SCDAH, Columbia, SC, 1995, 408 pages, FHL book 975.7 M2rd.

■ ***Cemetery Records of Confederate Soldiers Buried in South Carolina,*** author/publisher not named, published 1947, 46 pages, FHL book 975.7 V22c. Also on microfilm, FHL film #22822.

■ ***Confederate Service Records*** (for South Carolina soldiers who served in Alabama units), microfilm of original records compiled by the ADAH, filmed by the Genealogical Society of Utah, 1987, 1 roll, FHL film #1411532 (Item 14, South Carolina soldiers).

■ ***Recollections and Reminiscences, 1861-1865 Through World War I,*** United Daughters of the Confederacy, South Carolina Division, 12 vols. At the turn of the century, the Daughters of the Confederacy began compiling these recollections. From Intro: "Our purpose is to honor those women who collected the Original History, Reminiscences of Confederate Veterans, Letters written by Confederate Soldiers...Newspaper Accounts…The primary emphasis of vols. 1-7 is the Civil War. Beginning with part 8 of vol. 7 World War I is discussed. The Civil War remains the primary subject, however. Vol. 12 includes cemetery readings. Includes indexes. Some vols. include military rosters.
Includes personal recollections & biographical chronicles. FHL Library has: vols. 1-12, FHL book 975.7 M2rr v.1-12.

TENNESSEE

Online Tennessee Resources

■ **Tennessee State Library and Archives – History and Genealogy Webpage.**

www.state.tn.us/tsla/history/index.htm. At this webpage, go to the search box for "How Do I Find...? " which is categorized into the following record types:

- **Adoption Records** – link to the Dept. of Children's Services. Post-1951 Adoption Records may be available to qualified persons.
- **Birth and Death Certificates** – link to Genealogical Services Available by Mail – State Records; and Office of Vital Records, TN Dept. of Health. Includes information about delayed birth certificates, and information about obtaining birth and death records from the four larger cities in Tennessee (Nashville, Knoxville, Chattanooga, and Memphis) is also featured here. Death links are to the Index to Tennessee Death Records 1908-1912 (online) and Partial Index to Tennessee Death Records 1914-1925 (online); and a link to Selby County Register of Deeds.
- **Census Records** – all of Tennessee's federal censuses, 1820-1930. Information about using census indexes and link to Genealogical Services Available by Mail – Census Records.
- **Court Records** – Links to Courts Where Tennessee Court Cases Were Tried; Index to County Microfilm Reels; and Genealogical Fact Sheets About Tennessee Counties.
- **Deeds** – TSLA has microfilm of deeds from every county in Tennessee. The TSLA will conduct research in the deed records by a formal request form and fee. Links for deed information:
  - Early County Records Available on Interlibrary Loan
  - Genealogical Fact Sheets About Tennessee Counties
  - Genealogical Services Available by Mail – County Records (Deeds)
  - Index to County Microfilm Reels at TSLA
- **Divorce Records** – links:
  - Courts Where Tennessee Court Cases Were Tried
  - Earliest County Records at TSLA
  - Genealogical Services Available by Mail – County Records (Divorce)
  - Index to Names in the Acts of Tennessee 1796-1850
  - Index to County Microfilm Reels at TSLA
- **Land Grants** – Link to Genealogical Services Available by Mail – State Records (Land Grants)
- **Marriage Records** – Links:
  - Early County Records Available on Interlibrary Loan
  - Genealogical Fact Sheets About Tennessee Counties
  - Genealogical Services Available by Mail – County Records (Marriage)
  - Index to County Microfilm Reels at TSLA
  - Office of Vital Records, Tn. Department of Health

- **Military Records** – Links:
  - Genealogical Services Available by Mail – Military Records
  - National Personnel Records Center
- **Newspapers** – Links:
  - Genealogical Services Available by Mail – Miscellaneous Records (Newspapers)
  - Newspapers on Microfilm at TSLA
  - TSLA Interlibrary Loan Policies & Procedures
- **Probate Records** – Link to Genealogical Services Available by Mail – County Records (Probate)
- **Tax lists** – Links:
  - Early Tennessee Tax Lists at TSLA
  - Genealogical Fact Sheets About Tennessee Counties
  - Genealogical Services Available by Mail – County Records (Tax Lists)
  - Index to County Microfilm Reels at TSLA

For free-style searching in the TSLA county records, check out three webpages: 1) Early County Records Available on Interlibrary Loan, 2) Genealogical Fact Sheets About Tennessee Counties, and 3) Index to County Microfilm Reels at TSLA. Military records at the county level, in particular, Civil War era records such as county muster rolls, military lists, or pensions, can be found in the Genealogical Fact Sheets for each county – one of the best bibliographic listing from any state library in America. Instead of a cold search in Google or Catalog type searching, use the TSLA Genealogical Fact Sheet for any Tennessee county to see the incredible array of resources gathered together and made available at this outstanding state facility. The TSLA also provides an online search request, fees payable online, and covers virtually all of their resources. The webpages for "Genealogical Services Available by Mail" identify the records that will be searched, and number of copies that can be obtained for a basic fee.

■ **Tennessee State Library and Archives – Civil War Era Resources Online.** www.state.tn.us/tsla/history/military/index.htm. These resources are available at the TSLA:

- **Civil War Rosters** – Table and List of Titles. TSLA's collection includes many published rosters, pension applications, and other related lists from all states involved in the war, Union or Confederate.
- **Colored Confederate Pension Applications** – an online index.
- **Employment Rolls and Nonpayment Rolls of Negroes Employed in the Defenses of Nashville, 1862-1863** – an online index.
- **Members of the Confederate Relief and Historical Association of Memphis** – an online index.
- **Southern Claims Commission, Tennessee** – an online index.
- **Tennessee Confederate Pension Applications: Soldiers and Widows** – an online index.
- **Tennessee Confederate Physicians** – online index.

- **Tennessee Confederate Soldiers' Home Applications** – an online index.
- **Tennessee Civil War Flags** – icon images of each flag, click on the image to enlarge it to full screen, full color.
- **Tennessee Civil War Research Sources** – descriptions of Service Records, Pension Records, Biographical Sources, Unit Histories, and Manuscripts. Text for each category includes links to indexes, fact sheets, etc.
- **Tennessee Civil War Veterans' Questionnaires** – an online index. Beginning in 1914, an attempt was made to contact every living Confederate or Union veteran in Tennessee. They were asked to fill out a questionnaire and return it to Nashville. Over 1,650 completed forms were returned by 1922. The questionnaires were microfilmed, and this webpage has an index to the names. The responses are rich in detail about pre-war and post-war life, as well as military experiences. They include personal and family information; opinions about class and race distinctions; and details of agricultural, business and educational opportunities in nineteenth century Tennessee. Yes, 1,650 is a very small percentage of Tennessee's 195,000 Confederate and 55,000 Union soldiers, but if you are fortunate to find one of your relatives listed here, you will be handed one of the best (auto)biographical records of a person from any source.

■ **Tennessee and the Civil War.** www.tngenweb.org/civilwar/. This is a USGenNet website maintained by volunteers. Categories include:
- What's New
- Queries
- Confederate Records
- Union Records
- How-To
- Miscellaneous

■ **Civil War Rosters – Tennessee Links.** www.geocities.com/Area51/Lair/3680/cw/cw-tn.html. This site features links to 170 websites with Civil War rosters from Tennessee units, pensioners, and TN soldiers mentioned in other states.

Published Tennessee Resources

■ *Compiled Service Records of Confederate Soldiers Who Served in Organizations from the State of Tennessee,* microfilm of original records at the National Archives, Washington, D.C. The compiled service records consist of a jacket-envelope for each soldier, labeled with his name, his rank, and the unit in which he served. The jacket-envelope typically contains card abstracts of entries relating to the soldier as found in original muster rolls, returns, rosters, payrolls, appointment books, hospital registers, Union prison registers and rolls, parole rolls, and inspection reports; and the originals of any papers relating solely to the particular soldier. There are cross-reference cards and jacket-envelopes for soldiers' names that appear in the records under more than one spelling. Filmed by the National Archives, Series M268, 1959, 359 rolls. FHL has complete series, beginning with FHL film #880055 (A-An). See also, *Index to Compiled Service Records of Confederate Soldiers Who Served in Organizations from the State of Tennessee,* microfilm of original index cards at the National Archives, Washington, D.C. Filmed by the National Archives, 1956, Series M231, 48 rolls. FHL has entire series, beginning with FHL film #880055. This is the same list of names now online at the National Park Service website at: **www.civilwar.nps.gov/cwss/.**

■ *Compiled Service Records of Volunteer Union Soldiers Who Served in Organizations from the State of Tennessee,* microfilm of original records at the National Archives, Washington, D.C. Filmed by the National Archives, Series M395, 220 rolls. FHL has complete series, beginning with FHL film #821889 (A – Bl). See also, *Index to Compiled Service Records of Volunteer Union Soldiers Who Served in Organizations from the State of Tennessee,* microfilm of original index cards at the National Archives, Washington, D.C. Filmed by the National Archives, 1962, Series M392, 16 rolls. FHL has entire series, beginning with FHL film #821889. This is the same list of names now online at the National Park Service website at: **www.civilwar.nps.gov/cwss/.**

■ *Report of the Adjutant General of the State of Tennessee, of the Military Forces of the State, from 1861 to 1866,* microfiche of original published by S.C. Mercer, printer to the state, Nashville, 1966, 695 pages. Filmed by University Publications of America, Bethesda, MD, 1990, on 8 microfiche, FHL fiche #6082658.

■ *Tennesseans in the Civil War: A Military History of Confederate and Union Units with Available Rosters of Personnel,* compiled and published by the Civil War Centennial Commission, Nashville, TN, 1964, 2 vols. Includes index. FHL book 976.8 M2t v.1-2. Also on microfiche, FHL fiche #6046966.

■ *Tennessee's Confederate Dead,* compiled by Tony Hays, published by Tennessee River Press, Savannah, TN, 2000, 100 pages. FHL book 976.8 M2ht.

■ *1860-1861 John L. Mitchell's Tennessee State Gazetteer and Business Directory,* part of *Tennessee (State) Directories,* microfilm of originals published by various publishers, filmed by Research Publications, Woodbridge, CT, 1980-1984, on 8 microfiche. FHL fiche #6044535.

■ *Assessment Lists of the United States Direct Tax Commission for the District of Tennessee,* microfilm of originals at the National Archives, Washington, D.C. This assessment took place during the Civil War, 1861-1865. Filmed by the National Archives, Series T227, 6 rolls. FHL has entire series, as follows:
- Anderson County – Coffee County, FHL film #1578415.
- Coffee County – Gibson County, FHL film #1578416.
- Gibson County – Hancock County, FHL film #1578417.
- Hancock County – Madison County, FHL film #1578418.
- Marion County – Roane County, FHL film #1578419.
- Robertson County – Wilson County, FHL film #1578420.

■ *Confederate Service Records* (for Tennessee soldiers who served in Alabama units), microfilm of original records compiled by the ADAH, filmed by the Genealogical Society of Utah, 1987, 1 roll, FHL film #1411532 (Item 15, Tennessee soldiers).

■ *Confederate Veterans in Oklahoma: Tennessee,* compiled by Joe L. Todd, published by the Oklahoma Historical Society, Oklahoma City, 1996, 32 pages. This is a list of Confederate veterans living in Oklahoma (ca1910-1913), who served in Tennessee units during the Civil War. Arranged in alphabetical order by surname, the list gives name, rank unit, county of residence in Oklahoma, birth and death dates (if given) and the source of the information. The list was compiled from records of the United Confederate Veterans in the Archives Division of the Oklahoma Historical Society. FHL book 976.6 M2t.

■ *Tennessee Convicts: Early Records of the State Penitentiary*, by Charles A. Sherrill and Tomye M. Sherrill, published by C.A. Sherrill, Mt. Juliet, TN, 1997-2002, 2 vols. Includes index of places (vol. 1) and full-name indexes (vols. 1 & 2). Contents: vol. 1. 1831-1850; vol. 2. ca. 1850-1870. Vol. 2 has names in alphabetical order. FHL book 976.8 J6s.

■ *1890 Civil War Veterans Census, Tennessee*, transcribed and indexed by Byron and Barbara Sistler, published by Byron Sistler & Associates, Evanston, IL, 1978, 355 pages. FHL book 976.8 X2s. See also *Tennessee 1890 Census Index* [Union Veterans], Ronald Vern Jackson, editor, published by Accelerated Indexing Systems, Salt Lake City, UT, 1990, 376 pages, FHL book 976.8 X2j.

■ *The Tennessee Confederate Soldier's Home: Marching Out of the Mist Into the Light, Roster One and Roster Two, The Tennessee Confederate Veterans' Home*, by Judith A. Strange, published by Tennessee Tracers, Goodlettsville, TN, 1996. FHL book 976.8 M2s.

■ *Enumeration of Male Inhabitants of Twenty-One Years of Age and Upward, Citizens of Tennessee, January 1, 1891, as Provided for by an Act of General Assembly of Tennessee, Passed January 15, 1891, and Approved January 22, 1891*, extracted and published by Sue S. Reed, Houston, TX, 8 Vols. Each volume indexed. This is the only state census taken in Tennessee. Contents: Vol. 1: Anderson, Blount, Knox, and Sevier counties; vol. 2: Benton, Carroll, Henry, Houston, and Stewart counties; vol. 3: Dyer, Gibson, Lake, Obion, and Weakley counties; vol. 4: Shelby county; vol. 5: Cumberland, Fentress, Jackson, Loudon, Morgan, Overton, Putnam, Roane, and Scott counties; vol. 6: Campbell, Clay, Hancock, Macon, Pickett, Smith and Trousdale counties; vol. 7: Carter, Greene, Hawkins, Johnson, Sullivan,

Unicoi, and Washington counties; and vol. 8: Cheatham, Dickson, Hickman, Humphreys, Lawrence, Lewis, Perry, Wayne and Williamson counties. See FHL book 976.8 X2r v.1-8.

■ *Civil War Veterans Biographical and Genealogical Questionnaires, 1914-1922*, microfilm of original records at the Tennessee State Library and Archives, Nashville, TN. (See additional description in TN State Library and Archives online resources above. This microfilm series is for the original questionnaires, an online index to the names of the veterans is at the TSLA site). Filmed by the State Library, 1974, 9 rolls, copies at the FHL as follows:
- Federal, A – Z, FHL film #975591.
- Confederate, A – Bu, FHL film #975592.
- Confederate, By – Dor, FHL film #975593.
- Confederate, Dos – Go, FHL film #975594.
- Confederate, Gr – Ire, FHL film #975595.
- Confederate, Irw – McEl, FHL film #975596.
- Confederate, McEw – Picka, FHL film #975597.
- Confederate, Picke – So, FHL film #975598.
- Confederate, Sp – Y, FHL film #975599.

■ *Index to Tennessee Confederate Pension Applications*, transcribed and edited by Samuel D. Sistler, published by B. Sistler, Nashville, TN, 1995, 393 pages. FHL book 976.8 M22s. CD-ROM version: *Civil War Confederate Pension Applications Index*, Family Tree Maker's Family Archives. Military Records, No. 56. FHL CD-ROM No. 9, Part 155.

■ *Confederate Pension Applications: Soldiers and Widows, 1891- ca. 1965*, microfilm of original records at the Tennessee State Library and Archives, Nashville, TN. Tennessee began granting pensions to resident Confederate veterans in 1891 and to their widows in 1905. Includes indexes. Widows applications may include marriage certificates. Filmed by TSLA, 1975, 181 rolls. FHL has entire series, beginning with FHL film #978497 (Pensioners index) and FHL film #933353 (Index to soldier's applications, As-Gi). See also *Tennessee's Confederate Widows and Their Families: Abstracts of 11,190 Confederate Widows Pension Applications*, by Edna Wiefering, published by Cleveland Public Staff & Volunteers, Cleveland, TN, 1992, 479 pages. FHL book 976.8 M28w. Refer to item above for Tennessee State Library and Archives – Civil War Era Resources.

There is an online index to the names from Confederate Pension Applications: Soldiers and Widows.

TEXAS

Online Texas Resources

■ **Texas State Library and Archives – Genealogy Page.** www.tsl.state.tx.us/arc/ genfirst.html#cpi. The **Library Catalog of Texas State Agencies** is a searchable online card catalog. A search in the catalog for the keywords "civil war Texas" brought up 211 entries, including several roster lists, regimental histories, and Adjutant General name lists. A link to the catalog search form is available at the Genealogy Page. Genealogy resources available at the Texas State Library are extensive. At the Genealogy Page, each of the described record groups below includes references to people from the Civil War era:

■ **Texas State Library and Archives – Online Searchable Indexes:**
- **Index to Confederate Pension Applications (Online searchable index).** This is an interactive search to the names, county of residence, and pension number for some 54,634 approved, rejected, and home pensions issued by the Texas government between 1899 and 1975.
- **Index to Texas Adjutant General Service Records, 1836-1935. (Online searchable index).** The Service Records Series combines both official service record files from the Adjutant General's Office and alphabetical files created by other agencies which contain records related to an individual's service in a military unit.
- **Index to Republic Claims. (Online searchable index).** This series includes claims for payment, reimbursement, or restitution submitted by citizens to the Republic of Texas government from 1835 through 1846. It also includes records relating to Republic pensions and claims against the Republic submitted as public debt claims after 1846.
- **Confederate Indigent Families Lists. (Online searchable index).** View the names of families that received aid through the 1863 "Act to Support the Families and Dependents of Texas Soldiers." View the lists Alpha by County, or Alpha by Last name.

■ **Texans in the Civil War.** www.angelfire.com/ tx/RandysTexas/. This private civil war site features a combined index to rosters of all Texas Confederate units, with a search box for typing in a name. The indexed names are from various Texas civil war unit websites. Or, go to the links listed by the named divisions, brigades, or legions for infantry or cavalry units. As a portal to Texas civil war sites, both rosters and regimental histories, this service is very complete and very useful. Compare the names with those found at the National Park Service website at: **www.civilwar.nps.gov/cwss/.** Confederate unit histories are not complete at the NPS website, but this Texas site provides links to all known Texas regimental histories.

Published Texas Resources

■ **Texas State Library and Archives – On-site Resources:**
- **Vital Statistics Indexes.** The collection does not include the certificates themselves, but selected indexes to Texas births, deaths, marriages and divorces, all available for on-site use in the Genealogy Collection. This link gives complete information on accessing the vital statistics records.
- **Texas County Tax Rolls on Microfilm** are available for on-site use from the early years of each county through 1921. This link describes the records, the counties included, and any missing reels.
- **Index of County Records on Microfilm** is available online, along with instructions for borrowing rolls through interlibrary loan. Although the microfilm is housed in depository libraries throughout Texas, the Genealogy Collection houses the film for the following counties: Atascosa, Bandera, Bastrop, Bexar, Blanco, Caldwell, Comal, Frio, Gillespie, Guadalupe, Hays, Karnes, Kendall, Kerr, Kinney, Llano, McMullen, Medina, Uvalde, and Wilson. Click on a Texas county to see what records are available and the location of the microfilm in a Texas repository.
- **Selected Texas City Directories** from the past are available for on-site use in the Genealogy Reading Room. The link gives a complete list of Texas cities and years of publication for which any newspapers are available.
- **1867 Voters' Registration.** The Reconstruction Act of March 13, 1867 required the commanding officer in each military district to have, before September 1, a registration of all qualified voters in each county. These lists would be used to determine all who would be eligible to vote for any proposed Constitutional Convention in the state. Voter registrations took place between 1867 and 1869, with a few in 1870. This link shows the Texas counties and microfilm rolls on which they are organized. See the microfilmed and index resources

under the Published TX Resources below.

- **Texas Convict Record Ledgers and Indexes.** The record ledgers are excellent sources of individual convict descriptions and information regarding their incarceration. This series, available for use only on microfilm, may be viewed on-site in the Genealogy Reading Room or borrowed through the interlibrary loan program. This link describes the ledgers and indexes with the types of information, years of coverage, etc.

■ *Compiled Service Records of Confederate Soldiers Who Served in Organizations from the State of Texas,* microfilm of original records at the National Archives, Washington, D.C. The compiled service records consists of a jacket-envelope for each soldier, labeled with his name, his rank, and the unit in which he served. The jacket-envelope typically contains card abstracts of entries relating to the soldier as found in original muster rolls, returns, rosters, payrolls, appointment books, hospital registers, Union prison registers and rolls, parole rolls, and inspection reports; and the originals of any papers relating solely to the particular soldier. There are cross-reference cards and jacket-envelopes for soldiers' names that appear in the records under more than one spelling. Filmed by the National Archives, series M323, 445 rolls, 1965. FHL has entire series, beginning with FHL film #880014 (A – As).

■ *Index to Compiled Service Records of Confederate Soldiers Who Served in Organizations from the State of Texas,* microfilm of original records at the National Archives, Washington, D.C. Filmed by the National Archives, series M227, 41 rolls, 1955. FHL has entire series, beginning with FHL film #880014 (surnames A-As). This list of names is now online at the National Park Service website at: **www.civilwar.nps.gov/cwss/.**

■ *Texas Confederate Military Service Records Compiled from Muster Rolls in the Texas State Archives, 1860-1865,* microfilm of original records, now located at the National Archives, Washington, D.C. Filmed by the TX archives, 19--, 10 rolls. The first roll in the series contains an alphabetical list of company commanders; an alpha list of counties containing names of company commanders and muster roll numbers; and the start

of an alpha list of TX Confederate soldiers with service records taken from muster rolls. FHL has complete series, beginning with FHL film #2282486. See also *Muster Lists of the Texas Confederate Troops,* compiled by Sherman Lee Pompey, published by Historical and Genealogical Pub. Co., 1966, FHL has 8 vols. in 1, FHL book 976.4 M23p.

■ *Texas Confederate Index: Confederate Soldiers of the State of Texas,* microfilm of original manuscript. Includes name, rank, commission, enlistment date and place, discharge date and place, company, and description (age, residence, etc.). Filmed by Microfilm Service and Sales, Dallas, TX, 1961, 14 rolls. FHL has entire series, beginning with FHL film #227483 (A – Bradford).

■ *Index to Confederate Commanding Officers,* microfilm of original manuscript. Arranged alphabetically by surname, and gives the officer's military unit. Includes an index to names of commanding officers by Texas county. Filmed by Microfilm Service and Sales, Dallas, TX, 1961, 1 roll, FHL film #227482.

■ *Compiled Service Records of Volunteer Union Soldiers Who Served in Organizations from the State of Texas,* microfilm of original records at the National Archives, Washington, D.C. Filmed by the National Archives, series M402, 13 rolls, 1962. FHL has entire series, beginning with FHL film #1292646 (First Cavalry, A – Bo, 1861-1865).

■ *Index to Compiled Service Records of Volunteer Union Soldiers Who Served in Organizations from the State of Texas,* microfilm of original records at the National Archives, Washington, D.C. Filmed by the National Archives, series M393, 1963, 2 rolls. See FHL film #881592 (Index, A – Ma); and FHL film #881593 (Index, Mc – Z). This list of names included online at the National Park Service website at: **www.civilwar.nps.gov/cwss/.**

■ *Confederate Service Records* (for Texas soldiers who served in Alabama units), microfilm of original records compiled by the ADAH, filmed by the Genealogical Society of Utah, 1987, 1 roll, FHL film #1411532 (Item 16, Texas soldiers).

■ *Confederate Officers of Texas,* by Frances T. Ingmire, published by Mountain Press, Signal Mountain, TN, 1983, 107 pages. An alphabetical list of officers, giving date and company in which they served. A separate section lists officers by county. FHL book 976.4 M2iftc.

■ *Texas Confederate Home Roster: With Added Data from Confederate Home Ledgers,* compiled by Kathryn Hooper Davis, Linda Ericson Devereaux and Carolyn Reeves Ericson, published by Ericson Books, Nacogdoches, TX, 2003, 349 pages. Includes names of over 2,000 Confederate veterans and/or their wives who were cared for in their later years in the Confederate Home in Austin, Texas. See FHL book 976.4 M2dkh.

■ **Texas Confederate Scrip Grantees,** by Thomas Lloyd Miller, published by Ericson Books, Nacogdoches, TX, 1985, 165 pages. Grantees in alphabetical order by surname, giving the county where the land granted, certificate number, date issued, and whether the grant was given to the veteran or his widow. FHL book 976.4 R2mt.

■ **Civil War Burial Sites in Texas.** See 1), *Burial List of the Texas Confederate Troops,* compiled by Sherman Lee Pompey, published by Pacific Specialties, 1974, 1 vol., filmed by the Genealogical Society of Utah, 1975, 1 roll, FHL film #908986; and see 2), *Union Veterans of the Civil War: Buried in the State of Texas,* compiled by Kathy Wells, published by the Daughters of Union Veterans of the Civil War, 1861-1865, Latha Jane Boyd Tent #1 (Arlington, TX), 72 pages, includes index, FHL book 976.4 V3w; and see 3), *Texas Burial Sites of Civil War Notables: A Biographical and Pictorial Field Guide,* by James A. Mundie, Jr., published by Hill College Press, Hillsboro, TX, 2002, 414 pages. From book jacket: "The men and women covered, both Unionists and Confederates, include politicians, generals, naval officers, authors and civilians. A biography is given for each individual, along with directions to where he or she is buried. The book covers people in 290 cemeteries, in 131 counties, in every region of Texas." Includes index. FHL book 976.4 V3m.

■ *Confederate Indigent Families Lists of Texas, 1863-1865,* transcribed by Linda Mearse, published by the author, San Marcos, TX, 1995, 499 pages. (See the reference above for the Texas State Library and Archives, *Confederate Indigent Families Lists,* an online searchable index).

■ *Internal Revenue Assessment Lists for Texas, 1865-1866,* microfilm of original records at the National Archives, Washington, DC. Name lists are organized by federal districts/divisions, as follows: DISTRICT 2: Atascosas, Austin, Bee, Calhoun, Cameron, Colorado, De Witt, Duval, Encinal, Fayette, Fort Bend, Frio, Goliad, Gonzales, Hidalgo, Jackson, Karnes, La Salle, Lavaca, Live Oak, McMullin, Matagorda, Maverick, Nueces, Refugio, San Patricio, Starr, Victoria, Washington, Webb, Wharton, Zapata, and Zavala counties. DISTRICT 3: Archer, Bandera, Bastrop, Baylor, Bill, Bexar, Blanco, Bosque, Brown, Buchanan, Burleson, Burnet, Caldwell, Clay, Colahan (Callahan), Comal, Comanche, Concho, Cooke, Coryell, Dawson, Denton, Eastland, Edwards, El Paso, Erath, Falls, Gillespie, Guadalupe, Hamilton, Hardeman, Haskell, Hays, Hill, Jack, Johnson, Jones, Kemble (Kimble), Kerr, Kinney, Knox, Lampasas, Llano, McCulloch, Mason, Medina, Menard, Milam, Montague, Palo Pinto, Parker, Presidio, Runnels, San Saba, Shackelford, Tarrant, Taylor, Throckmorton, Travis, Uvalde, Wichita, Wilbargar (Wilbarger), Williamson, Wise, and Young counties. DISTRICT 4: Anderson, Bowie, Cass, Cherokee, Collin, Dallas, Ellis, Fannin, Freestone, Grayson, Harrison, Henderson, Hopkins, Hunt, Kaufman, Lamar, Limestone, Marion, Navarro, Panola, Red River, Rusk, Smith, Titus, Upshur, Van Zandt, and Wood counties. DISTRICT 4, DIVISION 15: Ellis, Freestone, Limestone, and Navarro counties. Filmed by the National Archives, series M791, 2 rolls, FHL #1578479 (District 2) & FHL film #1578480 (Districts 3-4).

■ *Texas 1867 Special Voter's Registration: Includes Information for 1867-1869,* microfilm of original records at the Texas State Library and Archives, Austin, TX. Registration forms include the name of the person, date of registration; county and precinct of residence; years resided in state; years resided in county; years resided in precinct; native of what state or county; how, when and where naturalized; signature; and general remarks. Filmed by the TX archives, 1984, 7 rolls. FHL has entire series, beginning with FHL film #1929135 (Anderson County – Caldwell County).

■ *An Index to the 1867 Voters Registration of Texas,* CD-ROM publication compiled by Donaly E. Brice and John C. Barron, published by Heritage Books, Bowie, MD, 2000. ISBN 0788413546. FHL has copy as CD-ROM No. 898. Voter lists are arranged by county, giving the person's name, date of registration, voting precinct, years of residence, and state or country of birth. This list includes the first statewide listing of freed slaves in Texas.

■ *Confederate Pensions (Texas): Applications Approved and Rejected,* microfilm of original records of the Comptroller's Office, Austin, TX. Applications are filed in numerical order by filing numbers, generally from the earliest to the latest, regardless of place of residence of applicant. (Texas granted a pension to any Civil War veteran living in Texas ca1870). Filmed by the Genealogical Society of Utah, 1974, 700 rolls, beginning with FHL film #960664 (Approved Applications, No. 1-132) through FHL film #975153 (Approved Applications, No. 52069-52094); followed by Rejected Applications, Abbe-Aker, FHL film #975154 through Woods-Yates, FHL film #976332; and Confederate Home Pension Applications and Miscellaneous Accepted/Rejected applications through the last three rolls, ending with FHL film #1027893.

■ **Indexes to Texas Confederate Pensions.** 1) Refer to *Confederate Pension Index for Texas, 1870-1930,* microfilm of original records at the Texas State Library and Archives, Austin, TX. Filmed by the Genealogical Society of Utah, 1966, 1 roll, FHL film #2031526. See also, 2) *Index to Applications for Texas Confederate Pensions,* compiled by John M. Kinney, published by the Archives, Austin, TX, 1975, 354 pages, FHL book 976.4 M22k 1975. Also, 3) a revised edition by Peggy Oakley was published in 1977, 357 pages, FHL book 976.4M22k 1977. See also 4), *Robert's Guide & Index to Texas Confederate Pension Application and Payment Records, 1899-1979,* compiled by Anthony Black, Robert de Berardinis and the Texas State Library and Archives staff. Published by Teckel Press, Houston, 2006, 6 vols., arranged alphabetically by surname of applicant: vol. 1, A; vol. 2, B-D; vol. 3, E-J; vol. 4, K-O; vol. 5, P-S, and vol. 6, T-Z. See FHL book 976.4 M22b v.1-6.

■ *1890 Texas Census Index of Civil War Veterans or their Widows,* compiled by Bryan Lee Dilts, published by Index Publishing, Salt Lake City, UT, 1984, 69 pages, FHL book 976.4 X22dv. See also *Texas 1890: Special Census of Veterans,* by

Ronald Vern Jackson, et al, published by Accelerated Indexing Systems, 1987, 136 pages, FHL book, 976.4 X22J. **Note:** Although the special 1890 Federal Census schedule specified that the veterans lists were to be used for Union veterans only, the Texas schedules included many Confederate soldiers and sailors as well.

■ *1895-1899 Rosters, United Confederate Veterans,* microfilm of manuscripts housed at the Jackson Barracks Military Library, New Orleans, LA. The first head of the United Confederate Veterans Association in 1895 was also at the time the Adjutant General of the state of Louisiana. As a result, the collection of original applications for membership from Confederate veterans from all over the country were gathered and maintained at the Louisiana Adjutant General's office; now located at Jackson Barracks, New Orleans, the present headquarters for the Louisiana National Guard. These original applications contain hidden genealogical information about a Confederate veteran that may not be known from any other source. The applications have never been microfilmed, but this series of rosters of membership would indicate if such a document exists, and a request for a copy could be made to the Jackson Barracks Military Library. Rosters filmed by the Genealogical Society of Utah, 1990, 2 rolls, FHL film #1710607 (Rosters 1895-1899, Alabama – Mississippi) and FHL film #1710608 (Rosters 1895-1899, Missouri – West Virginia, miscellaneous).

■ *Texas Division, United Daughters of the Confederacy Ancestor Roster,* edited by Loretta E. Burns, published by the Texas UDC, 1994-1996, 5 vols. Each volume is indexed. FHL book 976.4 D2u (v.1-5).

UTAH TERRITORY

Utah Territory's official involvement in the civil war consisted of the forming of one company of cavalry troops to support the Union army. After a request from President Abraham Lincoln to Brigham Young, the Lot Smith Company, Utah Cavalry was formed in the Spring of 1862 in Salt Lake City, and given the mission of protecting telegraph lines from Indian attacks. They were specifically charged with protecting the lines along the North Platte River in Nebraska Territory to Fort Bridger in Utah Territory (now in Wyoming). A footnote re Capt. Lot Smith: In 1857, Lot Smith was the leader of the Nauvoo Legion, a Mormon force sent by Brigham Young to attack the U.S. Army troops en route to Utah Territory – troops initially dispatched to take control of Utah Territory away from the Mormons. Lot Smith's rangers never found the main body of U.S. Army troops, but did manage to destroy several of the supply wagons of the Union wagon train, delaying the impending "Mormon War." The conflict was later diffused by the peaceful installment of a federally appointed governor, and the encampment of nearly 4,000 U.S. Army troops in Utah Territory. With the blessing of Brigham Young in 1862, Lot Smith joined the same army he had fought against in 1857.

Online Utah Resources

A list of 96 soldier records of Smith's Company of Cavalry is online at the National Park Service website at: **www.civilwar.nps.gov/cwss/**.

Published Utah Resources

■ *Compiled Service Records of Volunteer Union Soldiers Who Served in Organizations from the Territory of Utah: (Capt. Lot Smith's Company, Utah Calvary)*, microfilm of original records at the National Archives, Washington, D.C. Filmed by the National Archives, series M692, 1967, 1 roll. See FHL film #821588.

■ *Index to Compiled Service Records of Volunteer Union Soldiers Who Served in Organizations from the Territory of Utah*, microfilm of original records at the National Archives, Washington, D.C. Includes records from Captain Smith's Co., Utah Cavalry. Each index card gives name, rank, and unit in which the soldier served. Cross references are given for names that appear in record under different spellings. Filmed by the National Archives, series M556, 1964, 1 roll. See FHL film #1292645. The list of 96 soldiers of Smith's Company of Cavalry is now online at the National Park Service website at: **www.civilwar.nps.gov/cwss/**.

■ *Service Records of Indian Wars in Utah, 1853-1868,* microfilm of original records (Board of Commissioners of Indian War Records, Utah), filmed by the Genealogical Society of Utah, 1966, 11 rolls, beginning with FHL film #485506 (Index, Aag – Boo).

■ *Civil War Veteran Burials from the Arizona Territory, Nebraska, Nevada, New Mexico, Oregon, Utah and the Washington Territory,* manuscript compiled by Sherman Lee Pompey, filmed by the Genealogical Society of Utah, 1975, 1 roll, FHL film #908986.

■ *Records of Veterans with Federal Service Buried in Utah, Territorial to 1966,* microfilm of records at the Utah State Archives, Salt Lake City, UT. Index lists name, war served in, county, city, and cemetery of burial. Record may give name, rank, organization served with and branch of military, date of enlistment and discharge, date of birth and death, place of birth and death, place of burial and lot. Filmed by the Genealogical Society of Utah, 1966, 19 rolls, beginning with FHL film #485245 (name index for all UT counties). See also *Database-Alpha: Veteran Burials,* microfiche of original records at the Utah State Archives. Listing gives name, personal information such as birth and death dates, military information such as rank, unit, enlistment and discharge dates, and place buried. Filmed by the archives, 1986, 16 microfiche, FHL fiche #6331395. See also, *Veterans Buried in Utah,* microfiche of original records, "Military Department, Public Data" at the Utah State Archives, Salt Lake City, UT. Filmed by the archives, 1983, on 5 fiche, FHL fiche #6331396.

■ *Grand Army of the Republic – Utah Membership,* microfilm of original records at the Utah State Archives, Salt Lake City, UT. Contains membership records for GAR posts 1-5, 7, 22 in Utah. Membership records include town of residence, military unit, date of enlistment, date of discharge, and birthplace. Filmed by the archives, 1981, 2 rolls. See FHL films #1666083 and #1666089.

■ *Internal Revenue Assessment Lists for Utah* (microfilm of original state copy at the Utah State Archives with the title, *Assessment Book, Division No. 1, for the Territory of Utah 1867, 1862*).

Filmed by the Genealogical Society of Utah, 1956, 1 roll, FHL film #25780.

■ *The Saints and the Union: Utah Territory During the Civil War,* by E. B. Long, published by University of Illinois Press, Urbana, IL, 1981, 310 pages. Includes index. See FHL book 979.2 H2Le. (Also available at Amazon.com).

VERMONT

Online Vermont Resources

■ **Vermont State Archives – Genealogy Page.** http://vermont-archives.org/research/ genealogy/gene.htm. The Vermont State Archives provides an excellent library of materials useful for genealogical research, including the **Nye Index**, which is a name and subject index to 18th and 19th Century (mostly pre-1840) state records called the Manuscript Vermont State Papers. Civil War records held by state government are at the Reference and Research building. A link at this site to the Vermont Military Records Project includes a PDF textual finding aid online for "Records of the Adjutant and Inspector General," and another for "Military Records Collections." These downloadable PDF files are extensive, with details about the records available, including every Vermont regiment of the Civil War, rosters of soldiers, histories of the regiments, and more.

■ **Vermont Historical Society – Genealogy Page.** http://vermonthistory.org/index.php?option=com_ content&task=view&id=27&Itemid=230. This web-page presents a good review of the types of Vermont records available. Unlike most other New England states, Vermont's collection of indexed town records is small. But, serving as a unique alternative, Vermont's cemetery records database is huge, providing an index to Vermont's past in more detail than any other New England state. The VHS also has a card file created by the WPA during the 1930s that lists the men with military service buried in Vermont, available at the Reference Room of the VHS Library. The VHS online catalog is accessible from this webpage, and a keyword search in the catalog for "civil war Vermont" revealed 461 titles.

■ **Vermont in the Civil War Database Search.** http://vermontcivilwar.org/index/index.php. This VermontCivilWar.Org database has more than 35,500 names listed, including those who served in Vermont, U.S. and other States' units, those who were drafted (whether they served or not), and those from other States' units who are buried in Vermont. Entries contain name, town credited to (not necessarily town of residence), age at enlistment, and service information.

■ **Vermont Civil War Battles.** http://americancivilwar.com/statepic/vt.html. Part of the AmericanCivilWar.com battle sites section, this reference to Vermont's only battle of the Civil War is interesting because it was also the strangest battle of the war. 19 October 1864 was the date of a rather famous raid on St. Albans, Vermont. This was conducted by uniformed Confederates who were resisted poorly by a handful of Home Guards and the Invalid Corps (Veteran Reserves) – all of Vermont's regular troops were engaged in actions out of state. This armed incursion on the Union's northern border was an outgrowth of a large and complicated Confederate intelligence operation conducted in Canada throughout the war. Although the Confederates had plans to establish a northern front that would force a division of Union forces and support the Confederate cause in the South, the St. Albans raid was the only "invasion" conducted.

■ **The Civil War Archive – Union Regimental Histories – Vermont.** www.civilwararchive.com/Unreghst/uncttr1.htm#1 stcav. This website reproduces the regimental histories from Frederick H. Dyer's *A Compendium of the War of the Rebellion.* Each Vermont unit is described with a brief history of its formation date and place, marching orders, battles, number killed, wounded, and deaths by disease; and mustering out dates.

Published Vermont Resources

■ *Index to Compiled Service Records of Volunteer Union Soldiers Who Served in Organizations from the State of Vermont,* microfilm of original records at the National Archives, Washington, D.C. Filmed by the National Archives, 1964, series M557, 14 rolls. FHL has entire series, beginning with FHL film #882472 (A – Be). This list of names is included online at the National Park Service website at: **www.civilwar.nps.gov/cwss/**.

■ *Revised Roster of Vermont Volunteers: And Lists of Vermonters Who Served in the Army and Navy of the United States during the War of the Rebellion, 1861-66,* compiled by authority of the General Assembly under the direction of Theodore S. Peck, Adjutant-General, printed in 1892 by the Watchman Publishing Co., Montpelier, VT, 863 pages. Includes index. See FHL book 974.3 M2va. Also on microfilm, FHL film #1036000. Another filming, FHL film #1000623.

■ *Index to State of Vermont Military Records: Revolutionary War, Civil War, War of 1812: Salvaged from the State Arsenal Fire, September 1, 1945,* photocopy of typescript, FHL book 974.3 M22i. Also on microfilm, FHL film #824107.

■ *Internal Revenue Assessment Lists for Vermont, 1861-1866,* microfilm of original records at the National Archives, Washington, D.C. Filmed by the National Archives, 1980, series M792, 7 rolls. FHL has entire set, beginning with FHL film #1578444.

■ *General Index to Vital Records of Vermont, Early to 1870,* microfilm of original records in the Office of the Secretary of State, Montpelier, VT. Index includes births, deaths and marriages. Some cards filmed out of sequence. Filmed by the Genealogical Society of Utah, 1951, 287 rolls, beginning with FHL film #27455 (A – Adams, C). See also a CD-ROM publication entitled, *Index to Vermont Vital Records Early to 1870* compiled and published by D. R. King, Bountiful, UT, 1999, FHL CD-ROM No. 1309.

■ *1865 Vermont Directory,* reproduction of original book published 1865, prepared by Alice I. Noble, Atlanta, GA, 1994, 144 pages. FHL book 974.3 E4v.

■ *1890 Vermont Census Index: Special Schedule of the Eleventh Census (1890) Enumerating Union Veterans and of Union veterans of the Civil War,* by Ronald Vern Jackson, published by Accelerated Indexing Systems, Salt Lake City, UT, 1984, 156 pages, FHL book 974.3 X22j.

■ *Vermont in the Civil War: A History of the Part Taken by the Vermont Soldiers and Sailors in the War for the Union, 1861-65,* by G.G. Benedict, originally published by Free Press Association, Burlington, VT, 1886-1888, 2 vols., includes index. FHL has microfilm version, filmed by W.C. Cox Co., Tucson, AZ, 1975, 1 roll, FHL film #1000622.

■ *Vermont in the Great Rebellion: Containing Historical and Biographical Sketches, etc.,* by Otis F.R. Waite, originally published by Tracy, Chase and Company, Claremont, NH, 1869, 288 pages. Filmed by the Genealogical Society of Utah, 1991, 1 roll, FHL film #1697492.

■ *Full Duty: Vermonters in the Civil War,* by Howard Coffin, published by Countryman Press, Woodstock, VT, 1993, 376 pages, FHL book 974.3 M2ch.

VIRGINIA

Online Virginia Resources

■ **The Library of Virginia – Genealogical Research Page. www.lva.lib.va.us/whatwehave/ gene/index.htm.** The Library of Virginia and its extensive Archives Collections serves Virginia as both the state library and state archives. Located in downtown Richmond, the Library of Virginia holds one of America's greatest collection of genealogical materials. This webpage describes the basic genealogical resources at the Library of Virginia, including Census Records, Vital Records, County and City Records, Military Records, Bible Records, Genealogical Notes and Charts, and Published Family Histories. A 2-page PDF file is available, linked from the Genealogy Page, "Researching in the Archives Collections," and is nicely arranged in a Frequently Asked Questions (FAQ) format. Another link from this webpage will print an 8-page PDF file, "Published Materials for Genealogists," an outstanding review of the collections, with links to online databases, finding aids, and titles of useful guidebooks. For example, under the section, "Civil War," the following published references are highlighted:

- Wallace, Lee A. *Guide to Virginia Military Organizations, 1861–1865*. Rev. 2nd ed. Lynchburg, Va.: H.E. Howard Publishing, 1986. Call no. E581.4 W3 1986.
- Sifakis, Stewart. *Compendium of the Confederate Armies. Virginia.* New York: Facts on File, 1992. Call no. E581 S5 1992.
- United States. War Department. *The War of the Rebellion: A Compilation of the Official Records of the Union and Confederate Armies*. Harrisburg, Pa.: National Historical Society, distributed by Broadfoot Publishing, 1985. Call no. E464 A512.
- *Virginia Regimental History Series*. Lynchburg or Appomattox, Va.: H. E. Howard Publishing, 1982–. Call no. E581.5 1st–.
- Hewett, Janet B., ed. *Roster of Confederate Soldiers, 1861–1865*. Wilmington, N.C.: Broadfoot Publishing, 1995–. Call no. E548 H4 1995.
- ———. *Roster of Union Soldiers, 1861–1865*. Wilmington, N.C.: Broadfoot Publishing, 1997. Call no. E494 H4 1997.
- Spratt, Thomas. *Men in Gray Interments.* Athens, Ga.: Iberian Publishing, 1996–. Call no. E548 S67 1996.
- U.S. Quartermaster's Department. *Roll of Honor: Names of Soldiers Who Died in Defense of the American Union, Interred in the National Cemeteries.* Baltimore, Md.: Genealogical Publishing, 1994. Call no. E494 R653 R43 1994 (E494 R653 R43 1994 Index).

■   **The Library of Virginia – Military Records and Resources Page.   www.lva.lib.va.us/ whatwehave/mil/index.htm.** The Library of Virginia has done more to provide online indexes and images of military records online than any other state archives in America. Military records include official documentation of military service including muster and pay rolls and pension records. The linked titles at this webpage include military databases from the Colonial Wars era and the Revolutionary War era, through the World War II era. The following are links to databases related to the Civil War era. Many of the underlined database titles below begin with a search box for keywords or a browse feature within an alphabetical list, or, the link may go to an alpha index list to access a specific imaged document related to one person.
Searchable Databases and Guides Online:

- **Digitized Military Resources** – search across Library of Virginia military resources available online.
- **Archives and Manuscripts Catalog** – main access point for official state military records as well as individual regimental and personal service records.
- **Books, Journals... Catalog** – main access point for published materials, such as regimental histories and biographies.
- **Confederate Disability Applications and Receipts** – applications to the Board of Commissioners on Artificial Limbs from injured soldiers.
- **Confederate Pension Rolls, Veterans and Widows.** searchable database of pension applications and amended applications filed by resident Virginia Confederate veterans and their widows. See also **Card Index** below – it may contain different information.
- **Confederate Pension Rolls, Veterans and Widows Electronic Card Index** – index to pension applications and amended applications filed by resident Virginia Confederate veterans and their widows. See also Database above – it may contain different information.
- **Robert E. Lee Camp Confederate Soldiers' Home** Applications for Admission.
- **HarpWeek: The Civil War Era and Reconstruction (1857-1877)** – subscription database (You must visit the Library to use this resource).
- **Virginia Military Dead Database** – ongoing project indexing more than 744 sources and listing approximately 34,402 Virginians who have died in service.
- **Using Virginia Civil War Records** (PDF) – Research Notes Number 14.
- **Index to Virginia Confederate Rosters** – unofficial roster of soldiers from Virginia who served in the army of the Confederate States of America during the Civil War compiled between 1904 and 1918.
- **Selected Civil War Resources in the Personal Papers and Military Records Collections at the Library of Virginia** – (PDF) bibliography.
- **Confederate Navy Index** – searchable index created from a card file compiled primarily in 1924 as part of the United Confederate Veterans project to document Virginians' service during the Civil War.
- **Index to Confederate Veteran Magazine** – A fully-searchable index to the personal names of Confederate soldiers as they appear in the Confederate Veteran magazine published between 1893 and 1932.

■   **Virginia's Civil War – A Guide to Manuscripts at the Virginia Historical Society.** Browse Page: **www.vahistorical.org/cwg/ browse.htm.** This online guide to manuscripts is organized with a "browse" feature, with an alpha breakdown by subjects, titles, or family surnames. Another screen allows a keyword search. Each record found is described in detail, and the online guide is a real treasure for locating references to the Civil War in Virginia. The guide is also available as a 307-page book ($17.00) from the Museum Shop, Virginia Historical Society, PO Box 7311, Richmond, VA 23221-0311.

■ The Civil War Home Page.

http://sunsite.utk.edu/civil-war/warweb.html. This is a list of websites devoted to information about the American Civil War. Resources categorized as follows:

- General Resources
- The Secession Crisis and Before
- Images of Wartime
- Biographical Information
- Histories and Bibliographies
- Documentary Records
- State/Local Studies -- by State
- Battles & Campaigns
- Rosters & Regimental Histories
- Other Military Information
- Civil War Reenactors
- Civil War Round Tables
- Fictional Accounts of Wartime

Other General Resources
- Bob's Civil War Blog 23 April 2009
- The History Well
- Have Fun with History – the American Civil War American Civil War
- The American Civil War Research Database
- The Gilder Lehrman Institute of American History
- Civil War Talk
- John Tenniel and the American Civil War: Political Cartoons from Punch, 1860-1865
- TOCWOC (The Order of Civil War Obsessively Compulsed) [Blog]
- American Civil War Source
- Civil War Artifact Preservation Association
- Sons of Union Veterans of the Civil War
- Civil War Memorials (from dcMemorials.com)
- American Civil War in the News
- Daughters of the Union Veterans of the Civil War 1861-1865
- American Civil War: Comprehensive American Civil War site with forums at
- The Civil War: America Divided (traveling exhibit From Accessible Archives (NB: This site has a commercial character)
- Civil War Bookshelf: American Civil War historiography blogged daily
- American Civil War Search Directory (formerly DHQ's Civil War Portal)
- Official Register of the Government of the United States, 1861
- America's Civil War
- Gods and Generals: The Story Behind the Movie

■ Virginia Civil War Archive.

www.aladin.wrlc.org/gsdl/collect/vacw/vacw.shtml The Virginia Civil War Archive is a collection of 400 illustrations produced for the *Harper's Weekly* during 1861-1865 and which relate specifically to the Commonwealth of Virginia's involvement in the Civil War. From this group 100 images have been scanned for research and study by students and scholars on the World Wide Web. The images reflect the unfolding events and drama of the war as well as the superb artistry of the Weekly's many artists. There are 6 ways to find information in this collection:

- search for particular words that appear in the text by clicking the Search button
- browse documents by Title by clicking the Titles A-Z button
- browse documents by Subject by clicking the Subjects button
- browse documents by People by clicking the People A-Z button
- browse documents by Date by clicking the Dates button
- browse documents by Organization by clicking the Organizations button

■ The Civil War in Virginia.

www.virginiaplaces.org/military/civwar.html. This is a portal to over 270 websites related to the Civil War in Virginia. There are also some great articles about certain campaigns, railroads, and a very good collection of Civil War photographs, maps, and illustrations. The site is out of date, and many of the links no longer exist, but with a long list of websites to review, scan through the list for something of interest. A broken link may be repaired by going to Google for the site name.

■ The Virginia Regimental Histories Series.

http://www.bainesbooks.com/varegsrs.htm. This is a commercial bookstore site where the complete set of VA Regimental Histories is available for purchase. The series deals with each Virginia unit and Virginia soldier of the American Civil War. Individual volumes contain a unit history, an annotated muster roll of every man who served in that unit, and relevant photographs and maps. All of the printed histories from the series are available at The Library of Virginia, Virginia Historical Society, and the Family History Library in Salt

Lake City, Utah. This website is a place to purchase copies of the unit histories online, which are described briefly by title, author, page count, price, etc.

Published Virginia Resources

■ *Compiled Service Records of Confederate Soldiers Who Served in Organizations from the State of Virginia,* microfilm of original records at the National Archives, Washington, D.C. The compiled service records consists of a jacket-envelope for each soldier, labeled with his name, his rank, and the unit in which he served. The jacket-envelope typically contains card abstracts of entries relating to the soldier as found in original muster rolls, returns, rosters, payrolls, appointment books, hospital registers, Union prison registers and rolls, parole rolls, and inspection reports; and the originals of any papers relating solely to the particular soldier. There are cross-reference cards and jacket-envelopes for soldiers' names that appear in the records under more than one spelling. Filmed by the National Archives, series M324, 1,013 rolls, 1960. FHL has entire series, beginning with FHL film #1488739 (6th Cavalry, A – Be).

■ *Index to Compiled Service Records of Confederate Soldiers Who Served in Organizations from the State of Virginia,* microfilm of original records at the National Archives, Washington, D.C. Filmed by the National Archives, series M382, 62 rolls, 1962. FHL has entire series, beginning with FHL film #881395 (A – Am). This list of names is now online at the National Park Service website at: **www.civilwar.nps.gov/cwss/**.

■ *Index to Confederate Service Records of Virginia; Confederate Service Records of Virginia, 1861-1865,* microfilm of original records at the Library of Virginia, Richmond, VA. (These records were gathered after 1904, and are separate from the records of the National Archives). Filmed by the Genealogical Society of Utah, 1954, 42 rolls, beginning with FHL film #29777 (Index A – Balz, H.,); and FHL film #29767 (Service records, Vols. 1-2, 1st – 22nd regiments).

■ *Compiled Service Records of Volunteer Union Soldiers Who Served in Organizations from the State of Virginia,* microfilm of original records at the National Archives, Washington, D.C. Filmed by the National Archives, series M398, 7 rolls, 1962. FHL has entire series, beginning with FHL film #1292638 (First Infantry, 3 months, 1861).

■ *Index to Compiled Service Records of Volunteer Union Soldiers Who Served in Organizations from the State of Virginia,* microfilm of original records at the National Archives, Washington, D.C. Filmed by the National Archives, series M394, 1962, 1 roll. See FHL film #881594. This list of names included online at the National Park Service website at: **www.civilwar.nps.gov/cwss/**.

■ *Confederate Service Records* (for Virginia soldiers who served in Alabama units), microfilm of original records compiled by the ADAH, filmed by the Genealogical Society of Utah, 1987, 1 roll, FHL film #1411532 (Item 17, Virginia soldiers).

■ *A Guide to Virginia Military Organizations, 1861-1865,* by Lee A. Wallace, published by H.E. Howard, Lynchburg, VA, 1986, 372 pages, includes index. Part of Howard's *The Virginia Regimental Histories Series.* See FHL book 975.5 M2vr v.29.

■ **Virginia Regimental Histories.** There are unit histories, rosters, documents, photos, and more, for virtually every Confederate unit of the Civil War formed in Virginia. One large collection of unit histories is under the title, *Civil War Unit Histories,* with all known published histories represented at the Family History Library. At the **www.civilwar.nps.gov/cwss/** (National Park Service) website, the index to compiled service records will lead you to the name of a soldier/sailor, and the name of the regiment/unit in which he served. With that information, the same site has the roster names organized by regiment/unit. Included at the NPS site are complete Union regiments/unit histories from Frederick H. Dyer's *A Compendium of the War of the Rebellion,* but not all unit histories for Confederate units are available at the NPS site yet.

For all Virginia units of the Civil War, the individual published unit histories from Howard's *Virginia Regimental Histories Series* (website described above) can be found at the Family History Library catalog, organized under the category, Virginia – Military History – Civil War, 1861-1865 – Regimental histories.

■ *The Appomattox Roster: A List of the Paroles of the Army of Northern Virginia Issued at Appomattox Court House on April 9, 1865,* a photographic reprint of the edition of 1887 containing the original introduction by R. A. Brock and a foreword written for this edition by Philip Van Doren Stern, published by Antiquarian Press, New York, 1962, 508 pages, includes index. See FHL book 975.5 M23r. Also on microfilm, FHL film #896966.

■ *Roster of R.E. Lee Camp No. 1, Confederate Veterans, 1883-1919,* microfilm of the original records at the Virginia State Library and Archives, Richmond, VA. The Robert E. Lee Camp, No. 1, was organized in 1883. Contains lists of officers 1883-1919, contributing members, honorary members 1889-1907, and the roster of the R.E. Lee Camp, no. 1, for 1888 (1883-1919). Roster gives name, address, date of membership to camp and age at that time, recommended to camp by, enlistment in C.S.A., birthplace, rank, regiment, company, death date, and remarks. Filmed by the Genealogical Society of Utah, 1994, 1 roll, FHL film #2109655. Another filming, FHL film #2027899. See also, *Registers of Residents, 1885-1939,* filmed with *Roster,* same roll.

■ *Men in Gray Interments,* by Thomas M. Spratt, published by Iberian Publishing Co., Athens, GA, 1998, 11 vols. Gives name and location of cemetery, soldier's name, regiment, and any other information taken from tombstones, monuments and publications. Many of the soldiers served in regiments other than those from Virginia. See FHL book 975.5 V3s v. 1-11,

■ *Pardons by the President: Final Report of the Names of Persons Who Lived in Alabama, Virginia, West Virginia, or Georgia, Were Engaged in Rebellion and Pardoned by the President, Andrew Johnson,* Title of original document: *Message from the President of the United States, transmitting final report of the names of persons engaged in rebellion who have been pardoned by the President.* Original published Washington, D.C.: House of Representatives, 40th Congress, 2nd session, Executive document No. 16, December 4, 1867. Reprinted by Heritage Books, Bowie, MD, 1986, 147 pages. Many of these persons were engaged in military service for the Confederate government. See FHL book 973 M2par.

■ *Internal Revenue Assessment Lists for Virginia, 1865-1866,* microfilm of original records at the National Archives, Washington, D.C. See beginning of film for a lists of the districts and what counties are involved with each district. Filmed by the National Archives, series M793, 1988, 6 rolls. FHL has entire series, beginning with FHL film #1578235.

■ *Confederate Pension Applications, Virginia, Acts of 1888, 1900, 1902; Index, 1888-1934,* microfilm of original records at the Library of Virginia, Richmond, VA. The index was made by a member of the Comptroller's staff in the 1930's. In 1928 the Office of the Comptroller in the Department of Accounts assumed the functions of auditor with regard to pensions. Some applications and index cards may be out of order. From the introduction: "Virginia provided for her Confederate veterans and their widows and dependents with three pensions acts; 1888, 1900, 1902. These acts varied in the persons that they covered, what qualified a person for a pension, and the amount paid.... The Act of 1888 provided pensions for soldiers, sailors, and marines who were maimed or disabled during the war and for the widows of men who had been killed during the war. This act applied to natives of Virginia who enlisted from Virginia or any other state in Confederate service and who were residing in Virginia at the time of application. The act of 1900 was considered an extension of the act of 1888. The act of 1902 was basically the same as the act of 1888 but with additional restrictions on who could apply for the pensions. It was amended by later acts to lengthen the deadline for filing and to make minor changes. 1902 section for servant pensions appears to be for African Americans. In many cases pensions give age, place of birth, how many years they lived in the county, and what service they rendered. These applications are arranged alphabetically by locality and thereafter alphabetically by the surname of the applicant. Counties are not always in strict alphabetical order. Index is on cards which are arranged alphabetically by name of veteran, widow, or servant. It gives the names, county or city, year of act, whether soldier or widow is applying, usually a roll and page number, and if the applicant is a widow, sometimes gives her husband's name. Index is not complete. Disallowed pensions do not seem to appear in this index."

For the 1900 and 1902 acts, there are additional typed indexes before each county, independent city, and sections for servants and disallowed pensions. Filmed by the Genealogical Society of Utah, 1988-1992, 220 rolls, beginning the index on FHL film #1439763 (Index, Aaron – Bolton, 1888-1934); and the applications beginning on FHL film #1617178 (Accomack – Appomattox Counties).

■ *Commonwealth of Virginia Civil War Pensioners,* compiled by Ashley K. Nuckols, published by A.K. Nuckols, Family Roots, Tazewell, VA, 2003, 3 vols. The documents were found in the basement of the Tazewell County Courthouse in Tazewell, Virginia, and photocopied by the author. Vol. 1 contains photocopies of funeral expense accounts of Confederate pensioners, applications for pension, rerating applications, pension certificates, a list of ex-Confederate soldiers and sailors, and the 1917 roster of Confederate pensioners. The 1917 roster was published under: Roster of Confederate Pensioners of Virginia / compiled by the Auditor of Public Accounts (Richmond: Davis Bottom, Superintendent Public Printing, 1917). Vol. 2 contains photocopies of 3 rosters of pensioners for 1919-1921. Each roster was published under: Roster of Confederate Pensioners of Virginia / compiled by the Auditor of Public Accounts (Richmond: Davis Bottom, Superintendent Public Printing). Vol. 3 contains photocopies of 3 rosters of pensioners for 1922-1923, 1926. Each roster was published under: Roster of Confederate Pensioners of Virginia / compiled by the Auditor of Public Accounts (Richmond: Davis Bottom, Superintendent Public Printing). FHL book 975.5 M2n v.1-3).

■ *Application for the Relief of Needy Confederate Women, 1915-1967,* microfilm of original records at the Library of Virginia, Richmond, VA, obtained from the United Daughters of the Confederacy, Virginia Division, Richmond, VA. The application gives the name of soldier, what company and regiment, the applicant's physical condition, income, means of support, birthdate, and place of residence. Includes index. Applications for a Confederate pension granted to needy daughters and sisters of Confederate soldiers, sailors, and Marines. Filmed by the VA State Library, 1996, 27 rolls. FHL has entire series, beginning with FHL film #2031631 (Index to applications).

■ *The Eleventh Census of the United States 1890, Special Schedule, Union Veterans and Widows,* transcribed by Gail M. Walczyk, published by Peter's Row, Coram, NY, 2002, 2 vols. Arranged alphabetically by county, then by name of veteran or widow. Gives name of veteran or his widow's name if he is dead, veteran's rank, company, regiment or vessel, enlistment date, discharge date, length of service, address, disability and other information related to service. Sometimes gives aliases. A few Confederate veterans were included. FHL book 975.5 X2w v.1-2. See also, *Virginia's Union Veterans: Eleventh Census of the United States, 1890,* by Ronald Ray Turner, published by the author, Manassas, VA, 1994, 147 pages. Arranged in alphabetical order by name. Gives the name of the veteran (or the widow), the veteran's rank, company, regiment or vessel, and county. See FHL book 975.5 X2t. Also on microfilm, FHL film #1425065. See also *1890 Virginia Census Index of Civil War Veterans or Their Widows,* compiled by Bryan Lee Dilts, published by Index Publishing, Salt Lake City, UT, 1986, 32 pages. FHL book 975.5 X22d. See also, *Virginia 1890 Special Census of Veterans,* edited by Ronald Vern Jackson, et al, published by Accelerated Indexing Systems, North Salt Lake, UT, 1986, 109 pages, FHL book 975.5 X2j.

■ *Birth Records (Virginia), 1853-1941; indexes, 1853-1950; Delayed Birth Indexes, 1912-1950,* microfilm of the original records from the Virginia Bureau of Vital Statistics, now at the Library of Virginia, Richmond, VA. The Old birth indexes were made by the Works Project Administration (1936-1939) from birth registrations and cover 1853-1896. The Birth indexes of slaves cover 1853-1866. The commissioner of the revenue registered births for the county and then turned over his books to the clerk of the County Court. The clerk made abstracts to send to the state auditor and would also preserve the books in his office. Filmed by the Genealogical Society of Utah, 1996, 99 rolls, beginning with FHL film #2026327 (Old birth index, vol. 1, Aar – Car, 1853-1866).

WASHINGTON TERRITORY

Online Washington Resources

The Washington Secretary of State oversees the Washington State Library and Washington State Archives in Olympia, five regional archives facilities across the state, and the new Washington Digital Archives in Cheney, WA. All of these facilities are resource centers for research in Washington Territory during the era of the Civil War. These facilities each have websites with good descriptions of their holdings, and all sites are accessible from the Secretary of State's website at: **www.secstate.wa.gov/**, or go directly to each:

■ **Washington State Library – Search the Library Catalog. www.secstate.wa.gov/library/catalog.aspx.** A keyword search for "Civil War Washington Territory" brought up 27 items, including compiled service records, GAR membership rosters, and Army letters. Several of these items are available as digital images. **Genealogical Resources** at the Washington State Library and Washington State Archives are combined at one webpage: **www.secstate.wa.gov/history/genealogy.aspx**, and there is a good array of subjects to review. The **Classics in Washington History** page is another good review of historical titles, including several under "Military History."

■ **Washington State Archives – Search the Archives. www.secstate.wa.gov/archives/search.aspx.** A keyword search for "Washington Territory Civil War" brought up items from Territorial Records, Oral Histories, and Military Histories. One item of interest: *Civil War Clothing*

Registers 1862-1862, a microfilmed copy of an original register of clothing issued to the First Washington Volunteers during the Civil War. The register serves as a muster roll. The First Washington Territorial Volunteer Regiment was formed to man the U.S. Army forts and outposts in Washington Territory, allowing the regular U.S. Army troops to fight the Civil War in the east. The Regiment did not serve in battle. The register is arranged by company, then by name of soldier.

■ **Washington State Archives – Regional Branches. www.secstate.wa.gov/archives/.** At the **Archives Repositories** list, click on one of the regions: Northwest, Southwest, Central, Eastern, and Puget Sound Region. Each regional branch receives local government records from a number of counties within their area of coverage, including records from county offices such as the Auditor, the Clerk, the Treasurer, the Board of Commissioners; and from municipalities, school districts, and other service districts. As one of the five regional branches, the Northwest Regional Branch in Bellingham, WA, receives archival records from Clallam, Island, Jefferson, San Juan, Skagit, Snohomish, and Whatcom counties. Original records found here are typical of all of the regions, and include:
- Birth and death records from January, 1891 to July 1907.
- Marriage Records.
- Court Records including naturalizations, court dockets, civil and probate case files.
- Land records, including deed indexes, deeds, and patents.
- County commissioner's proceedings, ordinances, and resolutions.
- Real and personal property tax records.
- School district and Educational Service District records including school censuses.

■ **Search the Digital Archives. www.digitalarchives.wa.gov/default.aspx.** Opened in 2004, Washington State's **Digital Archives** is the nation's first archives dedicated specifically to the preservation of electronic records from both State and Local agencies that have permanent legal, fiscal or historical value. The goal is to digitize every historical document from the past, including territorial records dating from 1853, and state records since 1889. In its first four years of operation, the Digital Archives has digitized about 40 million pages of archival documents. For example, a program to digitize the images of all of Washington's Territorial Censuses is well under way, and name indexes to the censuses as well as many other resources are being combined in one Digital Archives search system. Of interest to genealogists, the other records being indexed include Marriage Records, Naturalization Records, Death Records, Birth Records, Military Records, Institution Records, Miscellaneous Historical Records, Physician Records, and Oaths of Office. Each of these categories have their own search screen, for example, search within "military records" for any Washington county. This is where lists of soldiers, veterans, discharge papers, etc., can be identified, and all names are included in the master index.

■ **The Civil War Home Page. www.civil-war.net/.** This is the most comprehensive national website for information about the Civil War, and includes a review of all Union regiments, battalions and companies furnished by all participating states, along with the numbers of soldiers who served, wounded, or died from each unit. Washington Territory's First Regiment, Washington Infantry is included with statistics.

Published Washington Resources

■ *Index to Compiled Service Records of Volunteer Union Soldiers Who Served in Organizations from the Territory of Washington,* microfilm of original records at the National Archives, Washington, D.C. Filmed by the National Archives, series M558, 1964, 1 roll, FHL film #821948.

■ *Washington Territory Census Index: 1857, 1860 and 1861 State Censuses,* edited by Ronald Vern Jackson, published by Accelerated Indexing Systems, Salt Lake City, UT, 1982, 50 pages. FHL book 979.7 X2j. Taken from the microfilm series, *Washington Territorial Census Rolls, 1857-1892,* microfilm of originals at the Washington State Archives, filmed by the archives, 1987, 20 rolls, beginning with FHL film #1841781 (Adams County, 1885-1889). Another series, *Washington Territorial County Census Microfilm,* was filmed by the Washington State Archives in 2003, 35 rolls, adding several county censuses (1871, 1881, 1883,

1885, and 1889) not in the FHL's set. WSL call no. 929.3797.

■ *Official Army Register of the Volunteer Force of the United States Army for the Years 1861, '62, '63, '64, '65,* United States Adjutant General's Office, originally published by the Government Printing Office, 1867, part of the series Civil War Unit histories. Part 4, The Union—Midwest and West: WT089, microfiche by University Publications of America, 1993, 1 fiche, Washington only. FHL fiche #6118466.

■ *Roster of Ellsworth Post No. 2: Department of Washington and Alaska, Grand Army of the Republic, Organized January 11th, 1881.* Published by the GAR, printed Schwab Bros., Portland, OR, 1889, 9 pages. See also, three original GAR books at the Washington State Library:
- *1883 Roster of Grand Army of the Republic Department of Washington Territory.* WSL call no. Rare V 369.1509 Grand 1883.
- *1884 Roster of Grand Army of the Republic Department of Washington Territory,* WSL call no. Rare V 369.1509 Grand 1884.
- *1885 Roster of Grand Army of the Republic Department of Washington Territory,* WSL call no. Rare V 369.1509 Grand 1885.

■ *Member Files at the Washington Soldiers Homes,* microfilm of original records at the Washington State Archives in Olympia, WA. Includes information from the State Soldiers' Home in Orting, the State Soldiers' Colony in Orting, and the Washington Veterans' Home in Retsil, Washington. Arranged by file number. Includes application for admission to home, lists military service, unit, date and place of enlistment and date and place of discharge, cause of discharge, name and address of nearest relative or friend, and miscellaneous information. Filmed by the Genealogical Society of Utah, 2005, 59 rolls, beginning with FHL film #1221583 (Orting Home, Stanton, Mahlon M.).

■ *Burial list of the Members of the 1st Washington Territory Infantry,* compiled by Sherman Lee Pompey, published by Pacific Specialties, Kingsburg, CA, 1972, 3 pages. FHL book 979.7 A1 no. 14. Also on microfiche, FHL fiche #6126329.

■ *Civil War Veteran Burials from the Arizona Territory, Nebraska, Nevada, New Mexico, Oregon, Utah and the Washington Territory,* compiled by Sherman Lee Pompey, text microfilmed by the Genealogical Society of Utah, 1975, 1 roll, FHL film #908986.

■ *Washington Internal Revenue Assessment Lists, 1869-1874,* microfilm of original records at the Seattle Branch, National Archives. Filmed by the Genealogical Society of Utah, 1989, 1 roll, FHL film #1639855.

WEST VIRGINIA

The state of West Virginia was admitted into the Union in June 1863 in the midst of the Civil War. From 1863-1865, West Virginia supplied only Union troops to the war. But several of the counties of Virginia before June 1863 had supplied Confederate troops, including a great number of men living in the Virginia counties that later became part of West Virginia. Therefore, a search for a Confederate soldier from West Virginia should begin with the Confederate regiments of Virginia.

Online West Virginia Resource

■ **West Virginia State Archives – Researching Your Civil War Ancestor.** www.wvculture.org/ HiStory/civwaran.html. This webpage should be mandatory reading for anyone interested in West Virginia's involvement in the Civil War. The types of records available are discussed, and a very thorough bibliography is included, with lists of publications such as the adjutant general reports of 1864 and 1865, regimental histories, county histories with soldier lists, and Civil War chronologies for both Union and Confederate units. There is also a bibliographic list from the *Virginia Regimental History Series* (published by H.E. Howard, Inc., mentioned in the Virginia section). A link to the Library of Virginia website is included here (as a recommendation for locating Confederate soldiers and Confederate Pension records online) and there is a link to the online reproduction of an article from *West Virginia History* with complete rosters of all Union soldiers

in the First West Virginia Infantry, extracted from the 1864 Adjutant General's report.

■ **West Virginia Archives & History – Genealogy Corner.** www.wvculture.org/history/ genealog.html. This site is a portal to the following webpages:
● Genealogy Surname Exchange
● AfriGeneas: African Ancestored Genealogy
● Archives and History News
● Cemeteries, West Virginia, Artificial Collection
● County Formations, West Virginia
● Counties of West Virginia
● Don Norman Files
● History of the American Negro
● Immigrant Ships Transcribers Guild
● Mining Your History Foundation
● On-Line Searchable Death Indexes and Records
● RootsWeb's Soundex Converter
● Researching an Adoption
● Researching Your Civil War Ancestor
● Researching Your Revolutionary War Ancestor
● RootsWeb.com
● State Archives and Libraries
● Upcoming Events
● US GenWeb Archives: West Virginia
● Virginia Marriage Laws
● Vital Registration
● Vital Research Records
● West Virginia GenWeb Project
● West Virginia Genealogy on GeneaSearch
● WV Union Militia – Civil War (Searchable database)

■ **West Virginia State Archives – Unclaimed Civil War Medals.** www.wvculture.org/ HISTORY/medals.html. In 1866, the state of West Virginia authorized the minting of over 26,000 medals to honor its Union Civil War soldiers. Today, over 4,000 medals remain unclaimed, physically located at the West Virginia State Archives. Each unclaimed medal is identified, linked to the name of a soldier, rank, company, and regiment; and a list of the unclaimed medals (by the name of the soldier) is searchable at this site Any direct descendant of a designated veteran is eligible to receive his medal. In order to claim an ancestor's medal, a claimant must submit his or her line of descent from the veteran along with documentation to support this line of descent. To establish line of descent, claimants must include *copies* of primary sources, including birth, death, marriage, will, deed, military, census, Bible records, etc. Old letters, diaries, marriage announcements, or obituaries may also prove helpful in verifying a descendant's claim. A more detailed set of instructions and an application form to apply for a Civil War Medal is available at this page.

■ **Civil War: West Virginia.**
www.lindapages.com/cwlist.htm.
The West Virginia Civil War Pages are all unique databases owned and/or created and maintained by Linda Cunningham Fluharty. The various links at this page are all to exclusive Fluharty sites, although many of them are for Fluharty databases offered through RootsWeb/GenWeb sites, and official West Virginia sites, such as the state archives and state library. The quality of the databases linked here are clearly superior to any other West Virginia name lists online. The featured sites include:

- 1st W. Va. Infantry Website – (Includes Book)
- 1st W. Va. Cavalry Website
- 12th W. Va. Infantry Website – (Includes Book)
- Carlin's Battery "D" – 1st W. Va. Lt. Art'y Website
- 5th W.Va. Cavalry (2nd Infantry) Regimental History Book
- The Civil War Medals of W. Va... Where Are They?
- ON THE WAY HOME – W.Va. Soldiers on the Sultana
- 7th W. Va. Infantry – Company "B"

In addition to the above, there are many more linked Fuharty sites specific to Rosters, General West Virginia Civil War Info; Biographies, Militia, Home Guards, Scouts; 1890 Census of Vets & Widows; Civil War: Other; Relatives in the Civil War; and Linda's Military Pages w/Civil War Sections. Fluharty databases specific to West Virginia counties include rosters, biographies, and general info on Calhoun, Marshall, Ohio, and Pleasants counties; as well as a WVGenWeb Military Page with several WV counties identified.

Published West Virginia Resources

■ *West Virginia in the Civil War,* by Boyd B. Stutler, published by the Education Foundation, Charleston, WV, 1963, 304 pages. Indexed. See FHL book 975.4 M2s.

■ *Compiled Service Records of Volunteer Union Soldiers Who Served in Organizations from the State of West Virginia,* microfilm of original records at the National Archives, Washington, D.C.

The compiled service records consist of a jacket-envelope for each soldier, labeled with his name, his rank, and the unit in which he served and typically containing card abstracts of entries relating to the soldier as found in original muster rolls, returns, hospital rolls, descriptive books, and lists of deserters; and the originals of any papers relating solely to the particular soldiers. The records are arranged according to an organizational breakdown ending with the regiment or the independent battalion or company. Under each unit the service records are arranged alphabetically by soldiers' surnames. Preceding the jacket-envelopes for the individual soldiers in each organizational unit are envelopes containing record-of-events cards giving the stations, movements, or activities of the unit or a part of it, and sometimes information relating to its organization or composition. In addition, there occasionally are envelopes containing general notation cards giving information relating to the entire organizational unit that sometimes was not stamped on or filed with the card abstracts. Filmed by the National Archives, 1963, series M508, 248 rolls. FHL has entire series, cataloged together with the *Index to Compiled Service Records,* beginning with FHL film #881595 (A – Bon). The organizations and compiled service records begin with FHL film #1478231 (1st Cavalry, A – Bi)

■ *Index to Compiled Service Records of Volunteer Union Soldiers Who Served in Organizations from the State of West Virginia,* microfilm of original records at the National Archives, Washington, D.C. Filmed by the National Archives, 1963, series M507, 13 rolls. FHL has complete series, beginning with FHL film #881595 (A – Bon). This list of names is now online at the National Park Service website at: **www.civilwar.nps.gov/cwss/**.

■ *Confederate Soldiers of Western Virginia,* by Jack Dickinson, published by the author, Barboursville, WV, 1986, 30+ pages, includes index. From Foreword: "This volume includes a combined, alphabetized index to the soldiers in the 8th. and 16th. Virginia Cavalry Regiments of the Confederate States Army. Both of these units filled their ranks with men from the western counties of Virginia....The combined index in this volume is not complete. Many Confederate Army records were lost or destroyed during and after the war. There were also some men from this geographical area who enlisted in other Confederate Army units, such as the 36th. Virginia Infantry and the 22nd. Virginia Infantry." See FHL book 975.5 M2d. Also on microfiche, FHL fiche #6093977.

■ *The Soldiery of West Virginia: In the French and Indian War, Lord Dunmore's War, the Revolution, the later Indian wars, the Whiskey Insurrection, the second war with England, the War with Mexico, and addenda relating to West Virginians in the Civil War,* the whole compiled from authentic sources by Virgil A. Lewis, reprinted by Genealogical Publishing Co, Baltimore, MD, 1967, 227 pages, from *The Third Biennial Report of the Department of Archives and History, State of West Virginia.* Contains rosters, pay lists, orders, letters, and other information about the regiments and soldiers who fought in the French and Indian War 1755-1763, Lord Dunmore's War 1774, the Revolutionary War 1775-1783, the later Indian wars 1783-1795, the Whiskey Insurrection 1794, the War of 1812, the War with Mexico 1846-1848, and the Civil War 1861-1865. FHL book 975.4 M2L Indexed in *Every Name Index to the Soldiery of West Virginia,* indexed by Donna Parker, published by Southern California Genealogical Society, Burbank, CA, 1993, 72 pages. FHL book 975.4 M2L.

■ *Annual Report of the Adjutant General of the State of West Virginia...,* microfiche of original published by the Adjutant General's Office, Wheeling, WV, 1863-1865, 3 vols. Filmed by University Publications of America, Bethesda, MD, 1992, on 14 microfiche. FHL has entire series, beginning with FHL fiche #6118872 (1864).

■ *Report of the Adjutant General of West Virginia, 1897-98,* microfilm of original published by the West Virginia Adjutant General's Office, Charleston, WV, 1898, 98 pages. Includes rosters of all West Virginia Union regiments of the Civil War. FHL copy obtained through the Library of Congress Photoduplication Service, 1989, 1 roll, FHL film #1550769.

■ *Internal Revenue Assessment Lists for West Virginia, 1862-1866,* microfilm of original records at the National Archives, Washington, D.C. Records include place of residence. Front of each roll includes an explanation of the set. Morgan, Berkley, Jefferson, Hampshire and Hardy counties are with district 3 of Virginia for 1862. DISTRICT 1 - Established 10 Oct. 1862 with Brooke, Hancock, Marion, Marshall, Ohio, Pleasants, Preston, Taylor Tyler & Wetzel counties. Reorganized 3 May 1865 with Brooke, Calhoun, Dodderidge, Gilmer, Hancock, Harrison, Marion, Marshall, Ohio, Pleasants, Ritchie, Roane, Tyler, Wetzel & Wirt counties. Louis County transferred to District 1 on 1 Aug. 1865 and Wood County on Mar. 14, 1866. DISTRICT 2 - Established 10 Oct 1862 with Barbour, Braxton, Cabell, Calhoun, Clay, Kanawha, Lewis, Mason, Putnam, Randolph, Ritchie, Roane, Tucker, Upshur, Webster, Wirt & Wood counties. Reorganized 3 May 1865 with Barbour, Berkeley, Hampshire, Hardy, Jefferson, Lewis, Monongalia, Morgan, Pendleton, Pocahontas, Preston, Randolph, Taylor, Tucker, Upshur & Webster counties. Marion County transferred here 1 Aug. 1865. DISTRICT 3 - Established 3 May 1865 with Boone, Braxton, Cabell, Clay, Fayette, Greenbrier, Jackson, Kanawha, Logan, McDowell, Mason, Mercer, Monroe, Nicholas, Putnam, Raleigh, Wayne, Wood and Wyoming counties. Districts are divided into divisions. The number of these may vary. Some may be missing or not be filmed in order. Includes an index of what counties are on which rolls and which kinds of reports are involved. Filmed by the National Archives, 1972, series M795, 4 rolls. FHL has complete series, beginning with FHL film #1578241 (District 1).

■ *Civil War - West Virginia: Union Lives Lost,* by Linda Cunningham Fluharty, published by the author, Baton Rouge, LA, 2004, 175 pages. Alphabetical listing of soldiers from West Virginia who were killed, mortally wounded, or died of disease or accident during the Civil War. Each entry includes name, age at death, rank, unit, date and place died, and cause of death. Includes biographical sketches of Enoch and John Basnett, John and George Bucher, Joseph Caldwell, Uriah

W. Halstead, Joseph Hervey, Alexander Hoback, Robert McLachlan, Jacob Conrad Smith, and Joseph Thoburn, unit history of Company C, 133rd West Virginia Militia, and historical notes on West Virginia soldiers' medals. See FHL book 975.4 M22f.

■ *West Virginia Civil War Almanac,* by Tim McKinney, published by Pictorial Histories Pub. Co., Charleston, WV, 1998, 2 vols. Vol. 1 contains the 1890 Civil War veterans census (arranged by state), 1890 census Confederate index, veteran distribution by county of residence, Civil War service medals, soldiers and citizens who died in federal prisons or military hospitals, Southern Claims Commission, SCC files of Joseph Caldwell and Logan Osburn, physicians in the Civil War, Ft. Delaware seventy-five, and letters of several veterans. Vol. 2 contains roster of U.S. soldiers from West Virginia, index of the Civil War veterans in the 1890 census, deceased Civil War veteran and their widows in the 1890 W.Va. census (arranged by county), index of deceased U.S. Civil War veteran in the 1890 W.Va. census, index of deceased Confederate veterans in the 1890 W.Va. census, index of black troops enlisted to the credit of West Virginia, veteran distribution by county of residence, statistical review of 1890 W.Va. Civil War veteran census, and addenda with corrections/additions to v. 1. See FHL book 975.4 M2M v.1-2.

■ *1890 West Virginia Census Index of Civil War Veterans or Their Widows,* compiled by Bryan Lee Dilts, published by Index Publishing, Salt Lake City, UT, 1986, 63 pages. FHL book 975.4 X22d. See also *West Virginia 1890 Veterans,* edited by Ronald Vern Jackson, et al, published by Accelerated Indexing Systems, 1986, 220 pages, FHL book 975.4 M2jv.

WISCONSIN

Online Wisconsin Resources

■ **Wisconsin Historical Society – Genealogy Page.** www.wisconsinhistory.org/genealogy/. Presents the following Genealogy Tools online:
  • **Wisconsin Genealogy Index**. Search more than 150,000 Wisconsin obituaries and biographical

sketches published before 1999, as well as 1,000,000 births, 400,000 deaths and 1,000,000 marriages registered before September 1907.
  • **Wisconsin Genealogical Research Service.** Search for and request copies of Civil War service records using our research service.
  • **Wisconsin Historical Images.** Browse our historic images from the 19th and 20th centuries. Find pictures of people and places or purchase reproductions.
  • **Wisconsin Historical Collections**. 1,000 articles, memoirs, interviews and other primary sources on early Wisconsin history.
  • **Roster of Wisconsin Volunteers, War of the Rebellion, 1861-1865**. Alphabetical and regimental lists of soldiers who served in Wisconsin units during the Civil War.
  • **More about Civil War Veterans**. Find every Civil War veteran, including former soldiers and sailors, who resided in the state of Wisconsin during the census years of 1885, 1895, and 1905.
  • **Wisconsin Local History & Biography Articles**. 16,000 historical and biographical articles. Search by name, location, or article subject(s).
  • **Turning Points in Wisconsin History**. Find eyewitness accounts and read background essays on events your ancestors experienced. Includes a large section for the Civil War Era with sub-categories of Abolition, Home Front, Military Affairs, and more.

■ **Wisconsin Department of Veterans Affairs – Civil War Regimental Histories. http://museum. dva.state.wi.us/Res_regiments.asp**. This site has state resources for Wisconsin's involvement in the Civil War, World War II, Korean War, Vietnam War, Memorials & Honors, and Veterans. A search for the Wisconsin regiments of the Civil War by Infantry, Artillery & Cavalry, and Miscellaneous Units has links to regimental histories adopted from Charles E. Estabrook, ed., *Records and Sketches of Military Organizations*, (Madison, 1914). For more general information on Wisconsin's Civil War units, they suggest the following works:
  • Dyer, Frederick, *Compendium of the War of the Rebellion*, (Des Moines, 1908).
  • Love, William DeLoss, *Wisconsin in the War of the Rebellion*, (Chicago, 1866).
  • Quiner, E.B., *The Military History of Wisconsin*, (Chicago, 1866).

■ **Civil War Rosters – Wisconsin State Links.** www.geocities.com/Area51/Lair/3680/cw/cw-wi.html. This is a private directory of Civil War Rosters/Muster Rolls that have been found on the Internet.

Published Wisconsin Resources

■ *Exploring Civil War Wisconsin: A Survival Guide for Researchers,* by Brett Barker; foreword by Alan T. Nolan, published by the Wisconsin Historical Society Press, Madison, WI, 2003, 127 pages, FHL book 977.5 M27b.

■ *Military Records, 1861-1865,* microfilm of original records at the State Historical Society of Wisconsin at Madison. For a general index see *Index to compiled service records of volunteer Union soldiers who served in organizations from the state of Wisconsin (1861-1865).* Filmed by the Genealogical Society of Utah, 1981, 32 rolls, beginning with FHL film #1311667 (regimental muster, and descriptive rolls, 1865, 1st Cavalry, more).

■ *Index to Compiled Service Records of Volunteer Union Soldiers Who Served in Organizations from the State of Wisconsin,* microfilm of original records in the National Archives, Washington, D.C. Filmed by the National Archives, series M559, 1964, 33 rolls. FHL has entire series, beginning with FHL film #882486 (Index, A – Bak). This list of names is now online at the National Park Service website at: **www.civilwar.nps.gov/cwss/**.

■ *Wisconsin Volunteers, War of the Rebellion, 1861-1865: Arranged Alphabetically,* compiled under the direction of the Adjutant General, microfilm of original published by the state printer, Democrat Printing Co., 1914, 1,137 pages. This list gives name, rank, company and regiment only. Filmed for the Family History Library by the Library of Congress, Photoduplication Service, 1988, 1 roll, FHL film #1550629.

■ *Annual Report of the Adjutant General of the State of Wisconsin for the Year Ending December 30th, 1865,* edited by Charles E. Estabrook, microfilm of reprint published 1866, state printer, Madison, WI. Includes index. Includes regimental rosters for all Wisconsin troops. Filmed by W.C. Cox, Tucson, AZ, 1974, 1 roll, FHL film #1000824.

■ *Official Army Registers of the Volunteer Force of the United States Army for the years 1861, '62, '63, '64, '65: [Wisconsin],* microfiche of original published by the U.S. Adjutant Generals' Office, 1865, 83 pages. Includes part 7, pp. 144-226 pertaining to Wisconsin. Filmed by University Publications of America, Bethesda, MD, 1993, 1 microfiche, FHL fiche #6118298.

■ *1865 Wisconsin State Census.* The state's original set was destroyed, but there are duplicate copies that exist for six counties, indexed in *1865 Wisconsin State Census: The Six Surviving Counties, Dunn, Green, Jackson, Kewaunee, Ozaukee, Sheboygan, Transcription and Index,* compiled by Barry Christopher Noonan, published by the author, Madison, WI, 1993, 353 pages. Copy at the State Historical Society library, call no. F580 N66 1993. The original manuscripts of the six surviving counties are available on microfilm, with copies at the FHL.

■ *Wisconsin Soldiers and Sailors Reunion: Containing the Post Office Address, Occupation and Name of Every Wisconsin Soldier and Sailor Now Living... Also the Name of Every Wisconsin Soldier Who Perished in the War... Also, a Complete Roster of Wisconsin's Armed Military Organizations,* microfiche of original compiled by J. A. Kellogg, et al, under the supervision of the president of the Wisconsin Soldiers Reunion. Original published by the Star Steam Job and Book Printing House, Fond du Lac, WI, 1880, 309 pages. Filmed by University Publications of American, Bethesda, MD, 1993, on 4 microfiche. FHL has complete set, beginning with FHL fiche #6118307.

■ *1885 Wisconsin State Census,* microfilm of original records at the Wisconsin State Historical Society, Madison, WI. Also includes county by county "Enumeration of Soldiers and Sailors of the Late War" (Civil War). Some counties are continued from one reel to the next. The city of Milwaukee is handled separately. Some counties are not in strict alphabetical order. Filmed by the Genealogical Society of Utah, 1979, 10 rolls, beginning with FHL film #1032695 (Adams– Clark Cos.). The last two rolls contain a separate list of soldier/sailors of the Civil War, enumerated by county. See also, *Alphabetical List of the Soldiers and Sailors of the Late War Residing in the State, June 20, 1885,* microfiche of original published by Wisconsin Dept. of State, Madison, WI, 1886.

Filmed by M.W. Johnson, Belvidere, IL, 1985, 3 microfiche, FHL fiche #6334309. See also, *Census Enumeration of Soldiers and Sailors of the Late War Residing in Wisconsin, June 20, 1885,* microfiche of original published: Madison, WI.: Authority, 1886. 387 pages. Published by Ancestor Pub., Arvada, CO, 2003. 11 microfiche, beginning with FHL fiche #6396515. FHL has the original book, published with the title, *Tabular Statements of the Census Enumeration, and the Agricultural, Mineral and Manufacturing Interests of the State: Also Alphabetical List of the Soldiers and Sailors of the Late War Residing in the State, June 20, 1885,* published by the state printer, Madison, WI, 1886, 387 pages, FHL book 977.5 X2w. Online facsimile: **www.wisconsinhistory.org/ turningpoints/search.asp?id=1617**.

■ *1890 Wisconsin Veterans Census Index,* edited by Ronald Vern Jackson, et al, published by Accelerated Indexing Systems, Salt Lake City, UT, 1988, 485 pages. See FHL book 977.5 X22w.

■ *1895 Wisconsin State Census,* microfilm of original records at the State Historical Society of Wisconsin – Archives Division, Madison, WI. Head of households census, complete for all Wisconsin counties. Also includes a separate name list of living veterans for each county. Filmed by the Genealogical Society of Utah, 1979, 12 rolls, beginning with FHL film #1032705 (Adams – Columbia counties). The scanned images from the microfilm of the *1895 Wisconsin State Census* are now available online at the **www.ancestry.com** site.

■ *Wisconsin Census Enumeration 1895. Names of Ex-Soldiers and Sailors Residing in Wisconsin, June 20, 1895: Compiled from the returns made by the County Clerks to the Secretary of State, as provided for by Chapter 161, Laws of 1885.* Alphabetically Arranged. Compiled and Published by Authority of Law, under Direction of Henry Casson, Secretary of State, Madison, Wis., Democrat Printing Company, State Printers, 1896. Online facsimile at: **www.wisconsinhistory.org/ turningpoints/search.asp?id=1617**.

■ *Wisconsin Civil War Veterans Living in Nebraska in 1893: Taken from the 1893 Nebraska Census (Internet), Supplemented by*

Volumes I & II, Wisconsin Civil War Roster, compiled by Bev Htzel, Published by the author, West Bend, WI, 2006, 45 pages. Names are listed alphabetically. Includes hometown, service dates, and where Veteran lived in Nebraska. Includes over 1100 veterans. See FHL book 977.5 M2hbn.

■ *Old Soldiers' Home: A History and Necrology of the Northwestern Branch National Home for Disabled Volunteer Soldiers Wauwatosa, Wisconsin, 1864-1900,* by Jeanette L. Jerger, published by Heritage Books, Bowie, MD, 2001, 240 pages. In addition to the Civil War, this necrology covers veterans of the War of 1812 and Mexican War. Although Wisconsin veterans are not in the majority, they are the sizeable minority. Veterans with roots in Illinois, New York and Pennsylvania are listed. Other states are also fairly well represented. See FHL book 977.5 M2j. See also, *Wisconsin Soldiers in Soldier Homes, 1895,* compiled by Bev Hetzel, published by the author, West Bend, WI, 1995, 24 pages. Names, with annotations, are in alphabetical order. The list was taken from a 1895 census report & from a two-vol. set on the Civil War. See FHL book 977.5 M2he.

■ *1905 Wisconsin State Census,* microfilm of original records at the State Historical Society of Wisconsin – Archives Division, Madison, WI. Contents: Name of each individual; relationship to head of household; color/race; sex; age at last birthday; marital status; place of birth, by state or country; place of birth of parents; occupation, if 14 years or older; number of months unemployed; and whether a home or farm was owned outright, mortgaged, or rented. Filmed by the State Historical Society, 1952, 36 rolls, beginning with FHL film #1020439 (Adams, Ashland, Barron counties). The scanned images from the microfilm of the *1905 Wisconsin State Census* are now available online at the **www.ancestry.com** site.

■ *1905 Wisconsin State Census Index,* microfilm of original card indexes (by county) at the State Historical Society of Wisconsin, Archives Division, Madison, WI. Surname, first name indexes in alphabetical order for each county. All county-wide indexes filmed by the Genealogical Society of Utah, 1978-1985, 444 rolls, 16mm film, beginning with FHL film #1266809 (Adams County).

■ *Wisconsin Census Enumeration 1905. Names of Ex-Soldiers and Sailors Residing in Wisconsin, June 20, 1905: Compiled from the returns made by the County Clerks to the Secretary of State, as provided for by Chapter 161, Laws of 1885.* Alphabetically Arranged. Compiled and Published by Authority of Law, under Direction of Henry Casson, Secretary of State, Madison, Wis., Democrat Printing Company, State Printers, 1896. Online facsimile at: **www.wisconsinhistory.org/ turningpoints/search.asp?id=1617**.

WYOMING TERRITORY

At the beginning of the Civil War era in 1861, the area that became Wyoming was part of Dakota and Nebraska Territories. After the creation of Idaho Territory in 1863, the present Wyoming and Montana areas were added to the original Idaho Territory area. In 1864, a new Montana Territory was taken from the large Idaho region, and the Wyoming portion returned to Dakota Territory, reducing Idaho Territory to its present state footprint. Wyoming became a territory in its own name in 1868, its bounds matching the current state boundaries. Wyoming was admitted to the Union as the 44th state in July 1890. No soldiers were drawn from Wyoming, but both Dakota Territory and Nebraska Territory supplied soldiers to the Union armies, and a good many of these men were from the area of present-day Wyoming. Soon after becoming a territory, Wyoming conducted a territory-wide census in 1869, the only territory or state census ever done in Wyoming. There are a few more resources related to Wyoming's veterans.

Online Wyoming Resources

■ **List of Civil War Pensioners, Wyoming, 1883.** ftp://ftp.rootsweb.com/pub/usgenweb/wy/pens188 3.txt. This is a transcribed list for the USGenWeb, organized by county, and showing the name of the pensioner, post office address, cause for which pensioned, monthly rate, and date of original allowance, for any pensioner living in Wyoming in 1883.

■ **Sons of Union Veterans of the Civil War – Colorado/Wyoming Department.** **http://suvcw. org/co/deptcowy.html**. The Sons of Union Veterans of the Civil War (SUVCW) is legally recognized as the heir to and representative of the Grand Army of the Republic (GAR), and oversees 26 Departments, each consisting of one or more states, and about 180 community based camps. The Department of Colorado/Wyoming covers the states of Colorado, Idaho, Montana, Utah, and Wyoming. CO/WY Department camps include Lot Smith Camp #1, Salt Lake City, UT; Centennial Camp #100, Denver, Colorado; Compliment-Chapman Camp #2, Billings, MT; Thomas E. Bowman Camp #12, Durango, CO; and Legion of the West Camp #7, Grand Junction, CO. Each of these camps are represented at this website with names and addresses of officers, encampment information, and camp descriptions.

Published Wyoming Resources

■ *Index to Compiled Service Records of Volunteer Union Soldiers Who Served in Organizations from the Territory of Dakota,* microfilm of original records at the National Archives, Washington, D.C. Includes soldiers who served from Wyoming areas, part of Dakota Territory until 1867. Filmed by the National Archives, 1 roll, Series M0536. FHL film #881616.

■ *Index to Compiled Service Records of Volunteer Union Soldiers Who Served in Organizations from the Territory of Nebraska,* microfilm of original records at the National Archives, Washington, D.C. Includes the soldiers from the part of Wyoming Territory taken from Dakota Territory in 1867. Filmed by the National Archives, Series M547, 1964, 2 rolls, Index, A-La, 1861-1865, FHL film #821905; and Index, Le-Z, 1861-1865, FHL film #821906. The above indexed names included in Index to Soldiers & Sailors of the Civil War, a searchable name index to 6.3 million Union and Confederate Civil War soldiers now available online at the National Park Service website (See RG1). Dakota Territory supplied 269 men; and Nebraska Territory supplied 5,275 men to the war (all Union). To search for one, go to the NPS website at: **www.civilwar.nps.gov/cwss/**.

■ *1869 Wyoming Territory Census,* microfilm of original records at the Wyoming State Archives and Historical Department, Cheyenne, WY. Filmed by the archives, 1 roll, FHL film #2261365.

■ *The Historical Encyclopedia of Wyoming,* edited by Thomas S. Chamblin, published by the Wyoming Historical Institute, Cheyenne, WY, 1970, 1,669 pages (2 vols.). Contains "representative citizens who have had an integral part in the growth and development of Wyoming and historical sketches of leading cities, counties and tabulated principal facts of interest regarding every city, town, county, and district of the state." 1,425 pages of biography. FHL book 978.7 D3h v.1-2.

■ *Wyoming Biographies,* by Lawrence M. Woods, published by High Plains Pub. Co., Worland, WY, 1991, 224 pages. Includes index. FHL book 978.7 D3w.

■ *1890 Wyoming Veterans Census Index,* edited by Ronald Vern Jackson, published by Accelerated Indexing Systems, Salt Lake City, UT, 1983, 57 pages (front matter), 19 pages (names). FHL book 978.7 X22j.

Part 4

The Best Civil War Resource Centers for Local & County Research

So far, we have identified the genealogical resources of the Civil War era as found in ten statewide and ten nationwide resource groups. The chances of success in finding references to an ancestor in any of the twenty resource groups are quite good. But, there is one important piece of information that can lead to still more references. That information is the exact location of the residence of an ancestor. Understanding the place of residence just before the war, during the war, or just after the war, will lead to still more published records – but records found at the local/county level, not the state/ national level.

Local resources are those that were first created at a village, city, or town/township, usually as sub-groups of a county. County resources are those that originated at one of the 3,141 counties in the United States, and the original records may still be stored at a county courthouse or local repository. We use the nationwide and statewide resources to help us identify the county where an ancestor lived, and any follow-up research into the records there may prove to be a very rewarding experience.

Some local and county resources may be identical to the resources found at the state level. In fact, the statewide resources were often originally created at the county level, then transferred to a state repository, such as county tax lists and other name lists transferred to a

state archives. However, there are still countywide resources that are unique to that county, e.g., tax lists, cemetery indexes, newspaper obituaries, funeral home records, vital records, land records, and perhaps many more records traditionally maintained at a county courthouse.

Certain resources relate to one particular county (or surrounding area) during the Civil War era. For example, local regiments raised in one or more counties recorded name lists of enrollments, issuing of uniforms and weapons, and other details concerning the formation of a regiment. These unique records generated at the county level may have never been transferred to a state archives, and if not, they may be still sitting in a county courthouse or local repository. This will be true for both Union and Confederate counties.

In some states, specific Civil War records relate to the smallest local government units. For example, New York's sixty-two counties are subdivided into about 3,000 minor civil divisions, including towns, villages, and unincorporated communities. Generally, records created at one of the minor civil divisions come to rest at the county courthouse. Such was the case for one of the best Militia Lists for the Civil War era, the New York Town Clerk's Registers (see example, RG16, page 43). Fortunately, those Town

Registers eventually were transferred from all New York counties to the state archives. But, other original records of the Civil War era may still be hiding at the New York town or county level.

Because of their ties to a particular county, some Civil War regiments may have historic records found in one county and nowhere else. For example, an obscure unpublished history of a regiment may have originated at the county, and the only copy of the manuscript may be in a local library, museum, college, or some other local repository.

To determine whether a county record exists that mentions an ancestor by name, the task is now one of taking an inventory of what is available within any county of interest.

Inventory Local & County Name Lists Online

Name lists of Civil War era residents from many of the American counties are found at specific county websites on the Internet. Included for the period 1861-1869 are possible censuses and tax lists, militia lists, regimental histories and name lists; or perhaps later veterans or pensioner databases.

As an example, inventory what is available online for Bourbon County, Kansas. Use your browser to search for the keywords "Bourbon County Kansas Genealogy." A Google search for just those keywords linked together will present over 1,600 items in the results/hit list. To review them all becomes a rather daunting task because many of the hits are repeats, most of them dozens of times each. After perhaps hours of reviewing the Google hit list in more detail, the unique genealogy links to Bourbon County will be condensed to about 200 different websites. Unfortunately, a general browser search may take hours, yet still miss many genealogy-related webpages. Therefore, it may be better to conduct the search using a browser specific to genealogy.

Of several genealogy search engines available online, **www.Linkpendium.com** is probably the most comprehensive locality portal site for genealogy on the Internet today.

At Linkpendium, the search for Bourbon County, Kansas references, for example, will reveal over 330 direct links to databases with Bourbon County information. They are all organized as follows:

Linkpendium Categories "Bourbon County Kansas Genealogy"

Projects:
- Bourbon County Information and Resources
- Bourbon County, Kansas
- Bourbon KS GenExchange

Adjacent counties:
- Allen County, KS to the west
- Anderson County, KS to the northwest
- Crawford County, KS to the south
- Linn County, KS to the north
- Neosho County, KS to the southwest
- Vernon County, MO to the east

Biographies, Oral Histories, Diaries, Memoirs, Genealogies, Correspondence:
- Bourbon County Biography Bibliography
- Bourbon County GEDCOM Index
- Fort Scott GEDCOM Index

Cemeteries: (12 databases)

Census Records and Indexes: (24 databases)

Directories:
- 1887 Bourbon County Farmers' Directory
- Fort Scott City Directories

Estate Records:
- Bourbon County, Kansas Will Testators Index 1867

Immigration and Naturalization Records:
- Name Index to Naturalizations for District of Kansas (1915-1967)

Introduction and Guides:
- Bourbon County Genealogy
- Bourbon County Kansas Genealogy, Resources for Family History Research
- Bourbon County Resources (RootsWeb)
- Cyndi's List of Kansas locality links

Land Patent Search: (BLM)

Libraries, Museums, Archives:
- Bourbon County
- Family History Library Holdings
- KSGenWeb Digital Library
- PERiodical Source Index Search, Bourbon County
- Southeast Kansas Library System SEKLS Genealogy Bibliography
- USGenWeb Archives

Mailing Lists and Message Boards:
- Bourbon County Genealogy Queries
- Bourbon County, KS
- GenForum Message

- RootsWeb Message
- KSBOURBO-L Bourbon County genealogy
- KSBOURBO-L Mailing List Homepage
- KSBOURBO-L Browsable Mailing List Archives
- KSBOURBO-L Searchable Mailing List Archives

Maps and Gazetteers: (16 digital documents)

Military Records and Histories:
- Pensioners on the Roll, 1 January 1883 Bourbon County
- World War I Draft Registration Cards, 1917-1918 Bourbon
- Bourbon County, Kansas World War II Casualties, Army and Army Air Corps
- World War II Casualties from Bourbon County, Kansas
- World War II Honor List of Dead and Missing Personnel

Miscellaneous Data: (14 databases)

Newspaper Records:
- Bourbon County Obituaries and Funeral Home Records
- Konantz-Cheney Funeral Home, Fort Scott, Kansas

Photographs, Postcards, Historical Images:
- Bourbon County (Built in America)
- Bourbon County (Kansas Memory)
- Bronson, Bourbon County Kansas and the West Photograph Collection
- Fort Scott Bourbon County Kansas and the West Photograph Collection
- Fort Scott, Kansas
- Garland, Kansas (Kansas Memory) Historical Postcards of Bourbon County
  - Marmaton (Kansas Memory)
  - Penny Postcards from Kansas

School Records and Histories:
- Custard School (Kansas One Room School House Project)
- Gwin School (Kansas One Room School House Project)
- Rocky Point (Hog Holler) School (Kansas One Room School House Project)

Societies:
- Molly Foster Berry Chapter, DAR, Fort Scott
- Old Fort Genealogical Society of Southeastern Kansas

Surnames Websites, Obituaries, Biographies, and other material specific to a surname:
- Transportation and Industry
- Bourbon County Bridges
- Building histories of Bourbon County
- Extant Railroad/Railway Structures
- Mines, Mining and Mineral Resources
- Patents, Bourbon County, Kansas

- Bourbon County Vital Records
- U.S. Federal Census Mortality Schedules, 1850-1880 Bourbon County, Kansas

At first look, it may appear that there is only one Civil War reference, that for the "1883 Pensioners on the Roll" under the Military Records and Histories category. However, note the array of name lists indicated in the other categories, such as biographies, censuses, deaths, burials, estates, land records, directories, obituaries, photos, school records, funeral homes, and more. Clearly, there is an abundance of references where Civil War era residents of Bourbon County, Kansas can be identified online.

Bourbon County, Kansas is a small county in population (about 16,000 in 2000), and the area is average in size by geographic area, or how far back the records may cover. Obviously, larger counties may have many more references listed in a Linkpendium search, as smaller counties will have less. This example indicates that there may be several references for virtually every county in the United States.

Inventory the Top Six Civil War Era Resource Centers

Continuing the inventory, we need to find any genealogical resources of the Civil War era in a library catalog. Which library catalog can be determined by knowing which libraries in the United States have the best collection of books, periodicals, documents, maps, or photographs relating to the Civil War era.

For this review, we have determined that the top resource centers are six very special facilities/institutions where Civil War materials can be found in great numbers. There are other very fine Civil War collections at the State Library or State Archives for virtually every state. The state facilities were identified in **Part 3 — Statewide Sources**.

All of the top facilities listed below have online catalogs or good descriptions of their holdings. They all offer many search options for locating a local/county resource without leaving home. Included are three large libraries, two specialized military collections, and several Civil War parks. Some are best visited in person, but all have Internet websites describing their holdings. The most important Civil War resource centers can be identified as the following:

1. Family History Library, Salt Lake City, Utah.

2. Allen County Public Library, Fort Wayne, Indiana.

3. Library of Congress, Washington, D.C.

4. U.S. Army Unit Histories at the Military History Institute of the U.S. Army Heritage and Education Center, Carlisle Barracks, Pennsylvania.

5. Confederate Unit Histories at the Historical Research Center of the Texas Heritage Museum, Hill College, Hillsboro, Texas.

6. Civil War Parks and Historic Sites of the National Park Service.

1. Family History Library
Salt Lake City, Utah

For local/county genealogical resources, no other facility in the U.S. comes even close to matching the huge collection at the Family History

Library (FHL), the largest library of its kind in the world. The collection includes over 2.4

million rolls of microfilmed genealogical records; 727,000 microfiche; 356,000 books, serials, and other formats; over 4,500 periodicals; and 3,725 electronic resources. Operated by The Church of Jesus Christ of Latter-day Saints, the library is open to anyone interested in their family history.

Incredibly, the FHL's microfilming arm, the Genealogical Society of Utah, has been visiting county courthouses in America for over seventy-five years, expressly for the purpose of filming original county records. Of the more than 2.4 million rolls of worldwide microfilm at the FHL, it is estimated that over 750,000 of them are from U.S. county records alone.

Virtually every county in the U.S. is represented with an array of county records on microfilm, including original vital records, tax lists, county censuses, land records, probate records, and military records in several categories. An average county may have over 250 rolls of microfilm of county records. The FHL also has a huge collection of printed books, many of which are extractions or indexes from the microfilmed records. To find any microfilmed records or books for one county, conduct an inventory using the Family History Library's online catalog.

Access the FHL's online catalog directly at: **www.familysearch.org/**. At this Home Page, click on Library Catalog under the pull-down Library tab. At the library catalog page, note that there are several search options, including searches by Place, Surname, Keyword, Title, Film/Fiche, Author, Subject, or Call Number.

Search FHL Catalog by Place

To test the steps and inventory resources available for Bourbon County, Kansas, for example, click on the "Place" search. The resulting page has a box for typing the name of a **Place** and an optional box to type **Part of** (a place). To test this example, type "Bourbon" in the first box and "Kansas" in the second box, then click on "Search."

The Place Search Results page will list all matching places, in this case, a single matching place identified as Kansas, Bourbon. Click on the underlined title to go to the Place Details page, which will present a list of categories or "Topics" for Bourbon County, Kansas. Note that you get to the list of Topics for a specific county in just three clicks. The Topics list for Bourbon County, Kansas appears in a box as shown below:

Place	Kansas, Bourbon
Notes	Created in 1855 as an original county under the territory of Kansas.
Topics	Kansas, Bourbon - Archives and libraries - Inventories, registers, catalogs Kansas, Bourbon - Biography Kansas, Bourbon - Cemeteries Kansas, Bourbon - Census - 1860 - Indexes Kansas, Bourbon - Court records Kansas, Bourbon - Directories Kansas, Bourbon - Genealogy Kansas, Bourbon - History Kansas, Bourbon - Land and property Kansas, Bourbon - Maps Kansas, Bourbon - Maps - Indexes Kansas, Bourbon - Military records - Civil War, 1861-1865 Kansas, Bourbon - Naturalization and citizenship Kansas, Bourbon - Probate records Kansas, Bourbon - Probate records - Indexes Kansas, Bourbon - Societies Kansas, Bourbon - Taxation Kansas, Bourbon - Vital records

Click on one of the underlined Topics to see a list of the actual titles of microfilm or printed books, periodicals, or other media cataloged under that Topic. Note that one of the Topics is labeled, Military records - Civil War, 1861-1865. Click on that Topic to see the following titles:

Topic	Kansas, Bourbon - Military records - Civil War, 1861-1865
Titles	Fifth Regiment, Kansas Volunteer Cavalry, 1861-1865 Graden, Debra F. Sixth Regiment, Kansas Volunteers, Cavalry 1861-1865 Graden, Debra F.

Click on the first title to see the details for a book by Debra F. Graden, as shown below:

Title	Fifth Regiment, Kansas Volunteer Cavalry, 1861-1865		
Stmnt.Resp.	extracted by Debra Graden		
Authors	Graden, Debra F. (Main Author)		
Notes	The Fifth Kansas Cavalry was mustered in at Barnesville, Kansas, in 1861. It was mustered out at Leavenworth, Kansas, in 1864. Gives name, rank, company, section, residence, date enlisted, date mustered, and remarks.		
Call Number	Location		Availability
978.197/B1 M2g	US/CAN Book		Available
Format	Books/Monographs		
Language	English		
Publication	Leavenworth, Kansas : D. Graden, c1997		
Physical	186 pages.		

The FHL catalog is organized in a hierarchical structure, and in the Place search, the largest geographic unit comes first, followed by any smaller political units. To see this organization, note the boxed tab, <u>View Related Places</u> in the top right hand corner of the Bourbon County Topics page. A click here will take you to a list of Bourbon County cities, towns, villages, etc., for which further records are available at the FHL, as shown below:

Place	Kansas, Bourbon
Part of	Kansas
Contains	Kansas, Bourbon, Barnesville Kansas, Bourbon, Fort Scott Kansas, Bourbon, Fulton Kansas, Bourbon, Mapleton

Several more Topics are listed for each of the underlined places, all part of Bourbon County, Kansas. The largest city in Bourbon County is Fort Scott, and there are ten topics listed under that city, as shown below:

Place	Kansas, Bourbon, Fort Scott
Topics	Bourbon, Fort Scott - Church history Bourbon, Fort Scott - Church records Bourbon, Fort Scott - Directories Bourbon, Fort Scott - Genealogy - Periodicals Bourbon, Fort Scott - History Bourbon, Fort Scott - Military records - Civil War, 1861-1865 Bourbon, Fort Scott - Military records - Civil War, 1861-1865 - Indexes Bourbon, Fort Scott - Naturalization and citizenship Bourbon, Fort Scott - Newspapers Bourbon, Fort Scott - Newspapers - Indexes

The power of the FHL catalog search lies in the ability to concentrate on a location, i.e., a place of residence for an ancestor. This library is oriented to genealogical research, and unlike many other large libraries, place searching has a priority here. Place searching gives any researcher some outstanding tools in finding resources that may mention your Civil War ancestors by name. And, the Place Search in the FHL catalog is easier to use than any other library in America.

Our goal is to locate records at the local/county level that mention the name of an ancestor. This example for Bourbon County, Kansas can be repeated for any of the 3,141 counties in the U.S.

Books and Films Online?

The Family History Library is currently engaged in an awesome program to digitize the images of a half-million books, and 2.5 million rolls of microfilm. At the same time, a huge indexing project using thousands of volunteers is underway. The FHL is committed to having all images and surname lists available at their **www.familysearch.org/** website some day. At the present rate of digitizing and indexing, it will take at least 20 years to complete. But, the FHL is famous for starting projects slowly and building up speed over time – if this pattern continues, expect this digitizing/indexing project to take less than ten years. For now, to review the majority of the FHL resource titles, one must still visit the FHL in Salt Lake City in person – or borrow a roll of film that can be used in your home town.

Borrowing Films Through a Family History Center

If your FHL catalog search reveals microfilm or microfiche titles you would like to see, you can request that a copy be loaned to a Family History Center, a branch facility of the Family History Library in Salt Lake City. There are more than 4,500 centers worldwide, all open to the public. Most centers are located in meetinghouses of the LDS Church, but there are a growing number of Family History Centers now part of public libraries, archives, and other institutions all over the country. There are three ways to find the nearest Family History Center:

• Go to the website at **www.familysearch.org/** and type in your locality in the box labeled <u>Find a Family History Center.</u> The information at each center listed includes the hours of service and a telephone number. Before you visit, contact the center to verify when it is open.

• If you live in North America, call 1-866-406-1830, and ask where the nearest Family History Center is located.

• Look in your local telephone book for "The Church of Jesus Christ of Latter-day Saints." Call and ask for the location of the nearest Family History Center in your area.

A nominal fee is charged for the loan. Ask the staff at the center for current fees and ordering procedures. The center staff will place the order for you, and when the film arrives, you can go back to the center and view it.

2. Allen County Public Library
Fort Wayne, Indiana

With one of the largest genealogical collections in the world, the Allen County Public Library

(ACPL) in Northeast Indiana has become a Mecca for amateur genealogists. This library has over 350,000 books, over 513,000 items of microfilm and microfiche, and over 10,000 Genealogy/Local History periodical titles. As a partner with the Family History Library in Salt Lake City, the Ft. Wayne library patrons have access to over 2.4 million rolls of microfilm as part of the FHL's Family History Center network.

On its own, the ACPL's Genealogy Center has one of the largest collections of published county histories, covering virtually all U.S. counties; and has one of the largest collections of family histories of any library in the U.S.

Search ACPL's Online Catalog

For locating any of the film or book titles, the ACPL's online catalog is the place to begin. To access the library's online catalog, go to **www.acpl.lib.in.us/**. At this ACPL Home Page, click on the box, <u>Search Catalog</u>. Search options here include Words or Phrase (keywords), Author, Title, Subject, Series, and Magazines. In the Advanced Search option, you can combine two or more of the search options with "and," as well as adding more options for a book's ISBN, language, location, age level, publication year, and sorting options. A place search can be done by using the Words or Phrase search option.

As a test, a search for the keywords "Bourbon Kansas" brought up a list of 15 book titles, including city directories, cemetery indexes, index to will books, index to surnames from the 1920 standard atlas, index to historical atlases, place names, plat books, county histories, family histories, and more. Testing more places, a search for "Albany County" had 160 titles, "San Francisco" had 3,344 titles, and a search for "Wake County" had 52 titles. Perhaps the U.S. place most distant from Ft. Wayne, Indiana is Honolulu, Hawaii. The search for just "Honolulu" brought up 232 titles, while "Hawaii" had 2,362 titles, and "Anchorage" brought up 126 titles, while "Alaska" revealed 2,943 titles.

This is a library with national significance, not just Indiana or the mid-west – there are genealogical titles from nearly every county in the United States. Doing the same Place Search in the FHL online catalog may present more titles for one county than are found at the Ft. Wayne library, but there will often be titles at the ACPL not found at the FHL. Therefore, it is recommended to include the ACPL catalog search to locate a more complete array of resources in print.

PERiodical Source Index (PERSI)

An important part of the ACPL's resources is the largest collection of Genealogy/Local History periodicals of any library in North America. The collection of periodicals includes American publications from thousands of genealogical societies, the earliest dating back to 1847; and similar Canadian periodicals from as far back as 1800.

The genealogical value of these periodicals is in the wealth of articles identifying the names of persons from a certain place at a certain time. Much of the content of Genealogy/Local History periodicals is made up of lists of names of people from census lists, tax lists, militia lists, burial lists, vital records, school memberships, church memberships, court records, biographies, deed records, land records, histories, naturalizations, directories, and many more local sources.

An extracted list of the names of deceased persons buried in a small cemetery is often a good subject for an article in one of these periodicals, rather than a book or monograph. As a result, a published list of names from that cemetery may appear nowhere else. To any serious genealogist, the need for finding an article that includes a name of an ancestor, or an article relating to a certain place, are compelling tasks that must be pursued. The ACPL understands this compelling need, perhaps better than anyone else.

Since 1980, the ACPL has published the *PERiodical Source Index* (PERSI), a database with nearly 2 million entries today. PERSI indexes individual surnames, article keywords, and genealogy subjects by category, found in over 10,000 periodicals. Created by the foundation and department staff of the Genealogy Center of the library in Fort Wayne, Indiana, PERSI is widely recognized as being a vital source for genealogical researchers. There are currently 29 annual PERSI volumes in print, found in libraries all over the U.S. and Canada.

PERSI Databases Online

For electronic access to the huge PERSI database, the ACPL has chosen to license the index to two large commercial genealogical services on the Internet. PERSI is one of the databases available at the **HeritageQuest Online** library service site, and the **Ancestry.com** subscription site. At both sites, the data in the printed volumes is merged into a single database. And, as annual volumes are completed by ACPL, the new data is provided to the two Internet services.

Access to the PERSI database at the Ancestry.com site requires a membership to the Ancestry subscription service. For an annual membership, the cost to an individual home user may exceed $200.00, but the service does have trial memberships, and monthly rates as well. The Ancestry databases may also be available through a subscribing library, limited to the use of the library's in-house computers.

The HeritageQuest Online service is available only to subscribing libraries, but in many libraries across the country, a library card holder is allowed remote access. If your local library has a website on the Internet, a visit there should tell you whether that library subscribes to the HeritageQuest Online service, and if so, whether the library allows remote access to patrons using a library card number.

Both services have the same PERSI database, provided by the ACPL, and updated annually. A search in both databases giving different results means one of the services was updated ahead of the other. The search engine to query the database is provided by Ancestry.com or HeritageQuest Online, and the search and results screens in each are somewhat different. But, in both systems, the options for searching include words from an article title, such as a Surname and Title Keyword; or by U.S. Place, Canadian Place; or by the article's Record Type (several genealogical record categories, such as Census, Tax, Military, Land, Court, etc.).

The index to surnames is limited to surnames mentioned in the article title only. Typically, in a list of the burials in a small cemetery, only the name of the cemetery from the article title will be in the index – perhaps hundreds of deceased persons names are not in the index. Surname searching is still important, because a biography of one person, or some other article that is mostly related to one person can be found in the index.

Search PERSI by Surname

As an example, let's say your main interest is to locate some reference to an Andrew Johnson, who you think lived in Bourbon County, Kansas at the time of the Civil War. Your first search in the PERSI database might start with a search using the Surname option only, with Johnson as the surname. The results for this search will bring up a total of 8,728 article titles. But, a different approach using the U.S. Locality section with the name Johnson as a keyword in the title, brings up over 11,670 entries. Narrow down this search by using Andrew Johnson as the title keywords, which brings up 127 article titles. The search still needs to be refined down to a specific place.

A search using the U.S. Locality section with the name Johnson as a keyword in the title, plus Kansas as the state, and Bourbon as the county, will bring up just one (1) article title, "Johnson Brick Yard," in the *Old Fort Log*, Vol. 11, No. 3 (Fall 1984), a periodical published by the Old Fort Genealogical Society of Southeast Kansas, located in Fort Scot, KS.

Search PERSI by Place

It could be that the best use of the PERSI index is to find any articles with a connection to a specific place. You are helped in that option by narrowing down the articles to a record type. So it is possible to locate, for example, any articles relating to the Civil War in Bourbon County, Kansas. Start the search with Military as the Record Type, and using the keywords Civil

War in the article title; and Kansas as the state and Bourbon as the county. The results for this particular search has a total of six (6) articles, listed at the Ancetry.com results page as shown below:

Ancestry.com Results List

Article Title: Civil War participants, 1861-65, A-G
Locality: United States, Kansas, Bourbon
Record Type: Military
Volume: 8
Number, Season, Year: 4 (Winter 1981)
Periodical Title: Old Fort Log

Article Title: Civil War veterans
Locality: United States, Kansas, Bourbon
Record Type: Military
Volume: 3
Number, Season, Year: 2 (July 1976)
Periodical Title: Old Fort Log

Article Title: Civil war veterans, 1861-65
Locality: United States, Kansas, Bourbon
Record Type: Military
Number, Season, Year: (1991)
Periodical Title: Old Fort Log

Article Title: Civil war veterans, 1861-65, J-Z
Locality: United States, Kansas, Bourbon
Record Type: Military
Volume: 18
Number, Season, Year: 2 (Summer 1991)
Periodical Title: Old Fort Log

Article Title: Civil War/Ft. Scott, Civil war in the West
Locality: United States, Kansas, Bourbon
Record Type: Military
Volume: 98
Number, Season, Year: 9 (November 1964)
Periodical Title: American Monthly Magazine

Article Title: History excerpts, Civil war
Locality: United States, Kansas, Bourbon
Record Type: Military
Volume: 6
Number, Season, Year: 4 (March 1972)
Periodical Title: Midwest Genealogical Register

The first four article titles above are from the *Old Fort Log* periodical. Click on the underlined name of the Periodical Title for more information about that periodical, as shown below:

Periodical Title: Old Fort Log
PERSI Code: KSOF
Topics: KS
Issues Per Year: 3x
ISSN Number: 0098-4760
ACPL Holdings: v.1- 1974-
ACPL Call Number: OPEN
Notes: numbering skips v.27n.2-v.28n.3
Repositories (in addition to ACPL): Library Of Congress
Publisher: Old Fort Genealogical Society of Southeast Kansas
Address: c/o Public Library, 210 S. National St., Fort Scott, KS 66701

HeritageQuest Online Results List

This same six articles appear in the HeritageQuest Online results list arranged in a somewhat different format, as shown below:

---

1. Civil War participants, 1861-65, A-G
   Old Fort Log. Fort Scott KS: Winter 1981. Vol. 8 Iss. 4

---

2. Civil War Veterans,
   Old Fort Log. Fort Scott KS: Jul 1976. Vol. 3 Iss. 3

---

3. Civil war veterans, 1861-65
   Old Fort Log. Fort Scott KS: 1991. Vol. - Iss. -

---

4. Civil war veterans, 1861-65, J-Z
   Old Fort Log. Fort Scott KS: Summer 1991. Vol. 18 Iss. 2

---

5. Fort Scott, Civil War in the West
   Daughters of the American Revolution Magazine. Washington DC: Nov 1964. Vol. 98 Iss. 9

---

6. History excerpts, Civil war
   Midwest Genealogical Register. Wichita KS: Mar 1972. Vol. 6 Iss. 4

Click on any underlined article title for more details, as shown below:

Article Details   Return to search results
☐ Add to Notebook

Title of Article	**Fort Scott, Civil War in the West**
Periodical	Daughters of the American Revolution Magazine Washington, DC: Nov 1964. Vol. 98, Iss. 9
Surname	-
Record Type	Military Records
Subject	Civil War
Locale	-
States/Prov.	Kansas
Counties	Bourbon
Countries	USA

Copies of this article may be obtained by completing the request form.

A click on the underlined Periodical title takes you to a "Periodical Details" page, expanding the information to include a PERSI Code, and all repositories holding the title with a complete list of volumes and issues.

Get a Copy of an Article

In both the Ancestry.com and HeritageQuest Online PERSI screens, a list of any repositories holding copies of a particular periodical can be seen, including all volumes and issues available. It may be difficult to get a copy of an article through the mail from any of the repositories except for the ACPL, which provides a service of making and mailing copies of articles from periodicals.

At both sites, a form can be accessed for the purpose of ordering copies of an article from the ACPL Foundation, up to six articles at a time. The PERSI Order Form is reproduced on the opposite page.

Periodical Source Index (PERSI) Order Form

Name:_____

Address:_____

_____

To obtain copies of articles in the PERSI index, contact the Allen County Public Library Foundation, P.O. Box 2270, Fort Wayne, IN 46801-2270. Send this form describing the articles to be copied, provide the full entry from PERSI and the name of the journal. Request only six articles at a time. The charge is $7.50 for each letter/form, pre-paid, plus $0.20 per page copied to be billed to you. Requests not acceptable by phone, fax, or e-mail. Please allow 6-8 weeks.

Title of article:_____
Title of Journal:_____
PERSI Code:_____ Volume:_____ No:_____ Month:_____ Year:_____

Title of article:_____
Title of journal:_____
PERSI Code:_____ Volume:_____ No:_____ Month:_____ Year:_____

Title of article:_____
Title of journal:_____
PERSI Code:_____ Volume:_____ No:_____ Month:_____ Year:_____

Title of article:_____
Title of journal:_____
PERSI Code:_____ Volume:_____ No:_____ Month:_____ Year:_____

Title of article:_____
Title of journal:_____
PERSI Code:_____ Volume:_____ No:_____ Month:_____ Year:_____

Title of article:_____
Title of journal:_____
PERSI Code:_____ Volume:_____ No:_____ Month:_____ Year:_____

3. Library of Congress
Washington, DC

The Library of Congress (LOC) is the world's largest library. The collection of books, periodicals, maps, photographs, and other

media related to the American Civil War is like no other library in the U.S. Many of the Civil War era photographs are now online.

Library Catalogs

Visit the main LOC online catalog at: **http://catalog.loc.gov/**. Your first two choices are for a Basic Search or Guided Search. A Basic Search option allows several search criteria, including Title, Author, and Keywords. A Guided Search allows more search limits for all searches. In either option, searching for just the keywords "Civil War" will display over 10,000 titles to review. Limit the search to "Civil War California" and there will be about 300 titles. Using "Civil War Virginia" brings up over 4,200 titles. Using "Bourbon County Kansas" will bring up 15 titles (but a somewhat different list than the 15 titles found at the ACPL catalog search).

Within the hit list of titles after any search, certain titles may display a logo for "Electronic Resource Available," which means the book, monograph, video, sound recording, etc., is fully online, and you can go directly to that resource with a mouse click.

The Library of Congress is on its way to become a completely digital library, including the full text of books, magazines, and monographs; and the reproductions of videos, movies, sound recordings, graphic arts, photographs, visual art, maps, and any other media that can be digitally reproduced and viewed on screen.

In addition to the main catalog searches, specialized searches can be done in the following catalogs:

● **Prints and Photographs.** The Prints and Photographs Online Catalog (PPOC) contains catalog records and digital images representing a cross-section of still pictures held by the Prints & Photographs Division and other units of the Library. The (full color) online picture reproduced below is one of over 10,000 prints.

● **Sound Online Inventory & Catalog (SONIC).** Collections in the Recorded Sound Section's SONIC database includes 78s, 45s and copyright cassettes, broadcast, and archival recordings.

• **Alternative Interface to the LC Online Catalog (Z39.50).** Access to other computer-to-computer systems sharing the Z39.50 format protocol.

• **Other Libraries' Catalogs.** Links to hundreds of online catalog websites from libraries all over the world.

LOC American Memories Photograph Collections

As perhaps the largest collection of historic photographs on the Internet, the LOC American Memories webpages are a mandatory visit to discover what photos may exist for people or places important to your genealogical research.

An important part of the American Memories collection is the Civil War photos at: **http://memory.loc.gov/ammem/cwphtml/ cwphomehtml**.

Left: *Portrait of Maj. Gen. Ulysses S. Grant, Officer of the Federal Army*, Brady National Photographic Art Gallery (Washington, D.C.), [Between 1860 and 1865]. LC-B8172-6371. **Right:** *Portrait of Gen. Robert E. Lee, Officer of the Confederate Army*, Julian Vannerson, 1863. LC-B8172-0001. Both photos are available without restriction at the **LOC American Memories** website.

The **Selected Civil War Photographs Collection** contains 1,118 photographs. Most of the images were made under the supervision of Mathew B. Brady, and include scenes of military personnel, preparations for battle, and battle after-effects.

An additional two hundred autographed portraits of army and navy officers, politicians, and cultural figures can be seen in the *Civil War*

Photograph Album, ca. 1861-65. (James Wadsworth Family Papers). The full album pages are displayed, revealing studio logos, addresses, and other imprint information on the approximately twenty photographers represented in the album.

---

4. U.S. Army Unit Histories
Military History Institute, U.S. Army Heritage and Education Center, Carlisle Barracks, Pennsylvania

Located in Ridgway Hall near the U.S. Army War College at Carlisle Barracks, Pennsylvania, the U.S. Army Military History Institute (a branch of the Army Heritage and Education Center) is a library, archive and research facility that deals mostly with military history and strategic studies.

The Military History Institute has the best collection of published unit histories for virtually all Union units (regiments, battalions, brigades, companies, etc.), as well as many Confederate

units. This is an outstanding library and archives, with histories, photographs, and Civil War memorabilia in great abundance. An online catalog search is very worthwhile, and a selected list of documents and photographs are accessible online as well. A civilian scholar, military officer, student, history buff, or amateur genealogist visiting Ridgway Hall will find a prodigious amount of material.

Finding aids and bibliographies are available, and a research historian with the job of providing patron assistance is always on duty in the reading room.

Army Heritage Collection Online

For accessing the Army Heritage resources, go to: **http://www.ahco.army.mil/site/index.jsp**, which presents the following choices:

● **Research Catalog.** Search the catalog for books, manuscripts, photographs, serials, microfilm, and more. An example here is to use "New York" as the keywords, and "Military Units" as the selected Search Type, which will bring up 1,156 titles, all related to histories, memories, memorials, letters, diaries, and many other topics related to Army units of New York, as well as references to soldiers, officers, or others with a connection to that New York unit.

● **Resource Guides & Finding Aids.** Search for subject bibliographies & collection descriptions of research sources.

You can search for **All Online Materials**, or search for selected **Digital Documents Online** in these categories:

● **Manuscripts/Archives.** Search for digitized personal papers, oral histories, letters & diaries of veterans, military units & associations.

● **Photos.** Search for digitized photograph images.

● **Artifacts.** Search for digital images of historical property of the Army Heritage Museum.

● **Military Publications.** Search for digitized Army Military Publications & selected defense agencies which include orders, regulations, doctrinal guidance & technical information.

For information and histories of any U.S. Army units during the Civil War era, the Military History Institute collection is more complete than any other library in the country. But, a researcher will find that units of the Confederate Army are also well represented.

5. Confederate Unit Histories
Historical Research Center, Texas Heritage Museum, Hill College, Hillsboro, Texas

Hill College at Hillsboro, Texas, is the home of the Texas Heritage Museum. The museum's Historical Research Center has one of the most

important collections for Civil War research in the nation. Established in 1963 and formerly called the Confederate Research Center, the collection has over 5,000 volumes dealing exclusively with the Civil War.

The highlight of the collection is a series of capsule histories for all 3,200 Confederate regiments, special units; and histories of all Confederate ships. The historic capsules include counties where companies mustered, alternate designations, higher commands, Civil War battles in which the unit participated, and a map of all locations where the unit served during the war. These Confederate unit histories are more complete and more useful than those found at the online Civil War Soldiers & Sailors System (RG1, p. 10), and make this library one of the top Civil War research centers in America. Like the

Army's Military History Institute, both Union and Confederate unit histories are here, but at this facility, the Confederate unit histories are virtually complete.

If you know the Confederate regiment of your ancestor, for a fee the Center will send you a copy of the capsule history for that unit. (Contact the Research Center for a fee schedule). If you do not know which regiment, the Center will provide a form for you to fill in and return. The Center will do the work for you for a fee. If nothing is found, the fee is waived. A form for requesting a capsule history and another one for requesting information on any Civil War veteran (Confederate or Union) are both available online as downloadable PDF files at the Texas Heritage Museum's website. Visit the website at **www.hillcollege.edu/Museum/** and review the fees for a capsule history or for a report on one Civil War veteran. You can also contact them by phone at (254) 659-7757, or visit the museum's Historical Research Center in person. See the museum's website for more information (such as directions, events, newsletter, email, phone, or mailing address). The website also has a contents list and index to the resources of the Historical Research Center.

A visit to the galleries of the Texas Heritage Museum has free admission. Both facilities are very up-to-date, with a shared theatre and many other military artifacts of special interest. This is a user-friendly museum and library, and genealogists are always welcome. The staff will usually try to help or guide any visitors in their research. The hours are Monday thru Thursday, 8am - 4:30pm; Friday, 8am - 4pm. From June thru August, the museum is open on Saturdays, 10am - 5pm (the Historical Research Center is not open on Saturdays).

Of related historical interest, the Texas Heritage Museum deals with wars in which Texans were involved. The museum commemorates the experiences of Texans during war times, featuring Civil War, World War II, Audie Murphy, and Vietnam exhibits; and includes a Weapons Gallery. The newly remodeled museum offers a new theatre featuring films highlighting the contents of the museum.

Outside of the museum is a new memorial honoring all native-born Texans awarded the Medal of Honor, including Audie Murphy, the most decorated soldier during WWII; and Samuel Dealey, the most decorated sailor of WWII.

A RootsWeb Civil War website features a selected bibliography of the resources available at the former Confederate Research Center (ca. 2004) at: **www.rootsweb.ancestry.com/ ~mscivilw/csa_resc.html**.

6. Civil War Parks and Historic Sites
National Park Service

The first national park established by any country in the world was Yellowstone National Park in 1872, under the direct supervision of the U.S. Secretary of the Interior. The U.S. Congress created several more national parks and monuments over the next forty-some years, administered by the Interior Department, War Department, or the U.S. Forest Service. In 1916, a much needed national park management system was implemented with the creation of the National Park Service (NPS). The NPS became a bureau within the U.S. Department of the Interior.

Since Yellowstone, over 100 countries have created some 1,200 national parks and monuments worldwide. Nearly 400 are now part of the U.S. National Park Service.

The NPS has fostered an educational and historical legacy, particularly with the many Civil War era resources found at certain NPS sites. For example, eighty-four (84) parks, monuments, or historic sites operated by the National Park Service have resources that are related to the history of the Civil War. Specific resources may spotlight a particular battlefield, biographies of soldiers and officers, histories, dioramas, lecture programs, and guided tours.

The Sesquicentennial of the American Civil War (2011-2015) offers the current generation of Americans an opportunity to commemorate this country's greatest national crisis. The NPS has enhanced the Civil War era displays and resources for the sesquicentennial in virtually all of its historic Civil War sites. Anyone who knows of an ancestor or relative who participated in a battle of the Civil War, Union or Confederate, must eventually visit that site in person – it becomes part of our personal history.

Ford's Theatre, ca.1870

Online Resources

As one of this nation's national treasures, the National Park Service has developed a presence online that is one of the most comprehensive of any government agency. There are two major NPS divisions online related to the American Civil War: **1)** the **Civil War Soldiers and Sailors System** (CWSS), an online searchable database with over six million names at: **www.civilwar.nps.gov/cwss**. The CWSS is described in detail in **Part 2 – Descriptions and Examples of Resource Groups Available**, RG 1, pp. 10-13. And, **2)** the official National Park Service Civil War website: **http://cwar.nps.gov/civilwar/**.

Of great value to genealogists, the latter site presents a list of all Civil War Parks, each with a direct link to a website devoted to one park, monument, or historic site. As an example, your curiosity about the historic site where Abraham Lincoln was assassinated can be satisfied by visiting the webpage for Ford's Theatre, a National Historic Site in Washington, DC. After a few good descriptive words and some general information at the Ford's Theatre webpage, Quicklinks at the site have <u>Directions</u>, <u>Operating Hours & Seasons</u>, <u>Fees & Reservations</u>, and a <u>Bookstore</u>.

The 84 Civil War parks/monuments on the list (each with a direct link to a webpage) are located at: **http://cwar.nps.gov/civilwar/cwparks.html** and are listed alphabetically as shown below:

● Abraham Lincoln Birthplace National Historic Site, KY
● African American Civil War Memorial, DC
● Andersonville National Historic Site, GA
● Andrew Johnson National Historic Site, TN
● Antietam National Battlefield, MD
● Appomattox Court House National Historical Park, VA
● Arkansas Post National Memorial, AR
● Arlington House, The Robert E. Lee Memorial, VA
● Booker T. Washington National Monument, VA
● Boston African American National Historic Site, MA
● Boston Harbor Islands National Recreation Area, MA
● Brice's Cross Roads National Battlefield Site, MS
● Buffalo National River, AR
● Cane River Creole National Historical Park, LA
● Cape Hatteras National Seashore, NC
● Cedar Creek and Belle Grove National Historical Park, VA
● Charles Pinckney National Historic Site, SC
● Chesapeake & Ohio Canal National Historical Park, DC, MD, WV
● Chickamauga & Chattanooga National Military Park, GA, TN
● Clara Barton National Historic Site, MD
● Colonial National Historical Park, VA
● Cumberland Gap National Historical Park, KY
● Dry Tortugas National Park, FL
● Ford's Theater National Historic Site, DC
● Fort Davis National Historic Site, TX
● Fort Donelson National Battlefield, TN
● Fort Larned National Historic Site, KS
● Fort McHenry National Monument Historic Shrine, MD
● Fort Pulaski National Monument, GA
● Fort Raleigh National Historic Site, NC
● Fort Scott National Historic Site, KS
● Fort Sumter National Monument, SC

- Fort Union National Monument, NM
- Frederick Douglas National Historic Site, DC
- Frederick Law Olmstead National Historic Site, MA
- Fredericksburg & Spotsylvania National Military Park, VA
- General Grant National Memorial, NY
- Gettysburg National Military Park, PA
- Golden Gate National Recreation Area, CA
  - Alcatraz Island, CA
  - Fort Point National Historic Site, CA
  - Presidio of San Francisco, CA
- Governor's Island National Monument, NY
- Gulf Islands National Seashore, FL, MS
- Hampton National Historic Site, MD
- Harpers Ferry National Historical Park, WV
- Homestead National Monument of America, NE
- Independence National Historical Park, PA
- James A. Garfield National Historic Site, OH
- Jefferson National Expansion Memorial, MO
- Jean Lafitte National Historical Park and Preserve, LA
- Kennesaw Mountain National Battlefield Park, GA
- Lincoln Boyhood National Memorial, IN
- Lincoln Home National Historic Site, IL
- Lincoln Memorial, DC
- Mammoth Cave National Park, KY
- Manassas National Battlefield Park, VA
- Marsh-Billings-Rockefeller National Historical Park, VT
- Martin Van Buren National Historic Site, NY
- Monocacy National Battlefield, MD
- Natchez National Historical Park, MS
- Natchez Trace Parkway, AL, MS, TN
  - Natchez Trace National Scenic Trail, MS, TN
  - Tupelo National Battlefield, MS
- National Capital Parks East, DC
  - Fort DuPont Park, DC
  - Fort Washington Park, MD
- New Bedford National Historical Park, MA
- Palo Alto Battlefield National Historic Site, TX
- Pea Ridge National Military Park, AR
- Pecos National Historical Park, NM
- Petersburg National Battlefield, VA
- Richmond National Battlefield, VA
- Rock Creek Park, DC
- San Juan Island National Historical Park, WA
- Sand Creek Massacre National Historic Site, CO
- Shiloh National Military Park, TN, MS
- Springfield Armory National Historic Site, MA
- Stones River National Battlefield, TN
- Tuskegee Institute National Historic Site, AL
- Ulysses S. Grant National Historic Site, MO
- Vicksburg National Military Park, MS
- Wilson's Creek National Battlefield, MO
- Women's Rights National Historical Park, NY